THE WOMEN'S ANNUAL | 1981: The Year in Review

G. K. Hall

WOMEN'S STUDIES

Publications

Barbara Haber
Editor

THE WOMEN'S ANNUAL

1981:
The Year in Review

Edited by
Barbara Haber

G.K. Hall & Company
70 Lincoln Street, Boston

ISBN 0-8161-8614-6

ISSN 0276-7988

CONTENTS

Introduction   1
 Barbara Haber

1   Domestic Life: The New Right
    and the Family   6
    Naomi R. Gerstel

2   Women and Education   24
    Polly Welts Kaufman

3   Women and Health   56
    Ann Conway

4   Third World Women in America   87
    Patricia Hill Collins

5   Women, Scholarship,
    and the Humanities   117
    Esther Stineman

6   Politics and Law   150
    Peggy Simpson

7   Popular Culture   193
    Michaele Weissman

8   Psychology of Women:
    Feminist Therapy   211
    Virginia K. Donovan and Ronnie Littenberg

9   Women and Religion   236
    Feminist Scholarship in Theology
    Constance H. Buchanan
    The Leadership and Empowerment
      of Women
    Sandra Hughes Boyd

10 Violence Against Women   270
    Freada Klein

11 Women and Work   303
    Sara Garrigan Burr

Contributors   321

Index   323

Introduction

In 1981 Americans experienced the first year of a new administration and in the course of that year became familiar with the term "Reaganomics." While the $35 billion in budget cuts that characterize the president's economic programs are no doubt affecting all Americans, evidence supports the fact that the overwhelming cuts came in the social welfare programs that serve mostly women and children. The bleak economic picture of 1981 inevitably puts a major focus in this book on the women's programs dangerously threatened by a conservative government; however, another focus is on the issues and trends that remain healthy. Most notably, scholarship about women continues to proliferate, and this volume attempts to document the work produced in major academic areas. In this second book of *The Women's Annual* series, contributors, from the vantage point of diverse perspectives, provide information and analyses that together offer a structured account of the year in review.

Almost everyone is effected by a bad economy and many suffer. Who can deny that men are also feeling the brunt of these hard times as businesses fail and employees are thrown out of work? While many of the problems facing Americans today are just plain human problems and not necessarily sex-specific, there remains an array of developments that can be separated and recognized as women's issues.

On the surface, it would appear that men are even worse off than women in the workplace, for their rate of unemployment exceeded women's in 1981 for the first time in twenty years. But as Sara Burr points out in her essay on women and work, those industries most affected by the 1981 recession are the ones that have been most resistant to females. Because more women than men work in low-paying service jobs, their rate of unemployment has trailed that of men in the high-paying industries and trades. What Burr suggests as the most significant trend for employed women is the growing hostility to their place in the economy. Affirmative Action plans are being shunted aside, and the omnibus budget reconciliation act of 1981, which Burr analyzes, reduces job

1

training opportunities for women at the same time that it reduces social services to them.

In her overview of politics and law, Peggy Simpson summarizes the prevailing government attitude toward women with a devastating comment attributed to Barbara R. Bergmann, professor of economics from the University of Maryland. Speaking before a congressional committee early in 1982 about the reversal of recent gains made by women, she said, "It is not an exaggeration to say that the Reagan administration has declared economic war on women, particularly on those women who do not have a man to depend on." Simpson documents this statement by listing cuts that are creating the most hardship:

400,000 families were removed from the Aid to Families with Dependent Children program
287,000 additional families received reduced benefits
$1 billion was cut from the Medicaid program
150,000 poor women were denied federal job training
100,000 displaced homemakers lost their job training program
14.5 million children were denied subsidized school lunches
Rents for public housing were increased, thus affecting women who head two-thirds of them

These hardships being foisted on all needy women are being felt most acutely by Third World women. Patricia Hill Collins points out that: "While whites generally outnumber nonwhites in the absolute number of persons benefiting from programs such as CETA, Aid to Families with Dependent Children, Medicaid . . . the percentage of Third World women receiving such benefits is higher than in comparable white communities." Collins analyzes other changes in government policy that will affect minorities: The federal government's indifference to Affirmative Action plans will reverse job gains made by minority women over the last decade; the move to reduce the size of the federal work force will mean the loss of new jobs for members of minority groups; and efforts to dismantle school desegregation programs will negate gains.

For the time being, other programs in education have survived drastic cuts. As Polly Kaufman explains in her chapter, some important programs were saved by the grass roots efforts of women who joined together to combat cuts. The women's educational equity act (WEEA) was scheduled to be diluted into the general block grants to states, but was rescued. Similarly, Congress extended the vocational education act of 1976 until 1984. (The act provides training for women in nontraditional careers as a way to rescue them from poverty.) Other programs have fared less well. Cuts in the National Institute of Education will halt basic research in sex equity areas, and funding for women's equity projects by the Department of Education will be less than the already low 0.2 percent of their budget. More serious is the proposed Hatch amendment to Title IX, which promises to curtail its ability to enforce equity by limiting its jurisdiction. Rather than affecting an entire institution, Title IX protection would touch on only those programs within the institution specifically funded by federal dollars.

Many of the economic, social and political changes that characterize 1981 are damaging the women's health movement. Although activists in this area hoped to concentrate their time and resources on the issues of reproductive rights and environmental and occupation health in 1981, they found it necessary to broaden their scope. In addition to looking ahead, they had to face old issues that were no longer resolved. In her chapter on women and health, Ann Conway lists some of the most alarming trends of 1981: The abatement of Social Security, Medicare and Medicaid benefits, proposed or passed governmental legislation including a right-to-life movement, reduction of primary care programs and family planning services, and the end of national health insurance considerations. In commenting on these trends, Conway says, "Acting under the so-called free market approach to health care, the Reagan administration demolished or diminished many programs extant since the Depression."

Advocates for women's rights to health care also deplore the government's proposed changes in drug regulation. Its move to lessen control of drug research and marketing could prove harmful to all consumers. Similarly, government relaxation of standards has had implications for the movement for environmental and occupational health. Conway points out that 5,000 new chemicals a year are added to the 500,000 that already exist. Without adequate testing, these chemicals could later prove to be harmful by causing birth defects or cancer.

Rural women and their families are another special group being denied services. Government reductions will imperil such basic programs as community health centers, alcoholism and drug abuse services, venereal disease prevention programs, black lung clinics, and migrant health centers.

Services to families are jeopardized in yet another area, as Freada Klein explains in her survey of the violence issues confronting American women. She offers the insight that, "The family, once viewed as the sanctuary from the harshness of urban, industrialized life, was exposed as the most violent unit in contemporary society." Klein describes how feminist activists increasingly have become involved in confronting such issues as marital rape, woman-battering, and child sexual abuse, thereby uncovering ominous aspects of family life. In the past, victims suffered alone; but growing feminist awareness has led to the development of essential services. As in so many other areas, funds for programs are being cut. Rape crises centers and battered women's shelters have closed or limited their services, and funds supporting regional networking and skill-sharing have been cut.

More encouraging is the creative legislation by some states that impose taxes to fund services. Many tax marriage licenses and divorce filings for this purpose, while Texas taxes liquor, Pennsylvania fines people convicted of violent crimes, and Wisconsin fines violators of their domestic violence law.

In her chapter on the New Right and the family, Naomi Gerstel distinguishes between the Old Right and the New by indicating that the latter is showing greater concern for social rather than economic matters. In addressing the crucial issue of the New Right's proprietary attitude toward the family, Gerstel makes the following observation: "Where feminists emphasize the oppressive aspects of family life and thus assert women's rights within and against the family, the New Right emphasizes the protective aspects of family life and attempts to revitalize its traditional form." To achieve this goal the New Right is trying to intercede through political methods in an attempt to control growing family crises. The most startling example of their work is the proposed family protection act, which would withhold federal funds from projects that "deny, diminish, or denigrate the role differences between the sexes as they have been historically understood in the United States."

While Gerstel concedes that the New Right may be accurate in its description of the changes in contemporary family life, she argues that they misunderstand the significance of these changes; and she is sure that their policies will never succeed in bringing back the traditional family. She provides, for example, an analysis of Phyllis Schlafly's zealous efforts to protect American women. About this, Gerstel says: "In her formulation New Right family policy is not directed at the control of women but at the control of men, and is best understood as an attempt to remind them of—indeed, to enforce—their obligations to women. For women to whom easily available divorce threatens impoverishment, this is a significant protection."

In this light it is perhaps possible at least to understand the basis for the New Right's attack on abortion, divorce, and all else they see as breaking down the fabric of American family life. What is lost on them, of course, is the fact that not all American women are married, with two children, and under the protection of an obliging male.

Very far removed from Schlafly and her followers are feminist psychologists Virginia Donovan and Ronnie Littenberg who work for change by helping women clients establish autonomy within a culture that seeks to maintain a sexist bias. In approaching a definition of feminist therapy in their essay, the authors state: "The feminist therapist's belief that the personal is political, that for fundamental changes to occur in the emotional lives of women basic social structures must change, has two direct implications for her work. The first is that she actively struggles with the manifestations of sexism, racism, and class oppression that affect her own attitudes and values. . . . The second is that she believes that there are no individual solutions for social, moral, and political problems."

Donovan and Littenberg provide a clear description of how feminist therapy differs from other forms of psychological counseling, and discuss issues that are of particular concern to them: Violence toward women, substance abuse, eating disorders, and lesbianism. Their feminism provides them with a framework essential for understanding what can be minimized or misunderstood by traditional counselors. Their aim is to connect the problems of the individual to the attitudes of society and thus establish theory in feminist therapy. Indeed, this linkage is crucial for the development of all feminist theory.

Esther Stineman's essay on new work in the humanities provides numerous examples of how gender has become an instrument for analyses in many academic disciplines. Feminist scholars routinely connect the personal with the political. For example, biographies of women have a richer perspective because their authors are asking new questions of the lives of their subjects. As Stineman states, they want to know: "Who had the power in the family? What was the nature and morality of such power? Was the woman abused in the family politics of the marital relationship? Was she denied the chance to make what might have been a fuller contribution to the world because of her life in the family?"

Feminist theologians are also bringing a new dimension to their field by examining issues of gender against the history and philosophy of religion. Constance Buchanan points out that a lively discourse is now occurring because of the examination of such questions as: What is the nature of women's religious experience? Does it liberate women or oppress them? Do race and class differences alter their religious experiences?

Feminist theologians are also examining current social issues and are taking political stands in controversial areas. Sandra Boyd examines several major issues of concern to women in religion and presents up-to-date information on the arguments surrounding ordination and the abortion debate. Boyd quotes at length from Beverly Harrison's "Theology of Pro-Choice: A Feminist Perspective," which points out the vicious irony of a society that wants to offer full human rights to a zygote at the moment of conception but will deny full social and political rights to women. Among Harrison's points is the fact that the same people who are against prochoice are also against the Equal Rights Amendment.

In all, 1981 has been a devastating year for those who care about women. The battle lines were drawn around every major issue and opposing forces clashed. In most areas women lost. While serious scholarship in women's studies continued, its impact on the mainstream of most disciplines remains minimal, with a fully integrated curriculum still a goal. For the most part, the general public continues to be misinformed about women's issues. As Michaele Weissman amply illustrates in her article on popular culture, serious matters are trivialized if not distorted by the media.

Every contributor would have preferred to report good news. What each offers instead is an analysis of the perplexing problems confronting women today. In sum, *The Women's Annual: 1981* brings to its readers a carefully documented and thoughtful overview of women's most recent history.

Barbara Haber
Cambridge, Massachusetts
April 1982

Domestic Life: The New Right and the Family

1

Naomi R. Gerstel

The elections of 1980 were the most dramatic triumph for the right in American politics at least since the early 1950s, and quite possibly since the heyday of pre-New Deal Republicanism in the 1920s. While there is considerable dispute as to whether or not the events of 1980 constitute a realigning election—one that results in the formation of electoral coalitions that are both new and lasting—there can be no dispute as to the immediate outcome: the incumbency of a Republican president who not only was elected with the support of his party's right wing but who also identifies with that wing; the defeat of a number of leading liberals in both the House and the Senate and their replacement with a freshman class of unusually conservative Republican legislators; and Republican control of the Senate for the first time since 1952 and by the largest margin since 1926.

What has come to be known as the New Right claims credit for much of the Republican victory—a judgment shared, albeit with far less enthusiasm, by many of the New Right's critics. What distinguishes the New Right from the Old Right is its greater concern for social rather than economic issues, a distinction explicit in the first use of the term by Kevin Phillips, a former Nixon aide and author of *The emerging republican majority*. It is the New Right that has led much of the opposition to both legalized abortion and to the ERA and, more generally, sought to reestablish through political methods what they see as the "traditional" American family.

Within the New Right, the most important organization formulating family policy has been the Library Court, a policy-planning and lobbying group begun in 1979 to coordinate the activities of what had been until that time a number of otherwise unconnected "profamily" groups. Over the past few years the Library Court has proposed a wide range of legislation, constitutional amendments, and administrative practices, all designed to protect what they see as the traditional family. The broadest of these proposals is the

6

Family Protection Act (FPA), a document of over fifty pages that was first introduced to Congress by Senator Laxalt of Nevada in 1979 and then reintroduced in the summer of 1980. It is now wending its way through the House and Senate.

This Act seeks to encourage and support the traditional heterosexual couple, permanently wed, in which the husband is the breadwinner and head of the household, the wife is a housekeeper and mother, and the children (of which there are always some) are subject to parental control. The FPA provides tax benefits for married couples filing joint returns, child care deductions for nonworking mothers, and tax exemptions to married couples who adopt a child.[1] In an attempt to preserve the traditional division of labor between husbands and wives, the act would withhold federal funds from projects that "deny, diminish, or denigrate the role differences between the sexes as they have been historically understood in the United States." It would prohibit the federal government from engaging in any litigation involving abortion or divorce. While the act's primary concern is with the nuclear unit, it also supports multigenerational families by providing tax credits for couples taking elderly parents into their homes.

The act also attempts to protect parental authority over their children against what they see as encroachments on the sanctity of the family by public agencies. It would deny federal funds to any groups that provide counseling services to minors about contraception or venereal disease without parental consent, would give parents the right to censor any school texts, and would prohibit federal funds to state or local educational agencies that limit parental visits to schools or access to records. Parents would receive a tax credit for sending their children to private and parochial schools, even schools that are racially or religiously segregated.

In addition, the FPA is directed against a number of groups, most notably homosexuals. Federal funding would be prohibited to anyone or any organization that "presents homosexuality, male or female, as an acceptable alternative life style or suggests that it can be an acceptable life style." No agency of the government would be allowed to seek enforcement of nondiscrimination against individuals who are homosexuals or who profess homosexual tendencies (Petchesky 1981; Schulman 1981; Wohl 1981a). In short, in the face of an apparently growing diversity of family patterns, the New Right seeks to restrict legitimacy to a single and traditional model of family life.

Following a brief description of some of the internal divisions within the New Right, this chapter suggests (1) that its policy on families and women is central to its beliefs; (2) that this policy is a response to real changes in the structure of American families and perhaps even includes a genuine concern for the position of women; but (3) that the New Right response to those changes is based on a misunderstanding of their meaning and its proposed policies would only exacerbate many of the problems they intend to solve.

The Contours of the New Right

We should not imagine that the New Right is monolithic. While the New Right (like the New Left before it) appears to have emerged out of a set of broad, shared sentiments and critical impulses, these sentiments and impulses are not sufficiently specific to translate into a program with which all New Right groups can agree. While some include more traditional conservative goals within their programs (e.g., opposition to welfare and support for the military), others concentrate more exclusively on social issues. Moreover, many of the organizations often included under the rubric of the New Right are single-issue groups that have little interest in joining a broader profamily coalition and in some cases (like the National Right to Life Committee, the largest antiabortion organization in the United States) have even publicly disavowed their support for other New Right issues.

The New Right consists of loosely knit affiliates, an uneasy coalition held together at times, as Frances Fitzgerald (1981) has suggested, by little more than shared mailing lists. Even the use of a single term, like the "New Right," to describe these groups may involve an analytic leap, suggesting a unity and stability that does not in fact exist. For the New Right includes both different types of organizations and different ideological strands. It includes religious organizations such as the Moral Majority and the Religious Roundtable, whose fundamentalist leaders, like Jerry Falwell (head of the Moral Majority and preacher on the "Old-Time Gospel Hour" that reaches as many as 50 million weekly), emphasize the scriptural basis of their positions. It includes single-issue groups whose members focus on specific concerns—antiabortion, stopping ERA, or forestalling homosexuality—but typically do not agree on the complete range of New Right issues. Some of the leaders of these groups, such as Phyllis Schlafly, leader of Stop ERA and the Eagle Forum, have refused to share membership lists with others. Finally, the New Right contains secular multi-issue groups such as the Conservative Caucus and the Committee for the Survival of a Free Congress. Although these organizations (unlike the religious groups or most single-issue groups) do not rely on mass membership, they have played an important role both in the formulation of New Right policy (the Library Court and the Family Protection Act) and as fund raisers (Richard Viguerie's company RAVCO).

Yet despite its internal divisions and disagreements—disagreements that undoubtedly seem more significant to its own members than to outsiders—some factions have managed to create a loose coalition. This is based in part on the interlocking character of New Right organization, with the directors of various organizations meeting regularly and speaking often at each others' functions. Many of the groups pool mailing lists; more important, though, they share common enemies—socialists, feminists, Eastern intellectuals, and "secular humanists"—and a common diagnosis of a moral crisis in which they see the decline of the traditional family as a cause and its restoration as a cure (Viguerie 1981; Kopkind 1977; Gordon and Hunter 1977/78; Crawford 1980; Sennett 1980; Hunter 1981; Riddiough 1981; Steinem 1981; Wohl 1981b; Range 1981).

Family and the Moral Order

Several critics and observers have suggested that the New Right's explicit concern for families and family policy is not to be taken seriously, that it is a Trojan horse of sorts used to conceal an attack on welfare and a defense of unreconstructed capitalism, which are both more serious and more important. Crawford argues that family issues are primarily "symbolic" and "often nonpolitical fringe issues at best" (1980, p. 149). Fitzgerald, too, suggests that "the very issues that distinguish the New Right seem to be an after-thought" (1981, p. 21). This interpretation seems mistaken on two grounds: first, it is mistaken as a "textual" reading of the New Right, and second, it ser-iously underestimates the social and political consequences of family policy, particularly for women.

The New Right does, to be sure, both attack the welfare state and defend unreconstituted capitalism. Yet many partisans also agree with Falwell that Americans are already "overly concerned about materialistic wealth" (1980, p. 126). For them, the crisis of American life is not primarily economic, it is that "we are quickly moving toward an amoral society where nothing is either absolutely right or absolutely wrong" (Falwell 1980, p. 117). At the core of the New Right's diagnosis of American society is a concern about the break-down of public and private morality, evidence for which can be found in the rise of pornography, violence and crime, illegitimate childbirths, drug use and alcoholism. Even more, the New Right is responding to the cultural upheavals of the 1960s and 1970s, and particularly to the emergence of an articulate and strong feminist movement (English 1981; Eisenstein 1981; Petchesky 1981). Such developments represent the disavowal of obligation and the dis-solution of a social order built on consensus and community. But because this crisis is primarily moral, they attempt neither to account for it nor to solve it in terms of strictly economic considerations. Rather, they respond to it in terms that speak directly to the moral order, calling for the renunciation of simple economic self-interest in favor of shared values and moral concerns.

In America as elsewhere, surely one source of moral order is religious belief and many of the New Right have placed the encouragement of religious belief high on their agenda. But this is only part of their program: equally if not more important is an emphasis on the family as both a source and an expression of reconstitution of the moral order.

The New Right Family

The family, as the New Right imagines it should be, is held together by both mutual obligation and mutual dependence. Unlike the feminist ideal of the family, which is egalitarian, the New Right ideal is hierarchical and based on a strict division of labor (Harding 1981). In some formulations the idealization of the differences between men and women is legitimated in religious terms, and in others by presumed biological conditions. Whatever the terms such a hierarchy is seen by the New Right as essential to the production and repro-duction of the moral order.

At the head of the New Right's ideal family stands the husband and father: he is the "decision maker," "protector," and "spiritual leader" (Falwell 1980, p. 129). He is responsible for the care and protection of his wife and children; but this responsibility also integrates him and controls his participation in the broader social order. As conservative theoretician George Gilder describes the process:

> A married man is spurred by the claims of his family to channel his otherwise disruptive male aggressiveness into his performance as a provider for his wife and children. . . . Most men make sacrifices necessary to reach the higher reaches of the American economy chiefly to support their wives and children. (1981, pp. 89, 191)

Thus, in the course of meeting his obligations as a husband and father, the married man must also become a good citizen.

In contrast, the ideal wife is submissive and domestic. As Schlafly would have it: "Everyone in the world has a boss of some kind . . . the family cannot be run by committee . . . if marriage is to be successful, it must have an ultimate decision maker, and that is the husband" (1977, pp. 60-61). While the wife is subordinate, this does not, to Schlafly and others, imply inferiority or debasement: in return for the care she receives from her husband, she also has her own important obligations.

Foremost among these is motherhood. It is here that women find their most important rights, duties, and responsibilities. As Falwell puts it: "Children deserve a well-educated, imaginative, full-time mother . . . the greatest investment a woman can ever make is in the lives of her precious children" (1980, p. 148). And as Schlafly says: "If her influence is limited to her immediate family, she knows that after all, nothing is more important than building the morals and integrity of the family unit, especially for its children" (1977, p. 177). Women who choose not to parent, women who put children in day-care centers, women who do not understand the moral obligations of parenting are selfish and sinful. As a mother, the New Right woman not only fulfills her own obligations but transmits a sense of responsibility to her children, ensuring that a moral order is reproduced from generation to generation.

In short, the mother should exercise unconditional authority over her children, and the husband, unconditional authority over his wife. This involves not only a rejection of both feminism and what Falwell has called "children's liberation philosophy," the idea that "children have rights separate from their family (sic)" (1980, p. 135), but also of the state's involvement in family matters. It is on these grounds that the New Right opposes both intrusions on parental authority—whether by schools, courts, or television—and intrusions on the husband's authority, as in their opposition to legislation attempting to control domestic violence (Eisenstein 1981; Petchesky 1981; Billings and Goldman 1979; Page and Clelland 1978).

To the New Right the family can and should be a critical source of moral order, but they do not imagine that American families are currently operating as they should. Quite the reverse:

> Since the family is the basic unit of society and since the family is in desperate trouble today, we can conclude that our society is in danger of total collapse. We are not moving towards an alternative life style. We are moving closer to the brink of destruction.
> (Falwell 1981, p. 254)

It is the crisis of the family—the rise of feminism and children's rights, egalitarianism, homosexuality, and sexual promiscuity—that is seen as the basis for a broader crisis of American social life.

The Crisis of the Family

In certain respects this analysis of the American family cannot be dismissed. If only on the level of description, the New Right successfully identifies a number of important trends concerning premarital sex, the relationship between husbands and wives, and between parents and children. I will argue later that the New Right has misunderstood the significance of changes in the family and that their policies would not succeed in reconstructing the family, even in their own terms.

The New Right points to acceptance of premarital sex as a cause of declining commitment to marriage, rising rates of abortion and single parenthood. Indeed, the number of teenagers who were sexually active increased by two-thirds in the last decade (Allan Gutmacher Institute 1981; Zelnick and Kanter 1981) and the increase was especially high among those aged ten to fourteen years old (Vinovskis 1981). It is now "the exceptional person who has not had premarital sex by age 19" (Allan Gutmacher Institute 1981, p. 3). Moreover, such activity is no longer simply a part of courtship in anticipation of marriage, as teenagers date and often sleep with a series of partners before marriage. Not surprisingly, the number of pregnancies among unmarried teenage women is also increasing. At the same time there has been a decline in the likelihood that teenagers will marry while pregnant: the proportion now is only 16 percent compared to 33 percent as recently as 1971. In addition, more of these young women are choosing abortion, 37 percent in 1980 compared to 23 percent in 1971 (Zelnick and Kanter 1981).

Not only are young people having sex in increasing numbers; they are living in decidedly untraditional ways. Between 1970 and 1980 the number of cohabiting couples tripled. The figures are even more startling when we look at those below twenty-five years of age, for whom the incidence of cohabitation increased tenfold over the last decade (U.S. Bureau of the Census 1981c).

While the young are clearly delaying marriage, they are not, as the New Right would suggest, rejecting marriage. Almost all eventually wed; however, the households they establish when they do marry tend not to fit the traditional form. By 1981 only 13 percent of American households consisted of a husband as sole wage earner, a wife as full-time homemaker and mother, and one or more children at home (U.S. Bureau of the Census 1981a, 1981b). Among married couples with children under age eighteen in the home, the majority (54%) of wives have jobs (U.S. Bureau of Census 1981b).

The New Right is also correct in asserting that couples in which the wife is employed are less stable than those in which she remains in the home: divorce rates are highest in families in which the wife works and has her own income (Cherlin 1981; Levitan and Belous 1981b). As they suggest, a strict division of labor (husband as wage earner and wife as homemaker) is likely to hold a family together out of mutual dependence.

Marriages of all sorts are increasingly unstable. While the divorce rate in the United States remained stable from 1951 to 1965, it has more than doubled since then (Kitagawa 1981). As a consequence, increasing numbers of children (20%) are now living with only one parent; most of these (90%) with only a mother (U.S. Bureau of the Census 1981c). As the New Right suggests, single parents seem less likely to expose their children to traditional values. While parenting typically fosters customary sex roles (Feldman 1981), divorced parents adopt less traditional views (Thornton and Freeman 1979). Moreover, without a second parent in the home, parental authority is likely to weaken: single mothers give their children greater rights and responsibilities and their children return less deference (Weiss 1979). Divorce does seem to entail a lowered commitment to the established social order on the part of both parents and children.

Only after recognizing the extent of the transformations that characterize contemporary American family life is it possible to make sense of New Right policy. It is not simply an attempt to defend an idealized traditional family. Rather, like the feminism it opposes, it is also a response to social dislocation. In this sense, it has an appreciable logic that appeals to quite genuine hopes and fears of both women and men. Its attraction for men is easy enough to see: as long as women remain in the home, men are protected from female competition in the marketplace, while benefiting from the highly personalized "consumption services" that wives provide (Hartmann 1981a, 1981b; Washington Area Marxist-Feminist Theory Study Group 1982). But New Right family policy is also attractive to certain women, especially those whose primary, or only, training was to be a housewife and mother. It is, in fact, these women who are the activists at New Right rallies and demonstrations (Brady and Tedins 1976; English 1981; Kopkind 1977). For them the current transformation of family life does not promise liberation, but threatens loneliness, abandonment, and poverty (Huber, Rexroat, and Spitze 1979; Dworkin 1979; Hacker 1980; Ault 1981).

Schlafly in particular has been sensitive to the significance of such threats. She asks, at one point: "Are you looking for security—emotional, social, financial?", and answers: "Nothing in the world is secure but death and taxes, but marriage and motherhood are the most reliable security the world can offer" (1977, p. 57). In her formulation New Right family policy is not directed at the control of women but at the control of men, and is best understood as an attempt to remind them of—indeed, to enforce—their obligations to women. For women to whom easily available divorce threatens impoverishment, this is a significant protection.

Even the New Right position on abortion may be understood as an attempt to dignify motherhood, and thus the situation of women, at a moment when the traditional sources of such dignity are under attack. As Blake and Del Pinal have suggested, "To have total discretion over reproduction may, for some women, seem to trivialize what they regard as the cosmic importance of motherhood" (1980, p. 49). Because relations with children are one clear sphere of women's power in the family, "for women who wish to use pregnancy as an instrumentality in their relations with husbands, easy access to abortion lessens rather than increases feminine power" (Blake and Del Pinal 1980, p. 49)[2].

There is, then, a surprising but nonetheless clear affinity between the goals of certain aspects of New Right family policy and the very feminism it apparently opposes, as both are strategies for the protection of women. Both have not only identified the family as the critical institutional setting in which the rights and needs of women are resolved, they have also argued that the family in its current form is inadequate to either these rights or needs. Where feminists emphasize the oppressive aspects of family life and thus assert women's rights within and against the family, the New Right emphasizes the protective aspects of family life and attempts to revitalize its traditional form.

The New Right and Public Opinion

According to many partisans of the New Right, their views have wide appeal. In Richard Viguerie's words: "The simple truth is that there is a new majority in America—and it is being led by the New Right" (1981, p. 7). This view is often accepted by critics of the New Right, implicit in references to its "ability to mobilize, not only as a backlash but as a mass movement" (Riddiough 1981, p. 30) and explicit in references to its "mass following" (Petchesky 1981, p. 237) or to its "great strength" (Gordon and Hunter 1977/78). Insofar as this assessment is based on the presumed appeal of New Right family programs in particular, it is a seriously mistaken reading of the American public and its response to the current transformation of family life. To most Americans family life as it is now evolving appears to offer liberation and opportunity as much as crisis.

Consider attitudes toward the employment of women. In both 1972 and 1978 a national sample of adult females and males was asked: "Do you approve of a married woman working if she has a husband capable of supporting her?" Already by 1972, 63 percent of the men and 68 percent of the women agreed. By 1978 positive response had increased to 72 percent of men and 78 percent of women (Cherlin and Walters 1981).

Even more impressive are the shifts on the harder questions of the employment of mothers. While in 1970 only one-half agreed with the statement "A working mother can establish just as warm and secure a relationship with her children as a mother who does not work," that number had increased to over two-thirds by 1977, the latest date for which data are available (Cherlin and Walters 1981). In an analysis of 1980 election data, I found that only 5.7 percent of males and 7.2 percent of females agreed with the New Right position by saying they strongly believed women's place was in the home.[3] As Thornton and Freeman (1979) have shown, the evidence of changing attitudes toward sex roles is not limited to certain classes or ethnic groups, but pervades all social strata.

Evidence for a rejection of the New Right construction of family life can also be seen in Americans' views on the ERA. Schlafly fights the ERA precisely because she believes it will destroy family life. This amendment, she argues, "loosens the legal bonds that keep families together" (1977, p. 94), "weakens the family" (1977, p. 116), "hurts husbands" (1977, p. 16), and "has no relevance to the 'big majority' of working women" (1977, p. 15). But the 'big majority' of Americans does not agree. In a 1978 National Opinion Research Center survey, 73 percent of males and 75 percent of females who had heard of the amendment approved of it and only 8 percent of men and 11 percent of women strongly opposed it.

Attitudes toward premarital sexual activity show the same rejection of the New Right agenda (de Boer 1981). Using data from five national surveys, Singh (1980) finds a steady increase in approval of premarital sex. The majority of males and females, of blacks and whites, of inhabitants of all regions of the nation, and even of Catholics and non-Catholics did not disapprove. Most do not view increases in sexual activity as evidence of moral disorder but apparently understand it as liberation.

There is perhaps somewhat more support for the New Right view that divorce should be more difficult. Indeed, in a 1978 national survey only 30 percent thought divorce should be made easier to obtain while 42 percent believed that divorce laws were not strict enough (U.S. Bureau of the Census 1980). Even these findings, however, represent a considerable liberalization of attitudes. Divorce has, in fact, become easier to obtain, in large part a consequence of no-fault laws, the first of which was not introduced until 1970. Yet in 1968, a time when laws were stricter, only 15 percent of the population believed divorce should be made easier while 60 percent believed the laws should be tightened (Cherlin 1981). Even though there is still considerable support for more restrictions on divorce, there is a clear trend away from such a position.

Only in regard to abortion does there seem to be evidence of widespread and possibly growing support for New Right positions. Despite the claims of many in the antiabortion movement that they represent a clear majority, the situation is, in fact, quite complex. From 1965 to 1973 the proportion of liberal attitudes on abortion increased dramatically, peaking in 1974. Stabilizing until 1977, 1978 brought a clear swing to the right when the population became increasingly divided. But by 1980 acceptance of abortion returned to the 1977 level (Granberg 1978; Granberg and Granberg 1980; Ebaugh and Haney 1980; Blake and Del Pinal 1980; Tedrow and Mahoney 1979). Today the large majority of Americans think that an abortion should be allowed if the mother's health is in danger, if the woman became pregnant as a result of rape, or if there is a "strong chance" that the baby will be born with a serious defect. Less than half of the population thinks that a woman should have a legal right to abortion simply because she is single and unwilling to marry the man responsible for the pregnancy or, if married, because she prefers not to have any more children. Most are also opposed to governmental support of abortion (Granberg and Granberg 1980; Baker, Epstein, and Forth 1981; Blake and Del Pinal 1981). The majority endorse some middle position: some justifications but not abortion on demand; support of private payment but opposition to public support. Furthermore, there is evidence that this majority—if forced to choose politically between the two polar positions represented by the New Right and Pro-Choice—may go with the Right (Blake and Del Pinal 1981).

If there is any wedge into public opinion for New Right positions, it would seem to be around abortions. Taken as a whole, however, the evidence from national sample surveys suggests that the New Right family program is hardly a majority position and that insofar as any trends are discernible, they are toward liberalization of attitudes toward family life.

Structural Trends

Even more important than attitudinal trends are the underlying structural trends to which attitudes are, at least in part, a response. These trends suggest that even if the New Right were successful in enacting its family program, that program would not be sufficient to restore the idealized traditional family of their imagination.

The most important structural trend undermining the tradtional family is the entrance of women into the labor force, a consequence not simply of changing attitudes but also of changes in the demand for and supply of women workers. The increased demand is in large part the result of rapid expansion since World War II of the service sector of the economy. Specifically, during the last decade the volume of patronage in eating places, health stores, and general businesses grew at a rate no less than sixteen times as fast as the industrial sector. These rapidly growing sectors of the economy contain a disproportionately large number of positions that have been defined as women's (Oppenheimer 1970; Rothschild 1981; Treiman and Hartmann 1981).

If the increased demand for women workers is accounted for by sectoral changes, the increased supply is in part accounted for by the inflationary pressures that accompany the rise of service industries and now seem endemic to advanced industrial societies. The most powerful predictor of women's employment is economic need (Gordon and Kammeyer 1980; Hiller and Philliber 1980; Levitan and Belous 1981a). With inflationary pressures, more and more families must depend on two wage earners to survive. Moreover, it is at the point at which children are born that economic pressures on the family are greatest. In addition to the cost of children themselves, they are most often born when the husband and father's career is still at an early and less well-paid stage. A "life cycle squeeze," as Valerie Oppenheimer (1974) and others have called it, impels women into the labor force at the same time that the New Right is insistent they should be in the home.

Once begun, a pattern of two-earner families tends to sustain itself. As Rothschild (1981) has argued, the very transformation of family life affected by the rise of the service sector supports the continued growth of that sector: as more women work and as more individuals live alone, the more people there are to buy services (for example, restaurant meals) that in the past were provided by women within the home and that are now provided by women employed outside the home. At the same time, as Oppenheimer (1979) has argued, young couples establish their expectations for a standard of living by looking to slightly older couples. Since most of these couples now have two incomes, newly married pairs are likely to feel pressure for both husband and wife to work. Nothing the New Right proposes or preaches is likely to arrest these trends.[4]

If the New Right is unlikely to slow the trend toward increased employment of women, it is equally unlikely to slow the increases in divorce. As recent studies show that liberalization of divorce laws results in no measurable increase in divorce rates (Wright and Stetson 1978), there is no reason to think that stricter laws would result in their decline. After extensive research in the United States and elsewhere, Max Rheinstein has concluded that "a strict statute law of divorce is not an effective means to prevent or even reduce the incidence of marital breakdown" (1972, p. 406). Indeed, it is likely that the only effect of stricter laws would be to stigmatize divorce and protract court proceedings, increasing the already significant distress suffered by those who do separate.

Passage of some form of antiabortion legislation would surely decrease the rate, yet many illegal abortions were performed before the Supreme Court's ruling in 1973, and it is likely that they would continue to be performed even if they were made illegal. Indeed, with a network of abortion counselors already in place and many doctors now experienced in the procedure, it seems unlikely that passage of antiabortion legislation could reduce the rate even to what it was before the Supreme Court ruling. While the amendment would make abortions more difficult, more expensive, and less safe, it would not stop them altogether (Donovan 1981; Glen 1978).

Conclusion

I have argued that family policy, far from an afterthought, is at the very core of New Right concerns about our society. New Right family policy is a response to a very real and ongoing transformation of family life and speaks directly to the dislocations suffered by a number of women in the course of this transformation. However, I have also argued that most Americans, women and men, neither share the New Right's attachment to an idealized traditional family nor accept its policy proposals for the family. Even if New Right policies were enacted, they would do little to realize the intended goals: prevention of women's entrance into the labor force, a decline in divorce rates, or an end to abortion.

If the New Right has neither mass appeal nor potentially effective policies, this does not mean that there are no grounds to fear its success. Although their family policy does not at the moment enjoy mass support, public opinion is an often unstable phenomenon and it is conceivable, although not likely, that it will shift. More important, American politics do not work by public opinion polls alone. At least in the election of 1980, various New Right organizations proved themselves highly effective in mobilizing support against those they opposed. It is yet to be seen how much influence they will exercise over the current Reagan administration, but it would be premature to rule out the possibility that they will be able to achieve many of their policy objectives even without public support. In fact, some of these policies are currently being enacted into law[1].

Similarly, although New Right programs are not likely to restore an idealized family, they might have other effects of equal importance. As mentioned, enactment of New Right legislation could make abortion and divorce, already difficult experiences, yet more painful. More important and more generally, New Right programs could result in the acceleration of a phenomenon most easily identified as "the feminization of poverty." Already, 30 percent of female-headed households are below the poverty line, and such households account for fully 51 percent of all those below that line (Levitan and Belous 1981b). This concentration is the result of child care burdens, insufficient skills and in at least some cases, simple discrimination. Yet, by denying abortions, a policy likely to be most effective among those already poor and unskilled, New Right policies would increase the burdens of childcare among those least able to afford them, and would, of course, do nothing either to encourage the upgrading of skills in the female labor force or discourage discrimination. They would, in short, do a great deal to exacerbate the problems of the large number of women—never married, newly divorced, widowed—who do not enjoy the "protection" (itself dubious at best) of an idealized traditional family. This can be prevented only by political organization and activity as effective as that of the New Right itself.

NOTES

[1] Some of these tax benefits have already become law. For example, in 1982 expenses for adopting a child with special needs may be deducted. The so-called Marriage Penalty Tax, in which a married couple paid higher taxes than an unmarried couple or

two single people with comparable income, was reduced as part of the Economic Recovery Act, signed into law by Congress in 1981. The New Right's policy of requiring parental consent for any counseling of teenagers about contraception is now before Congress.

[2] Linda Gordon has argued that in the nineteenth century, opposition to abortion was fueled by a desire to help "women strengthen their ability to say no to their husbands' sexual demands" (1981, p. 81; Gordon 1982). New Right discussions of women's sphere in contemporary society evoke, at least superficially, the nineteenth century. Historians maintain that creation of a separate women's sphere opened up avenues of power and influence to women (Cott 1977). Historically, in fact, it prepared the way for the emergence of feminism. Today such prescriptions are a backlash or reaction against a strong feminist movement rather than a prologue to it.

[3] Respondents were asked: "Recently there has been a lot of talk about women's rights. Some people feel that women should have an equal role with men in running business, industry, government. Others feel women's place is in the home. Where would you place yourself?" Responses ranged from one (equal role) to seven (women's place is in the home). Figures reported in the text are the percentage choosing the code seven, who took a position equivalent to that of the New Right. If we examine those who "lean" toward keeping women in the home (who chose a five, six, or seven), they are far from a majority, including only 21.4 percent of males and 18.7 percent of females. (Source: American Election Study, 1980, Center for Political Studies, Institute for Social Research, University of Michigan).

[4] In an interesting recent analysis, Clawson, Johnson, and Clawson (1982) suggest a different view. They argue that there is nothing inevitable about the continuing expansion of the service sector. Quite the reverse, they hold that the currently fashionable commitment to "reindustrialization" might, by political rather than strictly economic means, reverse the patterns of sectoral growth that have characterized the recent past. This would result in a declining demand for women workers.

REFERENCES

Allan Gutmacher Institute. 1981. *Teenage pregnancy: the problem that hasn't gone away.* New York: The Institute.

Ault, J. M. 1981. *Class differences in family structure and the social bases of modern feminism.* Unpublished doctoral dissertation, Brandeis University.

Baker, R. K.; Epstein, L. R.; and Forth, R. D. 1981. Matters of life and death. *American Politics Quarterly* 9:89-102.

Billings, D., and Goldman, R. 1979. Comment on the Kanawha County textbook controversy. *Social Forces* 57:1393-98.

Blake, J., and Del Pinal, J. H. 1980. Predicting polar attitudes toward abortion in the United States. In *Abortion parley*, ed. J. Burthcaell, pp. 27-56. New York: Andrews and McMeel.

Blake, J., and Del Pinal, J. H. 1981. Negativism, equivocation and wobbly assent: public support for the pro-choice platform on abortion. *Demography* 18:309-20.

Brady, D., and Tedins, K. 1976. Ladies in pink: religion and political ideology in the anti-ERA movement. *Social Science Quarterly* 56:564-76.

Cherlin, A. 1981. *Marriage, divorce, remarriage.* Cambridge: Harvard University Press.

Cherlin, A., and Walters, P. B. 1981. Trends in United States men's and women's sex role attitudes: 1972-1978. *American Sociological Review* 46:453-60.

Clawson, M. A.; Johnson, K.; and Clawson, D. 1982. Women, the new right, and reindustrialization. Paper to be presented at the Annual Meeting of the Society for the Study of Social Problems, San Francisco.

Cott, N. 1977. *The bonds of womanhood.* New Haven: Yale University Press.

Crawford, A. 1980. *Thunder on the right.* New York: Pantheon.

De Boer, C. 1981. The polls: marriage—a decaying institution? *Public Opinion Quarterly* 2:265-72.

Donovan, P. 1981. Half a loaf: a new anti-abortion strategy. *Family Planning Perspectives* 13:265-72.

Dworkin, A. 1979. Safety, shelter, rules, form, love: the promises of the ultra-right. *Ms.* 7:62-76.

Ebaugh, H. R. F., and Haney, C. 1980. Shift in abortion attitudes: 1972-1978. *Journal of Marriage and the Family* 42:491-500.

Eisenstein, Z. 1981. Antifeminism in the politics and elections of 1980. *Feminist Studies* 7:187-205.

English, D. 1981. The war against choice: inside the anti-abortion movement. *Mother Jones* 8:187-205.

Falwell, J. 1980. *Listen, America!* New York: Bantam.

Feldman, H. 1981. A comparison of intentional parents and intentionally childless parents. *Journal of Marriage and the Family* 43:593-600.

Fitzgerald, F. 1981. Triumph of the new right. *New York Review of Books* 28:19-26.

Gilder, G. 1981. *Wealth and power.* New York: Bantam.

Glen, K. B. 1978. Abortion in the courts: a laywoman's historical guide to the new disaster area. *Feminist Studies* 4:1-27.

Gordon, H. A., and Kammeyer, K. 1980. The gainful employment of women with young children. *Journal of Marriage and the Family* 42:327-36.

Gordon, L. 1981. The long struggle for reproductive rights. *Radical America* 15:75-88.

Gordon, L. 1982. Why nineteenth century feminists did not support "birth control" and twentieth century feminists do: feminism, reproduction and the family. In *Rethinking the family: some feminist questions*, ed. B. Thorne with M. Yalom, pp. 40-53. New York: Longman.

Gordon, L., and Hunter, A. 1977/78. Sex, family, and the new right. *Radical America* 11:1-17.

Granberg, D. 1978. Pro-life or reflection of conservative ideology. *Sociology and Social Research* 62:414-29.

Granberg, D., and Granberg, B. W. 1980. Abortion attitudes, 1965-1980: trends and determinants. *Family Planning Perspectives* 12:250-61.

Hacker, A. 1980. E.R.A.-R.I.P. *Harpers* September 10-14.

Harding, S. 1981. Family reform movements: recent feminism and its opposition. *Feminist studies* 7:57-75.

Hartmann, H. 1981a. The family as the locus of gender, class and political struggle: the example of housework. *Signs* 6:366-94.

Hartmann, H. 1981b. The unhappy marriage of marxism and feminism: towards a more progressive union. In *Women and Revolution*, ed. Lydia Sargent, pp. 1-42. Boston: South End Press.

Hiller, D. V., and Philliber, W. W. 1980. Necessity, compatibility, and status attainment as factors in the labor force participation of married women. *Journal of Marriage and the Family* 42:347-54.

Huber, J.; Rexroat, C.; and Spitze, G. 1979. A crucible of opinion on women's status: ERA in Illinois. *Social Forces* 57:549-65.

Hunter, A. 1981. In the wings: new right ideology and organization. *Radical America* 15:113-38.

Kitagawa, E. 1981. New life styles: marriage patterns, living arrangements, and fertility outside of marriage. *Annals of the American Academy of Science.* 453:1-17.

Kopkind, A. 1977. America's new right. *New Times* September 30:21-33.

Levitan, S. A., and Belous, R. S. 1981a. Working wives and mothers: what happens to family life? *Monthly Labor Review* 104:26-30.

Levitan, S. A., and Belous, R. S. 1981b. *What's happening to the American family?* Baltimore: Johns Hopkins University Press.

Oppenheimer, V. 1974. The life-cycle squeeze: the interaction of men's occupational and family life cycles. *Demography* 11:227-245.

Oppenheimer, V. 1979. Structural sources of economic pressure for wives to work: an analytical framework. *Journal of Family History* 4:177-97.

Oppenheimer, V. 1980. *The female labor force in the United States.* Westport, Conn.: Greenwood.

Page, A. L., and Clelland, D. A. 1978. The Kanawha County textbook controversy: a study of the politics of life style concern. *Social Forces* 57:265-81.

Phillips, K. 1970. *The emerging republican majority.* New York: Anchor.

Petchesky, R. 1981. Antiabortion, antifeminism, and the rise of the new right. *Feminist Studies* 7:206-46.

Range, P. R. 1981. Thunder from the right. *New York Times Magazine* February 8:22-25.

Rheinstein, M. 1972. *Marital stability, divorce, and the law.* Chicago: University of Chicago Press.

Riddiough, C. 1981. Women, feminism and the 1980 election. *Socialist Review* 11:71-95.

Rothschild, E. 1981. Reagan and the real economy. *New York Review of Books* 28:12-18.

Sennett, R. 1980. Power to the people. *New York Review of Books* 27:24-28.

Schulman, S. 1981. All in the family whether we like it or not. *WIN* May 15:5-7.

Schlafly, P. 1977. *The power of the positive woman.* New York: Jove.

Singh, B. K. 1980. Trends in attitudes toward premarital sexual relations. *Journal of Marriage and the Family* 42:387-94.

Steinem, G. 1982. Feminist notes: make war not love: a right wing lexicon. *Ms.* 10:93-102.

Tedrow, L. M., and Mahoney, E. R. 1979. Trends in attitudes toward abortion: 1972-1976. *Public Opinion Quarterly* 43:181-89.

Thornton, A., and Freeman, D. S. 1979. Changes in sex role attitudes of women, 1962-1977: evidence from a panel study. *American Sociological Review* 44:831-42.

Treiman, D., and Hartmann, H. 1981. *Women, work, and wages.* Washington, D.C.: National Academy.

U.S. Bureau of the Census. 1981o. *American families and living arrangements.* Current Population Reports, Special Studies, Series P-23, No. 104. Washington, D.C.: U.S. Government Printing Office.

U.S. Bureau of the Census. 1981a. *Households and families by type: March 1981.* Current Population Reports, Series P-20, No. 387. Washington, D.C.: U.S. Government Printing Office.

U.S. Bureau of the Census. 1981b. *Household and family characteristics.* Current Population Reports, Series P-20, No. 365. Washington, D.C.: U.S. Government Printing Office.

U.S. Bureau of the Census. 1981c. *Marital status and living arrangements: March 1980.* Current Population Reports, Series P-20, No. 365. Washington, D.C.: U.S. Government Printing Office.

Viguerie, R. A. 1981. *The new right: we're ready to lead.* Falls Church, Va.:Viguerie.

Vinovskis, M. A. 1981. An epidemic of adolescent pregnancy? Some historical considerations. *Journal of Family History* 6:205-30.

Washington Area Marxist-Feminist Theory Study Group. 1982. None dare call it patriarchy: a critique of the new immiseration. *Socialist Review* 61:105-112.

Weiss, R. 1979. *Going it alone. The family life and social situation of the single parent.* New York: Basic Books.

Wohl, L. 1981a. Watch on the right, can you protect your family from the family protection act? *Ms.* 9:76-77.

Wohl, L. 1981b. Backstage with the anti-abortion forces. *Ms.* 9:48-51.

Wright, G., and Stetson, D. 1978. The impact of no-fault divorce reform on divorce in American states. *Journal of Marriage and the Family* 40:575-80.

Zelnik, M., and Kanter, J. 1980. Sexual activity, contraceptive use, and pregnancy among metropolitan teenagers: 1971-79. *Family Planning Perspectives* 12:230-37.

SELECTED LISTINGS

New Right Activists, Organizations, and Leaders

Ehrenreich, B. The women's movements: feminist and anti-feminist. *Radical America* 15 (1981):93-105. Journalistic description of forces promoting antifeminist movement and undermining feminist movement.

Felsenthal, C. *The sweetheart of the silent majority: the biography of Phyllis Schlafly.* New York: Doubleday, 1981. A biography written by a journalist and supporter of the ERA. Useful for its discussion of Schlafly's earlier right-wing activities.

Goodman, W. R., and Price, J. J. H. *Jerry Falwell: an unauthorized profile.* Lynchburg, Va.: Paris Associates, 1981. An examination of Falwell's political and religious views. Relies on published material and interviews with individuals who either know Falwell or know of him. Contains a chapter on Falwell's position on women and families.

Granberg, D. The abortion activists. *Family Planning Perspectives.* Comparison of social characteristics and attitudes of members of one antiabortion group (NRLC) and one pro-choice group (NARAL). Finds NRLC activists, who are likely to be practicing Catholics, have consistently more conservative views than NARAL activists (they are more likely to oppose ERA, to favor restrictive divorce laws, to think homosexuality is wrong, and to oppose the availability of birth control for teenagers), but the majority of both groups favor political, social, and economic equality for women in other respects.

Hunter, W. A. *The new right: a growing force in state politics.* Washington, D.C.: Conference on Alternative State and Local Politics and Center to Protect Worker's Rights, 1980. Analyses of New Right's operation at state level. Contains ten case studies.

Tax, M., and Wallace, B. *The interlocking directorate.* 1980. A chart documenting the connections between leaders of conservative political organizations. Available from Bettie Wallace, Center for Constitutional Rights, 853 Broadway, New York, NY 10003.

Tedin, K. L.; Brady, M. E.; Gorman, B.; and Thompson, J. Social background and political differences between pro and anti-ERA activists. *American Politics Quarterly* 5 (1977):395-407. Examination of social and political differences between activists. Finds few educational or income differences but suggests that while pro-ERA activists tend to be secular, anti-ERA activists tend to be extremely religious and believe the ERA undermines authority both in the family and in the wider society.

Publications by and about the New Right

Conservative Digest. 7777 Leesburg Pike, Falls Church, VA 22043. A monthly magazine published by Richard Viguerie. (See especially vol. 6, May-June 1980, which provides profiles of profamily movement leaders, networks and aims.)

Group Research Reports. Group Research, Inc., 419 Jersey Avenue, SE, Washington, DC 20003. A monthly newsletter about the activities of the New Right.

Human Events. 422 First Avenue, SE, Washington, DC, 20003. A conservative monthly newsletter covering political events and activities.

Moral Majority. Moral Majority, Inc., 499 South Capitol Street, Suite 101, Washington, DC 20003. A free monthly publication covering profamily positions (as well as other views) of the religious Moral Majority.

2 | Women and Education

Polly Welts Kaufman

Throughout the year 1981 women continued to demonstrate in a variety of ways the depth of their commitment to equity for girls and women in the field of education. They could point to many results. More than one-half of college students are women. Their participation in law and medical schools has exceeded one-quarter of the total student body. Women who once thought their only options for training were in traditional fields entered programs to prepare themselves for scientific and technical careers. Girls and college women found greater access to athletic programs than ever before. School systems worked to foster sex-fair practices and to select sex-fair teaching materials.

Some areas proved more resistant to change than others. In the fields of administration in public education and librarianship, and at the highest levels of academic institutions women's progress could barely be measured. Declining budgets at local, state, and federal levels threatened goals already reached and new programs being planned. Women in collegiate athletics suffered a severe loss in their power to control their own competitions. Pressure increased from those who want to narrow the jurisdiction of Title IX. The Women's Educational Equity Act and Title IV of the Civil Rights Act were kept out of the block grants to states only after extraordinary lobbying efforts by organized women.

If women in education have learned one lesson in their efforts to achieve equity, it has been that all women at every level of society and in all ethnic groups must work together for change. When educational programs truly meet their needs, women come forward in surprising numbers to support the continuation of those programs. Only through grass-roots involvement in professional associations, educational institutions, and the broader community can women expect to develop a lasting constituency for educational equity.

24

Federal Programs

The importance of keeping the federal government involved in fostering sex equity for women and girls in educational programs and employment was underscored in the summer of 1981 by the successful mobilization to save the Women's Educational Equity Act (WEEA) from inclusion in the general block grants to states. Although the authorized funding level for WEEA was reduced from $8 million to $6 million and the level of actual funding was still in doubt, the grass-roots effort showed that women could demonstrate to Congress the strength of their constituency (Klein 1981; Simpson 1981). The Vocational Education Act was also kept independent from the block grants and was extended until 1984.

Programs sponsoring educational research suffered the most severe cuts in the 1982 federal budget, and the amount of basic research in sex equity areas undertaken by such programs as the National Institute of Education (NIE) will be greatly reduced. Overall funding for women's equity projects by the Department of Education (DE) was expected to decline in 1982 from the already low level of 0.2 percent of the DE budget in 1981 (Klein 1982). Women working in federal sex equity programs made plans to stretch scarce federal dollars by placing emphasis within allowable programs on identification and dissemination of effective practices and products rather than on the development of new products (Klein 1981).

Title IX

Recent efforts to limit the jurisdiction of Title IX, the basic statute enforcing the equitable treatment of girls and women on all levels of education, threatened to weaken the statute's effectiveness. Title IX, however, has been controversial from its beginning. Although it was passed in 1972 as part of the Education Amendments, guidelines for its general enforcement were not released for three years and for intercollegiate athletics not for seven years. The basic act prohibits discrimination on the basis of sex in educational programs or activities receiving federal financial assistance. The Office of Civil Rights (OCR) is responsible for investigating complaints and initiating compliance reviews (United States Commission on Civil Rights 1980).

A major strengthening of Title IX's effectiveness, however, occurred in May 1982, when the United States Supreme Court ruled that Title IX applies to employees of educational institutions as well as to students. In *North Haven Board of Education vs. Bell,* the Court supported a lower court's decision that Title IX did cover employment discrimination. A tenured North Haven, Connecticut, teacher had filed suit because she was not rehired after a one-year maternity leave (Fields 1981a,d; Greenhouse 1982; Hook 1981c).

On the other hand, court action continues to try to limit Title IX through redefinition of what constitutes federal financial assistance (Cusick 1981;

Mann 1981; Sandler 1981). The Grove City College court case is based on the contention that assistance does not include such indirect federal aid as guaranteed student loans (Hook 1981a). Court decisions in Michigan and Texas, currently being appealed, maintained that a school's athletic program need not comply if the program itself does not receive direct federal funds (Fields 1981c).

Despite these problems with enforcement there have been significant improvements in equity (National Advisory Council on Women's Educational Programs 1981a) in the areas of vocational, graduate, and professional education. Particular gains were noted in women's athletics. The proportion of girls in high school interscholastic sports increased from 7 percent in 1971 to 35 percent in 1981. Thirty percent of all participants in current intercollegiate athletic programs are women compared with 15 percent before Title IX; in 1981 women received 22 percent of all athletic scholarships compared with 1 percent in 1974. The Council noted the least progress in the area of women employed in education. They are only slowly gaining jobs in educational administration, and the percentage of women full professors showed no increase between 1975 and 1981.

Women's Educational Equity Act

First authorized in 1974, the Women's Educational Equity Act provides two basic approaches: advocacy and action. The advocacy arm of the National Advisory Council on Women's Educational Programs (NACWEP) consists of nineteen members appointed by the President. The Council works at every level of the federal government and incorporates into its policies special awareness of the needs of minority women. Subjects of recent reports include sexual harassment, vocational education, and the special needs of black and American Indian women. Although the Council sees a need to step up the effectiveness of Title IX in general, it reports that equity has been reached in the area of federal financial assistance to women college students (NACWEP 1981b).

The WEEA program sponsors new projects and disseminates completed products from its publishing center. The Resources section of this chapter includes some of the 200 products from the implementation of such programs as business management training for rural women, bilingual and multicultural programs, Title IX strategies, and guidelines for counseling and physical education.

Title IV of the Civil Rights Act supports ten centers for sex desegregation around the country that provide training and technical assistance to assist state and local education agencies in complying with federal laws that require equal opportunity for women and girls (Klein 1981b). Title IV was also funded as a separate program in the current federal budget.

Vocational Education

In July 1981 Congress extended the Vocational Education Act of 1976 until 1984. The continuing thrust of the act is to provide training for women in nontraditional careers as a way to address the growing problem of the feminization of poverty. States are required to establish programs to overcome sex discrimination and stereotyping in vocational education and to employ full-time sex equity coordinators. At least $50,000 of a state's vocational education grant must be spent to carry out sex equity activities. In addition, twenty-six states have set aside funding for these programs (Klein 1981b; National Advisory Council on Vocational Education 1980).

Late in 1981 there was a proposed change in the vocational education regulations that would disperse the responsibility for sex equity activities throughout the staff at the state level and eliminate the positions of coordinator. The League of Women Voters, whose Education Fund sponsors the monitoring of vocational education programs in five states, opposed the change. In testifying before the House Subcommittee on Vocational Education, Anne Schink (1981) of the League stated that nothing should be done to reduce the effectiveness of the act. Occupational segregation can only be reduced by eliminating segregation in vocational training programs, she said. She emphasized the need to narrow the gap between the earnings of men and women. Women trained in skilled trades and high technology can earn substantially better salaries than women trained to work in such traditional occupations as nurse's aides, sales clerks, and typists. The League found that the only actual gains in training women for nontraditional careers were in the fields of graphic arts, applied design, and electronic accounting. Administrators in each of these areas acknowledged that the sex equity coordinators had been most responsible for generating support.

A historical perspective on women entering clerical work is offered by Janice Weiss (1981) in her study of the rise of the nineteenth-century private commercial school. The first great increase in women clerical workers was in the decade between 1880 and 1890 when their numbers rose from 7,000 to 76,000, an increase of from 5 percent to 18 percent. Of the 76,000, 28 percent were stenographers and typists. Of all stenographers and typists, women represented 64 percent of the group. By 1900, 77 percent of all stenographers and typists were women. Despite their advertisements, private commercial schools existed to supply clerical workers for the bottom of the bureaucracy and did not expect them to become managers. By 1970 clerical workers accounted for one-third of all women workers.

Elementary and Secondary Education

Genuine efforts are being made throughout the country to reduce sex-role stereotyping practices in public schools. Change generally comes, as it did in the Philadelphia public schools (Mitchell 1981), when groups from outside the school system find acceptance from groups inside the school system and work together. In Philadelphia, the principal outside agents were the Education Committee of the local branch of the National Organization for Women (NOW) and the Equal Employment Opportunity Commission (EEOC). Inside groups included the Women's Rights Committee of the Philadelphia Federation of Teachers and Women in Education, a self-help group of women working to qualify for administrative positions. A Women's Studies Advisory Committee was formed, and to date public pressure has resulted in employment of a Title IX coordinator and a sex equity coordinator, the meeting of Title IX timetables for sex desegregation of physical education and vocational arts classes, development of a resource guide and curricular materials in women's studies (supported by a grant from WEAAP), workshops on sex-equity staff development for kindergarten and primary-level teachers, and the promotion of an increasing number of women to administrative positions.

Sex-Fair Resources for Teaching

Although such publishers as the Feminist Press and TABS (see Resources) continue to produce nonsexist materials for children and young adults, parents and educators still see the need to evaluate new materials that are used in schools. One parent of a New York public school student (Wagner 1981) organized a protest that stopped the publication of *Wildfire*, a new magazine published by Scholastic Press, a publisher selling primarily to schools through book clubs and subscriptions distributed in the classroom. Stating that it "read like a parody of the 1950s *True Romances*," Wagner organized the faculty in her daughter's school, the New York Board of Education, and the National Education Association to oppose it. The recent proliferation of preteen and teenage romances that stress "love as the career for girls" prompted the Council for Interracial Books to publish a double issue of its *Bulletin* on the subject. Suggestions for confronting the romances directly through classroom discussions and by substituting other popular books are included.

Kathryn P. Scott (1981) found that the image of girls and women in basal readers has improved, but that males are still subject to sex-role stereotyping. Females are used as main characters only slightly less frequently than males and are portrayed in some nontraditional roles, although not as often as in traditional roles. Males, however, are presented only in traditional roles that depict aggressiveness and competition as the norm and are not shown participating in any traditionally female activities. Project EMBERS (Meyers 1981) takes development of basal readers one step further by designing them to include materials that help students become aware of sexist and racist attitudes and practices in society. They also learn how to respond with political action appropriate to their age levels, such as letter-writing and leaflet-writing, interviewing, and planning petitions.

Recently published bibliographies of positive role models for girls and young women include heroines in young adult sports fiction (Unsworth 1981) and "Old girls with grit" (Drew 1980). Gloria and Esther Goldreich (1981) published *What can she be? a scientist*, the twelfth in their series for children depicting women in such nontraditional careers as geologists, legislators, police officers, and veterinarians.

Sex-Fair Teaching Methods

Specific teaching methods demonstrate strategies to reduce sex-role stereotyping in the classroom. Several 1981 studies, however, reveal the necessity for broader dissemination of information about successful practices and the continuing need to study the attitudes of school faculties. In their study of 400 educators, Tetenbaum, Lighter, and Travis (1981) found that the attitudes of administrators were significantly less positive toward working mothers than those of pupil personnel workers. Males in the group showed the least positive attitudes. Benz, Pfeiffer, and Newman (1981) discovered that teachers in a county school district in Ohio classed high-achieving students as either androgynous or masculine. The researchers postulate that the negative relationship between the feminine sex role and high achievement may be a factor in declining achievement as girls progress through the grades. Pamela Riley (1981) found that kindergarten children were strongly affected by sex-role stereotypes when asked to draw pictures of what they wanted to be when they grow up.

Several projects have been successful in reducing this role stereotyping in school systems. Five school districts in Florida, Oregon, Massachusetts, North Carolina, and Arizona have been chosen as sites to demonstrate nonsexist programs, activities, and teaching methods. The Quincy, Massachusetts, project Inter-Action (Kolb 1981) uses Women's History Week each March as a focus for activities, generating community interest with student-produced projects about townswomen. One elementary school sponsored a Grandmother's Day for which students developed photographic and taped oral histories. High school students used a variety of media to present the stories of Quincy women, including those who worked in the local shipyards in World War II and educators.

A physical education instructor in a Berkeley, California elementary school (Warren 1981) reduced both racial and sex segregation on the playground by using the "new games" philosophy that makes games less competitive and more cooperative. Everyone plays regardless of ability, and some games are played without keeping score. The entire school—staff and students—played kickball with the rules changed so that each person on the team was allowed to kick before the sides switched places.

With the help of concerned Baltimore elementary school teachers, Lynette Long (1981) devised a list to check the development of sex-fair practices in their own classrooms. She administered the checklist throughout the Baltimore school system and found there had been significant progress in reducing sexist practices.

Young Women and Mathematics

The contention by Johns Hopkins researchers Benbow and Stanley (1980) that genetic differences explain the lower achievement in mathematics of girls than boys has been challenged by mathematics educators. Benbow and Stanley measured a group of highly gifted seventh-grade and eighth-grade students on the mathematics portion of the Scholastic Aptitude Test and ascribed the difference to "greater male ability in spatial tasks." Elizabeth K. Stage (1981) from the University of California, Berkeley found problems with the experimental design and assumptions of the study, and Elizabeth Fennema (1981) from the University of Wisconsin, Madison argued that the researchers should have considered the social implications of their study.

Stage (1981) stated that Benbow and Stanley made an unwarranted assumption that they were measuring two groups who had received equivalent treatment in elementary schools, despite many studies demonstrating the opposite. They generalized from an unusual sample, she said, and used an unusual test as a measure. Her most important argument was that they drew a conclusion about inherent male superiority in spatial ability without testing it.

Fennema (1981) stated that the Benbow-Stanley conclusion was not new, but that their assumption of genetic differences as the cause was unproved. What started as "a moderate statement" on the part of the researchers was picked up by the national media as "an absolute fact." As a result, Fennema explained, women would perceive that any lack of ability in mathematics showed by them was because of immutable genetic characteristics. This view, she said, would have a detrimental impact on their performance in mathematics and related areas.

Teachers and Administrators

Despite awareness of the effects of declining school enrollments on their advancement, there is some reason to believe that the long decline in women's participation in top school positions may have been reversed or at least stabilized (Weeks 1981). On the level of school board membership, at least, the proportion of women members increased by 5.3 percent in 1981 to an all-time high of 32.8 percent—triple the 10 to 12 percent of 15 years ago (Underwood, Fortune, and Dodge 1982). Another trend was actually too small to count, but there was an increase in numbers of women school district superintendents in one year to 186 from 154 (Weeks 1981). The numbers are small, but in some states such as Massachusetts the rate of increase is substantial, from four to eleven in the past year. The pool of potential administrators, that is, women holding doctorates in education, also continues to rise, up to 44 percent from 39 percent two years ago.

If indeed, the decline from the late 1920s when 55 percent of elementary principals were women has leveled off, the disparity between the number of women who are teachers and the number who are administrators is still large

(Stockard and Kempner 1981). In 1978 the total number of administrative positions held by women was 16.3 percent compared with high school teaching positions at 48.6 percent, and elementary teaching positions at 83.6 percent (National Institute of Education 1980).

A report by the National Institute of Education (NIE) (1980) consolidates recent research on why women failed to hold their own in administration. The causes are a complex combination of historical events and social change in addition to the well-documented problems of women's socialization (Adkison 1981; Marshall 1981). With the passage of equal pay laws, any financial advantage to hiring women over men as administrators was lost, and school boards often perceived male candidates to have greater financial responsibilities than women candidates. Wider educational opportunities for men from the GI Bill increased the competition for positions. The social unrest of the late 1960s and early 1970s led many school systems to prefer male administrators because they believed them to be better disciplinarians. With the passage of Title IX, establishment of WEAAP, and hiring of state sex-equity coordinators, it is possible that the social trend is in women's favor for the first time in many decades.

The very fact that women did not hold administrative positions in school systems resulted in their being outside the "old boy" network. New networks of women administrators have been formed by Project AWARE of the American Association of School Administrators, with support from the Ford Foundation. Six regional centers in Arizona, North Carolina, Oregon, Georgia, Massachusetts, and Texas hold workshops, form support groups, and circulate information about job openings in educational administration. Several short-term model programs designed to increase the pool of women candidates for leadership positions in education are also described in the NIE report.

Child-Care Workers

The large numbers of women involved in paid, formal child-care systems would be difficult to count. They include mothers who are designated family day-care providers by the Administration for Children, Youth, and Families (ACYF), workers in day-care centers funded by Title XX, and Headstart staff. More than 8,000 persons who work with children between the ages of three and five years of age earned Child Development Associate (CDA) credentials since the program was established in 1975. More than 37,000 women are currently enrolled in training programs (Bank Street College of Education 1981a).

Directed by the Bank Street College of Education, the CDA National Credentialing Program also offers bilingual and bicultural CDA credentials. New programs are being developed for workers with infants and toddlers, for workers with special-needs preschool children, and for home visitors. Although training is offered in 350 institutions, child-care workers do not have to enroll in formal courses to be eligible for a credential. Each successful candidate completes an assessment demonstrating competencies in thirteen areas, including maintaining a safe, healthy learning environment, building positive self-concepts in children, and establishing productive relationships with families (Bank Street College of Education 1981b).

Community Education

Community-based educational programs have met a variety of women's needs all over the country. Organized by such diverse groups as community action committees, libraries, and YWCAs, the majority of programs arose out of frustration with courses and policies in established institutions. The common characteristic of community education is a response to the expressed needs of women by having them participate in every stage of their training from planning to implementation. Several federal and private sources have provided funding.

The National Congress of Neighborhood Women (NCNW) developed its college programs after it found that women in three Brooklyn neighborhoods had always wanted to go to college (Haywoode and Scanlon 1981). Neighborhood issues provide a focus, and the community is used as a learning resource. Linked with La Guardia Community College, the NCNW has graduated several classes with AA degrees and has helped groups in Pittsburgh and Rochester, New York to replicate its model. Their initial grant was from the Fund for the Improvement of Post-Secondary Education (FIPSE). Similar to the NCNW in goals, the Center for Self-Reliant Education is linked with De Anza Community College in Sunnyvale, California. The Center, which is funded by the Mott Foundation, works with community women to identify needs and use available resources to meet them. It sets up training programs and networks where none exist (Brody 1981).

Realizing the need for jobs for women that do not lead to dead ends and low pay, a former counselor for ex-offenders and a few colleagues established a program in Boston to train low-income women for well-paying technical jobs. Started as Women's Enterprises in 1975, the organization reopened as the Women's Technical Institute (Lowery 1982) in new quarters at the end of 1981. More than 300 women have been trained as electronics technicians, technical drafters, and machinists. In addition, career information resources, workshops, and counseling services have been used by 10,000 women. The Institute was started with support from CETA but has moved into funding from foundations and local businesses. Local YWCAs all over the country offer training in life management and job skills for displaced homemakers and underemployed women through the Second Wind program. Wider Opportunities for Women is a national advocacy organization providing technical assistance for training programs with a goal of increased employment opportunities for women.

Women workers over forty are receiving career and retirement education and counseling from the Working Women Education Fund, a project of the organization "Nine to Five." Developed by "Nine to Five" affiliates in Baltimore, Cleveland, and Los Angeles, the programs were expanded in 1982 to include Boston, Cincinnati, and Pittsburgh. The curriculum presents strategies for job advancement, assertiveness training, information about legal rights and retirement income, and educational and community resources.

Two programs funded to libraries by the National Endowment for the Humanities bring women's issues to the community. The project, "Humanities programs in Vermont public libraries" (Bates 1981), has involved nearly 5,000 participants in twenty-two communities. Women have literally come over the mountains in subzero weather to join a local scholar in discussion groups of such literature classics as *My Antonia* and *Jane Eyre.* The goal of the "Women in community project" (Haber 1981), organized by the Schlesinger Library at Radcliffe College, is to send women's studies back to the community. Grants were awarded on a nationwide basis to seven four-member community teams, each consisting of a women's studies scholar, a member of a community organization, and an academic and a public librarian. After a week-long training program at the Schlesinger Library, teams returned to their communities to develop public programs that include women's contributions to jazz and blues in Memphis, Tennessee; women coal miners in Morgantown, West Virginia; and women's networks, past and present, in Colorado Springs.

Community education is sometimes included under the category "service learning," a term used to describe various kinds of educational programs based on voluntary action and directed experiences. The National Women's Studies Association has published a handbook describing models, case studies, and resources (Fisher and Reuben 1981).

Women's Studies

A basic goal of scholars and teachers of women's studies is to integrate perspectives and information from new research into the standard curricula of schools, colleges, and universities. Separate programs continue to be considered essential as well, because they provide a base for conducting and stimulating research and offer courses that compensate for what is considered a male-centered bias in the rest of the curriculum (Hook 1981b).

A directory of programs aimed at integrating this material into college courses is available from Higher Education Resources Services (Tolpin 1981). More than thirty projects are listed, covering psychology, history, literature, western civilization, art education, and foreign languages. A report from a conference sponsored by the Southwest Institute for Research on Women at the University of Arizona (Dinnerstein, O'Donnell, MacCorquodale 1981) presents methods for implementing integration projects and gives examples from seventeen campuses. *HER story: 1620-1980,* is a curriculum guide prepared for American history courses by a committee of the Woodrow Wilson National Fellowship Foundation (1981). It includes units, documents, and bibliographies that can be adapted for use in a college or high school survey course. The Feminist Press continues to publish curriculum guides and primary source materials about women to use in teaching on all levels. New titles for 1981-1982 are listed in the Resource section.

A college-wide effort to integrate the study of women into the liberal arts curriculum at Wheaton College, Norton, Massachusetts, will culminate in a dissemination conference in 1983 (Association of American Colleges, October 1981). Supported by a three-year FIPSE grant, the Wheaton project includes such activities as a faculty and department self-assessment conference, a week-long intensive workshop for faculty with outside scholars and materials, stipends for visiting scholars, and released time for faculty. Although participation is voluntary, more than fifteen departments had instituted some kind of integration project by the end of the first year.

Reports from the field show mixed success in mainstreaming women's studies into college classrooms. In a survey of courses in nine southern states, Dean Cantrell (1981) found that half of the English departments now offer courses about women in literature. Cantrell believes these courses have been "the energizer of the sagging humanities." On the other hand, Carolyn Ruth Swift (1981) met with small success in attempting to introduce women authors into the survey of western literature at the University of Rhode Island. After a two-year struggle, Swift reported that Emily Dickinson was accepted as the token woman writer.

Donna J. Wood (1981) surveyed the national growth of women's studies programs and determined characteristics that made a college or university most likely to accept the courses. They include the existence of strong supporters of cultural diversity, large, heterogeneous student bodies, and a desire of the school to keep up with current trends. Barbara Hillyer Davis (1981) and Cynthia Kinnard and Jean Robinson (1981) suggest that teachers use women students' experiences and cultural backgrounds as positive material in their classes. Bettina Aptheker (1981) urges white scholars and teachers to acknowledge "the barriers to interracial solidarity" within themselves and their institutions and to work to overcome them.

Programs and centers for research on women are listed in the *Women's Studies Quarterly* (Women's studies programs 1981). "Feminist connections throughout education" is the theme of the 1982 women's studies convention at Humboldt State University, Arcata, California.

College Women

In the fall of 1981 college women outnumbered men on American campuses by nearly a half million, continuing a trend first noticed in 1979-1980, Although the number of men attending full-time and enrolled in universities still exceeds the number of women in those categories, the rate of increase for women is higher in each group and indicates a probable trend (Magarrell 1981). The section on reentry women analyzes the role of women as part-time and older students.

Of college degrees awarded in 1980, women received 49 percent of bachelor's degrees and 49.4 percent of master's degrees. At the doctorate level women earned 30 percent (College degrees awarded 1981). (For a breakdown on professional degrees awarded to women, see the section on academic and professional women.)

In looking for an explanation for the growth to near parity of women's enrollment in all but the doctoral levels, Heyns and Bird (1982) suggest that the economic benefits of a college education are greater for women than ever before. A useful index is the ratio of the median income between college and high school graduates. Heyns and Bird (1982) cite a study that shows an increase in that ratio for women college graduates between 1969 and 1975, a trend that appears to have been in effect since 1969. Between 1969 and 1975 the opposite effect was observed for men.

Sumru Erkut (1982a) believes that the basic dilemma facing college women today is no longer how to choose between a family and a career but how to combine the two. In their study of undergraduate women who identified women professors as role models, Erkut and Mokros (1981) found that these students look for different information from female mentors than from male mentors, in particular, the possibility of successfully combining professional and family life. Ekrut (1982b) suggests that career counselors should discuss family-life implications of different careers with male students, not just with female students. Colleges should help male faculty, administrators, and staff to serve as family and career role models by allowing paternity leaves, providing child care for meetings scheduled after business hours, and by offering flex-time and part-time careers to men as well as women. Ekrut concludes that only when women know they can use college to prepare for a working life not unequally burdened with family responsibilities can true equity in higher education be achieved for them and for men.

Reentry Women

The pressures for change in patterns of higher education continue to come from the large numbers of women over age thirty-five entering college for the first time or returning to finish an undergraduate degree. Enrollment of these women, which has doubled since 1972, is the reason women students now outnumber men students. Another trend affecting the character of the reentry programs is that 67 percent of reentry women over age thirty-five are also working (Women's Re-Entry Project 1981), and are depending on educational credentials to help them advance up the career ladder. (For a discussion of women returning for updating in science and engineering, see the section entitled Academic and Professional Women.)

Although specific groups of women face special barriers to their return to formal education, there are some general impediments, including the belief that continuing education programs are designed for bored middle-aged housewives, the concern that courses will not be relevant to their employment needs or cultural traditions, the fear that they will be different from other students, lack of support from home, and the need for child care and safe transportation. The Women's Re-Entry Project of the Project on the Status and Education of Women (1981) outlines strategies to combat the barriers to reentry women such as reaching out recruitment programs, connections with community organizations with similar goals, and such support services at the educational institution as special counseling and day care. Scheduling places and times of courses consistent with women's lifestyles, development of new curricula, and the acceptance of transfer credits are important. The Project has published a comprehensive list of sources of financial aid for reentry women.

Several recent studies analyze or suggest counseling programs geared to meet the needs of reentry women. DiNuzzo and Tolbert (1981) describe the success of a short-term group counseling program in developing self-understanding, help with decision-making, and provision of occupational information and job skills. Similar goals were achieved in a model for individual career counseling used by Seligman (1981). Ballmer and Cozby (1981) suggest the need for sensitivity to the problems arising from the inevitable restructuring of family relationships after a woman returns to school.

The Women's Re-Entry Project emphasizes the value of sensitivity to the needs of specific groups within the population of reentry women. Most are additionally disadvantaged by being members of a minority group, older, or single parents. The common bond is undereducation and underemployment. Black women have long sought education as a means for access to jobs other than unskilled labor or domestic work; professionals arriving from Indochina may need help with credentials or language; Hispanic and native American women may need the support of peer counseling to help handle cultural role expectations; and older women should not be assumed to be past the age for a new career.

Educational resources are among the services offered by the Displaced Homemakers Network to former homemakers who have lost their source of economic support. The Network provides a clearinghouse of information and acts as an advocacy group.

Women's Colleges

Defining themselves as institutions transformed by their central commitment to women, the 116 women's colleges currently in operation see themselves in a stronger position than they were in a decade ago, according to the results of a two-year study by the Women's College Coalition (Bales and Sharp 1981). Affirmation of the viability of women's colleges was given early in 1982 by the trustees of Barnard College in New York City, when they voted to continue Barnard as a single-sex institution, despite the decision of Columbia, its affiliated university, to become coeducational.

A summary of the enrollment data of the past ten years included in the Coalition's profile of women's colleges (Women's College Coalition 1981a) reveals a response to basic changes in women's enrollment patterns. Although the total gain in numbers of students at women's colleges is 25 percent, analysis reveals that the increases are from part-time and graduate students. The number of full-time undergraduates actually decreased by 15 percent in the ten-year period. The total increase in numbers of graduate and professional students was 178.4 percent. The largest increase combined the factors of part-time students and graduate students to make an increase of 223.4 percent.

The Coalition presents other data to demonstrate the strength of women's colleges and their commitment to women. Women control their institutions. Compared with 8 percent nationwide, 66 percent of the presidents of women's colleges are women. Half of the trustees and one-quarter of the chairpersons are women. Among the total faculties, 61 percent are women, as are nearly half of the full and associate professors. The Coalition's study of the colleges' learning environment (Women's College Coalition 1981b) found that the large majority of the faculties see their mission as raising women's aspirations. Although only 2.3 percent of college women are enrolled in women's institutions, the Coalition hopes to be able to isolate and describe the successful factors in the learning environment of women's colleges that can be adapted to meet the needs of women in coeducational institutions (Bales and Sharp 1981).

Collegiate Athletics

The loss in power and dissolution of the Association of Intercollegiate Athletics for Women (AIAW) appears to be unavoidable. The AIAW was formed in 1971 in response to the need for uniform rules related to competition, financial aid, and eligibility to play for the growing numbers of women athletes on campus. Early in 1971, the all-male National Collegiate Athletic Association (NCAA) voted to establish women's championships in Division I institutions (schools with the largest sports programs) and to add new championships to schools in Divisions II and III, which were set up in 1980 but have not yet begun. They also voted to guarantee women approximately one-third of the seats on the governing board and to require women's events to come under NCAA rules by 1985 (Middleton and Fields 1981; Hogan 1981).

The AIAW felt immediate repercussions. They lost 20 percent of their members; another 12 percent withdrew from AIAW competitions. Because head athletic directors are generally men, the decisions to withdraw were not always made by women, who are usually associate athletic directors. Most of the losses in membership came from Division I, with the result that NBC, a cable TV network, and commercial sponsors nullified their contracts with the AIAW. When the AIAW found that the NCAA had allocated $3 million to the new women's championships, they charged "unfair competition" and filed an anti-trust suit, hoping to gain an injunction to stop the NCAA-sponsored competitions (Fields 1981b).

The leadership of the AIAW believes that their organization has deep philosophical differences with the NCAA. From the beginning, a goal of the AIAW has been to avoid the excesses of male collegiate athletic programs. After they passed a student bill of rights at the January 1982 convention, Merily Baker, the new president, stated that the bill of rights reflected AIAW's view that athletic programs should be constructed for students "so that their time to develop as thinking and feeling human beings is not deformed by the demands of athletic pursuits" (Fields 1982). One example of a competitive program with a goal of mainstreaming its athletes into academic and student life is the women's sports program at the University of Texas in Austin, directed by AIAW's immediate past president, Donna Lopiano (Flocke 1981).

Academic and Professional Women

Academic and professional women continue to build networks of support, both internally within their institutions and externally within their professional associations. There is evidence, however, that the pool of women graduates in professional fields will not continue to grow indefinitely. Although women students continue to enter graduate programs, military academies, and medical, law, and business schools in numbers ranging from one-quarter to one-third of the students (Proportions of degrees awarded to women 1981), some observers are expecting this to level off.

Braslow and Heins (1981) note that the sharp increase in numbers of women admitted to medical schools appears to have tapered off. An American Bar Association survey (Female law enrollments 1982) comments that the rate of increase of women enrolled in law schools has dropped markedly. The gain in numbers in the first-year class in 1981 was only 3.4 percent compared with 13.2 percent in 1980. Women law school students represented 35.3 percent of the total in 1981–1982.

Women librarians see the development of links with other women's professional groups as one way to work on the problem of the disparity in pay and status between the sexes (Heim 1981). Although three-quarters of the members of the American Library Association are women, 28.9 percent of the men hold library directorships compared with 11.2 percent of the women. Women's positions are distributed throughout the profession, but 44.6 percent of men hold appointments in academic libraries. As a group, male librarians earn 25 percent more than female librarians (Heim 1981).

Women continue to enter Masters of Business Administration programs at an increasing rate. In 1970-1971 there were only 750 women MBA graduates compared with 12,332 in 1979-1980. A recent study of women in management positions, however, found that once they entered a management position they did not run into serious attitude problems from men until the number of women managers reached about 15 percent. At that point, many men, the study suggests, see too many women competing for positions (Carlson 1981).

Judith Stiehm (1981) found that the training in the United States Air Force Academy represents a two-track approach, one for men and one for women. Differences arise because women officers are not allowed to participate in combat flying, the core activity of the service. Although many women have received training in the military service in the past decade, it appears that the Department of Defense has decided to keep their numbers at 10 or 12 percent (Sawyer 1981).

Although Mary Fox (1981) found that achievement does govern advancement in colleges and universities for both men and women, her study revealed a dual salary structure. A survey of more than 4,000 faculty members at a number of colleges conducted by the *Chronicle of Higher Education* (Men's and women's salaries 1981) found that women on college and university faculties are paid 15 percent less than their male colleagues. The greatest gap occurs in the arts and sciences where women receive only 74 percent and 79 percent, respectively, as much as men. Women come the closest to matching men's salaries in physical education, business, economics, and vocational education. Lambert and Sandler (1981) suggest that women use prizes and awards to increase awareness of their programs and achievements and to legitimize activities designed to promote educational equity.

College Administration

Women's progress in gaining jobs in administration in higher education changed very little during the three-year period between 1975-1976 and 1978-1979, according to a survey conducted by the College and University Personnel Association (American Council on Education 1982). Based on data from 514 colleges and universities, the Association found that although women were employed in a wider range of positions than before, their numbers had increased by only 3.5 percent to a total of 22.9 percent of administrative jobs.

The study also found differences in salary and job responsibility between women and men. Women earned between 68 and 80 percent of the salaries of men holding the same positions. One-fourth of the women in top-level positions held one of four jobs: Dean of nursing, director of library services, bookstore manager, or registrar. Only 6 percent of the chief executive positions and 20 percent of administrative or academic affairs positions were held by women.

Five traditional reasons generally offered for the slow progress of women in higher education administration were tested by the Association. None was found to be valid. In answer to the explanation that women were paid lower salaries because they had not been on the job as long as men or because they were more often hired from inside institutions, the study found that neither factor made a difference in the sex or salary of the person hired. The Association reported that neither hiring trends nor salary appeared to be related to changes in financial conditions or enrollments of institutions, but that the increase in the number of jobs was consistently higher for men than for women. Finally, the study found that women did not necessarily gain positions in the areas with the highest rates of job openings.

Another explanation often cited for why women do not move into higher levels of educational administration is lack of mobility. Two studies found that women administrators were willing to move to new locations. A national survey with responses from approximately 1,000 women administrators (Curby 1980) showed that the women were willing to make changes for economic and job-related reasons not based on personal or social preferences. Moore and Sagaria (1981) found that many women administrators in Pennsylvania had recently changed positions or were anticipating a move. They believe that the women who built careers in a single institution represent a group of older women who responded in a different period in higher education.

The National Identification Program for Women Administrators conducted by the American Council on Education's Office of Women is a network of forty statewide coordinating committees to help women administrators locate new positions.

Social Sciences and the Humanities

Women historians (American Historical Association 1981) surveyed their own profession for the first time in ten years and found little evidence to support the contention that history departments have become "feminized." Although many women have entered the profession, their positions are concentrated at the lower levels. In 1979, 25 percent of all new history jobs went to women compared with 10 percent in 1969. The advance paralleled the increase in the number of women who earned history PhDs, which went from 10 percent in 1969 to 28 percent in 1978. On the other hand, one-third of the men and less than one-eighth of the women who earned doctorates in history between 1970 and 1974 held full professorships by 1980. Of those persons earning PhDs between 1975 and 1978, 27 percent of the men and only 9 percent of the women attained tenure-track positions.

The keynote speaker at the Fifth Berkshire Conference on the History of Women held at Vassar College in June 1981, Joan W. Scott (1981), added a historical perspective to these statistics. She warned that gains were won in the context of the economic, demographic, and ideological climate of the 1960s. Women historians need to continue to recognize the structural obstacles to their future employment, she said, and to recognize that any advances were built on long-established women's networks. Women should not delude themselves into thinking that their success depended only on "personal ingenuity, self-discipline, and cleverness."

In 1981 two women were elected to the top positions in the Organization of American Historians. Gerda Lerner of the University of Wisconsin was chosen president and Joan Hoff Wilson of Indiana University at Bloomington, executive secretary.

Employment patterns of women who received PhDs from 1973 to 1978 in English and modern languages show a significant level of underemployment (Committee on Women Historians 1981). Of 5,500 women receiving degrees in English, 17 percent are either teaching part time or are unemployed; in modern languages the figure is 24 percent.

Many underemployed women scholars, particularly in the humanities and the social sciences, have organized outside the academic profession as independent scholars. The purpose of the associations, which all welcome male members, is to provide a forum for intellectual exchange with a scholarly community. The oldest group is the Institute for Research in History in New York. Other groups include the Alliance of Independent Scholars in Cambridge, Mass., the Princeton (N.J.) Research Forum, the Center for Independent Study in New Haven, Conn., and the Academy of Independent Scholars in Boulder, Colorado (Gross 1981).

Science and Engineering

Although the number of women earning science and engineering degrees in proportion to the total degrees awarded in those fields has increased in the last decade, continued gains are threatened because important National Science Foundation (NSF) programs to prepare women for scientific careers suffered major cuts in 1981.

The NSF was directed by Congress, however, to appoint a new advisory committee on equal opportunities to monitor the progress of women and minority groups in science. According to the first report, *Women and Minorities in Science and Engineering*, released early in 1982, women earned 35 percent of bachelor's degrees awarded in science and engineering in 1980, up from 26 percent in 1970. On the graduate level in the same fields, women earned 27 percent of master's degrees, up from 17 percent; and 22 percent of the doctorates, up from 9 percent. The corresponding increase in the number of women scientists and engineers employed between 1974 and 1978 was almost 32 percent, and the proportion of women in the scientific work force grew from 7.8 percent to 9.4 percent. At 2 percent, engineering represented the lowest field of women's scientific employment.

Since 1976 the NSF has administered federal funding to train women through the Women in Science Program. Because of federal budget cuts, the last year for the awards was 1981 when the NSF granted thirty-four awards totaling nearly $2 million. The projects included twenty science career workshops designed to offer encouragement and counseling to women students, and fourteen career facilitation projects. The facilitation projects offered one to two years of training to nearly 500 women all over the country who had science degrees but who were not employed in technical fields or were underemployed. The projects ranged from a program updating women chemists and biologists for new careers in toxicology at American University, Washington, D.C., to ones training women to be mining engineers at Indiana State University at Evansville and computer scientists at the University of Denver. A summary of reentry programs in science (Lantz 1980) emphasizes the large numbers of women who desire updating in their skills and for whom the career facilitation model has proved successful.

The Women's Reentry Consortium was organized in 1981 to standardize and institutionalize reentry programs for women. Concentrating on such fields as engineering, chemistry, and computer science where women are underrepresented, the Consortium operates from regional centers in New York, Ohio, and California. The group publishes a quarterly newsletter, *Reentry*, runs seminars, and offers seed money for beginning reentry programs. A handbook for planning and implementing reentry projects is available from the Consortium (Lantz 1981).

Special reentry programs in science and engineering are the only way to overcome sex-role conditioning and career interruptions, according to Carol M. Shaw (1982). Successful programs, Shaw states, are based on a curricular response to an assessment of specific local, regional, and national needs. Programs can vary from simply bringing women up to date in their original fields of study to a combination of updating with a new component chosen to increase their employability.

Medical Education

In the past ten years, 20,000 women have graduated from medical school compared with a total of 14,000 in the four decades between 1930 and 1970 (Braslow and Heins 1981). Although 25 percent of the graduates of medical schools are now women, the authors believe it will take forty years before one-quarter of the practicing doctors will be female.

The number of women who have become full professors or achieved administrative positions in medical schools has grown very little in the last ten years, Braslow and Heins point out. Only 2 percent of department chairmen, 7 percent of associate deans, and 17 percent of assistant deans are women. Their numbers as full-time faculty members have only increased from 13 to 15 percent since 1968, although the absolute number increased from 2,365 to 6,170. On the other hand, Ferrer (1981) sees some cause for encouragement, pointing out that 56 departmental chairs are held by women, a 69 percent increase in two years.

Until the medical profession recognizes the special needs of the family, Marcia Angell (1981) believes that women will not reach the top of the medical profession, citing as reasons the need for part-time positions, leaves of absence to allow time to raise families, and reentry programs. Judith Lorber (1981) sees limits in the availability of sponsors for young women doctors by established physicians as a factor retarding development of women's medical careers.

A change in the choices of fields of specialization among female medical students has been noted (Kutner and Brogan 1981). In a study of recent entrants to two southern medical schools they found women less likely than before to choose the traditional specialties of pediatrics, anesthesiology, and psychiatry, with more entering the areas of family practice and internal medicine than in the past.

REFERENCES

Adkinson, J.A. 1981. Women in school administration: a review of the research. *Review of Educational Research* 51:311-43.

American Council on Education. 1982. *Women and Minorities in Administration of Higher Education and Institutions.* Washington, D.C.: College and University Personnel Association. Available from the Association at 11 Dupont Circle, Washington, DC 20036.

American Historical Association. 1981. *The status of women in the historical profession.* Washington, D.C.: The Association. Available from the Association at 400 A Street, SE, Washington, DC 20003.

Angell, M. 1981. Women in Medicine—beyond prejudice. *New England Journal of Medicine* 304:1161.

Aptheker, B. 1981. "Strong is what we make each other"; unlearning racism within women's studies. *Women's Studies Quarterly* 9:13-16.

Association of American Colleges. 1981. "The study of women in the liberal arts curriculum." *Forum for Liberal Education* 4. Entire issue is devoted to projects integrating the study of women into college curricula. Available from the Association at 1818 R Street, NW, Washington, DC 20009.

Bales, S.N. and Sharp, M. 1981. Women's colleges—weathering a difficult era with success and stamina. *Change* 13:53-56.

Ballmer, H. and Cozby, P.C. 1981. Family environments of women who return to college. *Sex Roles* 7:1019-26.

Bank Street College of Education. 1981a. CDA assessment and credentialing activities. Washington, D.C. Available from: CDA National Credentialing Program, 1341 G St., NW, Suite 802, Washington, DC 20005.

Bank Street College of Education. 1981b. Expansion of the CDA credential to new provider categories. Washington, D.C., October 1981.

Bates, P. 1981. Humanities programs in Vermont public libraries. Paper presented at the National Women's Studies Association meeting, June 2, Storrs, Conn.

Benbow, C. and Stanley, J.C. 1980. Sex differences in mathematical ability: fact or artifact? *Science* 210:1262-64.

Benz, C.R.; Pfeiffer, I.; and Newman, I. 1981. Sex role expectations of classroom teachers, grades 1-12. *American Educational Research Journal* 18:289-302.

Braslow, J.B., and Heins, M. 1981. Women in medical education: a decade of change. *New England Journal of Medicine* 304:1129-35.

Brody, C. 1981. An approach to community-based education for women. Paper presented at the National Women's Studies Association meeting, June 2, Storrs, Conn.

Cantrell, D. 1981. Women's studies as an energizer of the humanities in southern English departments. *Women's Studies Quarterly* 9:24-25.

Carlson, B. 1981. A long way. *New England Business* 3:15-19.

College degrees awarded in 1980. 1981. *Chronicle of Higher Education*, October 14, p. 10.

Committee on Women Historians, American Historical Association. 1981. "Guidelines on hiring women historians in academia," *Women's Studies Quarterly* 9:33-34.

Curby, V. 1980. *Women administrators in higher education: their geographic mobility.* Washington: D.C.: National Association for Women Deans, Administrators, and Counselors.

Cusick, T. 1981. Title IX under fire. *Peer Perspective* 7:3-5.

Davis, B. 1981. Teaching the feminist minority. *Women's Studies Quarterly* 9:7-9.

Dinnerstein, M.; O'Donnell, S.R.; and MacCorquodale, P. 1981. "How to Integrate Women's Studies into the Traditional Curriculum." Tucson: Southwest Institute for Research on Women (SIROW). Available from SIROW at the University of Arizona, Tucson, Ariz. 85721.

DiNuzzo, T.M., and Tolbert, E.L. 1981. Promoting the personal growth and vocational maturity of the re-entry woman: a group approach. *Journal of the National Association for Women Deans, Administrators, and Counselors* 45:26-31.

Drew, M. 1980. Old girls with grit. *Parents' Choice* 3, no. 3:8-9.

Erkut, S. 1982a. Social psychology looks at but does not see the undergraduate woman. In *The undergraduate woman: issues in educational equity*, ed P. Perrun, pp. 183-204. Lexington, Mass.: Heath.

Erkut, S. 1982b. Men have families, too. In *The undergraduate woman: issues in educational equity*, ed. P. Perrun, pp. 413-415. Lexington, Mass.: Heath.

Erkut, S. and, Mokros, J. 1981. Professors as models and mentors for college students. Working paper no. 65. Wellesely Mass.: Wellesley College Center for Research on Women. Available from the college at Wellesley, Mass. 02181.

Female law enrollments. 1982. *Chronicle of Higher Education* February 17, p. 2.

Fennema, E. 1981. Women and mathematics: does research matter? *Journal for Research in Mathematics Education* 12:380-85.

Ferrer, M. 1981. Women in medicine: has there been progress? *Journal of the American Medical Women's Association* 36:212.

Fields, C.M. 1981a. Administration moves to ease federal antibias regulations. *Chronicle of Higher Education* September 2, pp. 1, 21.

Fields, C.M. 1981b. Ban sought against NCAA's women's championships. *Chronicle of Higher Education*, October 21, pp. 1, 13.

Fields, C.M. 1981c. Judge says Title IX doesn't cover college's sports program. *Chronicle of Higher Education*, September 9, p. 8.

Fields, C.M. 1981d. Supreme Court hears sex-bias case: U.S. backs women's rights position. *Chronicle of Higher Education*, December 16, pp. 11, 12.

Fields, C.M. 1982. Women's sports group plans for possible dissolution. *Chronicle of Higher Education*, January 20, p. 5.

Fisher, J., and Reuben, E., eds. 1981. *Women's studies service learning handbook.* College Park, Md.: National Women's Studies Association.

Flocke, L. 1981. A winning game plan. *American Education* 17:6-12.

Fox, M.F. 1981. Sex, salary, and achievement: reward-dualism in academia. *Sociology of Education* 54:71-84.

Goldreich, E., and Goldreich, G. 1981. *What can she be? a scientist.* New York: Holt.

Greenhouse, L. 1982. Court says school anti-bias rules cover workers as well as pupils. *New York Times*, May 18, pp. 1, D23.

Gross, R. 1981. Independent scholarship: passion and pitfalls. *Chronicle of Higher Education,* June 8, p. 56.

Haber, B. 1981. Women in the community project. Paper presented at the American Historical Association meeting, December 28, Los Angeles.

Haywoode, T., and Scanlon, L. 1981. Planning to meet the changing needs of women: the national congress of neighborhood women neighborhood-based college program. Paper presented at the National Women's Studies Association meeting, June 2, Storrs, Conn.

Heim, K.M. 1981. Women in librarianship. In *The American library association yearbook: a review of library events,* pp. 299-303. Chicago: American Library Association.

Heyns, B., and Bird, J. 1982. Recent trends in the higher education of women. In *The undergraduate woman: issues in educational equity,* ed. P. Perrun, pp. 43-70. Lexington, Mass.: Heath.

Hogan, C.L. 1981. NCAA votes possible "takeover" of women's sports. *Peer Perspective* 7:5-6.

Hook, J. 1981a. Exemption from anti-bias rules proposed for colleges that don't get direct U.S. aid. *Chronicle of Higher Education,* October 7, pp. 9-10.

Hook, J. 1981b. Scholars wage campaign to integrate research on women into standard liberal-arts courses. *Chronicle of Higher Education,* November 4, p. 8.

Hook, J. 1981c. Title IX covers college employees. *Chronicle of Higher Education,* September 16, pp. 1, 17.

Kinnard, C., and Robinson, J. 1981. "It applies to me directly"—introducing students to women's studies. *Radical Teacher,* no. 18:15-23.

Klein, S.S. 1981. Summary of recent U.S. department of education activities to increase equal access and equal opportunities for women. Washington, D.C.: National Advisory Council on Women's Educational Programs.

Klein, S.S. 1982. Likely administration view of the federal role in education: implications for sex equity. Washington, D.C.: National Advisory Council on Women's Educational Programs.

Kolb, F. 1981. The integration of women's history into school and community. Paper presented at the American Historical Association meeting, December 28, Los Angeles.

Kutner, N.G., and Brogan, D.R. 1981. Occupational role innovation and secondary career choice among women medical students. *International Journal of Women's Studies* 4:157-66.

Lambert, B., and Sandler, B. 1981. Giving prizes and awards: a new way to recognize and encourage activities that promote equity for women in academe. Washington, D.C.: Project on the Status and Education of Women.

Lantz, A.E. 1980. *Reentry programs for female scientists.* New York: Praeger.

Lantz, A.E. 1981. *Planning for reentry programs: information from the projects.* Brooklyn, N.Y.: Women's Reentry Consortium. Available from the Consortium at Polytechnic Institute of New York, Box 83, 333 Jay St., Brooklyn, NY 11201.

Long, L. 1981. Sex-role stereotyping, how do you compare with other teachers? *Learning* 10:94-95.

Lorber, J. 1981. The limits of sponsorship for women physicians. *Journal of the American Medical Women's Association* 36:329-38.

Lowery. 1982. Women's jobs program banks on self-reliance. *Boston Globe,* January 29, p. 15.

Magarrell, J. 1981. Estimated college enrollment in fall 1981. *Chronicle of Higher Education,* December 9, p. 19.

Mann, J. 1981. Title IX. *Peer Perspective* 7:4.

Marshall, C. 1981. Organizational policy and women's socialization in administration. *Urban Education* 16:205-31.

Men's and women's 1981-82 salaries compared. 1981. *Chronicle of Higher Education,* November 25, p. 8.

Meyers, R.S. 1981. EMBERS: a project to develop elementary school readers. *Women's Studies Quarterly* 9:41-42.

Middleton, L., and Fields, C. 1981. NCAA votes to widen role in women's sports. *Chronicle of Higher Education,* January 19, p. 6.

Mitchell, B. A. 1981. Toward sex equity in the Philadelphia school system. *Women's Studies Quarterly* 9:18-19.

Moore, K. M., and Sagaria, M. A. D. 1981. Women administrators and mobility: the second struggle. *Journal of the National Association for Women Deans, Administrators, and Counselors* 44:21-28.

National Advisory Council on Vocational Education. 1980. *Increasing Sex Equity: the Impact of the 1976 Vocational Education Amendments on Sex Equity in Vocational Education.* Washington, D.C.: Institute for Women's Concerns. Available from the Institute at 1018 Wilson Blvd., Arlington, VA. 22209.

National Advisory Council on Women's Educational Programs. 1981a. *Title IX: the half full, half empty glass.* Washington, D.C.: Department of Education. Available from NACWEP, Suite 1821, 1832 M Street NW, Washington, DC 20036.

National Advisory Council on Women's Educational Programs. 1981b. *Women's education: the challenge of the 80s. Annual report.* Washington, D.C.: Department of Education.

National Institute of Education. 1980. *Women in educational administration: the principalship, a literature review.* Washington, D.C.: The Institute.

National Science Foundation. 1982. *Women and minorities in science and engineering.* Washington, D.C.: The Foundation. Available from Division of Science Resources Studies, National Science Foundation, 2000 L Street NW, Washington, DC 20550.

Proportion of degrees awarded to women. 1981. *Chronicle of Higher Education*, June 15, p. 8.

Riley, P. J. 1981. The influence of gender on occupational aspirations of kindergarten children. *Journal of Vocational Behavior* 19:244-50.

Sandler, B. 1981. Summary of proposed amendments to Title IX: impact on post-secondary institutions. Washington, D.C.: Project on the Status and Education of Women.

Sawyer, K. 1981. Military slows pace of recruiting women. *Boston Globe*, May 13, p. 10.

Schink, A. 1981. Testimony before the subcommittee on elementary, secondary, and vocational education of the House education and labor committee, December 17, 1981. Washington, D.C.: League of Women Voters, 1981. Available from the League, 1730 M Street NW, Washington, DC 20036.

Scott, J. W. 1981. Politics and professionalism: women historians in the 1980s. *Women's Studies Quarterly* 9:23-32.

Scott, K. 1981. Whatever happened to Jane and Dick? Sexism in texts reexamined. *Peabody Journal of Education* 58:135-39.

Seligman, L. 1981. Outcomes of career counseling with women. *Journal of the National Association for Women Deans, Administrators, and Counselors* 44:25-32.

Shaw, C. M. 1982. Reentry programs: their design and impact. *Engineering Education* 72 (April 1982):742-46.

Simpson, L. P. 1981. Saving WEEA from the block: a lesson in grassroots action. *TABS* 4, nos. 3 and 4:6-7.

Special double issue on preteen and teenage romance series. 1981. *Interracial Books for Children Bulletin* 12, nos. 4 and 5.

Stage, E. K. 1981. Commentary on women in math. *On Campus with Women* 29:2, 15.

Stiehm, J. H. 1981. *Bring me men and women: mandated change at the U.S. Air Force Academy*. Berkeley: University of California.

Stockard, J., and Kempner, K. 1981. women's representation in school administration: recent trends. *Educational Administration Quarterly* 17:81-91.

Swift, C. R. 1981. "Once more into the breach" of western literature courses. *Women's Studies Quarterly* 9:10-12, 33.

Tetenbaum, T. J.; Lighter, J.; and Travis, M. 1981. Educators' attitudes toward working mothers. *Journal of Educational Psychology* 73:369-75.

Tolpin, M. 1981. Directory of programs designed to integrate material on women into undergraduate curricular course offerings. Wellesley, Mass.: Higher Education Resource Services. Available from Wellesley College, Wellesley, MA 02181.

Underwood, K. E.; Fortune, J. C.; and Dodge, H. 1982. Your portrait: school boards have a brand-new look. *American School Board Journal* 169:17-18.

Unsworth, R. E. 1981. First baseperson? Heroines in YA sports fiction. *School Library Journal* 27:26-27.

United States Commission on Civil Rights. *Enforcing Title IX*. Washington, D.C.: The Commission. Available from the Commission at 621 N. Payne Street, Alexandria, VA 22314.

Useful statistics from recent national research council surveys. 1981. *Women's Studies Quarterly* 9:34.

Wagner, E. 1981. Protesting sexist materials—you can make a difference. *Interracial Books for Children Bulletin* 12, no. 3:3-6.

Warren, B. 1981. Using "new games" in school. *TABS* 4, nos. 3 and 4:11.

Weeks, M. L. 1981. Women administrators: leadership means going for the "top." *Education Week*, December 7, pp. 12-14.

Weiss, J. 1981. Educating for clerical work: the nineteenth-century private commercial school. *Journal of Social History* 14:407-23.

Women's College Coalition. 1981a. *Second profile of women's colleges*. Washington, D.C.: The Coalition. Available from the Coalition at Suite 1003, 1725 K Street NW, Washington, DC 20006.

Women's College Coalition. 1981b. *Study of the learning environment at women's colleges*. Washington, D.C.: The Coalition.

Women's Re-Entry Project of the Project on the Status and Education of Women. 1981. Association of American Colleges, 1818 R Street NW, Washington, DC 20009.

Women's studies program and centers for research on women. 1981. *Women's Studies Quarterly* 9:25-35.

Wood, D. J. 1981. Academic women's studies programs: a case of organizational innovation. *Journal of Higher Education* 52:155-72.

Woodrow Wilson National Fellowship Foundation. 1981. *Woman's place is in the history books. HER story: 1620-1980: a curriculum guide for American history teachers*. Princeton: The Foundation. Available from the Foundation at Box 642, Princeton, NJ 08540.

RESOURCES

Alliance of Independent Scholars, 6 Ash Street, Cambridge, MA 02138. Organization of scholars outside the academic profession who wish to continue intellectual exchange within a scholarly community.

American Historical Association. *Approaches to women's history: a resource book and teaching guide*. Washington, D.C.: The Association, 1979. Activities from a summer institution on integrating women's history into the high school curriculum. Available from the AHA at 400 A Street SE, Washington, DC 20003.

American Historical Association. "Guidelines on hiring women historians in academia." *Women's Studies Quarterly* 9 (Fall 1981):33-34.

Berry, Margaret C. *Women in educational administration: a book of readings*. Washington, D.C.: Association for Women Deans, Administrators, and Counselors, 1979. Collection of 29 essays on women in administration from public school to higher education. Available from NAWDAC, 1028 Connecticut Avenue NW, Washington, DC 20036.

Cain, Mary Alexander. *Boys and girls together: nonsexist activities for the elementary classroom.* Holmes Beach, Fla.: Learning Publications, 1981. Guide to inexpensive sex-fair games and activities available from publisher at Box 1326, Dept. C, Holmes Beach, FL 33509.

Campbell, Patricia B., and Scott, Elois. "Non-biased tests can change the scores." *Council for Interracial Books Bulletin* 11, no. 6 (1981):7-9. Gives tool for evaluating tests for bias against girls.

Center for Self-Reliant Education, 850 W. McKinley Street, Sunnyvale, CA 94086. Provides community-based activities, services, and training to meet needs of local women.

Child Development Associate National Credentialing Program, 1341 G Street NW, Suite 802, Washington, DC 20005. Offers assessment and training opportunities for child-care workers to qualify for national credential.

Committee on the Status of Women in Physics, American Physics Society, 335 E. 45th Street, New York, NY 10017. Supplies packet of information for junior high and high school counselors: "Wanted: more women in science and technology."

Council on Interracial Books for Children. "Identifying sexism and racism in children's books" and "Understanding institutional sexism" are sound/color film strips with booklets available from the Council at 1841 Broadway, New York, NY 10023.

Displaced Homemakers Network, Inc., 755 8th Street NW, Washington, DC 20001. National advocacy organization publishing *Network News*, program directories, and offering referral services for nationwide training programs.

Eliason, Carol, and Edmondson, Gloria. *Women in community and junior colleges.* ERIC: ED 196 456, 1980. Annotated review of works and programs relevant to educational opportunities for women at community colleges.

Epstein, Cynthia Fuchs. *Women in law.* New York: Basic Books, 1981. Outlines story of the growth of women lawyers from sociological and historical perspectives.

Feminist Press, Box 334, Old Westbury, NY 11568. Publishes materials for use in teaching women's studies at all levels. Some recent publications include:

    Abrams, Eileen. *A curriculum guide to women's studies for the middle school, grades 5-9.*

    Bracken, Jeanne; Wigutoff, Sharon; and Baker, Ilene. *Books for today's young readers.* Annotated bibliography of sex-fair fiction for ages 9 to 12.

Hull, Gloria; Smith, Barbara; and Scott, Patricia Bell. *All the women are white, all the blacks are men, but some of us are brave.* Curriculum guide to black women's studies.

Fox, Lynn H. *The problem of women in math.* New York: Ford Foundation, 1981. Available from the Foundation at Office of Reports, 320 E. 43rd Street, New York, NY 10017.

Francis, Lesley Lee. "Litigation on sex discrimination: an update." *Academe* 67 (August 1981):294-95. Includes summary of cases concerning sex discrimination in higher education.

Gallagher, Kathleen, and Peery, Alice. *Bibliography of materials on sexism and sex-role stereotyping in children's books.* Chapel Hill, N.C.: Lollipop Power, 1981. Available from publisher at P.O. Box 1171, Chapel Hill, NC 27514.

Gray, Mary W.; Nichols, Irene A.; and Schafer, Alice T. "Impact of the 1981 federal budget on women in higher education." *Academe* 67 (August 1981):202-04. Includes impact on women in science, student loans, and legal support for sex equity cases.

Heath, Kathryn G. "Educational equity: how long must women wait?" *Educational Studies* 12 (Spring 1981):1-21. Survey of federal programs supporting women's educational equity.

Holt, Margaret E. "Strategies for the 'ascent of woman' in higher education administration in the 80s." *Journal of the National Association for Women Deans, Administrators, and Counselors* 44 (Spring 1981):21-24. Among strategies suggested are the development of a "good new women's" network.

Humanities Programs in Vermont Public Libraries, c/o Rutland Free Library, Court Street, Rutland, VT 04701. Reading and discussion program on women and literature conducted in libraries all over the state.

Institute for Research in History, 432 Park Avenue S., New York, NY 10016. Organization of historians outside universities who share scholarly research and encourage publication of scholarship by persons outside academia.

Jacobs, Ruth H. "Out of the home to where?" Wellesley College Center for Research on Women, working paper no. 77, 1981. Available from the college at Wellesley, MA 02181. Checklist for counselors of displaced homemakers.

Klein, Susan S., and Thomas, Veronica G. *Sex equity in education: NIE-sponsored projects and publications.* Washington, D.C.: National Institute of Education, 1981. Update of 1980 NIE-sponsored projects and publications in sex equity.

League of Women Voters Education Fund, 1730 M Street NW, Washington, DC 20036. Sponsors publications, forums, and other activities to encourage women to participate in government at all levels.

Massachusetts Board of Education. *A guide for the evaluation of instructional materials under Chapter 622.* Boston: Massachusetts Board of Education. Revision of guide on evaluation of materials using standards of positive images of women and girls and minorities. Available from the Massachusetts Department of Education, Bureau of Equal Educational Opportunity, 1385 Hancock St., Quincy, MA 02169.

Moore, Kathryn M., and Wollitzer, Peter A. *Women in higher education: a contemporary bibliography.* Washington, D.C.: National Association of Women Deans, Administrators, and Counselors, 1979.

National Congress of Neighborhood Women, 11-29 Catherine Street, Brooklyn, NY 11211. Sets up community-based college programs, offers employment and counseling services, and publishes national newsletter.

National Identification Program for Women Administrators, American Council on Education, Office of Women, 11 Dupont Circle, Washington, DC 20036. Nationwide network to identify women candidates for administrative positions.

National Institutes of Health. *Women in biomedical research.* Papers from an NIH conference with goal of increasing the number of women in the field. Available from NIH, Bethesda, MD 20205.

National Women's History Week Project, P.O. Box 3716, Santa Rosa, CA 95402. Offers projects and materials for celebration of Women's History Week the second week in March.

Nemir, Rosa Lee. "Women physicians chairing pediatric departments in American medical schools, 1980." *Journal of the American Medical Woman's Association* 36 (June 1981):183-92. Biographies of the eight women who chair pediatric departments in United States medical schools.

Porter, Judie. "Sexism on instructional TV?" *Learning* 10 (October 1981):96. Discusses sex-role stereotyping on educational television programs.

Project AWARE, American Association of School Administrators, 1810 N. Moore Street, Arlington, VA 22209. Organization of women in school administration. Regional centers include:
AWARE West, 2604 W. Osborn Road, Phoenix AZ 85107.
Center for Women in Educational Leadership, University of North Carolina at Chapel Hill, Peabody Hall 201, Chapel Hill, NC 27514.
Northwest Women in Educational Administration, DEPM/College of

Education, University of Oregon, Eugene, OR 97403.

Southern Coalition for Educational Equity, Inc., P.O. Box 54426, Atlanta, GA 30308.

Northeast Coalition of Educational Leaders, Inc., 85 Speen St., Framingham, MA 01701.

Southwest Educational Development Laboratory, 211 East 7th Street, Austin, TX 78701.

Project HAVE Skills, Educational Testing Service, Princeton, NJ 08541. Produces three handbooks: For reentry women; their counselors, and their employers.

Project on Equal Education Rights (PEER), 1112 13th Street NW, Washington, DC 20005. Project of NOW Legal Defense and Education Fund, publishes *Peer Perspective* and resource guides, advocacy group especially concerned with implementation of Title IX.

Rural American Women. *Brake shoes, backhoes, and balance sheets: the changing vocational education of rural women.* Washington, D.C.: Rural American Women, 1981. Available from the organization at 1522 K Street NW, Washington, DC 20005. Outlines need for change in vocational education of rural women to address issues of marketing, management, and accounting.

Scott, Nancy A. *Returning women students: a review of research and descriptive studies.* Washington, D.C.: National Association of Women Deans, Administrators, and Counselors, 1980. Review of research on reentry women students.

Second Wind, West Suburban YWCA, 231 Beacon Street, Natick MA 01760. One of CETA training programs for displaced homemakers; includes training in life-skills management as well as for technical careers.

"Selected abstracts from the second national conference of the national women's studies association, May 16-20, 1980, Bloomington, Indiana." *Frontiers* 6 (Spring/Summer 1981):65-103.

Sex Desegregation Assistance Centers funded through Title IV of the Civil Rights Act of 1964 and administered by the Department of Education include (arranged by order of service areas 1 through 10):

New England Center for Equity Assistance, 290 S. Main Street, Andover, MA 01810.

Consortium for Educational Equity, Federation Hall, Douglass College, New Brunswick, NJ 08930.

Mid-Atlantic Sex Desegregation Assistance Center, American University, Foxhall Square Building, Suite 224, 3301 New Mexico Avenue NW, Washington, DC 20016.

Southeast Sex Desegregation Assistance Center, University of Miami, School of Education, P.O. Box 248065, Coral Gables, FL 33124.

Great Lakes Sex Desegregation Assistance Center, 1040 School of Education, University of Michigan, Ann Arbor, MI 48109.

Sex Desegregation Assistance Center of the Southwest, Stephen F. Austin State University, Box 13010A, Nacogdoches, TX 75962.

Sex Desegregation Assistance Center, Kansas State University College of Education, Holton Hall, Department of Administration, Manhattan, KS 66505.

Mountain West Sex Desegregation Assistance Center, Weber State College-1101, Ogden, UT 84408.

Sex Desegregation Assistance Center, Education Classroom Building, Room 327, California State University at Fullerton, Fullerton, CA 92634.

Far West Laboratory, 1855 Folsom Street, San Francisco, CA 94103.

Center for Sex Equity, Northwest Regional Education, 300 Southwest 6th Avenue, Portland, OR 97204.

Stoddard, Cynthia. *Sex discrimination in educational employment: legal alternatives and strategies.* Holmes Beach, Fla.: Learning Publications, 1981. Available from the publisher at P.O. Box 1326, Holmes Beach, FL 33509. Concise guide to legal strategies on all levels of educational employment to counter sex discrimination.

TABS, Aids for Ending Sexism in School, 744 Carroll Street, Brooklyn, NY 11215. Quarterly bulletin includes lesson plans, book reviews, and biographies suitable for use in elementary and secondary schools. Publishes women's poster set.

Terborg-Penn, Rosalyn. Teaching the history of black women: a bibliographical essay. *Women's Studies Quarterly* 9 (Summer 1981):16-17.

Tittle, Carol Kahn, and Denker, Eleanor Rubin. *Returning women students in higher education: defining policy issues.* New York: Praeger, 1980. Includes historical perspective, case studies, programs, and both institutional and situational barriers to reentry women.

United States Department of Labor, Women's Bureau. *The woman offender apprenticeship program: from inmate to skilled craft worker.* Washington, D.C.: U.S. Department of Labor, 1981. A step-by-step description on how to develop apprenticeship programs for women offenders. Includes case histories and list of nationwide apprenticeship centers.

Villadesen, Alice W., and Tack, Martha W. "Combining home and career responsibilities: the methods used by women executives in higher education:" *Journal of the National Association for Women Deans, Administrators, and Counselors* 45 (Fall 1981):20-25.

Waldenberg, Adair L. "Female representation in higher education, retrospect and prospect." ERIC: ED 205 156, 1981. Analysis of trends of representation of women in higher education.

Weibel, Kathleen, and Heim, Kathleen M. *The role of women in librarianship 1876-1976: the entry, advancement, and struggle for equalization in one profession*. Phoenix, Ariz.: Oryx Press, 1979. A collection of essays providing a comprehensive view of women in the library profession.

Wertheimer, Barbara Mayer. *Labor education for women workers*. Philadelphia: Temple University Press, 1981. Essays on history and present on worker education both inside and outside of unions to help women advance in their careers and in their unions.

Wheaton College. "Toward a Balanced Curriculum: Integrating the Study of Women into the Liberal Arts." A description of the three-year project to integrate the new scholarship on women into the entire liberal arts curriculum is available from the college at Norton, Mass. 02766.

Wider Opportunities for Women (WOW), 1511 K Street, NW, Suite 345, Washington, DC 20005. Independent employment resource for women workers; provides technical assistance for training programs; publishes national directories.

"Women and minorities in administration of higher education institutions." Report of participation of women and minorities in higher education administration. Available from College and University Personnel Association, American Council on Education, 11 Dupont Circle, Washington, DC 20036.

"Women in the community project." The Arthur and Elizabeth Schlesinger Library on the History of Women in America, 10 Garden Street, Cambridge, MA 02138.

Women's Action Alliance, Inc., 370 Lexington Avenue, Room 603, New York, NY 10017. Produces nonsexist materials for child development workers.

Women's Educational Equity Act Program. *Resources for educational equity, 1981-1982 catalog*. Available from WEEAP Publishing Center, 55 Chapel Street, Newton, MA 02160. Some 1981 WEEAP publications and their developers include:
Business management training for rural women. Southern Oregon State College, Ashland, OR 97520.
Connections: women and work and skills for good jobs. Boston YWCA, Boston, MA 02116.
Displaced homemakers: vo-tech workshop guide. Women's Resource Center, Norman, OK 73069.
Life skills for women in transition. University of Alaska, Juneau, AL 99801.
Options: a curriculum development program for rural high school students. Dartmouth College, Hanover, NH 03755.
Physical educators for equity. Eastern Kentucky University, Richmond, KY 40475.

Sexism in the classroom. Commission for the Betterment of Women's Rights of the Commonwealth of Puerto Rico, Santurce, PR 00908.

Toward equity: effective Title IX strategies, K-postsecondary. California State University, Fullerton, CA 92634.

Trabajamos: a bilingual/multicultural career awareness and language enrichment program. Washington, DC 20008.

What's new in sex equity curriculum? Arizona State University, Department of Education, Tempe, AZ 85281.

Women's Equity Action League, 805 15th Street NW, Suite 822, Washington, DC 20005. Educational and legal defense fund whose goal is to eliminate sex discrimination in education and employment. Sponsors intern program for students in Washington, monitors Congress, holds conferences, publishes *WEAL Washington Report* and *In the Running*, about women in sports.

Women's Reentry Consortium, Polytechnic Institute of New York, 333 Jay Street, Brooklyn, NY 11201. Designed for women and institutions involved in reentry training programs for women in science and engineering. Publishes quarterly newsletter, *Reentry.*

Women's Re-Entry Project of the Project on the Status and Education of Women, Association of American Colleges, 1818 R Street NW, Washington, DC 20009. Publications in 1981 include:
Financial Aid: a partial list of resources for women.
Re-entry women—getting an education without a degree.
Re-entry women: relevant statistics.
Re-entry women: special programs for special populations.

"Women's studies programs and centers for research on women." *Women's Studies Quarterly* 9 (Summer 1981):25-35. NWSA's annual listing of organized women's studies programs and centers for research is available from the Association at the University of Maryland, College Park, Md. 20742.

Women's Technical Institute, 1255 Boylston Street, Boston, MA 02215. Provides job skills training in nontraditional careers for women in woman-founded organization.

Working Women Education Fund, a project of "Nine to Five," 2000 Florida Avenue NW, Washington, DC 20009, offers career and retirement education and counseling for older women workers.

Yu, Joyce, "Finding funds for women's programs." *Educational Record* 62 (Summer 1981):58-59. Outlines steps for effective fund development, especially from the private sector.

3 | Women and Health

Ann Conway

For American women 1981 emerged as a year of extreme paradox, especially in regard to health care. Even as women became more aware of the special needs of older women, those with disabilities, and so on, the means of meeting those needs were dramatically reduced. The Reagan administration's destruction of health and social programs is nothing less than disastrous; the consequences will be felt for years to come. Yet many women are unaware of this. In 1981 it became more and more clear to the women's health movement that the task of this decade will be to promote cognizance of these matters.

Perhaps the most frightening aspect of the social, political, and economic changes that have swept the country is their scope: They affect almost every area of a woman's life. On a mundane level they mean a variety of concrete things. A teenage woman who has chosen to be sexually active will not be able to obtain family planning services as easily as before. An unemployed woman will find that a local employment office for women no longer exists. A recently divorced woman will find that companies are no longer required to hire her in well-paying nontraditional occupations. An older woman will have little control over how she is treated for menopause. A middle-class woman may not be able to obtain a safe abortion if she chooses to do so.

Although the women's health movement concentrated its resources on reproductive rights and environmental and occupational health in 1981, it became clear that it could not limit itself to these concerns. Proposed or passed governmental legislation included a right-to-life amendment, the reduction of primary care programs and family planning services, the end of national health insurance consideration, abatement of Social Security, Medicare, and Medicaid benefits, deregulation of environmental health programs—the list is endless. Acting under the so-called free market approach to health care, the Reagan administration demolished or diminished many programs extant since the Depression (What next for community health? 1980-1981).

In the 1960s and 1970s criticism of the women's health movement (and the women's movement in general) centered on the charge that it was elitist and overly concerned with the problems of white, middle-class women. Often, working-class white women and women of color were forced to address their economic problems first, leaving health and medical problems unattended; the problems of disabled and older women were largely disregarded. One of the heartening developments of the 1980s has been greater communication among these groups and a sense of their similar needs in the face of increasing oppression.

Ironically, this changing character has been concurrent with the shift toward conservatism in American life. Yet it has been influenced by several events. A rural women's health conference held in the summer of 1981 depicted enthusiastic rapport between urban health activists and their rural counterparts. Nurses, members of the traditionally most conservative of professions, have become more militant in their demands for increased wages and better working conditions. This is partially a result of their stronger identification with the women's health movement. The issue of reproductive rights remains a unifying force for women regardless of class, race, or occupation.

What is the direction of the movement in the 1980s? Women will continue to develop ways of health that emphasize the contribution of individuals and interaction between provider and consumer including nonallopathic approaches. Collectives, resource centers, health clinics, and consumer groups will continue to educate and support women. Umbrella organizations such as the National Women's Health Network (NWHN) will persist in their demands for a larger role in federal policymaking. Finally, activists will continue to identify and stress the unifying similarities among women. Over all, 1981 was not a good year, and it is to be hoped that a vastly different situation will prevail by the decade's end. It is up to all women concerned with health to make this hope a reality.

Abortion

The atmosphere of 1981, at least in regard to women fighting for their reproductive rights, was foreshadowed in the annual January March for Life held in Washington, D.C. Sixty thousand people took part in this march —not a great number; however, for the first time, the rally was addressed by Secretary of the Department of Health and Human Services Richard S. Schweiker. March representatives also met briefly with President Reagan.

The year saw political restrictions on women's reproductive rights: The appointment of ardent antiabortionists to influential government positions and the passage of federal and state legislation that curtails or eliminates a woman's right of choice to continue or interrupt pregnancy.

Federal funding for abortions was restricted in May by the passage of the Helms amendment. Building on a series of antiabortion riders attached to federal appropriations bills, this legislation discontinued funding of abortions for victims of rape or incest. Similar reduction of abortion benefits in federal employee health insurance was proposed during 1981.

Many other pieces of antiabortion legislation were introduced in the conservative 1981 Congress. These assumed three forms: The human life statute, which would use the fourteenth amendment to assure "equal protection" for the fetus; the human life amendment, which would establish the right to life for all persons from the moment of conception; and the human life federalism amendment, which was endorsed by the National Conference of Catholic Bishops (NCCB) in November. This amendment, passed by the influential Senate Judiciary Committee in March 1982, would give Congress and the states joint authority to regulate abortion, removing the subject from constitutional protection and judicial review.

Much of the responsibility for determining abortion availability was shifted to the states. Several states (among these Massachusetts, New York, and Minnesota) either passed or introduced parental consent statutes limiting the abortion rights of teenage women. In March the Supreme Court upheld the legality of laws requiring a physician to inform a teenager's parents before performing an abortion. Other states introduced their own versions of the Hyde or human life amendments.

Concurrent activities of the anitabortion movement included an unsuccessful attempt to block the nomination of the first woman appointee to the Supreme Court, Sandra Day O'Connor. The political "hit-listing" of prochoice candidates by conservative political coalitions also continued.

Despite these activities, opinion polls still showed a majority of Americans to be prochoice (Hatcher 1981). It is estimated that 1.5 million abortions were performed in 1981. Ironically, many of these were for poorer women whose federal funding had been eliminated. As a September study from the Center for Disease Control concluded, poorer women are still obtaining needed abortions through state funding or their own resources (Women on medicaid manage to get funding for abortion 1981).

The debate over the medical risks of repeat abortions continued with inconclusive results. Other studies focused on the emotional effects of the procedure. A British study of over 3,000 women who had terminated pregnancies found that while about one-third expressed mild psychological distress, very few experienced any form of psychosis. This finding refutes earlier allegations by antiabortionists that abortion often results in serious psychological disturbances (Peck 1981).

Birth Control

The Pill

Questions were raised concerning the conduct and conclusions of a twelve-year, $8.5 million study of the pill's effects. The "Walnut Creek study" was attacked on three fronts: (1) the validity of its conclusions (many of the women were past rather than present pill users); (2) its data analysis (the final report tended to obscure the seriousness of side effects found during the study); (3) the behavior of the researchers, who appeared at events sponsored by one manufacturer (G.D. Searle & Co.). Drug companies not only lent financial support to a part of the study dropped by the federal government, but also distorted the results of the study to their own advantage. The early publicity given to the study (a campaign funded by drug companies) declared pill risks to be minimal, although the study data directly contradicted this claim (Seaman 1981).

The conduct of this study and the overblown publicity about its "results" all point to the continuing need for women carefully to examine the claims of drug manufacturers and even scientific practice. Most scientists now agree "that the Pill's side effects include potentially fatal diseases: heart attacks, strokes, blood clots, brain hemorrhages and possibly cancer" (Okie 1981). The Walnut Creek study confirmed most of these risks, yet without the attention of the women's health movement, most women would not realize this.

In other research news, the World Health Organization (WHO) continued investigating the efficacy and safety of the pill according to hereditary and environmental differences. The result will be of interest and use to women in underdeveloped countries. Most other research to date has been conducted in more industrialized nations.

Depo-Provera

The "dumping" of Depo-Provera, a controversial injectable contraceptive, continued in African countries during 1981, as did intensified efforts by its manufacturer to legalize it in the United States. Headaches, nervousness, depression, weight gain, and heavy bleeding have all been associated with Depo-Provera. More serious side effects may include short-and long-term infertility and diabetes. There are also unresolved questions about the carcinogenicity of Depo in women.

During the summer the international women's health movement won a major victory when the government of Zimbabwe, using information partially supplied by the Boston Women's Health Book Collective, decided to ban use of Depo-Provera. At that time it was estimated that between ninety and one hundred thousand Zimbabwean women were using the drug. Late 1981 found women in Kenya and South Africa lobbying for its removal from their countries.

In the United States, the Michigan-based Upjohn Company continued to lobby for approval from the Food and Drug Administration (FDA). Selection of a public board of inquiry to evaluate the drug was completed in September. It is expected that NWHN and other groups will actively participate in the board's hearings.

IUD

Intrauterine devices (IUDs) were specifically linked with miscarriage risk and pelvic inflammatory disease (PID). They were also the object of a major lawsuit filed by the National Women's Health Network (Norsigian and Swenson 1981).

Published in late December, the report stated that miscarriage risk increases one and one-half times in the first trimester and ten times in the second trimester if pregnant women do not have the devices removed (Miscarriage risk 1981). Other research described calcium deposits that build up if the devices are not changed at regular intervals, and which can be linked to the development of severe PID; it had previously been thought that the IUD's plastic composition would prevent such deposits. Most physicians now recommend that women have IUDs replaced at least every three years.

Early in the year the National Women's Health Network sued A. H. Robins Co. for worldwide recall of the Dalkon shield IUD. This device has been associated with serious pelvic infection, inflammatory disease, and consequent infertility. It is expected that the suit will be in the courts for the next several years.

Barrier Methods

The cervical cap continued to be an effective and safe birth control method for those who had access to it. Since the FDA categorized it as an investigational device in January, the cap was often difficult to obtain. Premarketing safety data must now be gathered by the FDA; therefore the cap will not be marketed to the majority of women for one to three years. These facts are faintly ironic in light of the fact that the cap was popular before chemical birth control methods became available in the 1960s and 1970s (and United States drug companies reaped correspondingly high profits).

The risks of chemical spermicides were highlighted by a study sponsored by the Boston Collaborative Drug Surveillance Program. The study suggested that children conceived by women using spermicides ran a higher risk of being born with defects (Jick et al. 1981). Spermicides have also been linked to miscarriages and it has been suggested that they might also be carcinogenic to the fetus (Jick et al. 1981).

Other Methods

Interest was again centered on the possible uses of sponges for birth control, either natural (collagen) or artificial (collatex). One manufacturer reported 94 percent effectiveness for a collatex sponge soaked with spermicide. Plans have already begun to market such a sponge, although there are obvious questions about its safety. Other new barrier methods proposed include the development in London on a nonspermicide fit-free diaphragm (Report on non-spermicide fit-free diaphragm 1981).

Investigations continued into the feasibility of a male birth control pill. Although it is estimated that one-third of all people (worldwide) using contraception rely on male contraception, this percentage is steadily decreasing. In the United States, visits by men make up less than 1 percent of all family planning visits. Recent research on an effective male birth control pill may change these trends (Gardner 1981). One study examined the effects of hormone injection on men. Luteinizing hormone-releasing hormone acts to reduce sperm density in a variety of ways. Preliminary results indicate it may be effective, but that it carries with it a number of side effects. Other research into male birth control includes the future possibility of a reversible vasectomy (Contraceptives for men 1981).

Toxic Shock Syndrome

Concern over toxic shock syndrome (TSS) mounted during 1981. The syndrome is associated with the use of tampons and the bacteria *Staphylococcus aureus*. It is characterized by a broad spectrum of symptoms including high fever, vomiting, diarrhea, low blood pressure, and a sun-burnlike rash, usually on the palms of the hands or the soles of the feet (Norsigian and Swenson 1981). Research has posited that "there may be a unique toxin associated with the strain that causes TSS, but it is not clear whether it is a marker of disease or a cause of disease" (Women justifiably concerned 1981). While TSS is often associated with young menstruating women (although the reasons for this are not yet clear), it has also been found in women who have completed normal pregnancies and given birth (Hoffman and Slade 1981).

Studies presented in the *New England Journal of Medicine* and elsewhere (U.S. Department of Health and Human Services 1981) suggest that vagina size, use of highly absorbent tampons, age under 19 years, and perhaps other factors all play a causative role. Women can reduce the risk of TSS by alternating sanitary pads with tampons during their menstrual period, or by eliminating tampons altogether. Some women use sea sponges as an alternative to tampons, but at least one case of TSS has been associated with their use (U.S. Department of Health and Human Services 1981).

In 1980 women's health groups and other consumer activists called for research on the safety and efficacy of tampon use, and the FDA agreed to a warning label on tampon packages. In 1981, however, the FDA reopened the comment period on TSS. Citing widespread media attention to TSS and the "apparent decline in the number of cases during the last quarter of 1980" (U.S. Department of Health and Human Services, 1981), the FDA called into question the need for such a warning label and what segment of the female population it should address. Meanwhile, all the tampon manufacturers have voluntarily included package insert information on TSS. Once again, women's groups geared up to provide testimony concerning the very real danger TSS still presents. As in 1980, there are many questions regarding manufacturer accountability and the right of women to know what they are putting into their bodies. It is likely that similar cases will emerge throughout the decade.

Pregnancy and Childbirth

As a nationwide surplus of obstetricians was projected for the end of the decade, conflicts increased between physicians and nonphysician providers of women's health and medical care. There was also an increased backlash to home birth. A New York physician specializing in home births was temporarily suspended from practice by the local health commission (Whitehouse 1981). Also many nurse-midwives were subjected to harassment by physicians and health authorities, meeting with physician resistance in at least twelve states and the District of Columbia. Nevertheless, many parents continued to prefer the comfort, intimacy, and efficacy of deliveries by nurse-midwives and lay midwives, whether in the home, hospital, or birth center.

Studies demonstrate that nurse-midwives and nurse practitioners who provide obstetrical and gynecological care do so in an effective and economical manner (Nurse practitioners a big boon 1981). In Europe and other countries in which trained midwives provide a large proportion of care, infant mortality rates are lower than in the United States.

In December 1980 a House Commerce Subcommittee hearing zeroed in on what one Congressman deemed "restraint of trade" against nurse-midwives. A July 1981 joint meeting of the American College of Obstetricians and Gynecologists (ACOG) and the American College of Nurse-Midwives (ACOG), along with the Nurses Association of ACOG (NAACOG) attempted to clarify the changing character of the physician/nurse-midwife relationship. Many problems remained unresolved at the close of the meeting (Wood 1981b).

The physician/nurse-midwife debates point out the prevalence of territorial imperatives between the medical hierarchy and an increasingly militant and aware population of nurses and other female health providers. As more and more women demand childbirth experiences in which they are fully informed partners, this controversy is likely to continue.

Breast-feeding

The percentage of American women who choose to breast-feed their babies continues to rise, especially in the first few months following birth (Norsigian and Swenson 1981). The incidence of breast-feeding is directly related to social, racial, and economic factors (Mendershot 1981). New research indicates that vegetarian women who exclude eggs and dairy products as well as meat from their diets may run a risk of inducing vitamin B^{12} deficiencies in their breast-fed babies (Nutritional Vitamin B^{12} deficiency 1981).

In March 1982 the women's health movement and many other groups won a major victory when the Nestle Company agreed to adhere to the WHO/Unicef Code on the Marketing of Breast Milk Substitutes following a longstanding worldwide boycott of Nestle products and businesses. As of early 1982, however, the boycott will continue. In mid-1981 two prominent State Department officials resigned as a result of the Reagan administration's refusal to support the Code (APHA supports protest 1981).

Hormones and Drugs

Research continued into the pathogenic effects of DES (diethylstilbestrol), the artificial estrogen that has been linked with a rare form of vaginal cancer (adenocarcinoma). The cancer incidence is high among the daughters of women who took the drug to prevent miscarriage. The number of potentially affected women is in the millions.

Studies have corroborated earlier findings that DES causes ectopic pregnancy, infertility, intrauterine fetal death, and other reproductive complications (Norsigian and Swenson 1981). Withered fallopian tubes were found in some DES daughters, explaining both the higher risk of ectopic pregnancy and infertility (Some DES daughters 1981). A Stanford study found that rates of miscarriage and premature birth were also significantly higher for these daughters (Sandberg et al. 1981).

Not surprisingly, adverse effects of DES on men have emerged. Sons whose mothers took the drug not only run the risk of genital abnormalities (varicocele and epididymal cysts), but a preliminary study suggests that they may also have an increased risk of infertility. Further research on such effects remains to be done (Stenchever et al. 1981).

Abuse of DES and political action to deter its use continue. In addition to its illegal use in cattle feed, it has been used in at least one instance on humans to control behavior problems. For twenty years a University of Maryland Medical School professor has administered the drug to retarded youths in a state school (Engel 1981). It is probable that these and other injurious practices will become the objects of lawsuits by DES daughters and others throughout the 1980s.

There is also controversy over the safety of other drugs. Under pressure from women's groups and others, Merrell-National Laboratories, manufacturers of Bendectin (a drug used to control intractable nausea in pregnancy), agreed voluntarily, on a temporary basis to provide package inserts for its users. Bendectin has been tentatively associated with cleft palates, heart abnormalities, and other birth defects. Consumer activists continued to question the safety and efficacy of the drug, with the Public Citizen Health Research Groups demanding its removal on the grounds that one of its ingredients is ineffective (Bendectin 1981). Some physicians argued that it is necessary in cases of nausea and vomiting that are unresponsive to dietary changes. Nevertheless, many women questioned whether indiscriminate prescription of the drug would ultimately lead to abandonment of nondrug therapies. As this has happened in many other areas of women's health, it is hardly an idle concern.

The efficacy and safety of many other drugs associated with contraception and obstetrical care have been discussed. A Congressional hearing in July concluded that "none of the drugs used in obstetrical care today have been subjected to a well-controlled, scientific evaluation and found to be safe in regard to the neurological development of the child in utero" (Congressional hearing investigates 1981).

The treatment of contraceptive-related physical and emotional disorders also emerged as a concern. One physician warned against the "polypharmacy" approach to such disorders, stating that problems caused by contraception are best treated by changing the method (Hatcher 1981).

The Reagan administration proposed changes in drug regulation that will profoundly affect the lives of many women. Not only are certain dangerous drugs (like tranquilizers) likely to be prescribed for women, the action of many such drugs is not fully understood. The move to lessen regulatory control of research and marketing raises serious questions about political management of scientific investigations.

Proposed changes at the Food and Drug Administration (FDA) in 1981 included the following: Amount of time spent on review and approval of new drugs, amount of information required before a drug can be marketed, and FDA scrutiny of the early phases of clinical research. More concretely, the President's Health Policy Advisory Committee has proposed that the FDA eliminate its therapeutic equivalence list of generic drugs and the maximum allowable cost restrictions on drugs purchased by the federal government. Similarly, the committee recommended that the Health Care Financing Administration (HCFA) cease publication of its *Guide to prescription drug costs*.

As one might expect, the panel also called for deferment of FDA regulations requiring patient package inserts on a number of drugs, stating that they were costly and probably not read by many consumers (Howe 1981). Later in the year, a Rand Corporation study directly contradicted this position, finding that 70 percent of consumers read and understand the inserts, regardless of educational level and other factors (Drug information 1981).

Reproductive Technology

The evolution of reproductive technology is a growing concern. Since the birth of Louise Brown in 1978 it has become more and more clear that not only is laboratory conception possible, but that reproductive changes of frightening import are on the horizon. Most of these changes, which by and large are controlled by male scientists, will intimately affect the lives of all women.

Of the list of future reproductive possibilities, a variety of lesser known procedures have been added to in vitro fertilization and presex-selection techniques. Male pregnancy is already a reality in laboratory animals and viable embryos have been produced from the union of female mice (Kelly 1981). Surrogate parents (in which a woman is paid to be artificially inseminated and bear a child for an infertile woman) also became a subject of controversy during 1981. A cross between artificial insemination and surrogating is artificial embryonation, in which a surrogate's embryo is flushed out and implanted in an infertile woman. Embryo adoption would go one step further: The inseminated sperm would not come from the husband of an infertile wife, but from an anonymous donor (Kelly 1981).

Perhaps of greatest concern is the projected development of an artificial womb. Probably composed of silicone and amniotic fluid, the womb would hold embryos flushed out of the natural mother at an early stage of pregnancy. It is now predicted that such a womb will be a reality by the turn of the century.

Another form of this technology, genetic engineering, would bring about an end to birth defects and a host of hereditary disorders. There is a potential in such a process for tremendous abuse, for who is to decide what is or is not a "disorder"?

Clearly, these investigations pose many puzzling ethical and political dilemmas. While it is possible the freedom from childbearing will liberate women and that some lesbian couples would welcome the opportunities to conceive and bear children, feminists have identified the potential for further oppression of women through these techniques.

The area of reproductive technology must be closely monitored by women health activists, philosophers, and scientists. Six million American couples are infertile, a number that has risen markedly with the spread of venereal disease and increasing pollution of the environment. It must be remembered that consideration of these variables and their reduction is as important as the break-throughs of reproductive technology.

Teenage Pregnancy and Sexuality

The debate over adolescent pregnancy assumed an intensely paradoxical character in 1981. It is estimated that more than one million teenagers became pregnant in 1980; two-thirds of these pregnancies were unintended. Abortions terminated 38 percent of them. In the face of these figures, Congress and elected officials introduced legislation and regulation that would drastically limit the availability of contraception and abortion for young women in their teens (Rosenfield 1981).

In March the Supreme Court upheld the legality of a Utah law requiring teenagers to obtain parental consent before undergoing abortions. Several other states have such statutes in the planning stages. Later in the year, Congress passed a law the purpose of which was to "promote teenage chastity." In addition, Secretary Schweiker suggested that the government's role in providing contraceptives and sex education should be substantially reduced, which caused dismay among health workers and physicians alike (Wood 1981a; The ultimate chaperone 1981).

All of these developments ignore the facts and concerns that have been brought up over and over by the women's health movement. Two separate studies performed at Johns Hopkins University have stated that sexually active teenagers are still reluctant to get contraceptive advice for a number of reasons (Teen-age girls 1981), but that contraception is strikingly successful for those who do use some form of it. It was estimated by the latter study that teenage pregnancies would double without their use (Contraceptive held successful 1981).

On a brighter note, a comprehensive sex education text geared toward teenagers was published in early 1981. Written by several members of the Boston Women's Health Book Collective, *Changing bodies, changing lives: a book for teens on sex and relationships* is one of the first books on the subject to explore teen sexuality issues openly and compassionately. The women's health movement continued to fight for teen access to this book and *Our bodies our selves* in school and community libraries as attempts to ban such works increased nationwide. (See Bibliography for complete listings of these two titles.)

Breast Cancer

Breast cancer has been a major health concern for over a decade. The fears, death by cancer (over 30,000 women die annually from breast cancer) and mutilation by mastectomy, preoccupy many women as they move out of their 30s. Breast cancer is the leading cause of cancer death among women, and for women in their late 40s it is the leading cause of all deaths. By 1980 the American Cancer Society was estimating that one out of eleven women would develop the disease during her lifetime. (The incidence has been rising steadily for the past ten years.) (Norsigian and Swenson 1981).

Research on the relationship between genetic factors and the occurrence of breast cancer confirms that it is not a single disease, but several, with a number of causes (New research 1981). Unfortunately, researchers and consumer groups alike state that many clinicians are ignorant not only of the latest work on how to predict breast cancer but of its genetic and environmental origins. Studies have called for the need to consider the father's family and the grandfather's generation when seeking hereditary information (New research 1981). Another study found that the risk was four times higher for women using contraceptives whose grandmothers or aunts had the disease (previous research emphasized links with mothers or sisters) (The pill and breast cancer 1981). Health workers and women need to be further educated about these findings and the importance of genetic counseling in regard to diagnosis and treatment.

Women in several states (Massachusetts, California, and New York) fought long and hard to alter the inevitability of radical surgical procedures for breast cancer. As a result of intensive lobbying by businesswoman Juliet Ristow, the California legislature overcame the objections of the California Medical Association to enact an informed consent law regarding treatment. The law requires physicians to distribute a brochure that outlines several treatment options.

These developments stem from two 1979 Consensus Development Conferences of the National Institutes of Health. The meetings centered on two procedures: The estrogen receptor assay (to determine the appropriateness of hormone therapy) and mastectomy (surgical removal of the breast). The conferences recommended that the estrogen receptor be used primarily as a diagnostic procedure; that the Halsted radical mastectomy be eliminated; and that physicians adopt a two-step treatment procedure consisting of a biopsy preliminary to any treatment, including a possible mastectomy. This last innovation would increase accuracy of diagnosis and allow women to choose among a variety of treatments (Norsigian and Swenson 1981).

Unfortunately, many physicians are unaware of or unwilling to use the conference recommendations. Radical mastectomy is still frequently performed. Some physicians recommend "prophylactic" mastectomies for women at special risk of breast cancer; such practices are undertaken without adequate understanding by either doctors or patients of what the "risks" actually are.

A series of Senate hearings into the activities of the National Cancer Institute (NCI) were held late in the year. Questions revolved around the informed consent given by people who volunteer to test new drugs and the administration of these experimental agents. Some researchers charged that NCI research was considered "above the law" because of the FDA policy of waiving certain investigational rules in the case of cancer chemotherapy (Beset in the press 1981). As rates of the most common cancers (colon, lung, and breast) rise, the issue of ethical testing by researchers will be of more and more concern to women.

Infections and Sexually-Transmitted Diseases

Great attention was devoted in 1981 to infections common in women: Vaginal and bladder infections (vaginitis, monilia, trichomoniasis, and cervicitis), and cystic breast disease. It has been estimated that one out of every two women consulting a gynecologist does so because of vaginitis. Yet traditionally, the medical establishment has focused little attention on the disorder. "Only now is the National Center on Health Statistics compiling what is believed to be the first report on diseases of the female breast and genital tract" (Spratling 1981).

Lack of knowledge of these health problems, which manifests itself in the prescription of dangerous drugs (such as Flagyl for cystitis, known to cause cancer and gene mutations in mice) and questionable treatments (such as cervical cauterization to heal erosion), is of more and more concern. It is to be hoped that the increasing numbers of women in medicine will focus further research in these areas.

Attention has again centered on the prevalence of sexually transmitted ailments. Rates of well known venereal diseases (such as gonorrhea and syphilis) continued to be high, especially among adolescents. The biggest news, however, was not of these but of a previously obscure problem, genital herpes, a variety of HSV (herpes simplex virus) infection. Its manifestations include vesicular skin lesions, ulcers of the oropharynx and cervico vaginal mucosa, encephalitis, meningitis, hepatitis, pneumonitis, retinitis, eczema herpeticum, and shingles.

While genital herpes is much less frequent than facial herpes (the most common form of which is the cold sore), its incidence is increasing. One study found that genital herpes has occurred in one-tenth of a population attending communicable diseases clinics. Emotional stress, the menstrual cycle, and physical trauma have all been identified as precipitators of genital herpetic episodes.

Perhaps of most concern to women is HSV's effects on childbearing. Prenatal HSV is extremely rare but can cause abortion, fetal death, fetal microcephaly, cataracts, encephalitis, and fatal hepatitis. Neonatal infection is also uncommon, but carries with it a mortality rate of 60 percent to 70 percent (Hayes 1981). Preventive care, including abstinence from intercourse, is indicated for infected pregnant women, and cesarean section is the preferred means of delivery.

Women and Alcohol

The women's health movement paid increasing attention in 1981 to the problems of the female alcoholic. The Department of Health and Human Services estimates that of the ten million alcoholics in this country one-third are women. This percentage is continually increasing, particularly among teenagers (Sullivan 1982). Nevertheless, very little of the budget of the National Institute on Alcohol Abuse and Alcoholism is spent on research and programs concerning women and alcohol (Mann 1981).

Many misconceptions surround the experience of the female alcoholic:

> Not only are the vast majority of alcoholic women in hiding,
> unwilling to expose their problems to almost certain social
> contempt, but the whole subject is distorted by destructive stereo-
> types and by the wrong assumption that the experience of the
> alcoholic woman is identical to that of the alcoholic man.
> (Masterson 1981, quoting Marion Sandmaier)

Several recent studies have examined the specific dilemmas of black and elderly women alcoholics as well as those of the general female populace (Sullivan 1982; Alcoholism among blacks 1981). They conclude that women do not, as had been previously supposed, necessarily drink alone (thus being more "sick" than men) or in response to specific life crises. Feminist researchers have also pointed out that the polyaddictions characteristic of some female alcoholics are iatrogenic. Women are more likely to consult physicians for the anxiety and depression that cause and accompany their alcoholism; all too often they are treated with habit-forming drugs that add to their problems.

Women and Aging

The 1981 White House Conference on Aging focused greater attention on both medical and sociological health problems of older women.

Menopause remains one of the least understood of women's health issues. Too frequently physicians have little understanding of its accompanying physical and emotional changes. Consequently, symptoms are treated with hormones or tranquilizers whose long-term effects are either unknown or negative.

Research presented by Helen Roberts at the Third International Congress on Menopause (Ostend, Belgium) illuminated the subject (Women's views 1981). Dr. Roberts acknowledged the fundamental difference in the way that male physicians and older women view the menopause. The former see this as an intensely stressful period during which both full-time work and advice from well-meaning female friends add to the stress. She found, however, that both women's support and full-time employment tend to lessen tensions and physical symptoms. Roberts concluded that for many women menopause is a time of liberation from the responsibilities and worries of childbearing.

Other women researchers and writers continue to explore menopause, concentrating on sociocultural as well as physical manifestations (McPherson 1981). Many question the persistent categorization of older women's health issues under the broad headings of menopause and senility, both of which require further examination by feminist writers and health workers.

As the economy declines, the health problems of older women remain intimately linked to financial issues. The 1981 White House Conference on Aging established that not only is the American health care system ignorant of the symptomatology and treatment of the chronic conditions of older women, but that simple access to care is difficult, if not impossible, for many of them. Pension plans, Social Security benefits, and health insurance are all significant issues for older women. Since women over age sixty-five comprise the fastest-growing segment of the population (Chauncey 1982), this will become more, not less, of a dilemma in the future.

Fortunately, older women have steadily grown more conscious of the need to organize and lobby for their rights. The Gray Panthers have long been concerned with women's issues. The Older Women's League, established as a result of the 1980 White House Mini-Conference on Older Women, has now grown to fifty chapters. The National Organization for Women recently devoted more attention to the health and social concerns of these women (Klemsrud 1981). It is clear, however, that women must continue to organize and work together if they are to combat both ageism and sexism.

Women and Disabilities

The designation by the United Nations of 1981 as the International Year of Disabled Persons (IYDP) coincided with a greater emphasis on disabled women's concerns by the women's health movement. Almost 10 percent of all women have a disability. For this group perhaps more than any other, health becomes a matter of social structure and economics as well as clinical treatment. The average income of disabled women is a fraction of that earned by able-bodied women: $2,744 in 1980 (Asch and Fine 1981). Women with disabilities face discrimination in employment, counseling and training, health and social services, and housing. As in larger society, women working for the rights of disabled people have traditionally taken a back seat to male leaders, but recent developments have seen a major change in this.

In 1981 there was increasing inclusion of disabled women in administrative capacities in health-related organizations, the Boston Self-Help Center, for example. They also assumed decision-making roles in advocacy programs (Community Advocacy Program, Developmental Disabilities Law Center, Boston; and Project in Self-Advocacy, Boston). As in the larger women's health movement, disabled women began in the 1980s to organize self-help groups better to understand their physical condition and its treatment (Tapestry, Cambridge, Mass.).

Perhaps the greatest difficulty for these women lies in the attitudes of providers themselves: embarrassment, presumption of illness, and lack of understanding of disabled women's sexuality. Until recently, disbled women internalized the assumption that they had no sexual feelings, abilities, or reproductive capacity. For most this is simply untrue. In a related area, disabled and able-bodied women alike continued in 1981 to fight sterilization abuse, a particular concern for retarded women (Special issue on women and disability 1981). Drug-abuse (sometimes induced by providers) and alcohol addiction continue to be problems.

A major setback for institutionalized disabled women came in the form of an April Supreme Court decision that overturned the legality of a Bill of Rights provision in the 1975 Developmental Disabilities Act. This said that states must provide treatment for retarded persons in "the setting which is least restrictive of the persons' personal liberty." The Court found that Congress was stating a "preference," rather than a binding provision when it enacted the provision. Thus the Court obstructed the deinstitutionalization of an estimated 135,000 developmentally disabled people (including the retarded and those with autism, cerebral palsy, childhood psychoses, and cystic fibrosis) who reside in large public institutions (Sprague 1981).

Rural Women and Health

The first national gathering to focus on rural women's health was held in Hindman, Kentucky on June 19 to 21, 1981. Organized by members of the Rural Health Issues Committee of the National Women's Health Network (NWHN), the Appalachian Pathways Conference on Women and Health involved the participation of many Appalachian women's groups. It centered on the health, social, and economic problems of rural women, which are often neglected by the larger women's health movement, and the concurrent released report (*Patterns of change: rural women organizing for health* 1981). It concluded, "In general, health care is either inaccessible, unacceptable, inadequate or unavailable to large numbers of rural Americans, and the majority of those who need and actually receive care are women and children."

The difficulties urban American women experience in receiving adequate care are magnified in rural areas. In Appalachia, "occupational and environmental health problems are accentuated by the region's singular dependence on the coal industry and the relocation of chemical industries in the region with accompanying increased dumping of toxic wastes" (Batt 1981, p. 37). The poverty of the region, along with the educational and employment discrimination women traditionally face, contribute to their dilemmas. The NWHN report also pointed out that rural areas often lack special services for women, such as prenatal care, family planning services, mental health resources, rape crisis centers, and counseling for sexually abused children and victims of domestic violence (*Patterns of change: rural women organizing for health* 1981). Finally, the infant mortality rate is about twice as high as that in metropolitan centers.

The Appalachian Pathways Conference focused on these issues as well as the very real contributions country women have made to the women's health movement. Because of their isolation from the overly "scientific" orientation of urban medicine, Appalachian and other rural areas have maintained strong folk medicine traditions. Health care also tends to be more community-oriented and less profit-oriented. Such model systems as the United Mineworkers Clinics are found in Appalachia. In 1981, two Appalachian service organizations, the Frontier Nursing Service in Hyden, Kentucky and the Big Sandy Family and Childbirth Education Association, received 1981 Health Advocate of the Year Awards from the NWHN.

Already scarce services will be deeply affected by Reagan budget cuts proposed in 1981. Community health centers, alcoholism and drug abuse services, venereal disease prevention programs, black lung clinics, migrant health centers, and local health service associations will all be imperiled by reductions in government funding. The National Health Service Corporations and the Indian Health Service, both of which provide valuable and inexpensive medical care, will also lose money. Much of the conference discussion centered on these issues and on the serious threat of New Right legistlation such as the human life amendment (HLA).

Environmental and Occupational Health

Reproductive rights organizations and labor unions continue to work together to protect the rights of women in the workplace. The chemical threat to health, however, intensified in 1981 because of government relaxation of occupational health and safety standards.

While many women have entered the workplace in the last decade, only a small proportion of them have made it into the lucrative, "hazardous" occupations. Employers of women in these nontraditional jobs are likely to cite "reproductive hazards," ignoring the fact that "it has been estimated that approximately forty-five percent of women are actually risk-free—women who have been sterilized, passed through menopause or have no intention of becoming pregnant or completing a pregnancy to term" (Johnston, Peteros, and Pinto 1981). Companies such as American Cyanimid (against which five female workers won a lawsuit in 1980, charging that the company required them to be sterilized or lose their jobs); Bunker Hill Co.; E. I. Dupont de Nemours & Co.; Monsanto Co.; B. F. Goodrich; and General Motors practice policies that exclude pregnant and fertile women from exposure to toxic substances (Lee 1981).

This is not, however, to down-play the very real chemical dangers employment often poses. It is estimated that over 5,000 new chemicals yearly are added to the existing pool of 500,000, and very few are adequately tested. Birth defects of many kinds can originate from them. Also, a 1981 study reports that 20 percent to 38 percent of all cancers are linked to the workplace (Lee 1981). Lawyers predict that the number of lawsuits linking "latent diseases" with toxic exposure will vastly increase throughout the 1980s (Lee 1981).

Environmental contamination increases as much of the governmental pollution regulation is reduced or dismantled. Women's health groups were alarmed by the Environmental Protection Agency (EPA) consideration of a plan to lift the ban on the herbicide 2,3,4,T. This compound, which has been linked with miscarriage, contains traces of dioxin, one of the most toxic chemicals ever made. The prevalence of other toxic substances in the environment, such as DDE (a by-product of DDT), and PCB's are well known, as are the continual discoveries of toxic waste disposal sites.

The current Administration continued its "benign neglect" environmental policies in 1982. EPA faces cuts of $4 billion in 1982. The new heads of EPA and OSHA both wish to shift regulatory control back to the states (and corporate management). The President's Council on Environmental Quality lost 70 percent of its budget and two-thirds of its staff in 1981. All of these changes are predicated on greater "cost effectiveness." All pose serious risks to the renewal of the Clean Air Act and Clean Water Act, which comes up for passage in 1982 (Lee 1981). Also of concern to women antinuclear activists is the Administration's support of nuclear power, which is composed of three parts: acceleration of the licensing of nuclear power plants; encouragement of research and development of a system of breeder reactors and the institution of a federal disposal site for highly radioactive nuclear wastes (Marshall 1981).

REFERENCES

Alcoholism among blacks ignored. 1981. *U.S. Journal of Drug and Alcohol Dependence*, May.

APHA supports protest action. 1981. *Nation's Health*, July.

Asch, A. and Fine, M. 1981. Disabled women: sexism without the pedestal. *Journal of Sociology and Social Welfare* 8, no. 2:334-44.

Batt, L. 1981. National women's network focuses on rural health. *Mountain Life and Work*, July/August, pp. 36-38.

Bendectin—its safety now accepted—is challenged on efficacy. 1981. *Medical World News*, August 3, pp. 23-24.

Beset in the press, NCI faces foes in Congress. 1981. *Medical World News*, December 7, pp. 9-11.

Chauncey, C. 1982. The economics of aging. *Progress* 3, no. 4:1-3.

Congressional hearing investigates effects of obstetric drugs on child development. 1981. News release. American Foundation for Maternal and Child Health, Inc., Beekman Place, New York, NY 10022.

Contraceptives for men: researchers seek a birth control pill. 1981. *Contraceptive Technology Update*, December, pp. 160-61.

Contraceptives held successful for teenagers. 1981. *Family Practice News*, November 15.

Drug information inserts read and used, says study. 1981. *Nation's Health*, October.

Engel, M. 1981. U-Md. doctor gives DES to retarded youths. *Washington Post*, November 15.

Gardner, M. Study finds promise in male contraceptive hormone. 1981. *National Institute of Health News*, November, p. 9.

Hatcher, R. 1981. Commentary. *Contraceptive Technology Update*, November.

Hayes, K. 1981. Genital herpes simplex in midwifery practice. National Midwives Association, Second Annual Conference, February 27.

Hendershot, G. E. 1980. Trends in breast feeding. *Advance Data from Vital and Health Statistics*, National Center for Health Statistics, DHEW, No. 59, March 28.

Hendershot, G. E. 1981. Trends and differentials in breast feedings in the United States, 1970-75: Evidence from the National Survey of Family Growth, Cycle II. Paper presented at the annual meeting of the Population Association of America, March 26-28, Washington, D.C.

Hoffman, E., and Slade, M. 1981. Toxic shock's other victims. *New York Times*, December 27.

Howe, A. 1981. To drug firms, Reagan is a shot in the arm. *Philadelphia Inquirer*, January 11.

Jick, H. et al. 1981. Vaginal spermicides and congenital disorders. *Journal of the American Medical Association* 245:1329-32.

Johnston, B.; Peteros, K; and Pinto, J. 1981. Sorry, you can't work here. . . . *Second Opinion*, July.

Kelly, J. 1981. Lifeshock: how science is changing the human race. *Mademoiselle*, November, pp. 159-61.

Klemsrud, J. 1981. Improving the self-image of older women. *New York Times*, November 2.

Lee, M. M. 1981. The chemical threat to our reproductive health, parts 1 and 2. *Carasa News*, September and October.

Mann, J. 1981. Women's health needs a closer look. *Washington Post*, January 9.

Marshall, E. 1981. Reagan's plan for nuclear power. *Science* 214:419.

McPherson, K. 1981. Menopause as disease: the social construction of a metaphor. *Advances in Nursing Science*, January, pp. 95-113.

Masterson, P. 1981. Alcoholism: in the liquor closet. *Sojourner*, February, pp. 6-7.

Miscarriage risk linked to intrauterine device. 1981. *New York Times*, December 5.

New research about genetic factors in breast cancer. 1981. *Ms.*, September, p. 19.

Norsigian, J., and Swenson, N. 1981. Women and health. *The Women's Annual 1980: The Year in Review*. Boston: G. K. Hall.

Nurse practitioners a big boon to family planning. 1981. *Contraceptive Technology Update*, January.

Nutritional vitamin B12 deficiency in infants. 1981. *New Family Newsletter* 3, no. 2:3.

Okie, S. 1981. The pill: its perils, problems. *Washington Post*, February 15.

Patterns of change: rural women organizing for health. 1981. Rural Health Issues Committee, National Women's Health Network. Washington, D.C.: National Women's Health Network.

Peck, B. 1981. Few are depressed after termination. *Doctor*, September 4.

The pill and breast cancer: an odd family link. 1981. *Medical World News*, May 25.

Report on non-spermicide fit-free diaphragm. 1981. Untitled. *Family Planning Today* 3, no. 1.

Rosenfield, A. 1981. The adolescent and contraception: issues and controversies. *International Journal of Gynecology and Obstetrics* 19:57-64.

Sandberg, E. C. et al. 1981. Stanford University School of Medicine, Calif. Pregnancy outcome in women exposed to diethylstilbestrol in utero. *American Journal of Obstetrics and Gynecology* 140:194-205.

Seaman, B. 1980. Health group disputes drug company claims on oral contraceptive. Press release, National Women's Health Network, November 20.

Some DES daughters have withered tubes. 1981. *Medical World News*, June 8, p. 41.

Special issue on women and disability. 1981. *Off Our Backs* 11, no. 5:26.

Sprague, J. B. 1981. Access to care: disabled women and the health system. *Second Opinion*, May, pp. 1-3.

Spratling, C. 1981. Rx for women's health care. *Detroit Free Press*, July 19.

Stenchever, M. A. et al. 1981. University of Washington School of Medicine, Seattle, Wash. Possible relationship between in utero diethylstilbestrol exposure and male fertility. *American Journal of Obstetrics and Gynecology* 140:186-91.

Sullivan, T. 1982. A lonely road to recovery for women alcoholics. *Cambridge (Mass.)*

Chronicle, February 4.

Teen-age girls found reluctant to get sex advice. 1981. *New York Times*, October 27.

The ultimate chaperon. 1981. *Los Angeles Herald Examiner*, September 17, editorial.

U.S. Department of Health and Human Services. 1981. Public Health Service, Food and Drug Administration. Letter to consumers regarding TSS.

What next for community health? 1980-1981. *Community Health News* no. 3:1-3.

Whitehouse, F. 1981. Specialist in home births suspended. *New York Times*, December 2.

Women justifiably concerned. 1981. *Ob. Gyn. News*, November 15.

Women on medicaid manage to get funding for abortion. 1981. *The Nation's Health*, October.

Women's views on menopause devalued. 1981. *Family Practice News*, November 15, p. 48.

Wood, A. P. 1982. Hint of government cutback in teen contraceptive services alarms MDs. *Ob. Gyn. News* 16, no. 5:1, 11.

Wood, A. P. 1981. Obs. nurse-midwives labor to define new working relationship. *Ob. Gyn. News*, July 15.

BIBLIOGRAPHY

Barker-Benfield, G. J. *Horrors of the half-known life*. New York: Harper & Row, 1976; Harper Colophon, 1978. Documents medical misogyny.

Bart, Pauline, and Schlesinger, Melinda Bart. "Collective work and self-identity: the effect of working in a feminist illegal abortion collective." In *Workplace Democracy and Social Change*, eds. Frank Lindenfield and Joyce Rothschile-Whitt. Boston: Porter Sargent, 1980. Excellent exploration of social-psychological effects of collective work.

Bell, Ruth et al. *Changing bodies, changing lives: a book for teens on sex and relationships*. New York: Random House, 1981.

Bell, Susan. "Political gynecology: gynecological imperialism and the politics of self-help." *Science for the People* (January/February 1980). Women's political struggle for reproductive control.

Bell, Susan et al. "Reclaiming reproductive control: a feminist approach to fertility consciousness." *Science for the People* (January/February 1980).

Billings, E., and Westmore, A. *The Billings method*. Victoria, Australia: Anne O'Donovan Pty., 1980; New York: Random House, 1981. Fairly good but conservative approach to natural family planning.

Boston Women's Health Book Collective, Inc. *Nuestros Cuerpos, Nuestras Nuestras Vidas*. New York: Simon & Schuster, 1979. Spanish language edition of *Our Bodies, Our Selves*.

Boston Women's Health Book Collective. Our bodies, our selves: a book by and for women. New York: Simon & Schuster, 1973; revised and expanded, 1976; updated, 1979. Comprehensive health and sexuality information for women.

Boston Women's Health Book Collective. *Our selves and our children: A Book By and For Parents.* New York: Random House, 1978. Guide to parenting in all aspects of the word.

Boston Women's Health Book Collective, and ISIS, eds. *International women and health resource guide.* Boston: The Collective, 1980. Includes much information on international women's movement unavailable elsewhere.

Bunker, John et al. *Costs, risks and benefits of surgery.* New York: Oxford University Press, 1977. Documents much unnecessary reproductive surgery.

Cantarow, Ellen. "Dissecting the victim." *In These Times* (August 12-25, 1981). Personal account of the death of a parent by cancer; also analyzes the politics of cancer treatment.

Chaussey, Annette. "Deaf women and the women's movement." *Deaf American* 29 (April 1977): 10-11. One of the very rare analyses of deaf women's liberation.

Corsaro, M., and Korzeniowsky, C. *STD: a common sense guide.* New York: St. Martin's Press, 1980. Excellent overall guide to these diseases.

Donnison, Jean. *Midwives and medical men: a history of inter-professional rivalries and women's rights.* New York: Schocken Books, 1978. History of these conflicts from a British perspective.

Edelman, D. A. et al. *Intrauterine devices and their uses.* Boston: G.K. Hall, 1979. Good technical manual.

Edmonson, Barbara. "Sociosexual education for the handicapped." *Exceptional Education Quarterly* 1, no. 2 (August 1980): 67-76. Delineates growing need for sex education for the disabled community.

Ehrenreich, Barbara, and English, Deirdre. *Witches, midwives and nurses: a history of women healers.* Old Westbury, N.Y.: Feminist Press, 1973. Fascinating historical analysis and commentary on women as healers.

Ehrenreich, Barbara, and English, Deirdre. *Complaints and disorders: the sexual politics of sickness.* Old Westbury, N.Y.: The Feminist Press, 1974. Historical examination of the sex and class-based politics of disease diagnosis and treatment.

Ehrenreich, Barbara, and English, Deirdre. *For her own good: 150 years of the expert's advice to women.* New York: Doubleday/Anchor, 1978. Medical "expertise" and its iatrogenic effects on women.

Erlien, Marla et al. *More than a choice: women talk about abortion.* Boston: Abortion Action Coalition, 1979. Excellent pamphlet focusing on personal experience of abortion with section on political action.

Feminist Women's Health Center. *A new view of a woman's body: the totally illustrated guide of new information from the women's health movement.* New York: Simon and Schuster, 1982. Excellent annotations and some good descriptive material.

Fielding, Benjamin B. *Attitudes and aspects of orthopedically-handicapped women.* Doctoral dissertation. Columbia University, 1950. University Microfilms abstract ADG-01-72079. Classic work on how disability further affects women's life chances.

Gillespie, Patricia, and Fink, Albert. "The influence of sexism on the education of handicapped children." *Exceptional Children* 41 (November 1974): 155-162. Innovative study.

Gordon, Linda. *Woman's body, woman's right—a social history of birth control in America.* New York: Penguin books, 1977. Excellent discussion of the social, political, and economic factors influencing the kind of birth control available.

Gordon, Linda, and Hunter, Allen. "Sex, family and the New Right: antifeminism as a political force." *Radical America* (November 1977; February 1978).

Gray, Mary Jane. "Doctor recounts illegal abortions." *National Women's Health Network*, Fall 1981. Graphic account of the realities of illegal abortion.

Green, Nancy H. "Support group for women with physical disabilities." *Alert* 2 (Winter 1979): 7-8. Role of peer counseling in helping disabled women.

Greiner, Ted. *The promotion of bottle feeding by multinational corporations: how advertising and the health professions have contributed.* Cornell University International Nutrition Series No. 2. Ithaca, N.Y.: Cornell University Division of Nutritional Sciences, 1975. One of the few detailed historical analysis of infant formula abuse.

Gussow, Joan Dye. *The feeding web: issues in nutritional ecology.* Palo Alto, Calif.: Bull Publishing, 1978. Extremely valuable source book on environment, energy, population, and nutrition.

Gyorgy, Anna et al. *No nukes: everyone's guide to nuclear power.* Boston: South End Press, n.d.

Harrison, Michelle. *A woman in residence.* New York: Random House, 1982. Very good critique of the obstetrics/gynecology establishment by a female resident physician.

Henderson, Craig et al. *New England Journal of Medicine* 302 (January 3): 17-30; 302 (January 10):78-90. Comprehensive analysis of etiology and treatment of breast cancer.

Hite, Shere. *The Hite report.* New York: Macmillan, 1976; Dell, 1977. Innovative report of female sexuality.

ISIS. "Nuclear power and militarization." *ISIS International Bulletin*, no. 15 (1980). Available from ISIS, CP 50 (Cornavin) Geneva, Switzerland.

Journal of Sociology and Social Welfare. Special issue. "Women and disability: the double handicap." September 1981. Excellent overall view of women and disability.

Kaiser, Barbara, and Kaiser, Irwin. "The challenge of the women's movement to American gynecology." *American Journal of Obstetrics and Gynecology* 120 (November 1974): 652-61. Challenge to physician view of women's health movement.

Kent, Deborah. "In Search of Liberation." *Disabled USA* 3 (1977): 18-19. Connections and problems of disabled women with the women's movement.

Kitzinger, Sheila. *The experience of childbirth.* Harmondsworth, Middlesex, England: Penguin, rev. 1978. Technical and academic critique of childbirth experience.

Kitzinger, Sheila, and Davis, John, eds. *The place of birth.* New York: Oxford University Press, 1978.

Knox, Richard A. "Doctors: prevent N-war epidemic." *Boston Sunday Globe*, Mar. 21, 1981, p. 1. Report of Soviet/American physician conference on nuclear disarmament.

Kramer, Roz. "The great abortion battle of 1981." *Village Voice*, March 11, 1981. History and discussion of New Right involvement in antiabortion movement.

"Legal trends and issues in voluntary sterilization." *Population Reports* 9, no. 2 (March/April 1981). Global summation of voluntary sterilization laws, procedures and issues.

Lipnack, Jessica. "The women's health movement." *New Age Journal*, March 1980. Good overview.

"Medical schools: more women students but fewer women professors in USA." Excerpts from: *The Chronicle of Higher Education* (May 26, 1981). Current trends in medical school population projections of female percentage in physician population.

Milligan, Debi. "Pelvic inflammatory disease." Available from Boston Women's Health Book Collective, P.O. Box 192, W. Somerville, MA 02144.

Millman, Marcia. *The unkindest cut: life in the backrooms of medicine.* New York: Morrow, 1977. Excellent field study of modern medical practice.

National Women's Health Network, gen. ed. Health Resource Guides. No. 1: *Breast Cancer.* No. 2: *Hysterectomy.* No. 4: *Maternal health and childbirth.* No. 6: *DES.* No. 7: *Self-help.* No. 9: *Sterilization.* Washington, D.C.: NWHN, 1980.

Nellis, Muriel. *The female fix.* Boston: Houghton Mifflin, 1980. Comprehensive documentation and examination of drug and alcohol abuse among women.

Norsigian, Judith. "Redirecting contraceptive research." *Science for the People* 11, no. 1 (January/February 1979).

Oakley, Ann. *Women confined: toward a sociology of childbirth.* New York: Schocken Books, 1980. Excellent analysis of the birth experience.

O'Donnell, Mary et al. *Lesbian health matters!* Santa Cruz, Calif.: Santa Cruz Women's Center, 1979 (250 Locust St., Santa Cruz, Calif. 95060). Good overall guide.

Off Our Backs. Special issue on women and disability, May 1981. Excellent bibliography.

O'Toole, Corbett and Weeks, CeCe. *What happens after school? A study of disabled women and education.* San Francisco: Far West Laboratory for Women's Educational Equity Communications Network, 1978, 58 pp.

Parvati, Jeannine. *Hygeia: a woman's herbal.* Santa Rosa, Calif.: Freestone Collective, 1978. Interesting work on spirituality and the use of herbal remedies.

Petchessky, Ros. "Reproductive ethics and public policy: a look at the federal sterilization regulations." *Hastings Center Report*, October 1979.

Reproductive Health Resources. *Toward intimacy: family planning and sexuality concerns of physically disabled women.* New York: Human Sciences Press, 1979. Explodes myths surrounding sexuality, reproduction and disability.

Reproductive Health Resources. *Within reach: providing family planning services to physically disabled women.* New York: Human Sciences Press, 1979. Access and sexuality counseling.

Rich, Adrienne. *Of woman born.* New York: Bantam Books, 1977. Classic exploration of the "culture of motherhood" in Western society.

Rosoff, Jeannie J. "Abortion funding stopped for rape, incest victims." *Washington Memo* (May 29, 1981): 1-3. Summation of political machinations that resulted in passage of the Helms amendment.

Rural Health Issues Committee, NWHN. *Patterns of change: rural women organizing for health.* Washington, D.C.: NWHN, 1981. Guide to surmounting the unique organizing difficulties of rural women.

Sandmaier, Marian. *The invisible alcoholics: women and alcohol abuse in America.* New York: McGraw-Hill, 1980.

Santa Cruz Women's Health Collective. *Herpes.* Santa Cruz, Caif.: Women's Health Collective, 1977; rev. 1980.

Seaman, Barbara. *The doctor's case against the pill.* New York: Doubleday, rev. 1980. Excellent summary of health dangers of oral contraceptives.

Shaw, Nancy. *Forced labor: maternity care in the United States.* New York: Pergamon Press, 1974. Still one of the best documentations of the inadequacy of the hospital-based maternity experience.

Smith, R. Jeffrey. "Hayes intends modest reforms at FDA." *Science* 213 (Aug. 28, 1981). Excellent analysis of recent actual and proposed changes at FDA under Mr. Hayes's administration. Includes information on patient package inserts, testing and regulation.

Sommers, Tish, and Shields, Laurie. "Older Women and Health Care: Strategies for Survival." *Gray Paper*, no. 3 (1980).

Special Issue on Women and Deafness. *Gallaudet today.* Spring 1974. Slightly dated but extremely important writing on the relation of this neglected group to the women's movement at large.

Stellman, Jeanne. *Women's work, women's health: myths and realities.* New York: Pantheon, 1977. One of the rare books dealing exclusively with women's occupational health concerns.

Stokes, Bruce. *Men and family planning.* Worldwatch Paper 41, Dec. 1980. Documents male birth control use worldwide; posits efficacy of such methods when used correctly.

Turshen, Meredith. *Women, food and health in Tanzania: the political economy of disease.* London: Onyx Press, 1980.

United Nations. World Health Organization. *Meeting on infant and young child feeding.* Document FHE/ICF/79.3, (October 1979).

U.S. Congress. House of Representatives. Committee on Ways and Means. Subcommittee on Health. "Testimony on national health plans" by Norma Swenson, February 21, 1980.

U.S. Congress. "Testimony to subcommittee of oversight and investigations of the committee on interstate and foreign commerce, US House of Representatives, on nurse-midwifery: consumer's freedom of choice" by Judith Norsigian. December 18, 1980.

U.S. Department of Commerce, Census Bureau, 1970 Census of Population. *Persons with work disability,* Subject report PC(2)-6C. Washington, D.C.: Census Bureau, January 1973, 174 pp.

U.S. Department of Health, Education and Welfare. *An evaluation of cesarean section in the United States* by Helen Marieskind. Washington, D.C.: U.S. Government Printing Office, 1979.

U.S. Department of Health, Education and Welfare. National Institutes of Health, *DES task force summary report.* No. NIG-79-1688. Washington, D.C.: U.S. Government Printing Office, n.d.

U.S. Department of Health and Human Services. Public Health Service. Center for Disease Control. *Abortion surveillance.* Washington, D.C.: U.S. Government Printing Office, 1980.

U.S. Department of Health and Human Services. Public Health Service. Center for Disease Control. *Surgical sterilization surveillance: hysterectomy in women aged 15-44.* Washington, D.C.: U.S. Government Printing Office, 1980.

Walsh, Mary Roth. *Doctors wanted—no women need apply: sexual barriers in the medical profession 1835-1975.* New Haven: Yale University Press, 1977.

Wertz, Dorothy, and Wertz, Richard. *Lying-in: a history of childbirth in America.* New York: Free Press, 1977. Good historical overview; well-documented. Less feminist-oriented than other current works on this subject.

"Women and Disability. Special Problems of Disabled Women." *International Rehabilitation Review* (February 1977), pp. 1, 46.

"Women in crisis conference focuses on alcohol issues." National Institute on Alcohol Abuse and Alcoholism, Information and Feature Service, no. 88:1, September 29, 1981. This conference was one of the first to explore the unique social, psychological, and political dilemmas of women alcoholics.

Women Organized For Reproductive Choice. *The new right vs. women's rights.* Chicago: Women Organized for Reproductive Choice, 1980.

Zelnick, M. and Kantner, J. S. "Sexual activity, contraceptive use and pregnancy among metropolitan area teenagers, 1971-1979." *Family Planning Perspectives* 12 (1980). Good documentation of an often misrepresented area.

RESOURCES

Periodicals and Key Resource Organizations

American College of Nurse-Midwives, 1522 K Street N.W., Suite 1120, Washington, DC 20005.

Boston Self-Help Center, 18 Williston Road, Brookline, MA 02146. Counseling and advocacy services for people with disabilities.

Boston Women's Health Book Collective, P.O. Box 192, West Somerville, MA 02144. Authors of *Our bodies, our selves*; provide health and sexuality information to women.

CARASA (Coalition of Abortion Rights and Against Sterilization Abuse), 17 Murray Street, 5th floor, New York, NY 10007. Publishes *CARASA News*.

Center for Science in the Public Interest, 1757 S Street NW, Washington, DC 20009. Excellent resources, including posters on food and nutrition. Publishes *Nutrition Action*.

Coal Mining Women's Support Team News, Coal Employment Project, Box 3403, Oak Ridge, TN 37830.

Coalition for the Medical Rights of Women, 1638B Haight Street, San Francisco, CA 94114. Health advocacy and information resource. Publishes *Coalition News*.

Coalition for the Reproductive Rights of Workers (CRROW), 1126 16th Street NW, #316, Washington, DC 20036.

Disability Rights Education and Defense Fund, Inc. (DREDF), 2032 San Pablo Avenue, Berkeley, CA 94702.

Do It Now Foundation, Box 5115, Phoenix, AZ 85010. Substance abuse information.

Emma Goldman Clinic for Women, 715 N. Dodge, Iowa City, IA 52240. One of the oldest women's health centers in the United States; offers literature; major center for fitting cervical caps.

Feminist Resources on Energy and Ecology (FREE), Box 6098, Teall Station, Syracuse, NY 13217.

Feminist Women's Health Center, 6411 Hollywood Blvd., Los Angeles, CA 90028. Resource for organizing information and teaching materials basic to movement and philosophy of self-help; literature list.

Health Facts, Center for Medical Consumers and Health Care Information, 237 Thompson Street, New York, NY 10012. General bimonthly newsletter.

Health/PAC (Health Policy Advisory Center), 17 Murray Street, New York, NY 10007. Analyses and study of health issues from radical perspective; produces variety of publications.

Healthsharing, Women Healthsharing, Box 230, Station M, Toronto, Ontario M6S 4T3, Canada. Quarterly newsletter covering wide range of women's health concerns.

The Helper, American Social Health Association, Box 100, Palo Alto, CA 94302. About sexually transmitted diseases, particularly herpes.

The Hot Flash, Women's Health Services, 316 E. Marcy Street, Santa Fe, NM 87501. General monthly newsletter, frequent articles about herbs, massage, and nonallopathic approaches to healing as well as abortion and contraception updates.

ICASC Information, International Contraception, Abortion and Sterilization Campaign (ICASC), c/o NAC, 374 Grays Inn Road, London W.C. 1, England. Covers activities of governments, churches, the medical profession, drug companies, political parties, population control agencies, and antiabortion organizations, and what women are doing internationally to gain or preserve the right to control their fertility.

International Childbirth Education Association (ICEA), Box 20048, Minneapolis, MN 55420. Offers extensive annotated lists of publications and audiovisual resources; monthly newsletter covers wide range of childbirth issues.

National Women's Health Network, 224 Seventh Street SE, Washington, DC 20003. National membership consumer organization; monitors and works to influence government and industry policies. Publishes *Network News*.

New Hampshire Feminist Health Center, 38 S. Main Street, Concord, NH 03301. Publishes *Womenwise*, which covers wide variety of topics on women and health.

Off Our Backs, 1841 Columbia, Rm. 212, Washington, DC 20009. Probably the best feminist monthly newspaper, with excellent regular coverage of women's health issues.

Older Women's League (OWL), 3800 Harrison Street, Oakland, CA 94611. Publishes *Gray Papers: Issues for Action* (See Sommers in Bibliography).

The Practicing Midwife, 156 Drakes Lane, Summertown, TN 38483. Quarterly on alternative health issues, midwifery, primary health care, and public health field. Published by The Farm.

Reproductive Rights National Network (R_2N_2), 17 Murray Street, New York, NY 10007. Publishes *Reproductive Rights Newsletter*.

Resolve, Inc., Box 474, Belmont, MA 02178. Literature and resources on infertility, artificial insemination, and research into these and related issues. Publishes *Resolve Newsletter*.

Science for the People, 897 Main Street, Cambridge, MA 02139. Bimonthly offering analyses of politics of science, frequently examines women's health issues.

Union WAGE (Union Women's Alliance to Gain Equality), P.O. Box 40904, Berkeley CA 94701. Dedicated to fighting discrimination on the job, in unions, and in society. Publishes *Union WAGE*, which carries important articles on women and occupational health.

WIN News, Women's International Network, 187 Grant Street, Lexington, MA 02173. Carries wide range of topics of concern to women and reports from around the world.

Women and Health, Box 33790, Seattle, WA 98133 (editorial address); Haworth Press, 149 Fifth Avenue, New York, NY 10010 (subscription address). Academic journal with articles on all aspects of women's health.

Women for Environmental Health, 1747 Connecticut Avenue, NW, Washington, DC 20009.

Women in Medicine Newsletter, Women in Medicine Task Force, American Medical Student Association, 14650 Lee Road, Box 131, Chantilly, VA 22121.

Women of All Red Nations (WARN), Group of native American women seeking to improve health and living conditions of all native Americans; their work often emphasizes women and children.

Women's Committee, Mass. Coalition for Occupational Safety and Health, 718 Huntington Avenue, Boston, MA 02115. Broad spectrum of activities focusing on occupational health of women and other workers. Many health and safety materials available.

Women's Occupational Health Resource Center, School of Public Health, Columbia University, 60 Haven Avenue, B-1, New York, NY 10032.

Recommended Films

Abortion. By Jane Pincus et al. 1970. Available from Boston Women's Health Book Collective, P.O. Box 192, W. Somerville, MA 02144. Thirty minutes, 16-mm, black/white. Produced in 1970-71, this powerful film describes the plight of women denied access to legal abortion. Also covers sterilization abuse and experimentation on Third World women.

Blood of the condor. Available from Tricontinental Films, 333 Sixth Avenue,

New York, NY 10014. About the uprising of a Bolivian village after it is discovered that hundreds of their women were sterilized unknowingly at a U.S.-financed clinic.

Bottle babies. Available from American Baptist Films, Valley Forge, PA 19481. Twenty-minutes, black/white. About infant feeding formula abuse in Third World countries.

The Chicago maternity center story. By Jenny Rohrer and Suzanne Davenport. Available from Kartemquin Films Ltd., 1901 W. Wellington, Chicago, IL 60657. Sixty-minutes, 16-mm, black/white. Details the struggle of a community group that unsuccessfully attempts to preserve community-based childbirth options.

Daughters of time. By Ginny Durrin. Available from New Day Films, P.O. Box 315, Franklin Lakes, NJ 07417. Twenty-four-minutes, 16-mm, color. About nurse-midwives.

Formula factor. Available from California Newsreel, 630 Natoma Street, San Francisco, CA 94103. Thirty-minutes, 16-mm, color. Also about infant formula abuse.

Healthcaring from our end of the speculum. Available from Women Make Movies, 257 W. 19th Street, New York, NY 10011. Thirty-five-minutes, color. Excellent introductory film covering many different women's health concerns.

A new image of myself. Available from Feminist Women's Health Center, 6411 Hollywood Blvd., Los Angeles, CA 90028. Eight-minutes. Primarily about vaginal self-examination.

Menopause: a time of transition. By Sheryl Brown. Available from San Francisco Planned Parenthood, 1660 Bush Street, San Francisco, CA 94109. Slide and tape show covering what to expect in menopause.

Nursing: the politics of caring. 1978. Available from Fanlight Productions, P.O. Box 226, Cambridge, MA 02138. Twenty-two-minutes, 16-mm, color documentary about the struggles of nurses as advocates of patients. Explores attitudes of nurses toward their work.

La operacion. By Ana Maria Garia. Powerful documentary about sterilization abuse, particularly among Puerto Rican women. Further information available from the filmmaker, 733 Amsterdam Avenue, Apt. 12A, New York, NY 10025; or The Film Fund, 80 E. 11th Street, New York, NY 10003.

Our lives on the line. By Faye More and Linda Di Rocco. Available from the Media Group, Urban Planning Aid, Inc., 100 Arlington Street, 2nd floor, Boston, MA 02116. Forty-five-minute videotape explores abortion experiences of four black women living in Boston.

Period piece. By Emily Culpepper. Available from the author, 3726 Lake Shore Avenue, Oakland, CA 94610. Ten-minutes, 16-mm, color. About menstruation.

Taking our bodies back: the women's health movement. Available from Cambridge Documentary Films, Box 385, Cambridge, MA 02139. Thirty-three minutes, color. Somewhat dated (produced in 1973), but still a good general film on women's health.

Trying times: crisis in fertility. 1980. Available from Fanlight Productions, P.O. Box 226, Cambridge, MA 02138. Thirty-three-minutes, 16-mm, color. About infertility, produced in collaboration with Resolve.

VD and women. 1978. Available from Perennial Education, 477 Roger Williams, Box 855, Ravinia, Highland Park, IL 60035. Seventeen-minutes, 16-mm, color, includes good section on prevention.

Working for your life. By Andrea Hricko and Ken Light. Available from LOHP Films, Transit Media, 779 Susquehanna Avenue, Franklin Lakes, NJ 07417. Sixty-minutes, 16-mm, color introductory film about women and occupational health.

4 | Third World Women in America

Patricia Hill Collins

For Third World women in America, 1981 held few surprises. As the 1980 census data slowly found their way into the public record, black, Chicano, native American, and Asian-American women gained added confirmation of what was already thought to be true—the old problems in education, unemployment, and income remained. Nonetheless, there were some bright spots in this otherwise drab year. Pockets of nonwhite women continued to build local organizations in scattered American cities, and several seminal works by or about Third World women found their way to mass audiences for the first time. The overall record, however, was one of continued difficulty, with problems only aggravated by the 1981 recession.

By far the single most far-reaching event of the year affecting Third World women was the active effort of the newly inaugurated Reagan administration to redefine social welfare policy. As current policies are best evaluated in light of current realities, this essay first summarizes the socioeconomic position of Third World women in 1981 and then presents women's responses to that reality from federal, academic, and minority female points of view.

Assessing 1981: The Reality of Third World Women's Experience

General Population Trends

The 1980 population data released in 1981 unmistakenly confirmed what was suspected all along—the nonwhite proportion of the American population was growing larger. During the 1970s, native American, black, Asian-American, and Chicano populations all increased. Currently, nearly one out of five individuals residing in the United States is likely to be nonwhite (U.S. Bureau of the Census 1981b). Each Third World community has grown, but

87

the patterns of growth and the implications of those patterns for the women in them are quite different.

The Filipino and Korean communities have shown the highest percentage of growth, much of it due to more lenient immigration standards for Asians. Thus these women are more likely to need better jobs and adequate training programs and protection from exploitation from certain employers, for example sweat shop garment factories or low-wage domestic service. In contrast, high birth rates probably account for the 72 percent increase in the native American population over the past decade. As a group, these women are more likely to have children and demonstrate a need for child-related services such as perinatal health care, nutritional programs, elementary schools, day care, and so forth, in addition to needing training and education for themselves (Witt 1974; Medicine 1978).

Hispanic women appear to be affected by the demands of both high birth rates and immigration (Cotera 1976; Garcia-Bahne 1977; Acosta-Belen 1979; Mirande and Enriquez 1979). The growth rate of the Hispanic community is more difficult to measure because of the allegedly large numbers of uncounted Mexican nationals who reside in the United States whose entry was not made through formal channels. Thus the number of individuals dependent on family income may be even higher than is actually counted. This becomes especially significant when considering female-headed households. In addition to increases due to formal and informal immigration, the Hispanic community has a high percentage of children. The black community faces a similar situation (Brinkley-Carter 1980; Allen 1981). While only 21.3 percent of the white population is under age 16 years, 28.7 percent of blacks and 32 percent of Hispanics fall in this category (Table 1, Figure 1).

FIGURE 1.

Age Distribution by Race: 1980

15 years and under.

Age 16–64

Age 65 and over.

White	21.3	66.5	12.2
Black	28.7	63.4	7.9
Spanish origin[1]	32.0	63.1	4.9

Percent

[1] Householders of Spanish origin may be of any race.
Source: Table 32.

Table 1.
Population of the United States by age, sex, race, and Spanish origin: 1980

	Race					Spanish origin[1]
	White	Black	American Indian, Eskimo, Aleut	Asian and Pacific-islander	Other	
MALE						
Numbers by thousands	91,670	12,516	701	1,693	3,452	7,278
Percent distribution						
Under 19 years	31.8	42.5	44.9	35.1	44.5	43.9
Age 20–29	18.2	19.0	19.4	19.3	24.0	20.8
Age 30–39	14.3	12.2	13.2	17.7	13.8	13.4
Age 40–64	25.5	19.4	17.6	21.6	14.7	17.5
Age 65 and over	10.0	6.7	4.7	6.1	2.8	4.1
Median Age	30.0	23.6	22.4	27.8	22.2	22.7
FEMALE						
Numbers by thousands	96,671	13,972	717	1,807	3,305	7,328
Percent distribution						
Under 19 years	28.8	37.6	42.6	31.4	44.2	41.9
Age 20–29	17.1	19.0	19.1	20.0	21.9	19.7
Age 30–39	13.7	12.9	13.6	19.2	13.7	13.7
Age 40–65	26.0	21.4	18.5	23.3	16.2	19.0
Age 65 and over	14.2	8.8	5.7	5.9	3.9	5.5
Median age	32.6	26.2	23.5	29.3	22.4	23.8

Source: U.S. Bureau of the Census, 1980 Census of Population, Supplementary Report, PC80-S1-1.
[1]Persons of Spanish origin may be of any race.

Table 2.
School Enrollment of Persons 3 to 34 Years Old, by Level of School, Race, and Spanish Origin: October 1980, 1975, and 1970

Subject	1980	1975	1970	Percent Change 1970-80
ALL RACES				
Total enrolled	57,348	60,969	60,357	−5.0
Nursery school	1,987	1,748	1,096	81.3
Kindergarten	3,176	3,393	3,183	−2.0
Elementary school	27,449	30,446	33,950	−19.1
High school	14,556	15,683	14,715	−1.1
College	10,180	9,697	7,413	37.3
Male	5,025	5,342	4,401	14.2
Female	5,155	4,355	3,103	71.1
WHITE				
Total enrolled	47,673	51,430	51,719	−7.8
Nursery school	1,637	1,431	893	83.3
Kindergarten	2,595	2,845	2,706	−4.1
Elementary school	22,510	25,412	28,638	−21.4
High school	12,056	13,224	12,723	−5.2
College	8,875	8,516	6,759	31.3
Male	4,438	4,774	4,065	9.2
Female	4,436	3,743	2,693	64.7
BLACK				
Total enrolled	8,250	8,400	7,829	5.4
Nursery school	294	276	178	65.2
Kindergarten	490	468	426	15.0
Elementary school	4,259	4,509	4,868	−12.5
High school	2,200	2,199	1,834	20.0
College	1,007	948	522	92.9
Male	437	442	253	72.7
Female	570	506	269	111.9
SPANISH ORIGIN[1]				
Total enrolled	4,262	3,741	2,815	51.4
Nursery school	146	85	62	135.5
Kindergarten	263	235	184	42.9
Elementary school	2,363	2,062	1,805	30.9
High school	1,048	948	608	72.4
College	443	411	155	185.8
Male	223	219	(NA)	(X)
Female	221	192	(NA)	(X)

Sources: U.S. Bureau of the Census, Current Population Reports, Series P-20, Nos. 222, 303; 1970 Census of Population, Vol. II, 1C, *Persons of Spanish origin*; unpublished Current Population Survey data.
[1] Persons of Spanish origin may be of any race.

The implications of this are far-reaching. The black, Spanish-speaking, and native American communities are younger and have need for services connected with children, while the white population is older and has much more interest in programs benefiting older citizens. The fact that Third World groups are poorly represented in the over-65 age category only compounds the problem; one would expect protecting Social Security to be high on the list of an aging white community, with education, job training, day care, and other youth-related social welfare programs more important to minorities.

Black women share the concern of native American and Hispanic women for adequate child-related programs, but the age distribution data suggest that they have an additional problem. Currently, black women between the ages of 15 to 34 years outnumber black men by about 430,000. In spite of the acknowledged tendency to undercount inner-city, young black men, the surplus of young, black women is quite real and has profound implications for the black community. The gap existed in 1970 and widened during the past decade. For example, white females who date and marry black men may be increasingly resented by black women. Also, the attitude of black women toward black male homosexuals might be considerably less tolerant than what lesbian feminists of whatever color would like. More importantly, however, the percentage of black families headed by women who are separated, divorced, or single should be expected to increase.

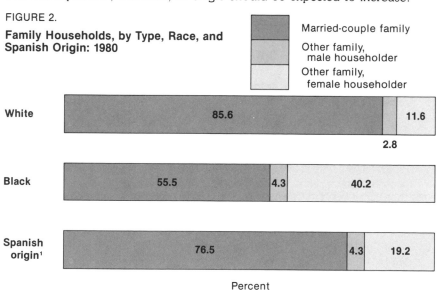

FIGURE 2.

Family Households, by Type, Race, and Spanish Origin: 1980

Married-couple family

Other family, male householder

Other family, female householder

White: 85.6 | 11.6 | 2.8

Black: 55.5 | 4.3 | 40.2

Spanish origin[1]: 76.5 | 4.3 | 19.2

Percent

[1] Householders of Spanish origin may be of any race.
Source: Table 32.

From 1970 to 1980, the proportion of black women heading households with no spouse present jumped from 28.3 percent in 1970 to a record 40.2 percent. It should be stressed that more than half of black households are populated by married-couple families; however, these data also mean that an increasing number of black females, for whatever reason, are choosing to head their own households. As the educational, employment, and income data reveal, for women with children, being a head of household has its own set of problems.

Education

The school enrollment data for both black and Hispanic communities are promising. Both groups showed increased school attendance on practically every educational level, with much of the increase due to population growth but a surprising amount reflecting people remaining longer in high school and college (Table 2). Of special note is black and Hispanic female college attendance—black women registered a 112 percent increase since 1970. This increase may itself aggravate the demographic imbalance in the black community, however, as the gap between male and female college enrollment is widening. A 1970 surplus of 16,000 black college women had mushroomed to 133,000 by 1980.

Also, while whites continue to reach higher levels of education than either blacks or Hispanics, both Third World groups have dramatically increased the percentages of their populations completing high school and some college (U.S. Bureau of the Census 1981b). In spite of these substantial gains, neither black nor Hispanic women have attained the educational level reached by white males and females ten years earlier.

Employment

Data on occupational distribution provide the most encouraging employment information for Third World women. Apparently, the educational achievements of nonwhite women, buttressed by stronger civil rights legislation, has spurred two trends—the exodus of Third World women from low-prestige domestic work and an increase of nonwhite women in clerical, technical, and professional positions (Table 3) (U.S. Department of Labor 1977, 1980b, 1981b, 1981d; Acosta-Belen and Sjostrom 1979; Wallace 1980). The white-collar areas especially showed promising increases. For example, 10.8 percent of Third World women held professional positions in 1970 compared to 16.3 percent in 1981, an increase to a level surpassing that of white males (14.6 percent). But these figures can be deceptive. White males predominate in the higher-paying white-collar positions, especially managerial and professional positions. They also dominate the lucrative blue-collar occupations, while Third World women remain clustered in service work. It appears that black and other nonwhite women have moved into traditionally female fields and, while the prestige attached to teaching, nursing, or clerical work may be high, the salary generally is not comparable to that earned by males of any race.

While this evaluation concerns women who are in the labor force, it says little about whether they are actually employed. Unemployment remains a

Table 3.
Percent Distribution of Employed Persons by Occupation, Race, and Sex

Occupation and Race	Males		Females	
	1970	**1981**	**1970**	**1981**
BLACK AND OTHER				
Totals 16 years and other (thousands)		5,675		5,333
Percent	100.0	100.0	100.0	100.0
White-collar workers	21.7	30.2	36.0	52.0
Professional and technical	7.8	12.1	10.8	16.3
Managers and administrators	4.7	6.8	1.9	4.4
Sales workers	1.8	2.8	2.5	3.4
Clerical workers	7.4	8.5	20.8	28.0
Blue-collar workers	59.6	51.6	19.2	18.8
Craft and kindred	13.8	15.8	0.8	1.2
Operatives, except transport	>28.4	15.6	>17.6	15.4
Transport equipment operatives		8.8		0.8
Nonfarm laborers	17.5	11.3	0.7	1.4
Service workers	13.1	15.9	43.1	28.8
Private household	0.3	0.2	17.5	5.3
Other	12.8	15.7	25.6	23.4
Farm workers	5.6	2.4	1.7	0.4
WHITE				
Totals 16 years and over (thousands)		50,594		37,299
Percent	100.0	100.0	100.0	100.0
White-collar workers	43.1	44.5	63.9	67.7
Professional and technical	14.6	16.4	15.0	17.6
Managers and administrators	15.3	15.6	4.8	7.7
Sales workers	6.1	6.4	7.7	7.2
Clerical workers	7.1	6.0	36.4	35.2
Blue-collar workers	45.6	43.1	15.7	12.8
Craft and kindred	20.8	20.9	1.2	1.8
Operatives, except transport	>8.7	10.4	>14.1	9.1
Transport equipment operatives		5.4		0.8
Nonfarm laborers	6.2	6.4	0.4	1.1
Service workers	6.0	8.0	18.7	18.0
Private household	0.1	—	3.4	1.9
Other	6.0	8.0	15.3	16.2
Farm worker	5.3	4.4	1.8	1.4

Sources: U.S. Department of Labor, Bureau of Labor Statistics, *Employment and Earnings*, 28, No. 11, November 1981; U.S. Bureau of the Census, Current Population Reports, Series P-23, No. 100.

Table 4.
Selected Unemployment Indicators

Selected Categories	Annual Average				January 1981	October 1981
	1970	1979	1980			
WHITE, Totals	4.5	5.1	6.3		6.7	6.9
Men 20 and over	3.2	3.6	5.2		5.5	5.9
Women 20 and over	4.4	5.0	5.6		6.0	6.1
Both (age 16-19)	13.5	13.9	14.8		16.8	17.6
BLACK AND OTHER, Totals	8.2	11.3	13.2		12.9	15.5
Men 20 and over	5.6	8.4	11.4		10.5	13.3
Women 20 and over	6.9	10.1	11.1		11.0	13.3
Both (age 16-19)	29.1	33.5	35.8		36.5	42.9

Sources: *Monthly Labor Review*, U.S. Department of Labor, November 1981, p. 66; U.S. Bureau of the Census, Current Population Reports, Series P-23, No. 80.

Unemployment rates seasonally adjusted.

crucial problem area for nonwhite communities generally and Third World women in particular (U.S. Department of Labor 1980b, 1981b). Third World women are slowly increasing their rate of participation in the labor force, showing a 1981 rate of 54.5 percent (U.S. Department of Labor 1981a). Black, Chicano, native American, and Asian-American women are as likely to be counted as part of the labor force as white females, but are nearly twice as likely as whites of either sex to be unemployed. Unemployment figures for nonwhite women were 16 percent in October 1981, while for women aged 16 to 21 they reached a whopping 42.2 percent—considerably higher than for any other group. This extremely high rate, seen in conjunction with the relatively low rate of labor force participation for this group (42.2 percent), suggests that young nonwhite women face considerable barriers in the labor market. They apparently cannot find jobs and it appears many have either given up looking or never began, thus joining the rank of "discouraged workers" (Bowers 1980; Newman 1980). Moreover, the employment situation for nonwhite workers of either sex is rapidly deteriorating. In 1970 black and other nonwhite females experienced an annual average unemployment rate of 6.9 percent (Table 4). The rate for January 1981 was 11 percent and for October, 13.3 percent. Having similar rates, both nonwhite women and nonwhite men are extremely hard-hit by the general upward creeping motion of unemployment.

Women experience some special problems resulting from either being clustered in lower-paying jobs or suffering unemployment in whatever category. It is well known that all women earn considerably less than all men, whether one examines income of all workers or isolates only year-round full-time employees (Table 5). But the crucial question for Third World women concerns the earnings of those who support families with no adult male earner present. More women than ever are either choosing or being forced to

Table 5.
Median Income by Sex and Race: 1980

Selected Characteristics	All Workers	Full-Time Year-Round Workers
MALES	12,530	19,173
White	13,328	19,720
Black	8,009	13,875
Spanish[1]	9,659	13,790
FEMALES	4,920	11,591
White	4,947	11,703
Black	4,580	10,915
Spanish	4,405	9,887

Source: U.S. Bureau of the Census, Current Population Reports, Series P-60, No. 127.

[1]Persons of Spanish origin may be of any race.

maintain their own households, and many of these support children (U.S. Department of Labor 1978; Waldman et al. 1980). Third World women appear to be well represented among this swelling group of female house-holders. For example, they make up 50 percent of all single women heading households. Similarly, 50 percent of all female householders in the labor force, whether single, separated, widowed, or divorced, are nonwhite. One crucial issue facing this group is employment, for these women, many of whom have children, must either support themselves or be supported by others, such as a spouse or the collective public (Sawhill 1975).

The racial and sexual unemployment patterns are revealing when focusing on this female householder category (Waldman 1980; U.S. Department of Labor 1981c; Grossman 1981). Although Third World women who head households are just as likely as white women to be seeking work, they are two to three times more likely to be unemployed. In October 1981 single Third World women age 20 years and over had an unemployment rate of 21.9 percent, more than three times the rate for a comparable group of white women (5.9 percent) and twice that of a comparable group of white males (10.1 percent) (Table 6) (U.S. Department of Labor 1980a). These statistics do not begin to address the question of whether single female householders support children, and many of them indeed do. Widowed, divorced, or sepa-

Table 6.
Unemployed Persons by Marital Status, Race, Age, and Sex: October 1981

Marital Status, Race, and Age	Males Unemployment Rates	Females Unemployment Rates
WHITE 16 years and over	6.0	7.1
Married, spouse present	3.6	5.8
Widowed, divorced, or separated	7.4	7.7
Single (never married)	12.2	9.5
BLACK AND OTHER 16 years and over	14.3	16.0
Married, spouse present	7.9	9.7
Widowed, divorced, or separated	15.4	11.3
Single (never married)	24.9	28.2
WHITE 20 to 64 years of age	5.2	6.2
Married, spouse present	3.7	5.7
Widowed, divorced, or separated	7.6	7.9
Single (never married)	10.1	5.9
BLACK AND OTHER 20 to 64 years of age	12.5	13.5
Married, spouse present	7.9	9.6
Widowed, divorced, or separated	14.9	11.4
Single (never married)	20.9	21.9

Source: U.S. Department of Labor, *Employment and Earnings*, November 1981.

rated minority women also have higher unemployment rates than either white males or females. If one examines the unemployment rate for nonwhite men who are widowed, divorced, or separated, the startling fact is that it is higher (14.9 percent) than for any other racial or sexaul combination with comparable marital status. All this results in Third World women being much more likely to end up as unemployed heads of households with children.

The case of black women illustrates this emerging family pattern. It has already been noted that they outnumber black men in the 15 to 34 years age category and that this demographic fact probably contributed to the increase in numbers of single black mothers over the past decade. It is not the unmarried status of these women that is the fundamental problem, however; it is their unemployment. A recent Department of Labor report on single women speculated on reasons for this:

> Contributing to the higher rate were the comparative youth and
> the family responsibilities of these black women. About 7 of 8
> blacks had children compared with 3 of 8 whites. Moreover, the
> majority of these unmarried black mothers were below age 35 and
> had children under 6. Historically, preschool age children have
> been a barrier to their mothers in obtaining employment. In addi-
> tion, the lack of formal education of these young mothers may be
> a marked hindrance in their attempts to find employment. (1980a,
> p. 48)

It appears that black and white mothers in one-parent families desire work equally. But the inability of black women in locating work has some major repercussions for black families specifically and black communities generally. Approximately one-half of all black children live in one-parent homes and are therefore highly dependent on the success of their mothers in finding employment. Children in such families are still less likely than white ones to have a mother employed in the labor force. As one researcher points out:

> Regardless of race or family type, children whose mothers were in
> the labor force were in families with considerably higher incomes,
> on average, than were children with non-working mothers.
> (Grossman 1981, p. 51)

These related issues of labor force participation rates, unemployment rates, occupational distribution, and family status all converge when one tries to get a clear view of a traditionally stereotyped person, the low-income Third World woman. The 1980 data for persons below the poverty level are especially revealing (Table 7).

While only 6.2 of white males and 9.5 percent of white females live below the poverty level, more than 31 percent of black women and 24 percent of Spanish women do (U.S. Bureau of the Census 1981c). These data exclude children and might be significantly higher if the minor dependents were counted. For example, while 8 percent of white families were classified below the poverty rate in 1980, 23.2 percent of all Spanish families and 28.9

Table 7
Persons Below the Poverty Level by Race and Sex: 1980

Persons 15 Years and Over	All Races	White	Black	Spanish[1] Origin
Totals below poverty level	16,907	11,704	4,763	2,863
Male	6,288	4,412	1,681	1,247
Female	10,618	7,291	3,082	1,616
Percent below poverty level	10.1	8.0	26.6	21.6
Male	7.8	6.2	20.8	18.9
Female	12.1	9.5	31.4	24.3

Source: U.S. Bureau of the Census, unpublished 1980 current population survey data.

[1]Persons of Spanish origin may be of any race.

Annual averages for all races, White, and Black, but unadjusted data as of March 1980 for persons of Spanish origin.

Table 8
Poverty Rate of Families by Race: 1981

Type of Family	All Families	White	Black	Spanish[1] Origin
ALL FAMILIES	10.3	8.0	28.9	23.2
Married-couple families	6.2	5.4	14.0	15.3
Male householder	6.1	5.4	13.4	15.0
Female householder	8.0	5.8	20.4	22.3
Male householder, no wife present	11.0	9.4	17.7	16.0
Female householder, no husband present	32.7	25.7	49.4	51.3

Source: U.S. Bureau of the Census, Current Population Reports, Series P-60, No. 127.

[1]Persons of Spanish origin may be of any race.

percent of all black families landed in this category (Table 8). Of families headed by women, however, 25.7 percent of the white families were below the poverty level as compared to 49.4 percent of black families and 51.3 percent of Spanish families. A closer look at female-headed families reveals few surprises—lower educational levels, high unemployment, and low-level occupations.

But the profile of the black and Hispanic female heading a family is far more complex than this. She is more likely than her white counterpart to have worked full time year-round. In fact, in approximately 10 percent of both black and Hispanic female-headed families below the poverty level, the heads of the households worked full time. As undesirable as it is to work and still be poor, the alternative of not working all but ensures black and Hispanic families of poverty. Forty-three percent of families headed by nonworking white women were below the poverty level as compared to 73.8 percent headed by nonworking black women and 76.7 percent headed by non-working Hispanic women.

In spite of the impressive gains made by Third World women in the areas of education and occupational prestige, the reality of their experience in 1981 has two elements. First, there is the tenuous security of the last-hired, often highly educated women, the two-thirds or so who have escaped poverty and hope to keep their hard-fought gains. Second, there is the alternative of being a statistic, one of the one-third or so nonwhite women who is likley to be young, a parent, less well educated, underemployed if not unemployed, and, if all these factors coalesce, dependent on public assistance. What has been the federal response, the scholarly interpretation, and the viewpoint of minority women themselves?

Third World Women and Changing Federal Policy

Three key contact points characterize the relationship of Chicano, native American, Asian-American, and black females with the federal government. First, the poverty of these women has led to their increased dependence on federal sources of both direct and indirect social welfare support. While whites generally outnumber nonwhites in the absolute number of persons benefiting from programs such as CETA, Aid to Families with Dependent Children, Medicaid, school lunch programs, Section 8 housing, and the like, the percentage of Third World women receiving such benefits is higher than in comparable white communites (U.S. Bureau of the Census 1981a 1981c). Moreover, even though many social welfare programs are administered by state and local governments, federal dollars pay for a significant portion of them. In addition, minority women are more likely to depend on other federal efforts not directly targeted to low-income populations, such as Basic Educational Opportunity Grants for college students, fellowship funds in graduate training, and loans to minority businesses.

Second, the federal government has a significant role in shaping and enforcing civil rights legislation. Specifically, it has actively encouraged or coerced states, local municipalities, and private organizations to adopt equal opportunity postures on issues such as affirmative action and school deseg-regation. It should be remembered that this strong federal presence devel-oped as a direct result of state and local unwillingness to root out discrim-inatory practices on their own.

These two well-known advocacy roles have overshadowed the third, lesser known contact—that of the federal government as an employer of minority women. Third World women are well represented among employees at all levels of government, and any shifts in this traditionally strong employment source is likely to be felt in their communities, particularly middle-class ones.

Reaganomics, as it has been called by the popular press, is the federal government's total program devoted to economic recovery for the United

States. In its early outlines, the program promised to reduce taxes, cut the federal budget, reduce inflation, reduce unemployment in the long run, and stimulate the private business sector. But as 1981 drew to a close, the early promises evaporated in the face of a December unemployment rate that was the second highest monthly rate since World War II. Simultaneously, cuts in government programs enacted on October 1 were just beginning to be felt as state and local governments rewrote their own rules to accommodate decreased federal spending. The promise of Reaganomics was that the cuts and hardships that the administration acknowledged were destined to come would be shared as equitably as possible by all segments of the population. The reality has been quite different and Third World women have been among the especially hard hit.

The relationship of these women to the federal government is undergoing some fundamental changes, and it appears that welfare programs will bear the brunt of federal cuts. Looking just in the area of noncash benefits, the dependence of Third World groups on federal programs becomes apparent (U.S. Bureau of the Census 1981a). For example, in March 1981, 35.1 percent of the food stamp program recipients were black and 10.8 percent were Hispanic; 34.1 percent of school lunch participants were black and 14.5 percent Hispanics; and approximately 40 percent of Medicaid recipients were black or Hispanic (U.S. Bureau of the Census 1981a). Seen another way, approximately 27 percent of black families receive food stamps, 28 percent benefit from Medicaid, and almost half participate in some portion of the school lunch program (Table 9). The very programs scheduled to be cut are those most heavily used by minority women heading households. In contrast, Social Security, another expensive program underused by nonwhites due to shorter life expectancies and ineligibility resulting from work histories, has been left relatively untouched.

The programs affected are widespread. The tighter income eligibility and applications procedures for the school lunch and breakfast programs have forced some schools to raise their meal prices; some plan to drop out of the program altogether. Proposed changes in the child-care feeding program that formerly provided three free meals and two free snacks to children in day-care centers and after-school programs include lowering income eligibility standards, reducing age limits for after-school programs, and decreasing the number of meals available from five to three. These changes suggest that day-care centers will be forced to serve less food or to absorb the extra cost by charging more for tuition. The need for day care by working mothers, especially heads of households, is acute. Tuition increases may force the children of working but low-wage mothers out of centers (Presser and Baldwin 1980; U.S. Commission on Civil Rights 1981). Cuts were proposed in the summer meals program that served free lunch to any child coming to a food center during an eight-week summer season and in the Women, Infants, and Children's Feeding Program aimed at high-risk pregnant women, nursing mothers, and infants.

Food programs are not alone in being targeted for cuts. Section 8 of the Federal Housing Act of 1974 is going to feel some of the Reagan administration's deepest cuts (Housing-aid 1982). For example, the percentage of income that tenants of public housing must contribute toward their rent will rise from the current 25 percent to 30 percent over the next five years. In spite of a growing shortage of low-income housing, funds for new construction and renovation of existing units seem destined for cuts. As Secretary of Housing and Urban Development Samuel R. Pierce, Jr.. put it. "Government-subsidized housing programs have been run inefficiently and, as a result, cost too damned much."

Taken separately, these changes do not appear to present a serious hardship to the Third World woman who makes use of only one service. But the issue seems to be the pattern of need by black, native American, and Hispanic women especially, the heads of household who currently are multi-service consumers. Many of these women cannot just get a job to supplement their income. Their unemployment rates are already high, their children are in subsidized day care, and training programs are becoming less accessible. Many of these women are already working.

The 1981 recession, growing unemployment, and proposed cuts in social welfare programs promise to aggravate existing problems for minority women. Even with existing levels of social services, black women currently give birth to babies who are twice as likely as white children to die at birth, and who are twice as likely as white babies to have dangerously low birth weights (Reid 1975; Allen 1981). The disadvantages of Third World women leap out from the federal government's own statistics. Cuts in social services promise dramatically to affect those 30 percent who are currently below the poverty line and that uncounted percentage who are just above it.

What of the other two-thirds of the minority female community? How will Reaganomics affect working-class and middle-class Third World women? Changes in the second contact point between them and federal policy speak to these questions. Clear signals have emerged from the Reagan administration that neither of the two action programs affecting minority women—affirmative action and school desegregation—will be vigorously enforced. In spite of the obvious patterns of income inequality and job inferiority exhibited by minority women, the Reagan formula argues for a more restrained conception of the role of the federal government and for more respect for local authority in the area of civil rights. This means that the Justice Department will no longer try to impose numerical goals or timetables for hiring, even though these remedies have been used extensively for at least ten years and are often imposed by courts. The irony is that affirmative action, taken in conjunction with gains in education, seems to be working inasmuch as Third World women experienced significant occupational mobility during the past decade. Assistant Attorney General for Civil Rights William Bradford Reynolds has indicated that numerical goals for hiring blacks and women will be opposed, even when such actions are voluntarily adopted by private industry with no government compulsion (Aides 1982; Bergman 1982). Mr. Reynolds also has taken some clear shots at school desegregation, stating that the Justice Department will no longer seek to desegregate an entire school district on the basis of segregation found to exist in one part of it. In his oft-quoted words, "We are not going to compel children who don't choose to have an integrated education to have one." Furthermore, late in 1981 the Reagan administration moved to restore tax-exempt status to over one hundred private schools and other organizations that were found to practice racial discrimination (School tax 1982). This was vigorously opposed by civil rights groups and coalitions of private schools and is unresolved as of this writing.

While the complexities of affirmative action programs and the morass of school desegration have generated widespread criticism, from the perspective of Third World women, the Reagan administration's track record on civil rights has been even more dismal. Ensuring a quality education for their children has long been a central concern of nonwhite mothers, so much so that the bulk of minority women's activism on the local level often focuses on the school system. Desegregation has long been at the heart of the matter. But while their children are of central concern for native American, black, Chicano, and Asian-American women, jobs are equally crucial. The attack on affirmative action could not have come at a worse time, for if the Reagan formula is followed, employers will be required not to discriminate, a position that is markedly different from that of taking positive action to seek out, train, and employ minority women. In the highly competitive job market and tight economy of 1981, the very real danger exists that without federal encouragement and coercion, employers may return to age-old practices of hiring friends and relatives and using unwritten yet effective racial and sexual criteria for promotion, salary determination, and layoff. If initiated, these practices promise to be especially troublesome to working-class and middle-class minority women. Those women currently protected by existing recruitment and promotional plans in blue-collar industries, those hoping to apply to graduate and professional school in preparation for prestigious white-male-dominated professions, and those women hoping to move up in their current professions may find the promise of equal opportunity frustratingly out of reach.

Working-class and middle-class black, native American, Chicano, and Asian-American women may also be affected by yet another planned change in federal policy—the move to reduce the size of the federal work force and the ripple effect this reduction might have on other levels of government. In the twelve months that ended November 1, 1981, the number of government employees declined by 316,000 — 40,000 on the federal level and the majority (246,000) on the local level. For the first time since World War II, government employment is declining (*New York Times*, December 27, 1981). Minorities as a group tend to be over-represented among federal employees, although the distribution patterns suggest some interesting possibilities if the layoff trend accelerates. More than 50 percent of minorities employed by the federal government are blue-collar, clerical, or other lower-grade staff. As one source notes:

... when government agencies decide to cut costs, the most ex-pendable employees (i.e. those at the lowest occupational posi-tions) are minorities. (Benokraitis and Feagin 1978, p. 28)

But a potentially more serious problem exists for the first-generation middle-class government employee. In his discussion of the new black "elite," Freeman (1973) concludes that public employers, especially the federal gov-ernment, offered qualified blacks better job opportunities than did the private sector. Thus government agencies have become a major source of black professional employment. But the problem may be more complex, as the distribution of professional, minority government employees is provocative.

... civil rights agencies may have large numbers of women and minorities—especially at higher grade levels—because these "embattled islands" in a hostile federal bureaucracy may be the few agencies in which women and minorities can attain upward mobility. Such agencies have become "federal ghettos" for qualified women and minorities who are not welcome in most other agencies. (Benokraitis and Feagin, 1978, p. 32)

The combination of plans to reduce the federal government's role in enforcing established equal opportunity legislation coupled with the projected decline in government employment, reflected in fewer new hiring and layoffs based on seniority, suggests that middle-class minority women may be especially affected. After noting that the now dismantled war on poverty provided an avenue for a sizeable number of minority individuals to establish middle-class lifestyles that are now proving difficult to sustain, Williams poses the following question:.

Will persons in equal opportunity programs experience a similar fate of containment, devaluation, and permanent margin-ality . . . as the mood of the nation turns reactionary? We need to examine the heavy dependence of the black middle class on race related programming and on public sector employment. (1980, p. 50)

In this era of government cutbacks, hiring freezes, and layoffs, this final area of contact between Third World women and the federal government is cer-tainly worth watching.

New Scholarship on Third World Women

Given the generally gloomy picture advanced for Third World women thus far, the academic community's 1981 achievements have been disappointing. Several problems continue to plague research on minority women. First, the relative scarcity of such research virtually ensures that any article published will be given more weight than it probably merits. While reams of articles dealing with *either* minorities or women appear to find their way into scholarly journals, serious attention to minority women remains elusive. For example, a late 1981 computer search of several estabished social science sources yielded a mere ten citations (see Selected Listings: New Scholarship on Minority Women, p. 114). This is not to say that other articles about Third World women are not being published, but it is to say that the distribution of new material remains limited. Journals that are willing to devote significant space to Third World issues are often difficult to locate through established sources such as libraries and bookstores.

A second and related problem concerns the subjects chosen for research. Very often the scholarly community either studies issues of interest to it but not to Third World women or selects topics that it thinks should be important to minority women. For example, the article by Temkingreener and associates, "Surgical fertility regulation among women on the Navajo Indian reservation," reflects concerns of the health bureaucracy. The continuing tendency to compare Third World groups to whites plus white society's concern with nonwhite fertility is evidenced in the work by Rochat and colleagues, "Family planning practices among Anglo and Hispanic women in United States counties bordering Mexico" (full citation in Selected Listings). In her excellent review of the literature of native American women, Green describes issues of concern for Indian communities, issues that are markedly different from those of the scholarly community.

> . . . Indian women and men are not very worried about unmarried mothers and illegitimate children, and receptivity to family-planning services. They point with pride to the growing and high birthrate among Native American populations. Yet they are terribly concerned about non-Indian adoption of Indian children, child-placement programs, sterilization abuse, clinical experimentation using Indians, diabetes, cervical cancer and missionary activity in the schools. (1980, p. 266)

There is obvious absence of work on any of these themes. When studying communities that have serious reservations about the nature and use of research, it may be more appropriate to select issues that are seen as important by Third World women themselves.

A third problem arises when one examines the dominant scholarly approach to topics that are of special concern to black, native American, Chicano, and Asian-American women. Each of these groups has been stereotyped differently and the biases of the researcher can easily intrude into both the way research design is constructed and the conclusions that are reached. Lyon and Rector-Owen's 1981 study is a typical case in point. Here is a work that examines a crucial concern—employment factors for young black women. It is characteristic of research on minorities in general and blacks in particular.

First, the primary interest of these researchers was to compare the earnings of black women with those of white women. But as Table 8 indicates, the real issue is not one of difference among women, but of differences between Third World women and white males. This is the crucial earnings gap. Second, the authors draw on a suspect body of scholarly work claiming that black women are actually *advantaged* in the labor market because of their dual minority status. In spite of overwhelming demographic data to the contrary cited earlier in this essay, the authors include the following among their findings:

> Both Farley and this study indicate that if black females possess the same human capital levels as white females, they will be paid more than their white counterparts. On sum, then, these comparisons indicate that the black female, because she possesses minority status in both race and sex, may receive advantages in the labor market not available to either black males or white females. (1981, p. 76)

They neglect to mention that women as a group earn substantially less than men.

Thus far the argument is quite interesting. Black women appear to be "advantaged" in comparison to white women. Also, the authors toss in, "relatively low levels of labor market discrimination" are found against black women. Based on these assumptions, the authors then ask their key question: if black women have an advantage in the labor market, why are they performing so poorly? By some quick maneuvering, they claim that black women lack certain qualities, or "human capital," possessed by whites, such as higher education, better socioeconomic backgrounds, higher IQs, and fewer children. One of the major policy implications should come as no surprise:

> For closing the racial gap in IQ and indirectly in pay and prestige, the key seems to lie in improving the social class level of the black family. (p. 74)

Once again, social science research has placed the blame for labor market disadvantage squarely at the doorstep of the sterotypical black family. The authors continue:

> . . . it becomes important to learn which changes in the characteristics or "human capital" of the individual black females will return the greatest amount of occupational prestige and income. (p. 70)

The message is clear—the problem is with the individual black female. The authors are not content to leave well enough alone. They go on to make their policy recommendations.

> . . . this study demonstrates that the labor market may no longer be the most efficacious arena in which to pursue racial equality, at

least by the traditional means of insuring equal treatment. We would argue that for these young black females, "equal" treatment is no longer the key issue. Rather, their disadvantages in pay and prestige stem largely from the lower levels of human capital they bring to the labor market. (p. 77)

The purpose here is not to denigrate the Lyon and Rector-Owen work, but to illustrate the entrenched biases in traditional scholarship on nonwhite communities generally and minority women particularly. Much of this work insists on seeing minority women as "deviant." Policy recommendations very often center on ways to make nonwhite women more like white women (who themselves are disadvantaged, albeit in different ways) or on ways to make Third World women adjust to a social system portrayed as virtually problem free. This victim-blaming bias blends beautifully with efforts to divorce the federal government from its role as social architect for equality. If the academic community provides the rationale that the recipients of social programs are somehow less worthy, it becomes somewhat easier on one's conscience when budget cuts are voted in.

Academic scholarship on Third World women is not all this disappointing. Fortunately, 1981 also saw the distribution of several different types of material by or about minority women. It is this exciting body of personal narratives, poetry, fiction, and analytical essays that gives a real feel for the nonwhite female perspectives.

The past few years have seen publication of several excellent works that deal with the Chicano experience (Cotera 1976; Sanchez and Cruz 1977; Mirande and Enriquez 1979; Loes 1980). Following in this tradition, *Las mujeres* by Elasser, Mackensie, and Trixier y Virgil (1980), is a collection of oral histories gathered from four generations of Chicana women in New Mexico. Five themes emerge: the shift from rural to urban environment, the struggle to preserve culture and tradition, new family patterns that result from these changes, efforts to cope with discrimination, and the struggle for jobs and education. As the interviewers note:

Our methods were informal, as were the settings and the circumstances in which the interviews took place. Gradually, the group of speakers grew by word of mouth as one woman after another asked her friends and relatives to talk. With these life stories came poems and recipes, invitations to dinners and fiestas, and friendships with women we would otherwise never have met. (1980, p. 39)

Las mujeres is a much-needed addition to Chicana scholarship. It provides a forum from which women can share their views of how it is to cope with some of the problems that exist in the Third World.

Two recently released works fill the void for anthologies of Third World women's literature. The first of these, *The third woman* (Fisher 1980), promises to be a mainstay of literature courses sensitive to the minority female experience. The editor argues:

... most minority women writers remain virtually unknown to students of literature. Their works are isolated in small-press publications or regional journals; all too frequently, their books go out of print and become inaccessible; most are neglected by anthologists, while those few who are regularly anthologized suffer because the same works are selected over and over again. All of this results in a common assumption that there is no literature by minority women. The purpose of *The third woman* is to demonstrate just the opposite. (1980, p. xxix)

The anthology does what it sets out to do. The narratives, poetry, and fiction are organized into one of four sections, each dealing with a specific Third World group and each containing background material establishing a context. The editor also chooses to avoid "selecting only pieces that are exclusively 'political' or 'feminist,' " and instead declares, "the political statement of this book derives from its existence as the first major collection of literature by American Indian, Afro-American, Chicano and Asian-American women" (p. xxx).

This work is clearly superlative—it is comprehensive and invaluable. But the editors of the second major anthology, *This bridge called my back: writings by radical women of color*, would definitely take issue with Fisher's treatment of feminism as "but one of many subjects." For Moraga and Anzaldua (1981) political issues lie at the core of all Third World women's writings. They argue that political issues both establish the context in which literature occurs and shape its developing themes. As they proclaim, "*This bridge called my back* intends to reflect an uncompromised definition of feminism by women of color in the U.S." (p. xxiii). Moraga and Anzaldua are quite clear about what an "uncompromised definition" should be and explain why they chose to name the anthology "radical."

We were interested in the writings of women of color who want nothing short of a revolution in the hands of women—who agree that this is the goal, no matter how we might disagree about getting there or the possibility of seeing it in our lifetimes. (p. xxiii)

As Donna Kate Dushin declares in "The bridge poem," after which the anthology is named:

I've had enough
I'm sick of seeing and touching
Both sides of things
Sick of being the damn bridge for everybody (p. xxi)

Third World women are "the colored in a white feminist movement, and the feminists among the people of our culture" (p. 23). The book intends to reverse this sense of invisibility, of falling through the cracks of society's definitions, always being defined as part of another group, never exploring an identity of one's own. As the editors state, a new type of bridging is needed, characterized by "naming ourselves and by telling our stories in our own words." In this sense, they develop ideas on Third World feminism sketched out in numerous earlier works by minority women (Cade 1970; *Asian Women* 1971; Shange 1975; Cotera 1977; Ferrer 1979; *Third World Women* 1979; Hemmons 1980; Lindsay 1980).

Moraga and Anzaldua are vitally concerned that Third World women in the United States form a broad-based political movement, which underlies their choice of themes in the anthology. First, the work discusses how visibility and invisibility shape the lives of Third World women and imbue all with either potential or realized radicalism. A second theme stresses ways in which these women should derive a feminist political theory specifically from their racial cultural background. The editors state "in leftist feminist circles we are dealt with as a political issue, rather than as flesh and blood human beings" (p. 61). While white feminists may find the discussion of the "destructive and demoralizing effects of racism in the women's movement" unsettling, the treatment of this third theme is candid and fair. Before building alliances among one another, Third World women must recognize and accept differences, hence, the attention to the fourth theme, that of cultural, class, and sexuality differences that divide women of color. Two final themes, Third World women's writing as a tool for self-preservation and revolution and an assessment of the ways and means of a Third World feminist future, develop the sense of perseverence and resilience of these women that is often so lacking in material about them.

Taken together, *The third woman* and *This bridge called my back* are elegant and complementary works. The former has an objective tone, is generally noncontroversial, and tries to expose the literature of minority women to a larger audience. In contrast, the latter is subjective and highly personal. It seeks out controversy and speaks to the actual and potential Third World feminist community and anyone else who is willing to listen. Both are invaluable, and taken together they present in two major sources what formerly had to be gleaned from small press publications, special issues of alternative journals, or the elusive literature of political action groups.

Two works published in 1981 on black women and feminism go a long way toward resolving the expectations raised by Michele Wallace's (1978) disappointing *Black macho and the myth of the superwoman*. The first, *Common differences: conflicts in black and white feminist perspectives* (Joseph and Lewis 1981), is an interesting dialogue between two feminists, one black and the other white. There are juxtaposed essays by each author, and the resulting discussions that culminate three years of "collaboration, criticism and caring" are lively. For example, Jill Lewis's chapter entitled "Sexual divisions of power: motivations of the women's liberation movement" compactly summarizes the diversity of feminist theory. If one considers that many black and Third World readers normally shy away from what are considered "white woman's books," the presentation of an accurate, objective synthesis of the basic tenets of feminism is refreshing. One cannot realistically talk about developing black feminism without some understanding of the sexual politics examined by feminist theory. Gloria Joseph's essay "Black mothers and daughters," while weakened by lack of information on her methodology, fills a significant need, especially in light of the recent feminist interest in mother-daughter relationships. Joseph defines the role of black mothers as one of contradiction, one that resists neat classification. She deplores scholarship's penchant of seeing them in myopically sterotypical ways.

> The multifaceted roles that Black mothers play as they visit one child in prison and another at college, and all in the same week, symbolize the continuous nurturing and caring roles that are often neglected by scholars in Black studies and women's studies. (1981, p. 93)

Like *This bridge called my back*, *Common differences* seeks to build a political coalition but of a slightly different nature. The authors are especially interested in the "role that capitalism plays in the politics of racism and sexism" (p. 274). Their book aims to be an exploration of the ways in which racial and sexual factors interact in the oppression of women in hopes that recognition of different yet common patterns of exploitation will clear the way for an interracial, feminist coalition.

Ain't I a woman, by Bell Hooks, the second major work on black women and feminism published in 1981, is complex. The chapters "Sexism and the black female slave experience" and "Continued devaluation of black womanhood" add little new actual material to the scholarly record. Rather, it is her interpretation that is novel. Hooks reexamines the slave experience and its aftermath in light of feminist views of patriarchy. Her discussion of sexual politics as applied to the black female experience is particularly revealing. For example, she zeros in on the meaning of the wide-scale rape of black women both during and after slavery:

> . . . the significance of the rape of enslaved black women was not simply that it "deliberately crushed" their sexual integrity for economic ends but that it led to a devaluation of black womanhood that permeated the psyches of all Americans and shaped the social status of all black women once slavery ended. (1981, p. 52)

Neither white women nor black men are let off easily, as even liberal-minded individuals have difficulty dealing with rape victims:

> . . . while many concerned citizens sympathized with the sexual exploitation of black women both during slavery and afterwards, like all rape victims in patriarchal society they were seen as having lost value and worth as a result of the humiliation they endured. (p. 53)

The implications of sexual politics for the black community and for black women specifically are gradually developed in Hooks's essay. Her work is controversial and provocative, but it is certainly worth reading.

REFERENCES

Acosta-Belen, E., ed. 1979. *The Puerto Rican woman*. New York: Praeger.

Acosta-Belen, E., and Sjostrom, B. R. 1979. The educational and professional status of Puerto Rican women. In *The Puerto Rican woman*, ed. E. Acosta-Belen, pp. 64-74. New York: Praeger.

Aides say president opposes quotas in affirmative action. *New York Times*, January 4, 1982.

Allen, W. 1981. The social and economic statuses of black women in the United States. *Phylon* 42, no. 1:26-40.

Asian women. 1971. Berkeley: Asian American Studies Center, University of California.

Benokraitis, N., and Feagin, J. 1978. *Affirmative action and equal opportunity: action, inaction, reaction*. Boulder, Colo.: Westview Press.

Bergmann, B. R. 1982. An affirmative look at hiring quotas. *New York Times*, January 10.

Bowers, N. 1980. Young and marginal: an overview of youth employment. In *Young workers and families: a special section*. Washington, D.C.: U.S. Department of Labor, Special Labor Force Report No. 233.

Brinkley-Carter, C. 1980. Black fertility: recent demographic and sociological influences. In *The black woman*, ed. L. F. Rodgers-Rose, pp. 43-66. Berkeley, Calif.: Sage.

Cade, T. ed. 1970. *The black woman: an anthology*. New York: Signet.

Cotera, M. P. 1976. *Diosa y hembra: the history and heritage of Chicanos in the U.S.* Austin, Texas: Information Systems Development.

Cotera, M. P. 1977. *The Chicano feminist*. Austin, Texas: Information Systems Development.

Elasser, N.; Mackensie, K.; and Trixier y Virgil, Y. 1980. *Las mujeres: conversations from a Hispanic community*. Westbury, N.Y.: Feminist Press.

Ferrer, N. V. 1979. Feminism and its influence on women's organizations in Puerto Rico. In *The Puerto Rican woman*, ed. E. Acosta-Belen, pp. 38-50. New York: Praeger.

Fisher, D., ed. 1980. *The third woman, minority women writers of the United States*. Boston: Houghton Mifflin.

Freeman, R. 1973. *Black elite: the new market for highly educated black Americans*. New York: McGraw-Hill.

Garcia-Bahne, B. 1977. La Chicana and the Chicano family. In *Essays on la mujer*, eds. R. Sanchez and R. M. Cruz, pp. 30-47. Los Angeles: Chicano Studies Center, University of California.

Green, R. 1980. Native American women. *Signs* 6, no. 2:248-67.

Grossman, A. S. 1981. Working mothers and their children. *Monthly Labor Review* May:49-54.

Hemmons, W. M. 1980. The women's liberation movement: understanding black women's attitudes. In *The black woman*, ed. L. F. Rodgers-Rose, pp. 285-99. Beverly Hills: Sage.

Hooks, B. 1981. *Ain't I a woman*. Boston: South End Press.

Housing aid cuts affect poor individually and collectively. *New York Times*, January 3, 1982, p. 8E.

Joseph, G., and Lewis, J. 1981. *Common differences: conflicts in black and white feminist perspectives*. Garden City, N.Y.: Anchor.

Lindsay, B., ed. 1980. *Comparative perspectives of third world women: the impact of race, sex, and class*. New York: Praeger.

Loes, C. 1980. La Chicana: a bibliographic survey. *Frontiers* 5, no. 2:59-74.

Lyon, L., and Rector-Owen, H. 1981. Labor-market mobility among young black and white women—longitudinal models of occupational prestige and income. *Social Science Quarterly* 62, no. 1:64-78.

Medicine, B. 1978. *The native American woman: a perspective*. Austin, Texas: ERIC.

Mirande, A., and Enriquez, E. 1979. *La Chicana: the Mexican-American woman*. Chicago: University of Chicago Press.

Moraga, C., and Anzaldua, G., eds. 1981. *This bridge called my back. Writings by radical women of color*. Watertown, Mass.: Persephone Press.

Newman, M. 1980. The labor market experience of black youth, 1954-78. In *Young workers and families: a special section*. Washington, D.C.: U.S. Department of Labor, Special Labor Force Report 233.

Presser, H., and Baldwin, W. 1980. Child care as a constraint on employment: prevalence, correlates, and bearing on the work and fertility nexus. *American Journal of Sociology* 85, no. 5:1202-13.

Reid, I. 1975. Health issues facing black women. In *Conference on the educational and occupational needs of black women*, vol. 2. Washington, D.C.: U.S. Department of Health, Education and Welfare, pp. 203-26.

Sanchez, R., and Cruz, R. H., eds. 1977. *Essays on la mujer*. Los Angeles: Chicano Studies Center Publications, University of California.

Sawhill, I. V. 1975. Black women who head families: economic needs and economic resources. In *Conference on the educational and occupational needs of black women*, vol. 2. Washington, D.C.: U.S. Department of Health, Education and Welfare, pp. 169-82.

School tax ruling faces test. *New York Times*, January 10, 1982.

Shange, N. 1975. *For colored girls who have considered suicide when the rainbow is enuf*. New York: Macmillan.

Third world women, the politics of being other. 1979. *Heresies* 2, no. 4, issue 8.

U.S. Bureau of the Census. 1981a. *Characteristics of households receiving noncash benefits: 1980*. Current Population Reports, Series P-60, No. 128. Washington, D.C.: U.S. Government Printing Office.

U.S. Bureau of the Census. 1981b. *Population profile of the United States: 1980*. Current Population Reports, Series P-20, No. 363. Washington, D.C.: U.S. Government Printing Office.

U.S. Bureau of the Census. 1981c. *Money income and poverty status of families and persons in the United States: 1980*. Current Population Reports, Series P-60, No. 127. Washington, D.C.: U.S. Government Printing Office.

U.S. Commission on Civil Rights. 1981. *Child care and equal opportunity for women*. Washington, D.C.: Clearinghouse Publication No. 67.

U.S. Department of Labor. 1977. *Minority women workers: a statistical overview* rev. Washington, D.C.: U.S. Government Printing Office.

U.S. Department of Labor. 1978. *Women who head families: a socioeconomic analysis.* Washington, D.C.: Special Labor Force Report No. 213.

U.S. Department of Labor. 1980a. *Labor force patterns of single women.* Washington, D.C.: Special Labor Force Report No. 228.

U.S. Department of Labor. 1980b. *Perspectives on working women: a databook.* Washington, D.C.: Bulletin 2080.

U.S. Department of Labor, Bureau of Labor Statistics. 1981a. *Employment and Earnings.* Washington, D.C.: vol. 28, no. 11, November.

U.S. Department of Labor, Bureau of Labor Statistics. 1981b. *Employment and unemployment: a report on 1980.* Washington, D.C.: Special Labor Force Report 244.

U.S. Department of Labor. 1981c. *Marital and family characteristics of the labor force, March 1979.* Washington, D.C.: Special Labor Force Report No. 237.

U.S. Department of Labor. 1981d. *Women in domestic work: yesterday and today.* Special Labor Force Report No. 242, Washington, D.C.: Bureau of Labor Statistics.

Waldman, E. et al. 1980. Working mothers in the 1970s: a look at the statistics. In *Young workers and families: a special section.* Washington, D.C.: U.S. Department of Labor, Special Labor Force Report 233.

Wallace, M. 1978. *Black macho and the myth of the superwoman.* New York: Dial.

Wallace, P. 1980. *Black women in the labor force.* Cambridge. MIT Press.

Williams, L. 1980. In *Dilemmas of the new black middle class,* ed. Joseph Washington, pp. 43-64. Philadelphia: University of Pennsylvania, Afro-American Studies Department.

Witt, S. H. 1974. Native women today. *Civil Rights Digest* vol. 6, no. 3:29-35.

BIBLIOGRAPHY

The following books are highly recommended for further reading.

Acosta-Belen, Edna, ed. *The Puerto Rican woman.* New York: Praeger, 1979. A collection of essays covering diverse issues such as women in the labor force, educational and professional status, the growth of Puerto Rican feminism, the black Puerto Rican woman, and the reponse of the Puerto Rican community to female homosexuality. Contains a brief bibliography.

Almquist, Elizabeth McTaggart. *Minorities, gender, and work.* Lexington, Mass.: Heath, 1979. A scholarly work evaluating the status of minority groups in the workforce. Contains material on lesser-known groups such as Cuban Americans and Filipino Americans. Also discusses barriers to equality and the legal status of minority populations.

Cotera, Martha P. *Diosa y hembra: the history and heritage of Chicanas in the U.S.* Austin, Texas: Information Systems Development, 1976. A comprehensive profile of the Mexican-American woman containing a detailed overview of Chicana history, a socioeconomic profile of Chicanas in the United States, La Chicanas and the family, and contemporary issues affecting Mexican-American women. Includes a useful listing of Chicana organizations, material on farmworkers and migrant women, and Chicana achievement in professions.

Fisher, Dexter, ed. *The third woman, minority women writers of the United States.* Boston: Houghton Mifflin, 1980. A comprehensive anthology of writings by American Indian, black, Chicana, and Asian-American women writers. Includes poetry, narratives, fiction, and background articles on each group.

Harley, Sharon, and Terborg-Penn, Rosalyn, eds. *The Afro-American woman: struggles and images.* Port Washington, N.Y.: Kennikat Press, 1978. A scholarly collection of historical essays on diverse topics, among them, discrimination against black women in the women's movement, images of black women in Afro-American poetry, and black male perspectives on the nineteenth-century woman.

Lindsay, Beverly, ed. *Comparative perspectives of third world women: the impact of race, sex, and class.* New York: Praeger, 1980. An excellent anthology linking the status of women in developing countries to that of minority women in the United States. Contains material on Caribbean women, women in Cuba, and Vietnamese immigrants.

Mirande, Alfredo, and Enriquez, Evangelina. *La Chicana: the Mexican-American woman.* Chicago: University of Chicago Press, 1977. A solid, basic text surveying the history and status of Mexican-American women. Contains chapters on the family, images in literature, work, and education, and Chicana feminism.

Moraga, Cherrie, and Anzaldua, Gloria, eds. *This bridge called my back. Writings by radical women of color.* Watertown, Mass.: Persephone Press, 1981. An important collection of writings by radical Third World women. Contains material on culture, the roots of minority female radicalism, and racism in the women's movement.

Niethammer, Carolyn. *Daughters of the earth: the lives and legends of American Indian women.* New York: Collier, 1977. An artful blend of text, source material, and photographs characterizes this sensitive portrayal of native American women's life in traditional societies. Contains material on child rearing, woman's economic role, women leaders, women doctors, and a section on women and war.

Rodgers-Rose, La Frances, ed. *The black woman*. Beverly Hills: Sage, 1980. A scholarly, comprehensive anthology with topics ranging from black female professionals to depression and suicide. Contains a solid section of black women and the family.

SELECTED LISTINGS

New Scholarship on Minority Women

Allen, W. R. The social and economic statuses of black women in the United States. *Phylon* 42, no. 1:26-40.

Alston, D., and Rose, N. Perceptions of middle-aged black women as related to selected background factors. *Journal of General Psychology* 104, no. 2:167-71.

Gonzalez, D., and Page, J. Cuban women, sex-role conflicts and the use of prescription drugs. *Journal of Psychoactive Drugs* 13, no. 1:47-51.

Jaskowski, H. My heart will go out—healing songs of native-American women. *International Journal of Women's Studies* 4, no. 2:118-34.

Lyon, L., and Rector-Owen, H. Labor-market mobility among young black and white women—longitudinal models of occupational prestige and income. *Social Science Quarterly* 62, no. 1:64-78.

McNally, M. J. The church, black Catholic women religious in antebellum period. *Negro History Bulletin* 44, no. 1:19-20.

Rochat, R.W.; Warren, C. W.; Smith, J.C.; Holck, S. E.; and Friedman, J. S. Family planning practices among Anglo and Hispanic women in United States counties bordering Mexico. *Family Planning Perspectives* 13, no. 4:176-80.

Temkingreener, H.; Kunitz, S. J.; Broudy, D.; and Haffner, M. Surgical fertility regulation among women on the Navajo Indian reservation. *American Journal of Public Health* 71, no. 4: 403-7.

Ward, C. M., and Walsh, W. B. Concurrent validity of Holland theory for non-college degreed black women. *Journal of Vocational Behavior* 18, no. 3:356-61.

Zuckerman, D. M. Sex role related goals and attitudes of minority students—a study of black college women and reentry students. *Journal of College Student Personnel* 22, no. 1:23-30.

Minority Women's Organizations

Native Americans

Native American Indian Women's Association. c/o Dorothy Davids, Community Dynamics Institute, University of Wisconsin Extension, 610 Langdon St., Room 532, Madison, WI 53706. Issues of interest to the organization include educational needs of tribal women and strategies for economic development.

North American Indian Women's Association. 720 E. Spruce St., Sisseton, SD 57262. The organization is concerned with the education, health, and family life of Indians. It also promotes communication among native American women and a greater appreciation of Indian culture.

Asians

Chinese Women's Benevolent Association. 22 Pell St., Suite 3, New York, NY 10013. Working with Chinese women who need short-term or long-term assistance, the organization helps in the areas of fund raising, student aid, interpreting, and translating.

Organization of Chinese-American Women. 3214 Quesada St. NW, Washington, DC 20015. The organization was formed in 1977 to foster fuller participation of Chinese-American women in American life.

Organization of Pan-Asian-American Women. 2025 I St. NW, Suite 926, Washington, DC 20006. Issues of interest to the organization are unemployment and underemployment among recent immigrants and refugees and the language and cultural barriers Asian and Pacific women face in finding jobs, training, and services.

Hispanics

Chicana Rights Project, Mexican-American Legal Defense and Education Fund. 517 Petroleum Commerce Building, 210 N. Mary's St., San Antonio, TX 78205. Concerned with helping Mexican-American women obtain their full civil rights, this organization collects data on Hispanic women.

Comision Nacional Feminil Mexicana. 379 S. Lona Dr., Los Angeles, CA 90017. Founded in 1970, this organization helps Chicana women prepare for and attain leadership status. Chapters located in several California communities provide training assistance and information.

National Conference of Puerto Rican Women. P.O. Box 464, Radio City Station, New York, NY 10019. This organization seeks to increase participation by Puerto Rican and other Hispanic women in the social, economic, and political life of the United States.

Blacks

Black Career Women, Inc. 706 Walnut St., Suite 804, Cincinnati, OH 45202. Provides career counseling and seminars, and publishes a newsletter about black women and employment.

Black Women's Educational Policy and Research Center. Center for Research on Women, Wellesley College, Wellesley, MA 02181. Collects data on current research and projects concerning black women's educational and employment needs. This organization publishes a newsletter three times each year and also offers workshops and seminars.

Black Women Entrepreneurs, Inc. 2200 Woodward Towers, Detroit, MI 48226. Publishes a monthly newsletter and sponsors quarterly conferences for women in business.

Coalition of 100 Black Women. 60 East 86th St., New York, NY 10028. This organization consists of a national network of black women focused on economic and political development.

League of Black Women. 111 East Wacker Drive, Suite 321, Chicago, IL 60601. Provides counseling for women in business. It also offers workshops and job placement.

Links, Inc. 1522 K St. NW, Suite 404, Washington, DC 20005. Founded in 1946, Links has 4,000 members organized in 162 chapters in various parts of the country. It promotes educational, cultural, and civic activities to aid black youth, and publishes a newsletter.

National Alliance of Black Feminists. 202 S. State St., Suite 1024, Chicago, IL 60604. This is a nonprofit, nonpartisan organization dedicated to achieving full equality for black women. Formed in 1975, NABF maintains a speakers bureau and provides other services.

National Association of Negro Professional Women's Clubs. 1843 Chelan St., Flint, MI 48503. The association seeks to strengthen ties between black professional women and to encourage young women to enter the field. Its various chapters sponsor a variety of activities.

National Council of Negro Women. 1346 Connecticut Ave. NW, Washington, DC 20036. The NCNW is a large coalition organization of twenty-seven affiliated organizations and over four million members. It operates a Black Women's Institute in Washington, sponsors conferences, and currently supports an archives collection of papers of black women. Other programs include assistance with day care, health, job training, and counseling of juvenile offenders.

National Hook-Up of Black Women. 2021 K St. NW, Washington, DC 20005. Founded in 1975, this group aims to influence the political process by lobbying for black women's concerns.

Women, Scholarship, and the Humanities

5

Esther Stineman

Will you tell us, that women have no Newtons, Shakespeares, and Byrons? Greater natural powers than even those possessed may have been destroyed in woman for want of proper culture, a just appreciation, reward for merit as an incentive to exertion, and freedom of action . . . ; and yet, amid all blighting, crushing circumstances—confined within the narrowest possible limits, trampled upon by prejudice and injustice, from her education and position forced to occupy herself almost exclusively with the most trivial affairs—in spite of all these difficulties, her intellect is as good as his. Ernestine L. Rose 1851

Few of us have even heard of Ernestine L. Rose whose passionate protest on behalf of women's creative intellect electrified her audience at the Second National Convention, Friends of Woman Suffrage, in 1851. Because reformer, freethinker, and feminist Rose was much more a speaker than a writer (indeed, she apparently left no papers when she died in 1892), we would probably not even have this comment of the "queen of the platform" during the mid-1800s were it not for the massive *History of woman suffrage* edited by Elizabeth Cady Stanton, the first volume of which was published one hundred years ago in 1881. Rose's comments appear prominently in this rich source to which contemporary feminist scholars owe their understanding of what the first wave of feminism was about. Much debate surrounded the publication of the *History of woman suffrage*. Critics claimed that it was impossible to write a credible history when a movement was still in progress. Others felt that under no circumstances should those involved actively in the movement be permitted to write the history of which they were so much a part. Stanton and Anthony's correspondence gives us an intimate perspective in their roles as historical conservators (Stanton 1981). We see clearly a

117

hundred years later the vision that Stanton and her collaborators shared; if they had not assembled the speeches, documents, clippings, and proceedings of the woman movement, it is likely that we would not have fallen heir to this accurate, painstaking organic history, a project that in its six volumes went beyond the lifetimes of Stanton and Anthony, and which evolved into the centerpiece around which modern feminist historians began to examine the new American women's history in the late 1960s and early 1970s.

It seems particularly important to return to Rose's remark and Stanton's central historical project in these initial comments on the unwieldly topic of women, the humanities, and scholarship for 1981. The new women's scholarship has its critics in this year who say that women involved in feminism's second wave should not be its historians, that those whose lives are bound up in correcting and confronting issues of inequality should not be its poets, artists, and humanists.

As we review the first year in the second decade of feminism's second wave, we will turn away from such criticism much as Stanton happily did, and instead ask some critical questions about the importance of generating a literature of our own, one that confronts inequalities and how they are perpetuated and that asks probing questions about their genesis. This is a literature that corrects the record, but also one that creates a record where none existed.

In 1981 there is a sense of self-confidence about the direction of women and the humanities. "The 1970s witnessed enormous growth in women's studies. Although much remains to be achieved, the subjects studied under its rubric provoke few sneers and less condescension. Correspondingly, male as well as female scholars are turning their attention to analyses which take women as well as men into account. These inquiries are here to stay" (Bell and Rosenhan 1981, p. 540).

This necessarily selective review concentrates on influential work that might be read with interest by specialists and nonspecialists in women's studies; works that promise to be durable additions to the field; that take risks and chart the new frontiers of women-related scholarship; and finally, works in the humanities (excepting fiction) that sum up what came before and point to new developments and trends not fully worked out.

The pitfall in capsulizing new scholarship lies in the easy generalization that feminist humanists think alike about women, and that their subjects, women, have regarded and do regard their lives and goals as somehow bearing a resemblance to one another simply because of gender. The danger is to shove new theoretical discussions and discoveries into "feminist" slots in the same manner as forcing round pegs into square holes. The 1981 scholarship under review, whether written by men or women, testifies to the originality of and differences between women's experiences of the world and refuses to be distorted into a ruling "feminist" paradigm. Like the humanities themselves, these studies construct a house of many rooms with many windows, no window in any room commanding a loftier view than any other.

This chapter tends to focus on American work and looks to the type of feminist interdisciplinary inquiry that one encounters chiefly in the university. With the advent of women's studies programs "the classroom has become a major locus for the elaboration of feminist thinking," where applied criticisms, theories, and studies are the pragmatic order (Gaudin et al. 1981).

History

Women and work

Perhaps no single area in women's history has emerged so strongly this year as the historical reconstruction of women and their work. The Feminist Press, now in its eleventh year, introduced its list for 1981 with the announcement that it would complete the last few works in its twelve-volume project, *Women's lives/women's work*, with important contributions to the history of women's labor in the American classroom (Hoffman 1981); their work on the land (Jensen 1981b); and their overall contributions in both volunteer and remunerated labor. "Women have always worked," states Kessler-Harris (1981). In the classroom, teachers are finding that students taking courses on women in literature are responding more readily to approaches that highlight the positive victories of women who have worked than to the negative image of women as victims (Radner 1981).

Indeed, the study not simply of working women, but of working-class women has increasingly interested social historians, as evidenced by works such as Barbara Wertheimer's *Labor and education for women workers* (1981) and a substantial new bibliography, *America's white working-class women* (Kennedy 1981), in which the author suggests, ". . . the richness of the emerging literature on white working-class women tantalizes more than it satisfies" (p. xxiii). Only in the last few years, for example, has substantial work been done on the invisible corps of women in domestic service as maids, laundresses, and cooks—an army of underpaid, overworked women (Katzman 1978). Katzman finds that such jobs as women's occupations persisted in the face of industrialization and despite reform efforts. His first chapter allows the domestics to speak for themselves, which attests persuasively to the scorn and negativism heaped on them by women factory workers and even by the women who depended on their services, negative projections often internalized by the servants themselves. Sutherland (1981) goes further back into the early nineteenth century to study the attitudes of society toward servants and servants toward their jobs. Interestingly, when Katzman and Sutherland discuss the demise of domestic service in the 1920s they neglect to point out that the servant's replacement in most cases was the housewife.

A different twist on women's work patterns emerges in Louis J. Kern's *An ordered love: sex roles and sexuality in Victorian utopias* (1981), which looks at Shakers, Mormons, and the Oneida community. In the Mormon and

Oneida utopias life for women was not simply erotic subjugation, their work-load was often staggering. Although Kern's use of sources is impressive, feminists may differ with his assessment of these communities as "a remark-able and noble achievement."

In *Farm and factory* (1981) Dublin presents the lives of women in the Yankee mills from 1830 to 1860 as revealed through their correspondence. They suffered the loss of family closeness because their work in urban areas necessitated leaving their rural homes. In four sets of letters written by such women or members of their immediate families, concerns about sickness and death, the centrality of religion especially in times of sickness, and the importance of family and kinship bonds are repeated. Especially vivid is the grim portrayal of paternalistic factory boarding houses in which these women who often worked a seventy-hour week at a nickel an hour were forced to live. Describing an event as if it were a common, inevitable occurrence, Mary Paul writes home in 1845: "Last Thursday one girl fell down and broke her neck which caused instant death. She was going in or coming out of the mill and slipped down, it being very icy" (p.103).

More recent in its focus, and somewhat conservative in its conclusions, Winifred Wandersee's *Women's work and family values, 1920-1940* (1981) makes the case that historically, women's work outside the home is most often a reflection of a commitment to family values. A woman's desire to work and her movement into the labor force during the 1920s and 1930s was prompted by economic necessity in working-class homes even when the male worked. She argues that feminism as an ideology suffered a setback in the interwar years because its proponents refused to come to grips with the deep family values nurtured by most American women, and she hints darkly that current feminist theorists persist in ignoring family-centered attitudes still prevalent among working women. While Wandersee is interested chiefly in the interwar years, a new corpus of scholarship in 1981 clustered around women's working roles during World War II (Anderson 1981; Skold 1980; Honey 1981). For a moving account of post-World War II *hibakusha*, literally "A-bomb-received persons," many of them women, Bruin and Salaff (1981) have documented first-person experiences of Osaka victims and their attempts to work and support themselves after the horrors of the bomb. *Falkland Road* (Mark 1981), another international document, is a grim photographic documentary of life as a prostitute in a notorious section of Bombay.

Women of the republic: intellect and ideology in revolutionary America (Kerber 1980) is a work that testifies to the dangerous, demanding, and dif-ficult work women performed during the early years of the republic, including a revisionist account of the life of women campfollowers. This year an important revisionist contribution (Hacker 1981) expands to women's part in the military institutions of early modern Europe, asking who these women were who participated in military institutions, and what was the nature of the work they did. He reminds us that although the military institutions with which we are familiar have played a formidable part in the creation of Western civilization, we will have no true understanding of them if women's part is deleted from their history.

Temperance

There exists a sizeable literature about women and temperance. This year, however, two new approaches to the subject suggest that there is still much to say on the topic. Ruth Bordin has taken a controversial slant in her study of the Women's Christian Temperance Union (WCTU)(1981). She looks to the historiography of the WCTU and finds previous inquiries have neglected to ask why women embraced this particular cause or investigated its deeper relationship to the women's movement. Her conclusion is that women used the issue to gain a foothold in public life and to participate in a broad range of reformist and philanthropic causes. Historians have overlooked what Bordin deems to be WCTU leader Frances Willard's radical social philosophy, preferring to see her as the incarnation of nineteenth-century "idealized womanhood." Bordin's analysis credits the WCTU with its massive membership for getting things done, in contrast to the suffrage movement with its narrower, single-issue focus. Her book deserves to be read against both Epstein's *The politics of domesticity* (1981) with its delineation of "proto-feminism," and Mitchinson's organizational study of the WCTU (1981).

Women on the left, immigrant women, and oral history

"Women are the real Left," wrote Robin Morgan (1970) in *Rat*, an underground newspaper. "We are rising powerful in our unclean bodies; bright glowing mad in our inferior brains; wild hair flying, wild eyes staring, wild voices keening. . . . " Historians have lagged behind in their documentation of what Morgan knew in 1970. In a new book *Women and American Socialism, 1870-1920*, influential historian Mari Jo Buhle (1981) builds her thesis on the blindness of historians of American Socialism to see the crucial split among Socialist women that resulted in their disenchantment with the Party. Her reading of Socialist periodicals leads her to the conclusion that to write the history of women who participated in the movement from the late nineteenth century to the early decades of the twentieth ". . . is to rewrite the history of American Socialism" (Buhle 1981, p. xiii). Native-born women clung to their sisterhood and espoused a distinct strain of Socialism in contrast to immigrant women, who often did not understand the feminist agenda of their American sisters and who objected to what they perceived as stridency in the demands of these women on Party leaders. Feminists gave the impression that they did not have much use for the immigrant women who did not participate in their strategies for internal change within the Party along sexual lines. Misreadings of feminism by the Party, the feminists' mistrust of the male power elite within the Party, elaborate machinations by the Women's National Committee to bring male-dominated leadership to its knees, and misunderstandings of the goals of the various women's groups all contributed to a net membership loss for the Socialist Party and its women's committees. What women were doing while the Party was falling apart escaped scholarly notice until quite recently. A recent literature review (de Grazia and Hicks 1980) is illuminating for its annotated segment on the historical role of women in Western communism. Individual biographical and autobiographical treatments of socialist and anarchist women have been more plentiful; *Anarchist women, 1870-1920* (March 1981) is a substantial addition.

A posthumous autobiography that stands in a special class is Eugenia Ginzburg's *Within the whirlwind* (1981), a memorable account of her years in slave labor and exile in Siberia during the Stalinist reign of terror. A university teacher and a loyal Communist Party member, she was inexplicably arrested by Stalin's secret police during the purges of the late 1930s, and finally charged with terrorism. Her first book *Journey into the whirlwind* (1967) chronicled the first three of her eighteen years in a concentration camp separated from her husband and two children. Ginzburg's tragic and intense description of prison life and thoughts during these years of separation from everyone and everything she held dear is stunning personal history. She died in 1977.

A significant scholarly contribution in 1981 to theoretical work about women on the left is Kraditor's *The radical persuasion, 1890-1917*. Subtitled "Aspects of the intellectual history and historiography of three American radical organizations," on the surface it deals only with the Socialist Labor Party, the Socialist Party, and the Industrial Workers of the World. But Kraditor seizes on some significant historiographical questions. Where are the studies of religion, families, immigration, communities, and recreational activities? she asks of those who have written radical history. In the chapter "The radicals' perceptions of nonwhite and women workers" she argues that historians have not understood the average worker's nonradicalism because the social context of the average worker (whom she unhappily names *John Q. Worker*) has been overlooked in favor of an unfortunate emphasis on official documents that record the history of imbroglios within radical organizations. The influence of immigrant women on these organizations is not to be underestimated according to Kraditor's calculations, and she laments the lack of documentation on them and their differences.

Maxine Seller remarks on this dearth from a different perspective in her introduction to *Immigrant women* (1981):

> Much of the voluminous literature on immigration has been male-centered, taking man's experience as the norm and assuming that women's experience was either identical to men's or not important enough to warrant separate and serious attention (p. 5).

Seller's approach underscores some key concepts in the newer scholarship about women: Immigrant women become subjects in her work, and their ethnicity offers valuable insights. Her anthology is organized around a cele-bration of diversity—German women on the Utah frontier, European women in the city, and Japanese "picture brides" all have a place in her schema. Contributors to this anthology are scholars, activists, politicians, and women who kept diaries. Marie Zakrzewska, Anzia Yezierska, Emma Goldman, Mother Jones, Maxine Hong Kingston, Paule Marshall, and Barbara Mikulski are here, but so is Innocencia Flores, a Harlem rent striker. *Born of the same roots* (Hsu 1981) has selections on Chinese immigrant women.

Kraditor's conviction that the story of radical movements is not wholly told in the archives of printed and typed documents is shared by those doing women's oral history, which is saying, if you want to understand the truth of women in specific contexts, first you must listen to and comprehend her experience as an ordinary woman. Her life is important. *Las mujeres* (Elsasser, Mackenzie, and Tixler y Virgil 1981) and "Motherlogues" (Rubin and Friedensohn 1981) speak of the vitality inherent in oral history to the preservation of women's lives. The best documentary approach is a comparative American and European nineteenth-century collection *Victorian women* (Hellerstein, Hume, and Offen 1981).

Women and the West

To see the evidence of 1981 scholarship on American Western women is to wonder whether a certain glamor does not still cling to the notion of the journey across the country. Susan Armitage (1981) verifies this in a recent review essay. Joanna Stratton wrote *Pioneer Women* (1981) after she discovered a cache of more than 600 stories about "the woman side of pioneer life," painstakingly collected over the years by her great-grandmother, Lilla Day Monroe, a lawyer, editor, suffrage leader, and family woman. These stories reveal the tone and texture of life for many women during the settlement of the Kansas frontier from 1854 to 1890. Wonderful photographs accompany these reminiscences (they are neither letters nor diaries, but recollections many years following the events) about the journey Westward and its accompanying rigors of settling the towns, fighting off the wild animals, maintaining culture, and beginning reforms.

Historians are discovering that women were keen observers of the territories they traveled and the people they encountered along the journey (Roe 1981; Schlissel 1982). Goldman (1981) reports with clarity about the more active roles of some women who entered the rugged prostitution business on the American frontier. In photographs and text, a group of Canadian women pay tribute to those who traveled by the Canadian Pacific Railway to homestead on the Canadian frontier (Rasmussen et al. 1975, 1981). Books that previously were thought to be male autobiographies of pioneer life are being recognized now as the lively accounts of observant, diarist wives (Poe 1981).

Autobiography and biography, letters and diaries

Perhaps because the work being done on Western women is largely biographical and autobiographical rather than theoretical, it appeals to more people than does the vanguard theoretical work in history and literature. We are approaching a time when the quality of women's biographies is improving. Biographers are beginning to ask more probing questions about their subjects, a reflection of the new women's scholarship. Who had the power in the family? What was the nature and morality of such power? Was the woman abused in the family politics of the marital relationship? Was she denied the chance to make what might have been a fuller contribution to the world around her because of her life in the family? These are a few of the newer concerns reflected in 1981 biographical and autobiographical works written for a public who cannot seem to get enough on such women as Virginia Woolf, Anaïs Nin, the Beecher, Alcott, and Adams families, Eva Peron, Lidian Emerson, Simone de Beauvoir, Isadora Duncan, and others, some feminists, others not.

Anne Winifred Gerin (1981) has written a popular, impressively researched biography about Anne Thackeray Ritchie, daughter of William Makepeace Thackeray. Virginia Woolf, Ritchie's niece, wrote of her aunt, "She will be the unacknowledged source of much that remains in men's minds about the Victorian age. She will be a transport medium through which we behold the dead. . . . Above all and forever she will be the companion and interpreter of her father, whose spirit she has made to walk among us not only because she wrote of him but because even more wonderfully she lived in him" (p. vi). This biography tells us what Woolf admired in her aunt (in *Night and day*, published in 1919, Anne Ritchie is immortalized in the character of Mrs. Hilbery), a woman who was always a thoroughly devoted daughter. In the late nineteenth century Ritchie devoted herself to bringing out a thirteen-volume edition of her father's works for which she wrote biographical introductions. She counted among her friends the literary luminaries of her day—Charles Dickens, Tennyson, Henry James, and the Brownings. To her niece Virginia, Anne Ritchie herself was larger than life, a noble, writing woman. She died in 1919 in her seventies. This biography is a signal event because it celebrates the genius of the brilliant daughter of a brilliant man, and suggests that fathers and daughters are worthy of consideration, even though women's studies have been preoccupied almost exclusively with the mother-daughter relationship.

Another popular and praiseworthy biography, this time of a notable American family, is *The Beechers* (Rugoff 1981). It dissects the tyrannical patriarchal force of a nineteenth-century minister, and reveals a man whose unbearable personality created a domestic climate that nurtured the spectacular accomplishments of daughters Catharine (1800-1878), the educationist, and Harriet Beecher Stowe (1811-1896), the novelist. One might say this father frightened his daughters into careers and his sons into the ministry.

Bedell's biography of the Alcott family (1981) fixes a lens on a little known member of the Alcott clan, Louisa May's mother, Abbie May, whose activist dedication to Boston's poor and homeless has so far not received much attention. Bedell's work (the first of two projected volumes) is an important feminist restoration of an important American family portrait. Still another legendary family receives a surprising reexamination from a long-time student of the Adamses. *Cannibals of the heart* (Shepherd 1981) narrates the somewhat unhappy family saga of President John Quincy Adams and his wife Louisa Johnson Adams. The biographer is on the side of Louisa throughout, and confirms Louisa's view that John Quincy's ambitions left the family in their wake. Their eldest son committed suicide and the family endured long separations for the sake of the patriarch's career. To Shepherd, John Quincy was a great figure, but Louisa's contributions were also remarkable. Later in her life, for example, she championed the reformist causes of abolition and the rights of women.

This year saw the publication of two significant works on Mary Boykin Chesnut, a definitive scholarly edition of the diaries and a biography (Chesnut 1981; Muhlenfeld 1981). Daughter of an aristocratic South Carolinian family, spouse of a high-ranking member of Jefferson Davis's Confederate government, Mary Chesnut was at the eye of the hurricane during the Civil War, and was somewhat of a paradox because of her horror of slavery and her outspoken views on the abhorrent conditions of patriarchy. "There is no slave like a wife," she writes in 1861. Her diary, edited by the prominent historian C. Vann Woodward, is a colorful tapestry of Southern humanity—slaves, soldiers, poor whites, and aristocrats all marching across her design.

A different sort of political wife emerges in Woodrow Wilson's *A President in love* (1981), published in the same year as Shachtman's biography *Edith and Woodrow* (1981). The focus in the letters is on Wilson the man. "I love the way you put your dear hand on mine while with the other you turn the pages of history," Edith Bolling Galt wrote during their short courtship of 1915, a period during which the White House was operating at white heat with the matters of wartime. Tribble, the editor of the correspondence, places the letters and Mrs. Galt in the context of the presidential day. Clearly, Wilson was a romantic man who demonstrated a surprising interest in the personal and passionate during this crucial moment in history. Edith Galt Wilson, who undertook to act as his official go-between with key advisers from October 1919 to April 1920 during her husband's illness from a stroke has been called by some historians "the first woman President of the United States." Her side of the correspondence is interesting for the insight it provides about her as a political wife in the making, who considered anyone who disagreed with her lover as a traitor to his cause.

One would like to see more extensive work done on Edith Wilson by feminist historians, just as one would like to see further analysis on Alice Roosevelt Longworth about whom a book came out this year (Teague 1981).

Her witty and ferocious commentaries on personalities in Washington survived her long life (1884-1980).

Many biographies, diaries, and letters were published in 1981 about literary women. Dorothy Sayers and Katherine Anne Porter were sketched by friends with access to their papers (Brabazon 1981; Lopez 1981). Sayers's portrait shows her to be a woman of wide-ranging talents as a mystery writer and medieval scholar, with extreme conflicts in her personal life as a lover and mother. Porter's self-portraiture (these are mainly transcribed oral recollections) reveals her deep grief in having lost major female figures early in her life — her mother and grandmother — bereavements so intense that her writing became her umbilical cord with the world.

The Brontës, George Eliot, Josephine Butler, Annie Besant, Ellen Terry, Harriet Beecher Stowe, and Florence Nightingale receive elegant, concise, thoughtful biographical treatment from Elizabeth Longford in *Eminent Victorian women* (1981). This is also a compelling picture book with illustrations from *Punch* cartoons, portraits, photographs, and illustrations of Victorian fiction. Though Longford shows her subjects as real women with faults as well as virtues, she does not get inside someone such as Florence Nightingale with anything like the intensity that Elaine Showalter manages in an essay about Nightingale and her miserable relationship with her mother and sister (1981). Showalter sees a feminist lesson in Nightingale's nightmare of a mother-daughter relationship: "If we fail to respond to Nightingale, we betray a Cassandra, whose complaint came from a female experience as authentic and profoundly felt as that of any of our cherished heroines" (p. 412).

Showalter seems to suggest that feminist scholarship cannot itself remain authentic and vigorous if it simply stands at the shrines of a "cherished" few whose lives conform to certain ideological expectations that we have come to call feminist. Margaret Sanger, for example, becomes a more sympathetic figure when seen as a woman with severe personal as well as political pressures bearing down on her (Jensen 1981a).

Increasingly, feminist historians are writing about women who have successfully combined their feminist undertakings with marriages. Lucy Sprague Mitchell, the educator who with her husband established the experimental Bank Street School in New York City in the 1920s, neither wrote about nor actively espoused feminism, according to a recent study (Antler 1981). She had children, a career, and a husband who emotionally and intellectually supported her endeavors. Her papers document a desire for autonomy similar to that sought but apparently not achieved by Charlotte Perkins Gilman, whose "intellectual dilemmas related to her private ones . . . [whose] keen professional ambition confronted—head on—her intense desire for love" (Hill 1980, Introduction). Gilman's letters and private writings show a woman very different from the public, intellectual self that emerged from her published work as do Margaret Sanger's (Jensen 1981a). Similar complexities of shaping an egalitarian relationship between married lovers were worked through a half-century earlier in the correspondence of two "loving warriors," Lucy Stone and Henry Blackwell (1981).

Isak Dinesen (Karen Blixen) the Danish writer (her memoir *Out of Africa* was published in 1938) emerges as a woman who successfully concealed her personal anguish beneath her measured prose. *Letters from Africa 1914-1931* (1981) unmasks the almost frighteningly stoic coffee plantation manager in Kenya to reveal a woman whose life was beset with tragedy. Her father committed suicide because of his depression over syphilis contracted as a young man; her husband infected her with syphilis, then divorced her. Although treated successfully, the disease affected her spine and contributed to invalidism in her later years. A colonialist herself, she protested against the injustices of colonialism. For all the miseries and financial failures she suffered in Africa, however, her letters are full of references to the Africans whom she respected, and to the literary matters that absorbed and ennobled her.

Among contemporary literary autobiographies, Maya Angelou's *The heart of a woman* (1981) is most consistent with the power and truth of her writing. In her first autobiography (*I know why the caged bird sings*, published in 1970), Angelou's gift as a superb story teller became evident. In this book Angelou practices with dedication her writing craft and acknowledges the awesome responsibility of raising a teenage black son as a single parent.

A biography of Simone de Beauvoir (Ascher 1981) self-consciously becomes autobiography. Ascher confesses, "One of the greatest gifts Simone de Beauvoir has given me . . . is her conviction that it is all right to be an intellectual." Except for one letter from Beauvoir telling Ascher that she is sure the biography will be a good one, the biographer admits that she has had no conversation, no communication with her subject, a gap that she remarkably incorporates into her work as a frustrating yet exhilarating aspect of it, and an experiment in biographical form. This book, she writes in her introduction, is "my own mixture and invention: part biography, part literary criticism, part political and personal commentary, it is not exactly any of these."

Biography of the inaccessible contemporary can be effective, especially if it is the most carefully researched scholarship available. Georgia O'Keeffe, whose reclusive style of life in New Mexico is well known, is the subject of a major biography by a young journalist who is neither art critic nor scholar (Lisle 1981). While Lisle reveres her subject, her research is sound and she does as much as one could expect given the lack of contact with O'Keeffe, who, in her nineties, prefers to paint rather than to give interviews. O'Keeffe in the past has strongly asserted that her flowers admit no specifically feminist interpretation: "Well—I make you take time to look at what I saw and when you took time to really notice my flower you hung all your own associations with flowers on my flower and you write about my flower as if I think and see what you think and see of the flower—and I don't" (O'Keeffe 1976, plate 24).

Mary Lou Shields's *Sea run: surviving my mother's madness* (1981) is a beautifully written autobiography that looks back on the early 1970s when the author simultaneously entered psychoanalysis and became involved with radical feminism. Shields felt that her mother's madness threatened her own survival as a functioning person and as an artist. She breaks through to a new form of autobiography using descriptions of sessions with her male analyst as the backdrop against which her life is illuminated—a narrative of eventual victory over the self-doubt and anguish that frighten those who experience mental illness in their own families.

H.D. (Hilda Doolittle), the acclaimed poet most known for her connections with the *imagiste* movement of the second and third decades of the 1900s, was also deeply involved with psychoanalysis as an analysand of Freud. Susan Freidman's biography, *Psyche reborn* (1981), discovers the "woman-centered mythmaking" of H.D. in her poetry of life, although on the surface the poet appeared steeped in androcentric traditions of the humanities and psychoanalysis. A more popular biography of H.D. without the feminist theory and probing of Friedman's work has been published by Robinson (1981), and reflects the recently greater accessibility to the poet's papers at Yale University.

That some women are not standing as far behind the great men in their lives as previously supposed by historians and scholars is evident in four recent major biographical works (Edwards 1981; Emerson 1980; Hoge 1981; Marek 1981). George Marek demonstrates the high price of servitude Cosima Wagner paid to become a collaborator with her husband Richard Wagner. Cosima was not unused to the trials of living with difficult and talented men; her father was Franz Liszt. Although the entries in Lady Tennyson's journal, edited by James Hoge, are difficult going and boring sometimes, the composite picture lays to rest the "maligned" reputation of Emily Tennyson as the wife who ruined the artistry of her husband poet Alfred Lord Tennyson. The journal shows this simply isn't so. She acted as his most intimate confidante, his secretary and amanuensis. As for Lidian Jackson Emerson (married to Ralph Waldo), her daughter says, "She longed to speak out, to become a writer," but worried "how Papa would like that" (28 April 1873). A restored picture of Lidian Emerson, a woman admired by her contemporaries for her verbal abilities, emerges from the source materials, mainly letters preserved at the Houghton Library at Harvard. Among her circle she was thought to be the force that made Emerson a recognized public success. Finally, a revisionist biography by Anne Edwards about Sonya Tolstoy (miserably married to Leo) makes one wonder what he was complaining about when he reviled her in his letters and memoirs. Her own correspondence and diaries, somehow written in the spare moments when her thirteen children and the family estate did not require her attention, indicate that she was greatly distorted by her husband into the image of a shrew. Although Tolstoy wrote of Sonya's lack of passion, it was actually he who was unable to comprehend his agonizing sexual conflict, and she appears in this biography to have been a rather passionate woman. She worked beside him tirelessly as a transcriber and editor for his most important work, including *War and peace*.

Drama and Poetry

"We should have literature of our own, a printing-press and a publishing house, and tract writers and distributors, as well as lectures and conventions," exhorted Elizabeth Oakes Smith at the Women's Rights Convention of 1852, recorded in the *History of woman suffrage* (1881); "and yet I say this to a race of beggers, for women have no pecuniary resources." A great deal of the new women's work in the humanities, especially drama and poetry, is often published on a shoestring. Drama, except rarely, is generally performed in drama collectives and women's theaters. A "literature of our own" has not been forged without grave financial problems. Corinne Jacker (1981), a dramatist, writes, "What we women who write plays are not insisting on is that we have to make these explorations our way. I cannot go on imitating what I have seen, trying to make my plays neat and predictable. . . . (p.33).

A few years ago it was difficult to arrive at a representative listing of plays written by women; few had been published and many were circulated in manuscript or photocopy form. Because they have established a starting point for looking at women's contributions to the theater, *Plays by American women* and *Women in American theater* are signal publications (Barlow 1981; Chinoy and Jenkins 1981). The latter is a reference source with invaluable information on actresses; women playwrights, critics, and teachers; minority and feminist women in the theater, and images of women which is in itself a fine thing. That they compiled a list of 700 American women playwrights and their thousands of plays is of the greatest importance to researchers and teachers of theater, an accomplishment made possible by pooling the lists of many women to achieve as comprehensive a tally as possible.

It is more rare for female poets than for male poets to have their work accepted by major publishing houses. June Jordan (1980), Marilyn Hacker (1981), and Adrienne Rich (1981) are three exceptions. Unless a poet is as well established as Rich, many larger publishers are wary of a strong statement of sexual preference as she renders in these lines to her mother-in-law: "Your son is dead/ten years, I am a lesbian,/my children are themselves. . . ." Perhaps, too, publishers are uncertain of taking risks with poets who take risks, as Hacker does: "Poets, and poems, are not/apolitical."

Prominent feminist poets are usually published in feminist journals and by feminist presses. Persephone Press has pioneered in the effort to publish fine lesbian poetry (Bulkin and Larkin 1981). Feminist poets often appeared as subjects of interviews (Hammond 1981b; Lorde 1981); or one poet interviews another (Lorde and Rich 1981). Lynda Koolish (1981) frequently takes the accompanying photographs. What is the specific task of feminist poets? Audre Lorde approaches this question in a way that has interesting implications for those who would give her labels. "There's always someone asking you to underline one piece of yourself—whether it's *Black, woman, mother, dyke, teacher,* etc.—because that's the piece they need to key into," she told Hammond in a *Denver Quarterly* interview. "They want you to dismiss everything else. But once you do that, then you've lost because then you become acquired or bought by that particular essence of yourself. . . ." (Hammond 1981, p. 15).

Conditions consistently publishes fine poetry by women. In the Spring 1981 issue, for example, it included work by Joy Harjo, Martha Courtot, Stephanie Strickland, Mariam Sagan, Wendy Rose, Paula Gunn Allen, Cherrie Moraga, Jacqueline Lapidus, and Adrienne Rich. An accomplished poet whose first collection of poetry appeared this year is Elizabeth Spires (1981). Spires is an award-winning poet who often works with formal structures and traditional subjects. Anthologies of work by neglected poets, for example, *Black sister* (Stetson 1981), resurrect a unique literary tradition.

Poets rarely published in their lifetime, Anne Bradstreet and Emily Dickinson, both received major editions in 1981. The expensive fascimile edition of Dickinson's poems is of particular interest to scholars as one can see her unusual punctuation, strange capitalizations, stanza divisions, and idiosyncratic mechanics. Others might do well to stick to the 1955 authoritative edition (Harvard University Press, edited by Thomas Johnson). Much published during her life, Anne Sexton's ten books of poetry from her prolific career have been gathered for the first time in one edition (Sexton 1981).

Music, Art, and Architecture

The question here, as in drama and poetry, must be: Is there a female aesthetic? The answer at least in music seems to be that not enough has been written to know. In the last ten years major studies have underscored the bad treatment received by women in music at the hands of historians, and of the discrimination they have suffered during their creative lives (Wood 1980). We are just beginning to learn about the importance of mothers to women artists and the crucial role of older female mentors in encouraging musical careers. Feminist scholarship is on-going to correct a false record of women's invisibility from musical history through the compilation of bibliographies, discographies, and the like, as well as by amending and adding to existing dictionary and reference sources. Wood's 1980 review essay on music in *Signs* is important, as it points to the slow scholarly progress in this area and suggests possible avenues for theoretical expansion that will "link the work of feminists in music to what is emerging elsewhere in the new feminist scholarship. Musicologists can help examine those transitions, for example, between the household as a center of musical production and the public stage; between performers and composers as amateurs and professionals" (pp. 296-97). *Sojourner* centered its July 1981 issue on music, including profiles of June Millington, Wood Simons, Hazel Dickins, Kristen Lems, and Karen Kane among twentieth century musical women, and an article entitled "Regaining composers."

At the Bloomington National Women's Studies Association Convention, 1980, Heidi Von Gunden analysed the problem during a session called

"Feminist critical perspectives in arts and culture" (*Frontiers* 1981). "Music," Von Gunden said, "has traditionally been about fifty years behind the visual arts in stylistic changes and theoretical developments. It is too early for a feminist criticism. Important changes begun in the 1950s will lead to a feminist criticism" (p. 97). She then went on to define these changes as a reexamination of the roles of the composer, performers, and audience, which has begun to regard the nonlinear, intuitive, and improvisational in music as important as the rational, systemic, and structural modes held sacrosanct before the 1950s.

By contrast, a female aesthetic in visual arts seems more explicable, perhaps because the work can be photographed, reproduced, and viewed again and again. During 1981 there has been significantly increased visibility in feminist journals of the work of minority artists (Nelson 1981); of art clusters around political themes (Withers 1981); of the work of feminist photographers on other feminists (Koolish 1981); and of work celebrating women's architecture (Kennedy 1981; *Heresies II* 1981). A feminist analysis of architecture intersects the fields of economics, feminist theory, and social history, as Delores Hayden's *The grand domestic revolution* (1981) brilliantly demonstrates.

An essay on literary criticism asserted that the qualities of sensitivity, intuition, and expressiveness granted to women by the patriarchal culture allowed a certain toleration for the woman artist (Sherman and Beck 1979). Not so for the woman critic. Although women art historians make up 50 percent of membership in the College Art Association, only a small number have been able to achieve the exalted status of recognized art theorist. Much of this has to do with the relegation of certain genres of art-interior design, the decorative arts, and crafts to an inferior position in art-historiographic literature. For the first time a discussion of these issues has been aired, and women scholars in art historiography are given their due through a series of biographical and critical essays accompanied by bibliographies in a book called *Women as interpreters of the visual arts* (Sherman and Holcomb 1981). Perhaps a discussion of the exclusion of women artists from the canon begins here, for it is art historians who become the curators and the directors of museums, and it is women who have frequently been excluded from the most prestigious institutional affiliations.

French and American Feminism

The lively debate centering on new French feminism continues to spark in American feminist journals, the aftermath of Marks and de Courtivron's anthology, *New French feminism* (1980). In the introduction to their volume the editors differentiate French from American feminist modes of inquiry: Americans seek to ressurect invisible women and to construct a usable past, while the much more radical (and perhaps more playful) French choose to deconstruct the texts of Western civilization. Theirs intends to be an atheistic, antibourgeois methodology, making our classroom-centered feminism look rather tame by comparison. Catharine Stimpson (1981b) elegantly outlined the major issues in her essay on the humanities in *The Women's Annual: 1980.* The beat goes on. Monique Wittig and Hélène Cixous, though on two different "sides" of the French debate, are celebrities in this international feminist scuffle, which has at its root the imperative to look at linguistic differences between genders in order to begin to understand gender differences. Only then can one learn that control of the language signals control of societal power.

In their introduction to the *Yale French studies* special issue devoted to "Feminist readings: French texts/American contexts" (Gaudin et al. 1981) the editors noted their special issue coincided with similarly focused issues of *Signs, Feminist Studies*, and *Critical Inquiry.* In their collective introduction the editors write, "This is indeed a special moment which occurs in a context of such rapid change that any fixed description will by nature misrepresent its movement" (p. 5). Although there is a sense among American feminist intellectuals (who are usually employed in universities and involved in the daily duties of teaching women's studies courses) that what Sandra Gilbert calls the "word-play" of people like Irigaray and Cixous is an indulgence American feminists often do not have time for, still we find Hélène Wenzel (1981) writing an appreciation for Monique Wittig's "text as body/politics" in one journal; and Ann Rosalind Jones (1981) publishing an article on *l'ecriture feminine* in another. Carolyn Burke (1981) pursues "Irigaray through the looking glass," while Rosenfeld (1981) writes a fairly clear explication of the "lexical and syntactic innovations" in an article about Wittig's experiments in liberating the text. Jones perhaps hits closest to the mark in her capsulization of the new French feminism as a feminism of "intertextual games" although the French see the feminist annihilation of the male monopoly of text as a deadly serious enterprise.

Closer to home, articles on Canadian and Quebecoise writers appear throughout 1981 in *Frontiers, Signs,* and the *Journal of Popular Culture* (a special issue). Gould (1981b) in "Setting words free: feminist writing in Quebec" clarifies theoretical trends in recent feminist literature in France, Canada, and the United States and does an admirable service in naming contemporary writers in Quebec. In another article on Marie-Claire Blais, Gould (1981a) measures Blais's feminine vision "by the extent to which she forges new hopes, for both her female characters and readers in a language born of the joys and anguish of the feminine body" (pp. 26–27).

While the editors of the special issue on Canadian women in the *Journal of Popular Culture* explain that the self-confidence of Canadian women writers is due to a strong female literary lineage (Davidson 1981), Louise Forsythe (1981) concedes that ". . . there is no example in recent Quebec literature of a woman writer who has been able to affirm a strong and authentic relationship with her own mother." An article in praise of the strength in

Canadian women writers' natural imagery suggests that they ". . . make use of the clash between American/masculine and Canadian/feminine perspectives" (Irvine 1981, p. 73).

Feminist Literary Criticism and Theory

As the centenary of Virginia Woolf's birth approaches, literary studies about her work and its connection with her life continue to proliferate. One wonders what she would have thought of the celebratory outpouring from the presses, not only the new editions of her work such as Harcourt Brace Jovanovich's announced deluxe volumes of her major novels with new forewords written by influential contemporary writers (Maureen Howard for *Mrs. Dalloway*; Eudora Welty for *To the lighthouse*; and Mary Gordon for *A Room of one's own*), but also calendars, T-shirts, and the like. The scholarship on Woolf often tends to rework old ground. Those familiar with her bibliography will see that new work clusters in well-tilled patches—reminiscences from Bloomsbury (Partridge 1981); psychological exhumation of her search for the mother (Strouse 1981); attempts to locate the *real* Virginia Woolf (Poole 1981), and specialized thematic studies of her fiction (Spilka 1980). *New feminist essays on Virginia Woolf* (Marcus 1981) offers twelve fresh readings of Woolf including an essay by Ruddick on her real and fictionalized brothers and Little's reading of *Jacob's room* as parody. Edna O'Brien's new play *Virginia* (1981) is based on Woolf's life, much of it using her prose as monologue. Volume IV of *The Diary of Virginia Woolf* for the years 1931-1935, promised for 1981, will appear early in 1982.

Notable 1981 contributions to literary scholarship about individual authors include work on Zora Neale Hurston (Howard 1981); Jane Austen (Monaghan 1981), which includes a particularly fine essay by Nina Auerbach on Austen's "romantic imprisonment"; Harriet Beecher Stowe (Ammons 1981), which looks at Stowe through our eyes and those of her contemporaries; Sappho (Stigers 1981); Gayl Jones (Harris 1981); Jean Rhys (Nebeker 1981); Ellen Glasgow (Raper 1981); Marianne Moore (Costello 1981); Sherwood Anderson (Rigsbee 1981); and Willa Cather (Rosowski 1981). Some of these studies, for example Schlueter's (1981) book on Shirley Ann Grau, comment on careers of little known but important authors.

The bifurcated image studies (woman as madonna/whore) so popular in the earlier women's studies literature have given way to more labyrinthine treatments, often using the tools of psychoanalysis (Storch 1981). American feminists no longer look to Freud as the bogey man of feminology and begin to define female tropes and rhetorical figures using feminist revisions of Freudianism. Schor (1981) suggests that synecdoche, the figure of speech in which the part substitutes for the whole or vice versa, may be considered the rhetorical figure of clitoral theory in the same way that metonymy, the use of the name of one object for another, has come to represent the phallus. Fictional characters, however, are not case studies for psychoanalysis, as Judith

Gardiner (1981) reminds us. "In . . . books we join the narrator in reconstructing the other woman by whom we know ourselves" (p. 442).

Women critics must often defend their ground in mainstream journals of literary criticism. In an indictment against the male myth of fathering oneself which Nina Baym perceives as the principal theory of American literature, she writes, "If literature is the attempt to *father* oneself by the author, then every act of writing by a woman is both perverse and absurd" (1981a, p. 139). The irony she sees in the present criticism is that as feminists rediscover women writers, a male-dominated critical theory allows "women less and less presence" (p. 139). Where Baym criticizes the ruling male paradigm in critical theory, Jehlen (1981) addresses the paradox of feminist criticism: How does a feminist deal with the issues of "good" or "bad" literature when an honest appraisal may run against the grain of feminism? Using Shakespeare as an example, Jehlen sees the bard ". . . working within his own ideology that defined bastards, Jews, and women as by nature deformed or inferior, and as understanding the contradictions of that ideology without rejecting its basic tenets—so that, from a feminist standpoint, he was a misogynist—and as being nonetheless a great poet" (p. 579). She calls for a new methodological focus for feminist criticism.

Some feminist scholars, although interested in a new epistemology, focus their writing on minority issues within feminism lest entire groups of women be overlooked in new debates. Costa-Cãardenas (1981) writes of the Chicana and her literature; Beck (1981) of recent texts in lesbian studies; and Christian (1980) of black novelists. Other specialized literary studies select a life-cycle issue important to women as a theme of critical inquiry: Aging in the work of May Sarton (Springer 1981), or a new vision of mothers and daughters (Forsythe 1981).

Reception of literary studies by the world outside feminist scholarly circles is often not encouraging. In a lengthy representative review article on new Shakespearean scholarship in the *New York Review of Books*, Anne Barton takes two feminist writers to task for distortion of their critical faculties to suit feminist theory. "In her eagerness to sustain a theory, "she writes of Coppelia Kahn's *Man's estate: masculine identity in Shakespeare* (1981), "she sometimes distorts or suppresses facts of the play . . ." (Barton 1981, p. 22). Marilyn French's *Shakespeare's division of experience* (1980) is "a stubborn one-sided view. It is clear," criticizes Barton, "that the qualities French values, and according to which she would like to see life lived by both sexes, are all, in her [French's] terms—feminine" (p. 21). Norman Rabkin's *Shakespeare and the problem of meaning* (1981), however, is "brilliant: taut, concise, beautifully argued, and sensitively responsive to the individuality of particular Shakespeare plays" (p. 22). One wonders what Barton would do with the special issue of *Women's Studies* (1981) with essays on Shakespeare by a variety of feminist scholars.

Women's Relationships With Each Other

Perhaps no single issue in the last few years has so effectively divided feminist scholars as the nature of friendships among women. One side of the argument claims female friendship, indeed female creativity, to be specifically lesbian in orientation, while the other side posits a more conventional view of women's relationships to one another. Lillian Faderman's ambitious study of mainly literary female friends and the changing historical and cultural views of closely alligned women takes a specifically lesbian position on the question.

Emily Dickinson, Sarah Orne Jewett, Willa Cather, Gertrude Stein, Djuna Barnes, and Anaïs Nin are among the more familiar literary women in a study that extends from the renaissance to the present. Faderman begins, "I venture to guess that had romantic friends of other eras lived today, many of them would have been lesbian-feminists, and had the lesbian-feminists of our day lived in other eras, most of them would have been romantic friends" (Faderman 1981, Preface). Reviewing the book, Nina Baym (1981b) admires it for its "moderate lesbian-feminist point of view" but finds "many errors and much oversimplification in the area I know best. . . ." The notable aspect of the new scholarship in Faderman's book is her focus on the female couple as a contained unit. If these women had difficulties in their lesbian identities, Faderman says, then we should look to the phallocentric milieu in which they struggled. Other controversial articles elsewhere further the debate on the historiographical discussion of women's relationships and friendships with one another (Rupp 1981).

Elizabeth Abel (1981) extends the work of Louise Bernikow (1980) by moving beyond a discussion of the friendships among novelists into their works of fiction and the heterosexual women's friendships they create (Abel 1981).

Moving away from specific relationships among women toward a definition of "the relationships between sexuality and creativity gender and genre," critic Sandra Gilbert (1981) asks, "Is language in its essence patriarchal and, if so, how can 'masculinist' language create female poetic identity?" (p. 39). Susan Kissel (1981) asks what accounts for the difference in authorial intention of contemporary American women writers from those of men, and concludes "purposeful" and "committed" anger. Todd (1981) and Homans (1981) are other prominent voices in the controversy about "gender and literary voice."

Conclusion

To make conclusions about 1981's scholarship in the humanities is difficult. Surveying the territory is exhilarating. Everywhere there is evidence of hard thought and strong ideas. Is there—or even should there be—a unity to all this.

On the institutional level there have been some important changes this year. *Signs*, the most prestigious women's studies journal, moved from East coast to West, and is now edited by Barbara Charlesworth Gelpi; Spring 1981 marked her inaugural issue. Feminist historian Gerda Lerner assumed the presidency of the Organization of American Historians, the first woman to serve in that capacity in the association's long and somewhat conservative history (Stimpson 1981a). On the surface at least, these changes speak of vitality.

Theory in feminist scholarship, especially in literature, began to take on riskier issues. The material on French feminism is one example. The feminist view increasingly seen on lesbian history and literature is another. As theoretical imperatives become ever more absorbing to scholars, laywomen who do not specialize in feminist scholarship might well ask whether they will be left behind in the dust of theoretical debates. Will the theorizing effect change in the real world?

The year 1981 began and ended with the recognition that feminist values are not at the core of social policy in the United States. Input from the New Right threatens to dry up sources that have funded the new women's scholarship in the past (Wohl 1981). While moderate feminists prophesy a harmonious blending of feminist and "feminine" discourse in public forums (Friedan 1981), others are more skeptical. Catharine Stimpson, in leaving *Signs*, paused to note that "we must recognize . . . that the opposition to sexual justice, to equality for women, and to the full search for scholarly truth about the female in culture and in society is careening with fresh belligerence and zeal across the public land cape" (Stimpson 1980, p. 188). In universities, undergraduate majors in the humanities are dwindling in number (Lougee 1981). Yet it is in undergraduate humanities courses that feminist scholars have the greatest potential to pass on the new scholarship.

At the end of 1981 the overriding question about the new women's scholarship, which began so promisingly a decade ago, was will it continue to flourish and to prosper? Will the extraordinary outpouring of feminist documentation currently being produced in the humanities help to ensure the social changes on behalf of feminism that women like Ernestine Rose looked for in the midnineteenth century?

REFERENCES

Abel, E. 1981. (E)merging identities: the dynamics of female friendship in contemporary fiction by women. *Signs* 6:413-35.

Ammons, E., ed. 1980. *Critical essays on Harriet Beecher Stowe*. Boston: G. K. Hall.

Anderson, K. 1981. *Wartime women: sex roles, family relations, and the status of women during World War II*. Westport, Conn.: Greenwood Press.

Angelou, M. 1981. *The heart of a woman*. New York: Random House.

Antler, J. 1981. Feminism as life-process: the life and career of Lucy Sprague Mitchell. *Feminist Studies* 7, no. 1:134-57.

Armitage, S. 1981. Western women's history: a review essay. *Frontiers* 5, no. 3:71-73.

Ascher, C. 1981. *Simone de Beauvoir: a life of freedom.* Boston: Beacon.

Barlow, J., ed. 1981. *Plays by American women.* New York: Bard/Avon.

Barton, A. 1981. Was Shakespeare a chauvinist? *The New York Review of Books*, June 11, pp. 20-22.

Baym, N. 1981a. Melodramas of beset manhood: how theories of American fiction exclude women authors. *American Quarterly* 33, no. 2:123-39.

Baym, N. 1981b. Review: Faderman, Lillian: *Surpassing the love of women. Studies In American Fiction* 9, no. 2.

Beck, E. 1981. Review: selected texts in lesbian studies. *Feminist Collections: Women's Studies Library Resources in Wisconsin* 3, no. 1:22-26. Available from Women's Studies Librarian, UW System, Memorial Library, Madison WI 53706.

Bedell, M. 1981. *The Alcotts: biography of a family.* New York: Clarkson N. Potter.

Bell, S. G., and Rosenhan, M. 1981. A problem in naming: women studies— women's studies? *Signs* 6:540-42.

Bernikow, L. 1980. *Among Women.* New York: Crown.

Bordin, R. 1981. *Woman and temperance: the quest for power and liberty, 1873-1900.* Philadelphia: Temple University Press.

Brabazon, J. 1981. *Dorothy Sayers: a biography.* New York: Charles Scribner's Sons.

Bradstreet, A. D. 1981. *The complete works of Anne Bradstreet*, edited by J. R. McElrath, Jr. and A. P. Robb. Boston: Twayne.

Bruin, J. and Salaff, S. 1981. Never again: the organization of women atomic bomb victims in Osaka. *Feminist Studies* 7, no. 1:1-18.

Buhle, M. J. 1981. *Women and American socialism, 1870-1920.* Urbana: University of Illinois Press.

Bulkin, E., and Larkin, J. 1981. *Lesbian poetry: an anthology.* Watertown, Mass.: Persephone Press.

Burke, C. 1981. Irigaray through the looking glass. *Feminist Studies* 7, no. 2:288-306.

Chesnut, M. B. M. 1981. *Mary Chesnut's Civil War*, edited by C. V. Woodward. New Haven, Conn.: Yale Univeristy Press.

Chinoy, H. K. and Jenkins, L. 1981. *Women in American theater.* New York: Crown.

Christian, B. 1980. *Black women novelists: the development of a tradition, 1892-1976.* Westport, Conn.: Greenwood Press.

Conditions: Seven 3,1 (1981). Special issue. Poetry.

Costa-Cãardenas, M. 1981. The Chicana in the city as seen in her literature. *Frontiers* 6, nos. 1 and 2:13-18.

Costello, B. 1981. *Marianne Moore: imaginary possessions.* Cambridge: Harvard University Press.

Davidson, C. 1981. Introduction. *Journal of Popular Culture* 15, no. 3.

de Grazia, V., and Hicks, L. 1980. Women and communism in advanced capitalist societies: readings and resources. *Radical History Review* 23:80-101.

Dickinson, E. 1981. *The manuscript books of Emily Dickinson*, edited by R. W. Franklin. Boston: Harvard/Belknap.

Dinesen, I. [Blixen, Karen]. 1981. *Letters from Africa, 1914-1931*, edited by F. Lasson, translated from Danish by Anne Born. Chicago: University of Chicago Press.

Dublin, T. 1980. *Farm and factory: the mill experience and women's lives in New England, 1830-1860.* New York: Columbia University Press.

Edwards, A. 1981. *Sonya: the life of Countess Tolstoy.* New York: Simon & Schuster.

Elsasser, N.; MacKenzie, K.; and Tixler y Virgil, Y. 1981. *Las mujeres: conversations from a Hispanic community.* Old Westbury, N.Y.: Feminist Press.

Emerson, E. T. 1980. *The life of Lidian Jackson Emerson*, edited by D. B. Carpenter. Boston: Twayne.

Epstein, B. L. 1981. *The politics of domesticity: women, evangelism, and temperance in nineteenth-century America.* Middletown, Conn.: Wesleyan University Press.

Faderman, L. 1981. *Surpassing the love of men.* New York: William Morrow.

Forsythe, L. H. 1981. The radical transformation of the mother-daughter relationship in some women writers of Quebec. *Frontiers* 6, nos. 1 and 2:44-49.

French, M. 1980. *Shakespeare's division of experience.* New York: Summit.

Friedan, B. 1981. *The second stage.* New York: Summit.

Friedman, S. S. 1981. *Psyche reborn: the emergence of H.D.* Bloomington: Indiana University Press.

Frontiers. 1980. Selected proceedings of the National Women's Studies Association. 6, nos. 1 and 2:60-100.

Gardiner, J. K. 1981. The (us)es of (i)dentity: a response to Abel on (e)merging identities. *Signs* 6:436-44.

Gaudin, C. et al. 1981. Introduction. *Yale French Studies.* 62:2-18.

Gerin, W. 1981. *Anne Thackeray Ritchie: a biography.* New York: Oxford University Press.

Gilbert, S. M. 1981. Speaking in mother tongues. *Ms.* 9, no. 12 (June):39-40.

Ginzburg, E. 1967. *Journey into the whirlwind.* New York: Harcourt Brace Jovanovich.

Ginzburg, E. 1981. *Within the whirlwind.* New York: Harcourt Brace Jovanovich.

Goldman, M. S. 1981. *Gold diggers & silver miners: prostitution and social life on the Comstock.* Ann Arbor: University of Michigan Press.

Gould, K. 1981a. The censored world and the body politic: reconsidering the fiction of Marie-Claire Blais. *Journal of Popular Culture* 15, no 3:14-27.

Gould, K. 1981b. Setting words free: feminist writing in Quebec. *Signs* 6:617-42.

Hacker, B. C. 1981. Women and military institutions in early modern Europe: a reconnaissance. *Signs* 6:643-71.

Hacker, M. 1981. *Taking notice.* New York: Knopf.

Hammond, K. 1981a. An interview with Marilyn Hacker. *Frontiers* 5, no. 3:22-27.

Hammond, K. 1981b. Audre Lorde: interview. *Denver Quarterly* 16, no 1:10-27.

Harris, J. 1981. Gayl Jones' *Corregidora*. *Frontiers* 5, no. 3:1-5.

Hayden D. 1981. *The grand domestic revolution.* Boston: MIT Press.

Hellerstein, E. O.; Hume, L. P.; and Offen, K. M., eds. 1981. *Victorian women: a documentary account of women's lives in nineteenth-century England, France and the United States.* Stanford, Calif.: Stanford University Press.

Heresies II. 1981. 3, no. 3. Special issue. Making room: women and architecture.

Hill, M. A. 1980. *Charlotte Perkins Gilman: the making of a radical feminist, 1860-1896.* Philadelphia: Temple University Press.

Hoffman, N. 1981. "Women's true profession": voices from the history of teaching. Old Westbury, N.Y.: Feminist Press.

Hoge, J. O., ed. 1981. *Lady Tennyson's journal.* Charlottesville: University Press of Virginia.

Homans, M. 1980. *Women writers and poetic identity: Dorothy Wordsworth, Emily Brontë, and Emily Dickinson.* Princeton, N.J.: Princeton University Press.

Honey, M. 1981. The "womanpower" campaign: advertising and recruitment propaganda during World War II. *Frontiers* 6, nos. 1 and 2:50-56.

Howard, L. P. 1981. *Zora Neale Hurston.* Boston: Twayne.

Hsu, V. L., ed. 1981. *Born of the same roots: stories of modern Chinese women.* Bloomington: Indiana University Press.

Irvine, L. 1981. Surfacing, surviving, surpassing: Canada's women writers. *Journal of Popular Culture* 15, no. 3:70-77.

Jacker, C. 1981. Better than a shriveled husk: new forms for the theater. In *Toward the second decade,* edited by B. Justice and R. Pore. Westport, Conn.: Westport Press.

Jehlen, M. 1981. Archimedes and the paradox of feminist criticism. *Signs* 6:575-601.

Jensen, J. M. 1981a. The evolution of Margaret Sanger's *Family limitation* pamphlet, 1914-1921. *Signs* 6:548-67.

Jensen, J. M. 1981b. *With these hands: women working on the land.* Old Westbury, N.Y.: Feminist Press; New York: McGraw-Hill.

Jones, A. R. 1981. Writing the body: toward an understanding of *l'ecriture feminine. Feminist Studies* 7, no. 2:247-63.

Jordan, J. 1980. *Passion: new poems, 1977-1980.* Boston: Beacon.

Kahn, C. 1981. *Man's estate: masculine identity in Shakespeare.* Berkeley: University of California Press.

Katzman, D. M. 1981. *Seven days a week: women and domestic service in industrializing America.* Urbana: University of Illinois Press.

Kennedy, M. I. 1981. Toward a rediscovery of "feminine" principles in architecture and planning. *Women's Studies International Quarterly* 4, no. 1:75-82.

Kennedy, S. E. 1981. *America's white working-class women: a historical bibliography.* New York: Garland.

140 Esther Stineman

Kerber, L. K. 1980. *Women of the republic: intellect and ideology in revolutionary America.* Chapel Hill: University of North Carolina Press.

Kern, L. J. 1981. *An ordered love: sex roles and sexuality in Victorian utopias—the Shakers, the Mormons, and the Oneida community.* Chapel Hill: University of North Carolina Press.

Kessler-Harris, A. 1981. *Women have always worked: an historical overview.* Old Westbury, N.Y.: Feminist Press; New York: McGraw-Hill.

Kissel, S. 1981. Double vision: the differing views of contemporary male and female writers. *Frontiers* 6, nos. 1 and 2:39-43.

Koolish, L. 1981. Photographs. Introduction by Josephine Withers. *Feminist Studies* 7, no. 2:305-17.

Kraditor, A. S. 1981. *The radical persuasion, 1890-1917.* Baton Rouge: Louisiana State University Press.

Lisle, L. 1981. *Portrait of an artist: a biography of Georgia O'Keeffe.* New York: Washington Square.

Longford, E. 1981. *Eminent Victorian women.* New York: Knopf.

Lopez, E. H. 1981. *Conversations with Katherine Anne Porter: refugee from Indian Creek.* Boston: Little, Brown.

Lorde, A. Poetry. *Denver Quarterly* 16, no. 1:28-35.

Lorde, A., and Rich, A. 1981. An interview with Audre Lorde. *Signs* 6:713-36.

Lougee, C. C. 1981. Women, history, and the humanities: an argument in favor of the general studies curriculum. *Women's Studies Quarterly* 9, no. 1.

Marcus, J. 1981. *New feminist essays on Virginia Woolf.* Lincoln: University of Nebraska Press.

Marek, G. 1981. *Cosima Wagner.* New York: Harper & Row.

Mark, M. E. 1981. *Falkland road: prostitutes of Bombay.* New York: Knopf.

Marks, E., and de Courtivron, I., eds. 1981. *New French feminisms.* New York: Schocken.

Marsh, M. S. 1981. *Anarchist women, 1870-1920.* Philadelphia: Temple University Press.

Mitchinson, W. 1981. The women's Christian temperance union: a study in organization. *International Journal of Women's Studies* 4, no. 2:143-56.

Monaghan, D., ed. 1981. *Jane Austen in a social context.* New York: Barnes & Noble.

Muhlenfeld, E. 1981. *Mary Boykin Chesnut: a biography.* Baton Rouge: Louisiana State University Press.

Nebeker, H. 1981. *Jean Rhys woman in passage: a critical study of the novels of Jean Rhys.* Montreal: Eden Press Women's Publications.

Nelson, K. 1981. Hispanic folk artists of the San Luis Valley, Colorado. *Frontiers* 5, no. 3:34-43.

O'Brien, E. 1981. *Virginia: a play.* New York: Harcourt Brace Jovanovich.

O'Keeffe, G. 1976. *Georgia O'Keeffe.* New York: Viking.

Partridge, F. 1981. *Love in Bloomsbury: memories.* Boston: Little, Brown.

Poe, S. 1981. *Buckboard days,* edited by E. Cunningham, new introduction by Sandra L. Myres. Albuquerque: University of New Mexico Press.

Poole, R. 1981. *The unknown Virginia Woolf.* New York: Cambridge University Press.

Rabkin, N. 1981. *Shakespeare and the problem of meaning.* Chicago: University of Chicago Press.

Radner, S. 1981. Changing approaches to teaching "Women in Literature." *Frontiers* 6, nos. 1 and 2:3-5.

Raper, J. R. 1981. *Without shelter: the early career of Ellen Glasgow.* Baton Rouge: Louisiana State University Press.

Rich, A. 1981. *A wild patience has taken me this far: poems 1978-1981.* New York: Norton.

Rasmussen, L. et al., comps. 1981, 1975. *A harvest yet to reap.* Lincoln: University of Nebraska, Toronto: Women's Press.

Rigsbee, S. A. 1981. The feminine in Winesburg, Ohio. *Studies in American Fiction* 9, no. 2:233-44.

Robinson, J. S. 1981. *H.D., the life and work of an American Poet.* Boston: Houghton Mifflin.

Roe, F. 1981. *Army letters from an officer's wife, 1871-1888,* introduction by Sandra L. Myres. Lincoln: University of Nebraska Press.

Rosenfeld, M. 1981. Language and the vision of a lesbian-feminist utopia in Wittig's *Les guérillères. Frontiers* 6, no. 1:6-9.

Rosowski, S. 1981. Willa Cather's women. *Studies in American Fiction* 9, no. 2:261-75.

Rubin, B., and Friedensohn, D. 1981. Motherlogues. *Women's Studies Quarterly* 9, no. 2:4-13.

Rugoff, M. 1981. *The Beechers.* New York: Harper & Row.

Rupp, L. J. 1981. "Imagine my surprise": women's relationships in historical perspective. *Frontiers* 5, no. 3:61-70.

Schlissel, L. 1982. *Women's diaries of the westward journey,* preface by Carl N. Degler. New York: Schocken.

Schlueter, P. 1981. *Shirley Ann Grau.* Boston: Twayne.

Schor, N. 1981. Female paranoia: the case for psychoanalytic feminist criticism. *Yale French Studies* 62:204-19.

Seller, M. S. 1981. *Immigrant women.* Philadelphia: Temple University Press.

Sexton, A. 1981. *Collected poems,* foreword by Maxine Kumin. Boston: Houghton Mifflin.

Schachtman, T. 1981. *Edith and Woodrow.* New York: Putnam.

Shepherd, J. 1981. *Cannibals of the heart: a personal biography of Louisa Catherine and John Quincy Adams.* New York: McGraw-Hill.

Sherman, C. R., and Holcomb, A. M., eds. 1981. *Women as interpreters of the visual arts.* Westport, Conn.: Greenwood Press.

Sherman, J. A., and Beck, E. T. 1979. *The prism of sex: essays on the sociology of knowledge.* Madison, Wisc.: University of Wisconsin Press.

Shields, M. L. 1981. *Sea run: surviving my mother's madness.* New York: Seaview.

Showalter, E. 1981. Florence Nightingale's feminist complaint: women, religion and suggestions for thought. *Signs* 6:395-412.

Skold, K. B. 1980. The job he left behind: American women in the shipyards during World War II. In *Women, war & revolution*, edited by C. R. Berkin and C. M. Lovett. New York: Holmes & Meier.

Sojourner 1981. 6, no. 12. Special issue. Music.

Spilka, M. 1980. *Virginia Woolf's quarrel with grieving.* Lincoln: University of Nebraska Press.

Spires, E. 1981. *Globe.* Middletown, Conn.: Wesleyan University Press.

Springer, M. 1981. "As we shall be": May Sarton and aging. *Frontiers* 5, no. 3:46-49.

Stanton, E. C. 1981. *Elizabeth Cady Stanton-Susan B. Anthony: correspondence, writing, speeches*, edited by E. C. DuBois, foreword by Gerda Lerner. New York: Schocken.

Stanton, E. C. et al., eds. 1969. *History of woman suffrage.* New York: Arno Press. Repr. of 1881-1922 ed.

Stigers, E. S. 1981. Sappho's private world. *Women's Studies* 8, nos. 1 and 2:47-64.

Stimpson, C. R. 1980. Editorial. *Signs* 6:187-88.

Stimpson, C. R. 1981a. Gerda Lerner on the future of our past. *Ms.* 10, no. 3:50-55.

Stimpson, C. R. 1981b. Women, scholarship and the humanities (1980): a review essay. In *The women's annual: 1980—the year in review*, edited by B. Haber. Boston: G. K. Hall.

Stone, L., and Blackwell, H. 1981. *Loving warriors: selected letters of Lucy Stone and Henry B. Blackwell, 1853 to 1893*, edited by L. Wheeler. New York: Dial.

Storch, M. 1981. Blake and women: "Nature's Cruel Holiness." *American Imago* 38, no. 2:221-46.

Stratton, J. L. 1981. *Pioneer women: voices from the Kansas frontier*, introduction by A. Schlesinger. New York: Simon & Schuster.

Strouse, L. F. 1981. Virginia Woolf and her voyage out. *American Imago* 38, no. 2:185-202.

Sutherland, D. E. 1981. *Americans and their servants: domestic service in the United States for 1800-1920.* Baton Rouge: Louisiana University Press.

Teague, M. 1981. *Mrs. L.: conversations with Alice Roosevelt Longworth.* New York: Doubleday.

Todd, J., ed. 1981. *Gender and literary voice.* New York: Holmes & Meier.

Wandersee, W. D. 1981. *Women's work and family values, 1920-1940.* Cambridge: Harvard University Press.

Wenzel, H. V. 1981. The text as body/politics: an appreciation of Monique Wittig's writings in context. *Feminist Studies* 7, no. 2:264-87.

Wertheimer, B. M., ed. 1981. *Labor education for women workers.* Philadelphia: Temple University Press.

Wilson, W. 1981. *A President in love: the courtship letters of Woodrow Wilson and Edith Bolling Galt*, edited by E. Tribble. Boston: Houghton Mifflin.

Withers, J. 1981. No more war: an art essay. *Feminist Studies* 7, no. 1:76-88.

Wohl, L. C. 1981. Holding our own against a conservative tide. *Ms.* 9, no. 12:50-53.

Women's Studies 1981. 9, no. 1. Special issue. Shakespeare.

Wood, E. 1980. Women in music: review essay. *Signs* 6:283-97.

Woolf, V. 1981a. *The diary of Virginia Woolf*, Volume IV, 1931-1935, edited by A. O. Bell, assisted by A. McNellie. New York: Harcourt Brace Jovanovich.

Woolf, V. 1981b. *Mrs. Dalloway*, foreword by Maureen Howard. New York: Harcourt Brace Jovanovich.

Woolf, V. 1981c. *A room of one's own*, foreword by Mary Gordon. New York: Harcourt Brace Jovanovich.

Woolf, V. 1981d. *To the lighthouse*, foreword by Eudora Welty. New York: Harcourt Brace Jovanovich.

Yale French Studies 1981. 62. Special issue. Feminist readings: French texts/American contexts.

SUGGESTED READING

Ashton, Dore, and Hare, Denise Browne. *Rosa Bonheur: a life and legend.* New York: Viking, 1981. The best available source on Bonheur in a beautiful editon.

Bartlett, Elizabeth. *Memory is no stranger.* Athens: Ohio University Press, 1981. Although Bartlett is not considered a feminist poet, her work is original. She is known for the twelve-tone poem.

Battiscombe, Georgina. *Christina Rossetti: a divided life.* New York: Holt, Rinehart & Winston, 1981. A popular biography explores the knots of family obligations that at once constricted Rossetti and provided a climate of creativity.

Brown, Lloyd W. *Women writers in black Africa.* Westport, Conn.: Greenwood Press, 1981.

Cazden, Elizabeth. *Antoinette Brown Blackwell: a biography.* Old Westbury, N.Y.: Feminist Press, 1982. The first biography of this feminist who was the first ordained woman Christian minister in America.

Chernin, Kim. *The obsession: reflections on the tyranny of slenderness.* New York: Harper & Row, 1981. The chapter on anorexia, "The hunger artist," may be of particular interest to humanists studying the relationship of creative women to anorexia. Chernin uses literature and myth to support her thesis that women in western society have been culturally forced to dislike their bodies.

Cheyfitz, Eric. *The trans-parent: sexual politics in the language of Emerson.* Baltimore: Johns Hopkins, 1981. Cheyfitz examines the obsession with manliness in Emerson's work using a psychoanalytic approach. Most interesting in its work on woman and her link with nature in American thought.

Dahlberg, Frances. *Woman the gatherer.* New Haven: Yale University Press, 1981. An anthology of data and theories describing women in evolution. The focus is on women who live in hunting and gathering societies.

Estrada, Alvaro. *Maria Sabina: her life & chants.* New York: Ross-Erikson, 1981. Maria Sabina is a Mazatec Indian shaman whose chants are beautiful poetry of interest to humanists and anthropologists. Jerome Rothenberg's preface puts Sabina's role as a shaman into cultural context.

Frontiers 1982. 6, no. 3. Special issue. Native Amerian Women.

Gay, Jane W. *With the Nez Perces: Alice Fletcher in the field, 1889-92.* Lincoln: University of Nebraska Press, 1981. This remarkable document records the adventures of two outstanding women of the late nineteenth century: Anthropologist Alice Fletcher, whose task it was to assign Indians to specific tracts of land for the government; and her companion E. Jane Gay, who took photographs of the work in the field and who wrote long letters to Eastern friends about their work and experiences.

Glendinning, Victoria. *Edith Sitwell: a unicorn among lions.* New York: Knopf, 1981. This is excellent for the way it captures the rather eccentric Edith in her early twentieth-century, British literary milieu.

Green, Rayna. "Native American women: review essay." *Signs.* 6 (1980):248-67. A significant contribution to the documentation of work in this area.

Haber, Barbara. *Women in America: a guide to books, 1963-1975*, with an appendix on books published 1976-1979. Urbana: University of Illinois Press, 1981. This is a most readable and select bibliography, and is possibly the only paperback bibliography in women's studies.

Hamalian, Leo. *Ladies on the loose: women travellers of the 18th and 19th centuries.* New York: Dodd, 1981. A wonderfully entertaining and informative collection of travels to the four corners of the earth in diary form. Margaret Fuller's observations of Italy and Mary Kingsey's observations of the African jungle are among the seventeen selections.

Hess, Karen. *Martha Washington's book of cookery.* New York: Columbia University Press, 1981. Hess's work represents what is being done in the field of culinary history.

Hrdy, Sarah Blaffer. *The woman that never evolved.* Cambridge: Harvard University Press, 1981. A sociobiologist and feminist, Hrdy believes that evolutionary biology can prove that the sexually passive, noncompetitive, all-nurturing woman of prevailing myth could never have evolved with the primate order, although males are universally dominant over females in the primate species.

Hull, Gloria; Smith, Barbara; and Scott, Patricia Bell, eds. *Black women's studies*. Old Westbury, N.Y.: Feminist Press, 1981. This is the most nearly definitive treatment of black women in the area of feminist scholarship.

Jordan, June. *Civil wars*. Boston: Beacon, 1981. One of the most compelling books of 1981. Jordan's essays of the 1960s and 1970s are collected here—everything from a plan for Harlem she devised with Buckminster Fuller to black studies and black feminism.

Journal of Popular Culture 15, no. 3 (1981). This special issue on Canadian women writers explores the work of Antonine Maillet, Marie-Claire Blais, Susanna Moodie, Catharine Parr Traill, Emily Carr, Martha Ostenso, Dorothy Livesay, and Margaret Laurence.

Kennaway, James, and Kennaway, Susan. *The Kennaway papers*. New York: Holt, Rhinehart & Winston, 1981. Although this autobiography is not precisely humanities scholarship, its documentation of a marriage is highly literary and filled with tragedy.

Koehler, Lyle. *A search for power: the "weaker sex" in seventeenth-century New England*. Urbana: University of Illinois Press, 1980. Little was availalbe on women in seventeenth-century studies during 1981 besides this incredible study of sex, sexism, women's work, sex-role stereotyping, religious rebels, and witchcraft in early New England. The book is heavily documented and has a first-rate bibliography.

Kersey, Shirley Nelson. *Classics in the education of girls and women*. Metuchen, N.J.: Scarecrow Press, 1981. Kersey has assembled a book of readings by famous men and women on the education of women—Plato, St. Jerome, Erasmus, Sir Thomas More, Rousseau, Emma Willard, and Catharine Beecher.

Mainiero, Linda, ed. *American women writers*. Vol. 3. New York: Ungar, 1981. This volume of the series begins with Laura Jean Libbey and ends with Joanna Russ. Poet Amy Lowell, novelist Carson McCullers, journalist Aimee Semple McPhearson, and anthropologist Margaret Mead are among the women who get competent biographical and bibliographic treatment in this excellent tool for beginning research.

McAlexander, Hubert Horton. *The prodigal daughter: a biography of Sherwood Bonner*. Baton Rouge: Louisiana State University Press, 1981. Bonner's novels (*Like unto like* [1878] and *The Valcours* [1881]) are all but forgotten. Bonner, herself a radical and an outcast from Southern society because of her decision to become a writer after abandoning her marriage, lived a painful, romantic, exciting life. McAlexander's scholarship is representative of the research that is being undertaken to recover the lives of forgotten American women writers.

McCullough, Joan. *First of all: significant "firsts" by American women.* New York: Holt, Rinehart & Winston, 1981. A reference source that says what it does. These sorts of references are invaluable for checking sources, names, and dates.

Maenad: A Women's Literary Journal. A feminist quarterly featuring splendid visuals. Volume 1 began in 1980. Maenad, P.O. Box 738, Gloucester, MA 01930. $16.00 per year.

Mebane, Mary E. *An autobiography.* New York: Viking, 1981. Mary Mebane writes of growing up in the 1930s in rural North Carolina. Although her descriptions of black girlhood in the country are notable for their splendid portraits of nature, one is drawn to this for its human conflict between the author and her mother. Mebane is an educator living in Wisconsin.

Miller, Sally M. *Flawed liberation: socialism and feminism.* Westport, Conn.: Greenwood Press, 1981. Miller has assembled a path-breaking group of essays that "demonstrate conclusively . . . the Socialist party of Eugene V. Debs, Morris Hillquit, and Victor Berger was also the party of May Wood Simons, Lena Morrow Lewis, and Kate Richards O'Hare." One of the chief criticisms leveled against the new social history of the Socialist Party has been the exclusion, not only of the contributions of the most visible Socialist women, but of rank-and-file women who worked mainly in their local communities. Much of the work in this volume traces these lost women through letters, diaries, Socialist periodicals, and other primary sources. The bibliographic essay will be important for those doing research in this relatively untouched area.

Moraga, Cherrie, and Moraga, Anzaldua, eds. *This bridge called my back: writing by radical women of color.* Watertown, Mass.: Persephone Press. 1981. Many first-person accounts of the lesbian experience by women of color.

Nin, Anaïs. *The diary of Anaïs Nin,* Volume VII, 1966-1974, edited and with a preface by G. Stuhlmann. New York: Harcourt Brace Jovanovich, 1981. This is the last volume of one of the most remarkable diaries in twentieth-century letters. In *Toward a new poetry* (Ann Arbor: University of Michigan, 1981), Diane Wakoski writes, "I see Anaïs Nin as a symbol . . . her spirit prevailing all this time and helping all serious experimenters to see their own possibilities."

Oakley, Ann. *Subject women.* Oxford: Martin Robertson, 1981. Oakley calls this "a history and sociology of late twentieth-century industrialized society." She writes of women's studies, the rise of women's liberation in the 1960s, of Freudian analysis, education for women, domestic work, and male politics. Her table of types of feminisms is an extremely useful reference source. A most provocative contemporary history of feminism.

Paige, Karen Ericksen, and Paige, Jeffery M. *The politics of reproductive ritual.* Berkeley: University of California Press, 1981. This new anthropological study inquires into the theory of origins and purposes of reproductive rituals—male circumcision, menstrual taboo, and birth practices. The central question is why these practices are present in some cultures, absent in others.

Pearson, Carol, and Pope, Katherine. *The female hero in American and British literature.* New York: Bowker, 1981. Pearson and Pope continue the work they began in *Who am I this time? Female portraits in British and American literature* (New York: McGraw-Hill, 1976). Women heroes are defined as females on their own quests.

Radway, Janice. "The utopian impulse in popular literature: gothic romances and 'feminist' protest." *American Quarterly* 33, no. 2 (1981):140-62. This analysis of popular 1960s and 1970s romances hinges its arguments on the popularity of these formulaic narratives concurrent with the new social mores developing with 1960s and 1970s feminism. The appendix of novels includes works by Victoria Holt, Mary Stewart, Phyllis Whitney, Dorothy Eden, Norah Lofts, and Andre Norton.

Raven, Susan, and Weir, Alison. *Women of achievement: thirty-five centuries of history.* New York: Harmony/Crown, 1981. An attractive biographical, picture-book compilation. Arranged along predictable lines, it includes sections on politics and power, education and social reform, the written word, travel and exploration, and performing arts.

Register, Cheri. "Literary criticism: a review essay." *Signs* 6 (1980):268-82.

Roberts, J. R., comp. *Black lesbians: an annotated bibliography.* Tallahassee, Fla.: Naiad Press, 1981. Well-annotated bibliography of material that is probably not found readily in other bibliographic sources. Chapters are topical: Liberation, literature and criticism, music, oppression, photography, and periodicals.

Robinson, William H. *Phillis Wheatley: a bio-bibliography.* Boston: G. K. Hall, 1981. A splendid job of organizing and placing in context the existing scholarship on Wheatley.

A selected bibliography of works by Chicanas. New York: Vance, 1981.

Seligman, Dee. *Doris Lessing: an annotated bibliography of criticism.* Westport, Conn.: Greenwood Press, 1981. An important bibliography on Lessing, this is the first major organization of her scholarship and fiction since Selma R. Burkom's *Doris Lessing: a checklist of primary and sec-*

ondary sources (New York: Whitson, 1973). This is the place to start on Lessing research.

Shostak, Marjorie. *Nisa: the life and words of a !Kung woman.* Cambridge: Harvard University Press, 1981. Shostak profiles the life of a woman in a hunting and gathering society who lives in the Kalahari Desert of southern Africa. This is a magnificent documentation of the difficult life of an independent woman, a mother of five children, none of whom survived the rigors of the hostile environment in which Nisa makes her way.

Signs 7, no. 1 (Autumn 1981). Contains a special section on "French feminist theory." Essays on and by Luce Irigaray, Hélène Cixous, and Julia Kristeva, among others participating in the "intellectual crisis of French feminism."

Silko, Leslie Marmon. *Storyteller.* New York: Seaver, 1981. The fabulous aspect of Silko's work here—the retelling of folktales from her childhood on the Luguna Pueblo in New Mexico—seems more akin to poetry than to fiction. Silko is interested in the process os storytelling and how one transcribes the vitality of the spoken story or legend into the written word.

Slaughter, Jane, and Kern, Robert. *European women on the left.* Westport, Conn.: Greenwood Press, 1981. In scope and treatment this is similar to Marsh's *Anarchist women* (1981) cited in References.

Stetson, E., ed. *Black sister: poetry by American black women, 1746-1980.* Bloomington: Indiana University Press, 1981.

Terborg-Penn, Rosalyn. "Teaching the history of black women: a bibliographic essay." *Women's Studies Quarterly* 9, no. 2 (1981):16-17. The author acknowledges the lack of secondary material in black women's history and proceeds to do an excellent job in outlining what is available. Black women have been overlooked even in the traditional scholarship, so in a sense talking about the new scholarship continues to be the task of recovering lost women. Sources here include material on black women in religion, in the family, and in the women's and civil rights movements.

Thurin, Erik Ingvar. *Emerson as priest of Pan: a study in the metaphysics of sex.* Lawrence: The Regents Press of Kansas, 1981. Although feminists might take exception with various aspects of Thurin's analysis and illuminate others by asking different questions, he discusses Emerson's views of love and sex in a thorough and detailed manner new to Emersonian scholarship. The chapter "Sexual polarity and sexual politics: Emerson and the emancipation of women" holds particular interest for feminist scholars.

Tingley, Elizabeth, and Tingley, Donald F. *Women and feminism in American history: a guide to information sources.* Detroit: Gale, 1981. Clearly a reference source, major bibliographies, biographical directories, periodicals, and manuscript collections of interest to women's historians are identified with brief annotations. Tingley and Tingley cite a feast of titles under the topics romantic, Victorian, colonial eras; arts, science, politics; ethnic and minority women; prostitution; violence; and motherhood. The materials are mainly books, a few articles, and a very few dissertations.

Trilling, Diana. *Mrs. Harris: the death of the Scarsdale diet doctor.* New York: Harcourt Brace Jovanovich, 1981. Literary critic Trilling's handling of this sensational crime of the 1980s makes this a book of compelling, most contemporary social history.

Weiser, Marjorie P. K., and Arbiter, Jean S. *Womanlist.* New York: Atheneum, 1981. An interesting and entertaining reference book.

Williams, Selma. *Divine rebel: the life of Anne Marbury Hutchinson.* New York: Holt, Rinehart & Winston, 1981. An exploration of Anne Hutchinson of the seventeenth-century Antinomian controversy. Although not an in-depth scholarly treatment, Williams does a fine job in establishing Hutchinson as a woman ahead of her time.

Wilson, Gilbert. *Waheenee: an Indian girl's story*, introduction by Gilbert Hanson. Lincoln: University of Nebraska Press/Bison, 1981. This is a resurrection of an anthropologist's transcription of Waheenee-wea or Buffalo-Bird Woman's story first published in 1921. Waheenee was a woman of the Hidatsa tribe killed off by smallpox in what is now North Dakota. Her story illuminates the experience of being a woman of the Hidatsa.

Women's Studies 8, nos. 1 and 2 (1981). Special issue. Women of classical Greece and Rome.

Women's Studies 8, no 3 (1981). Special issue. Colette's novels.

Women's Studies Monograph Series. National Institute of Education, U.S. Department of Education, 1980, 1981. For sale by the Superintendent of Documents, U.S. Government Printing Office, Washington, DC 20401. The eighth monograph in this series, *Minority women in women's studies*, is a summary of issues in the humanities and other disciplines of crucial concern to minority women.

Yeazell, Ruth. *The death and letters of Alice James.* Berkeley: University of California Press, 1981. Following on the heels of Jean Strouse's major biography (1980), Yeazell's work present new letters that fill out the portrait of the almost forgotten, gifted sister of Henry and William James. Yeazell's thesis is built around Alice's central project: A life spent in learning how to die. She finds that "the record is generally blank" when it comes to the "acutely intelligent" James' attempts to figure out the causes of sister Alice's life-long invalidism. Yeazell's work is a notable achievement in recovering the story of a forgotten woman in a major American family.

6 | Politics and Law

Peggy Simpson

Overview

On the first Monday in October 1981, Sandra Day O'Connor took the oath as the first woman justice on the Supreme Court, shattering a sex barrier of 191 years. The evening of her ninety-nine to zero Senate confirmation, celebrating with a candlelight dinner, she said: "Thomas Jefferson and James Madison would be turning over in their graves right now—but let's hope that Abigail Adams would be pleased."

It was a rare breakthrough for women in a year noted most for urgent efforts to control damage from an across-the-board onslaught by President Reagan's administration against decades of gains made by women.

It was a year when the role of women in society—today as well as in the future—was once again a hotly debated topic. On the positive side, a feminist who mastered stump-speaking by campaigning for the Equal Rights Amendment was elected mayor of Houston, confounding the odds. The public supported stronger measures against rape and sexual harassment. Courts continued to knock down barriers that kept women from nontraditional "male" jobs. The pay equity frontier was widened slightly when the city of San Jose and then the state of California ordered revision of wage scales along a comparable worth measure of jobs done by men and women.

But the year was full of reversals. The ERA remained blocked in state legislatures with scant chance of approval before the June 30, 1982, deadline. The Supreme Court ruled that women could be excluded from registration for a military draft and that women who had followed a traditional role as dependent spouses of military men could not share in their husbands' pensions if they divorced. In Congress there was a standoff between beleagured defenders of women's rights and New Right activists advocating a constitutional amendment banning abortion and a proposed family protection act.

150

The most radical and wrenching reversals, however, occurred in the Reagan administration itself. By year's end the government appeared to have abdicated its decades-old advocacy of wider options for women and minorities. Those seeking sex equity would have to do so without the help of government, and in some cases they would have to fight to stop the government from dismantling structures and tools that had been put in place with bipartisan support.

Reagan's candidacy had been opposed by virtually all feminist and minority groups but most expected he would moderate his conservative views when he took office, as he had done as governor of California presiding over a liberal Democratic legislature. He seemed to be trying to reassure critics in his inaugural address when he asked: "How can we love our country and not love our countrymen and, loving them, not reach out a hand when they fall, heal them when they're sick and provide opportunity to make them self-sufficient so they will be equal in fact and not just in theory?"

As 1981 evolved Reagan critics assumed he had meant that the private sector—and those much-ballyhooed volunteers—would provide that healing help, not the federal government.

Reagan broke the tradition of the two previous administrations and chose an all-male cabinet. Republican feminists had no entree to the White House and, paradoxically, neither did antifeminist Phyllis Schlafly who had wanted to be Secretary of Defense. Women were left out of the top decision-making levels despite the selection of political scientist Jeane Kirkpatrick as ambassador to the United Nations.

The problem posed by the scarcity of women appointees paled, however, compared to the thundering impact of Reagan's retreat from policies shaped by bipartisan majorities for twenty years to help remedy inequities faced by women and minorities.

Reversals came through a combination of methods: Budget cuts targeted toward social welfare programs that disproportionately affect women; appointment of conservative ideologues—or, as in the case of major civil rights agencies, the lack of any appointees, which crippled their ability to function; rejection of class action suits and back pay remedies for most job equity cases; and a stated attempt to overturn the Supreme Court's recent endorsement of affirmative action.

Reagan's two core constituencies, business and New Right conservatives, applauded these reversals, although for different reasons. Business expected Reagan to dilute or abolish affirmative action goals they considered burdensome. Social conservatives, especially a newly invigorated and heavily financed religious Right, favored a dramatically restricted role for women that focused on their childbearing functions and their dependent, submissive role in the family.

The New Right's goals included constitutional bans on abortion and affirmative action..They fought laws that would guard against child abuse or domestic violence, saying this abrogated parental rights to punish their children—or a husband's right to beat his wife, presumbly. Sen. Jeremiah Denton (R-Ala.) a former prisoner-of-war recruited in 1980 by the Moral Majority, opposed legislation making marital rape a crime, saying he considered rape a hideous act but that a husband guilty of "a little coercion" should not be in the same category as criminal rapists, adding, "Dammit, when you get married you kind of expect you are going to get a little sex."

The Reagan Revolution and the rise of the New Right occurred against a backdrop of historic shifts in lives of women and men. Women have made dramatic gains in most segments of society. They have tripled their numbers in elected political office since 1970. With the help of new laws and the government as an advocate, they have broken into higher-paying nontraditional jobs ranging from coal miners to bank executives. Women now make up 43 percent of the full-time work force (an unprecedented 45,760,000 women workers), often taking time out to have children but then returning to the job market. They also are having fewer children. As they become a more significant and established part of society outside the home, they have made their case, again with the help of the government, against pay inequities, sexual harassment on the job and violence against women ranging from rape to wife-battering.

These are the trends the New Right wants to change or reverse. Clearly, 1981 was a time of great flux for women in the political and economic sphere, with Reagan and the New Right drawing a line in the dirt dividing those who favored expanded options for women in society and those who insisted on a return to more traditional roles.

Antifeminist Phyllis Schlafly, who won notoriety for her Senate testimony that "sexual harassment . . . is not a problem for the virtuous woman," led the New Right's attack on affirmative action as the root of the current evil. She said it constitutes "sexual harassment of the role of motherhood and of the traditional family lifestyle."

Neoconservative Midge Decter ridiculed feminists as misguided "haters" who kept feminine women captive rather than freeing them, convincing them they were victims of society's discrimination rather than enabling them to fight against their bondage. In 1981 conservatives loved to quote Betty Friedan, the theorist of the modern women's movement, and her new arguments that women must not be "antifamily" and must build bridges with men to secure their own future.

But conservatives were not the only critics made uneasy by women's gains and the claims they put on the future. The "neoliberal" group of moderate Democrats, for instance, talked about social reforms of the 1960s as aberrations that must be set aside. They spoke with disdain of "special interests" who clamored for "equality of results, not equality of opportunity" (Rothenberg 1982). They talked about the need to scuttle the Democratic Party's 1972 reform rule that had mandated an equal division of women and men convention delegates, and late in 1981 the party leaders took the first steps to do just that. The neoliberal guru, Washington Monthly editor Charles Peters, questioned why, in the depths of the current recession, any employers would hire women. The clear implication: That women would stay at home again, as they did with society's blessing after both world wars.

As the year evolved, public opinion about Reagan began to shift dramatically. Voters began to draw distinctions between their affection for a personable, gregarious president who had survived an assassination attempt with courage and humor, and his policies that would take the country back to a simpler day.

A "gender gap" emerged. Women supported Reagan in fewer numbers than men did. The year-end differences measured up to 16 percent, a historic polling phenomenon that political scientists said was not duplicated in polls going back to President Eisenhower. Reagan supporters dismissed the gender gap as insignificant, saying it was partly a war-and-peace difference but also that women were "lagging" indicators compared to men and ultimately would vote in similar ways as men. Women's rights groups ridiculed that interpretation; but both sides knew that the proving ground for the existence of a gender gap as well as the test of Reagan's policies would be the 1982 elections.

Reagan Administration

Appointments

Despite the near-unanimous acclaim for President Reagan's selection of Sandra Day O'Connor for the Supreme Court, both the ideological bent of many of his other appointees and the scarcity of women to appointed posts came under attack. Known feminist ties or support of the Equal Rights Amendment appeared almost automatically to disqualify contenders for top jobs in the Reagan regime despite White House denials. This helped eliminate many nationally known GOP feminists, including the thirty who had formed a Reagan-Bush Women's Advisory Task Force after the 1980 Republican convention to demonstrate solidarity with the ticket despite their differences with Reagan over his opposition to the ERA and abortion.

By the end of 1981 Reagan had named forty-four women to positions requiring Senate confirmation, 11 percent of the 400 selected. The White House contested that figure, compiled by the Coalition on Women's Appointments representing nearly 100 groups, saying if women named to boards and part-time commissions were included the total number was closer to seventy, which matched the record of former President Carter.

The appointments were to vastly different levels of jobs, however. Carter had two women in his cabinet; Reagan had no women heading cabinet agencies, although U.N. Ambassador Kirkpatrick was given cabinet rank. Carter named three women as under-secretaries, Reagan none; Carter named seven women as general counsels in cabinet agencies. Reagan none; Carter chose five women as inspectors general, Reagan one. Thirteen women served as ambassador under Carter. By year's end Reagan had named three.

Another major change came in appointments to the federal judiciary. Of forty-three federal district or circuit level judges named by Reagan in his first year, only one was a woman. It appeared that women candidates for judgeships underwent a rigorous scrutiny on their abortion views, in contrast to male contenders.

Many who did get jobs were New Right activists who had led the fight against the ERA, abortion, and affirmative action. The most notable was Interior Secretary James Watt, who founded the Mountain States Legal Foundation (MSLF) in Denver that mounted legal challenges against affirmative action and Title IX, and helped orchestrate the suit against the ERA time extension. Another key appointee, Solicitor General Rex Lee, was a board member of the MSLF and wrote a major book criticizing the ERA while dean of the law school at Brigham Young University in Utah.

Another major New Right appointee was Donald Devine, a board member of the Young Americans for Freedom, who became director of the Office of Personnel Management that oversees federal employees and their health insurance. A nationally known crusader against abortion and affirmative action, Devine set about to eliminate abortion coverage from federal health plans. He also moved swiftly to try to purge Planned Parenthood from groups eligible for the federal charitable donation drive. That did not succeed but he promised to renew his attempt in 1982, as well as to oust such new arrivals in the federal funds campaign as the Women's Legal Defense Fund.

Other members of the New Right who received Reagan appointments were Everett Koop as surgeon general, who in his national campaign against abortion had criticized birth control and reproductive health research and had branded amniocentesis as little more than a "search and destroy" operation; JoAnn Gasper, who headed a fundamentalist group called The Right Woman, to be a deputy assistant secretary for social services policy working on children and family issues; Marjory Mecklenberg, another leading anti-abortion activist, to head the office on adolescents and youths; and Robert Billings, the Moral Majority's first executive director, as liaison officer for a 10-state region of the Department of Education.

Budget Cuts and Policies

Women took a major beating in Reagan's $35 billion budget cuts. The overwhelming majority of cuts came in the social welfare programs that serve mostly women and children. Others were targeted at programs that carried little money but had been enacted especially to widen options for women or to end inequities against them in sports, education, science, or small business. Women's groups called the cuts a devastating frontal attack on the safety net built up over decades to deal with problems of women, including the very elderly and the very young. University of Maryland economics professor Barbara R. Bergmann told the Joint Economic Committee of Congress early in 1982 that the Reagan administration, in reversing recent gains made by women, was exacerbating the already precarious economic status of millions of women, adding, "it is not an exaggeration to say that the Reagan administration has declared economic war on women, particularly on those women who do not have a man to depend on" (Bergmann 1982).

Reagan proposed even more drastic cuts for 1983. For the budget that covered 1982, these hurt the most: 400,000 families were ousted from rolls of the Aid to Families with Dependent Children program and another 287,000 families found benefits reduced; $1 billion was cut from the Medicaid program, mostly by making ineligible the families losing AFDC benefits; 150,000 women were booted from federal job training programs that were ended; a related program that had trained and placed 100,000 displaced homemakers in 1980 also was ended; 14.5 million children were shorn from the subsidized school lunch program and millions more lost free milk and snacks at day-care and summer-school programs. The previously open-ended $900 million nutrition program for Women, Infants, and Children (WIC) was restricted despite proof this innovative new program had headed off malnutrition and related health problems for infants and children in low-income families.

Rents were increased for families in public housing units, two-thirds of which are headed by women, and money was curbed for construction of further low-income subsidized housing. The Women's Bureau in the Department of Labor was cut by nearly one-third compared to a 5.5 percent cut for other Labor agencies. Across the government, enforcement and investigative funds for civil rights agencies were reduced although Congress restored some funds against Reagan's will.

One clear target was money for family planning. Funds were reduced sharply, but Congress refused to go along with Reagan's plan to wrap this program into an amorphous block grant that states could use as they wished, thus leaving family planning subject to total extinction as New Right lobbyists wanted. About 4.5 million girls and women benefit from medical services and educational counseling provided by funds under Title X. In exchange for preserving the program intact, sponsors agreed to accept a new so-called "chastity" program, a $30 million experiment that will attempt to offer alternatives (not including abortion) to pregnant or sexually active teenagers. Early in 1982 new restrictions were imposed on family planning centers, one of which being that officials must notify parents of birth control advice or devices given minors. Reagan defended this as "parental rights." This proposal, which the president attempted to implement without legislation, is one of the key proposals in the New Right's Family Protection Act. The very publicity over the parental notification proposal caused a sharp drop-off in requests by teenagers for help from family planning centers in February.

Older women were especially hard-hit by budget cuts and the pain may increase for them in the future. Sixty percent of women older than sixty-five who are unmarried, widowed, divorced, or separated rely totally on Social Security as their source of income. Because they held lower-paying jobs than men did or because they were out of the labor force for many years, their benefits averaged only $230 a month compared to $339 for men. Nearly three million elderly women receive only the minimum Social Security benefit of $122 a month. Reagan proposed to eliminate that, saying those who were poor enough could apply for other forms of welfare. After a national outcry, he was forced to preserve the minimum benefit for those currently receiving it, but he will permit no others to become eligible after 1981.

Another Reagan reduction hit widowed mothers particularly hard. Social Security benefits to finance college costs were curtailed for children older than eighteen and were to be phased out entirely by 1985. Widows' sustenance benefits also were diminished. When her children turn sixteen the widow must find work or a training program that will lead to employment.

One reason why a successful across-the-board assault could be mounted only months after Reagan took office was because a New Right think tank, the Heritage Foundation, had prepared a 1,093-page road-map for conservative change. It outlined the dismantling of much of the civilian part of government and detailed reversals of policies. To an astounding degree, the Reagan team followed this blueprint. The massive budget cuts were part of the plan. So were the three-year individual tax cuts (which were expanded to a $750 billion package once Reagan and the Congress finished their bidding war) to spur savings and business investment, but also to deplete the federal treasury so significantly that there would be little money to continue social programs or to start new ones.

Heritage criticized some programs in revealing specifity. It damned the Women's Educational Equity Act (WEEA) as "a top priority for the feminist network . . . an important resource for the practice of feminist policies and politics. Its programs require immediate scrutiny and its budget should be drastically cut" (Heatherly 1981). Reagan proposed doing just that but congressional supporters, led by Rep. Margaret Heckler (R-Mass.), salvaged a $6 million budget for the activity.

For the Heritage Foundation, however, "affirmative action is the sorest point of all . . . it should be jettisoned as soon as it is politically possible to do so. In the meantime, it should not be administered with a heavy hand."

This advice was carried out with a vengeance and with disregard for recent Supreme Court mandates supporting remedial hiring of women or minorities and the use of goals and timetables in which to do so. In some cases the Reagan administration simply stopped enforcing antibias laws. In others, decisions on filing suits or awarding back pay as remedies for discrimination were centralized in the agency headqauarters, thus effectively creating a backlog and eliminating much action. Key policy jobs were left vacant, paralyzing entire agencies such as the Equal Employment Opportunity Commission (EEOC)

By the fall, the Justice Department had taken the lead in the civil rights rollback. It disputed the EEOC's authority to require federal agencies to set goals and timetables for increasing employment for women and minorities. It abandoned these tools in its own efforts to correct systemic discrimination in employment bias suits, with Assistant Attorney General William Bradford

Reynolds saying employers must include women or minorities in an applicant pool, but there apparently would be no penalty if employers never hired them.

In December, Reynolds went further, saying the government will seek to reverse the Supreme Court's 1979 ruling in *Steelworkers* v. *Weber* that upheld voluntarily established affirmative action plans to remedy previous discrimination practices, even though the company was under no court mandate to take such steps.

As in most of these rollbacks, Reagan's own influence was unclear. When asked at a news conference about Reynolds's intent to overturn the Weber ruling Reagan was unfamiliar with both what Reynolds was doing and with the Weber issue. After the reporter explained, the president said he couldn't disagree with voluntary attempts to remedy past inequities. Only days later, however, the White House "corrected" the record, and the attempt to undermine affirmative action was resumed.

One agency's change in course was likely to have damaging impact on efforts by women to get jobs in nontraditional fields. The Office of Federal Contract Compliance Program (OFCCP) created by executive orders dating back nearly twenty years, has the power to cut off federal contracts from employers who discriminate in employment. Due to court suits and congressional prodding, the OFCCP had become a formidable lever for opening doors in mostly male occupations including construction, mining, chemical company assembly lines, and finance. When voluntary efforts to get jobs in these areas and isolated suits did not work, OFCCP used industry wide probes and the threat of contract cutoffs to persuade employers to start hiring women. It was the threat of losing lucrative federal contracts that proved instrumental in getting the employers to begin training programs and to hire and promote women.

Under the leadership of former corporate executive Ellen Shong, the OFCCP said it no longer would pursue industrywide investigations, would rely on the good faith of employers to hire more women and minorities, would suggest dropping back pay as a penalty against employers who discriminated, and would propose to eliminate regular scrutiny of three-fourths of the 350,000 federal contractors. Neither business nor civil rights groups were pleased.

In early 1982 the OFCCP settled a long-pending complaint against the National City Bank of Cleveland, which it earlier concluded had discriminated against women and minorities. The preliminary back-pay liability had been projected at $15 million, but the Reagan administration settled the case with no back pay penalty at all. This left the government agreeing there had been discrimination but refusing to punish the offenders or compensate the victims.

One other vehicle for freezing civil rights enforcement, at least temporarily, was a year-long study, with Vice President Bush heading the task force, of regulations or laws the administration found objectionable. Among those under study — and therefore left in legal limbo for much of 1981—were the sports provisions of Title IX and the newly adopted EEOC regulations that put the burden on employers to protect workers from sexual harassment by coworkers. Education Secretary Terrel Bell attempted to win other changes in Title IX to exempt faculty hiring and firing decisions from the jurisdiction of the antibias law and to restrict the scope further by contending that the law covered only a specific program that received federal funds rather than the college as a whole when, for instance, only subsidized student loans may have been received.

Although civil rights retrenchment has received the most attention, significant shifts in policy also occurred for women in the military. Within weeks after Reagan took office the armed services put a hold on recruiting women and began closing some specialties to women that had taken decades to open. Reagan's supporters argued that women had weakened the capability of the military and that, since they were barred from combat, they should also be barred from most other military jobs.

Lt. Col. David Evans, writing in the Naval Institute magazine *Proceedings*, said women undercut morale, drop out at higher rates than men, put undue pressure on males to pick up the slack when they are ill or pregnant, spawn sexual harassment complaints because they fraternize with men, and require separate sanitary facilities even in the field. He said, "The folk wisdom of an enlisted male Marine leaves little room for argument: 'When the platoon goes to field, she doesn't go. If they go to combat, she doesn't go. If they go aboard a ship, she doesn't go. Why is she in this platoon?'"

The number of women in uniform more than tripled since 1971 to 150,000 in 1979. The Carter administration, moving to strengthen the all-volunteer service, projected an increase by 1986 to 225,000 women, or 12 percent of the total. But in 1981 the number of female recruits dropped 15 percent. The Army signed up 4,000 fewer women than it had the year before and planned to cut back by another 1,500 in 1982. The Air Force recruited only 11,000 women, 3,000 fewer than the year before; the Navy decreased its recruitment by about 7 percent. A Reagan-appointed Defense Advisory Committee on Women in the Services was studying such issues as the pregnancy rate, physical fitness, child care, sea-shore rotation, and retention.

A retired Army general, Andrew J. Gatsis (1981), writing in the *Conservative Digest*, stated the objections against women in the military in blunt terms, saying it is linked to the move to "unisex the society through the women's movement." He said women cannot do the heavy work required in most field operations and the sexual abuse from their male colleagues makes them "an even greater liability." His most emotional argument against women in the military was a traditional plea to protect them from such hard realities as war.

> Are they ready to see their daughters and wives exposed to the
> wrath of the enemy because they could not dig into the hard
> ground in time for protection? Do they desire to have them sub-

jected to the stench of bloated and ripened bodies left in the sun several days? . . . Do they want their daughters out on recovery patrols to shovel up decomposed human flesh into rubber sacks for evidence identification? Have the ERA proponents thought about what our women would suffer from the dregs of our own army alone, not to speak of what the enemy would do to them as POWs? How can we reconcile our moral perceptions of women with these immoralities of war? . . . We just understand what is at stake. One does not send in the second team when our national survival is in jeopardy, just to satisfy the whims of a disgruntled group of women liberationists. No matter how hard the feminists try to achieve total equality in the armed forces, the most they can hope to become is second-class men. (Gatsis 1981).

Reagan's position on women in the military remained unclear as the year ended. Although the hold on recruiting women apparently remained firm, in early February Secretary of Defense Casper W. Weinberger ordered the services: "Aggressively break down those remaining barriers that prevent us from making the fullest use of the capabilities of women."

Retrenchment and erosion were the bywords of 1981. With two exceptions, the Reagan administration cut back rather than began new programs or policies for women. In the early fall, he launched a Fifty States Project by appointing a White House assistant as liaison to governors to help them identify laws or policies that discriminate. No federal action would be contemplated but a clearinghouse of information could result. In late December, Reagan formed a twenty-one-member White House Task Force on Legal Equity and gave it "a clear presidential mandate" to extinguish sex discrimination. The task force will not actively review rules and regulations, however, but will forward proposed rule revisions to pertinent agencies after approval by several strata of Justice Department and cabinet level agencies.

Legislation

Although he did not specifically sponsor the New Right's legislative agenda, Reagan endorsed most of it and said he would sign it if it came to the White House. This included laws on proposed constitutional bans on abortion, busing, and affirmative action, and the family protection act, or restrictions on such sex equity programs as Title IX.

The year ended with a standoff between women's rights advocates and those favoring a restricted role for women, however. Most of the New Right's social agenda was left for 1982, and although he backed it publicly, Reagan was advised not to appear to sponsor any of its controversial items that polls say the majority does not favor.

In addition to budget cuts that furthered the New Right's goals of curbing Planned Parenthood, Legal Services, and other "agents of change," they won adoption of a $30 million so-called chastity program for teenage women and new tax breaks for families that adopt children.

Extensive hearings were held on abortion amendments, including a bill by Senator Jesse Helms (R-N.C.) that would declare Congress's conclusion that life begins at conception and that fetuses are "persons" protected by the Fourteenth Amendment, thus making abortion murder. By the end of the year antiabortion measures had been approved by two subcommittees, paving the way for possible action by Congress in 1982.

A bipartisan coalition of 24 senators and 64 representatives, together with the Congresswoman's Caucus, presented a twelve-part women's rights legislative package, the economic equity act. It included bans on bias in the insurance industry and guarantees of pension rights for military spouses. These were opposed by the administration and the industry. Three other provisions, however, were added to the 1981 tax bill with very little debate: To expand the tax credit for child care for working parents from $800 to $1,200; to make a nonworking spouse eligible for an individual retirement account (IRA) in her own name, based on the working spouse's income but with a requirement that both spouses must participate; and repeal of the widow's tax that had forced many farm widows to sell their property to pay inheritance or estate taxes because tax laws assumed they had contributed little or nothing to its value.

In addition, the tax tables were changed to lessen the marriage penalty assessed a two-earner married couple who paid higher joint taxes than did two single persons earning the same amount. Reagan had campaigned for this, the New Right opposed it, and many women's rights groups kept a hands-off posture because the change automatically put single taxpayers at a relative disadvantage.

Legal Implications

Sandra Day O'Connor

Reagan called her a "person for all seasons" and said he selected her not only to fulfill his 1980 campaign pledge to appoint "the most qualified woman I could possibly find," but because she met his very high standards for any nominee to the high court.

The unexpected nomination of O'Connor came 112 years after the Supreme Court denied Myra Bradwell the right to practice law, saying that Illinois could limit membership in the bar to men only in a ruling that read in part: "Man is, or should be, woman's protector and defender. The natural and proper timidity and delicacy which belongs to the female sex evidently unfits it for many of the occupations of civil life. The constitution of the family organization, which is founded in the divine ordinance as well as in the nature of things, indicates the domestic sphere as that which properly belongs to the domain and function of womanhood. . . . The paramount destiny and mission of woman are to fulfill the noble and benign office of wife and mother."

O'Connor is a wife and mother of three, but she also is an accomplished attorney, legislator, and judge. In an era when sex discrimination was pervasive against women in the law, she was a civilian lawyer for the army, a deputy county attorney, a lawyer in private practice, an assistant attorney general in Arizona, a state senator (and first woman majority leader), a superior-court judge, and a judge on the Arizona Court of Appeals. The granddaughter of an Arizona pioneer, O'Connor left the 150,000-acre family ranch to attend Stanford University, graduating "with great distinction" from law school in 1952. Her classmates included her future husband John, and William Rehnquist, currently the Supreme Court's most conservative member.

She apparently was an early "super-mom" model, rearing three children while returning first to private law practice and then political life, and continuing as an active community volunteer as well. She experienced discrimination first hand in her early job applications. As a state senator she worked to enact many bills to advance the legal status of women such as revising the community property laws, repealing restrictive labor laws that limited the hours women could work, and passing state equal pay laws. She voted for a bill allowing family planning information to be given to minors without parental consent.

Because she had not consistently opposed family planning and abortion measures, and because in Arizona she was known as a moderate who also was a feminist, the entire array of New Right groups crusaded vigorously against her, thus winning the enmity of Reagan, who moved up her nomination after antiabortion crusaders insisted he hold off. They prompted the godfather of modern political conservatism, Sen. Barry Goldwater (R-Ariz.), to say in a fit of rage that "Every good Christian ought to kick [Moral Majority leader] Jerry Falwell right in the ass." Their opposition made O'Connor look even more impressive at the tense Senate confirmation hearings in her even-tempered refusal to be pushed into revealing her personal views on abortion.

O'Connor brought to the court an extraordinary rich mix of experiences, a judicial track record as a pragmatic conservative rather than as an ideologue, and a collegiality that could be invaluable on the splintered, leaderless court. In her first months on the bench she voted most often with Rehnquist and Chief Justice William Burger. She took pains to separate herself from them on several occasions, however, and at least once even sided with the court's two liberals, Justices William Brennan and Thurgood Marshall. By the year's end she had not voted on such controversies as sex discrimination, school desegregation, affirmative action, or abortion, but she was developing a position as a centrist similar to that of the justice she replaced, Potter Stewart, which would preserve the court's ideological line-up rather than make it far more conservative.

O'Connor was elevated to the Supreme Court as barriers to women in the law were slowly being toppled. There had been 101 male Supreme Court justices. Of the 670 federal judges, only fifty-two had been women, and forty-eight of them currently are serving; all but three were appointed by President Carter during a major expansion of the judiciary (Table 1). Reagan seemed intent on pulling back from that pattern, naming only one woman out of his

Table 1.
Women on the Federal Bench

Name	Court
Sandra Day O'Connor*	Supreme Court
Betty Fletcher	Ninth Circuit
Ruth B. Ginsburg	D.C. Circuit
Amalya Kearse	Second Circuit
Cornelia Kennedy†	Sixth Circuit
Phyllis Kravitch	Fifth Circuit
Dorothy Nelson	Ninth Circuit
Carolyn Randall	Eleventh Circuit
Mary Schroeder	Ninth Circuit
Stephanie Seymour	Tenth Circuit
Dolores Sloviter	Third Circuit
Patricia Wald	D.C. Circuit
Ann Aldrich	N.D. Ohio
Susan Black	M.D. Florida
Patricia Boyle	E.D. Michigan
Ellen Burns	D. Connecticut
Carmen Cerezo	D. Puerto Rico
Barbara Crabb	W.D. Wisconsin
Orinda Evans	N.D. Georgia
Helen Frye	D. Oregon
Susan Getzendanner	N.D. Illinois
Joyce Green	District of Columbia
June Green‡	District of Columbia
Cynthia H. Hall*	C.D. California
Norma Johnson	District of Columbia
Shirley Jones	D. Maryland
Judy Keep	S.D. California
Mary Lowe	S.D. California
Consuelo Marshall	C.D. California
Gabrielle McDonald	S.D. Texas
Constance Motley‡	S.D. New York
Diana Murphy	D. Minnesota
Marilyn Patel	N.D. California
Mariana Pfaelzer	C.D. California
Sylvia Rambo	M.D. Pennsylvania
Mary Anne Rickey§	D. Arizona
Mary Lou Robinson	N.D. Texas
Barbara Rothstein	W.D. Washington
Elsijane Roy	E. and W.D. Arizona
Norma Shapiro	E.D. Pennsylvania

Table 1. (continued)

Anna Taylor	E.D. Minnesota
Anne Thompson‡	D. New Jersey
Zita Weinshienk	D. Colorado
Veronica Wicker	E.D. Louisiana
Rya Zobel	D. Massachusetts
Helen Neis	Court of Customs and Patent Appeals

Source: The National Women's Political Caucus, January 12, 1982.
*Reagan appointees.
†Originally appointed by Nixon, elevated to circuit court by Carter.
‡Appointed by Lyndon Johnson.
§Appointed by Gerald Ford.
All others were appointed by Carter.

Table 2.
Women on Highest State Courts

Name	Court
Shirley Abrahamson	Wisconsin Supreme Court
Ruth I. Abrams	Massachusetts Supreme Judicial Court
Rose Elizabeth Bird	California Supreme Court (chief judge)
Mary S. Coleman	Michigan Supreme Court (chief judge)
Rita C. Davidson	Maryland Court of Appeals
Carolyn Dimmick	Washington Supreme Court
Jean Dubofsky	Colorado Supreme Court
Christine Durham	Utah Supreme Court
Catherine B. Kelly	District of Columbia Court of Appeals
Blanche Krupansky	Ohio Supreme Court
Julia Cooper Mack	District of Columbia Court of Appeals
Kay E. McFarland	Kansas Supreme Court
Florence Murray	Rhode Island Supreme Court
Ellen A. Peters	Connecticut Supreme Court
Betty Roberts	Oregon Supreme Court
Susie Sharp	North Carolina Supreme Court
Janie L. Shores	Alabama Supreme Court
Rosalie Wahl	Minnesota Supreme Court
Alma Wilson	Oklahoma Supreme Court

Source: The National Women's Political Caucus, 1982.

There are nineteen women out of 350 serving on the highest courts in states. There are no women on highest courts of thirty-three states.

forty-three selections in 1981 to the federal bench. Reagan also dismantled the system by which Carter had pressured senators to take extra steps to seek out women and members of minority groups for judgeships. Although civil rights and women's groups continued to put pressure on individual senators, there was fear that without help from the White House the results would culminate in the kind of recommendation GOP Sen. John Warner of Virginia submitted: A list of white males.

The judiciary remains a mostly male bastion (Table 2). No women serve on federal district courts in twenty-eight states, three-fourths of the total; none serve on one-third of the circuit courts. There are 700 women judges in courts of record and they now comprise 13 percent of the bar, or 70,000 lawyers.

Trends and Cases

The first year of the Reagan administration dramatized the fragility of many legal protections that women's rights activists had taken for granted. Some antibias regulations were frozen for review by Reagan policy makers and others were undercut by budget reductions for enforcement staffs. Still others were weakened by diminished use of such key remedial and investigatory tools as class action suits, hiring goals, timetables, and back pay penalites. The retreat by the federal government, which had taken the lead in helping women and minorities expand their rights, was sure to retard grass-roots efforts by women as well.

As many events in 1981 showed, women were breaking down discriminatory barriers across the country with lawsuits, lobbying activities, and trade union and political strength. They continued to topple protectionist practices that had kept them out of higher-paying, male-dominated trades and professions. They strengthened their legal remedies against sexual harassment and rape. They broke new legal ground in ways to remedy pay inequities between women and men, which new studies have documented to be pervasive even in the same occupations, let alone between jobs that are different but are of "comparable worth" (Treiman 1981).

There were setbacks as well in 1981. Some major ones came from the Supreme Court in rulings handed down before O'Connor joined the high bench.

Two legal blows came a day apart in June and affected women who sought nontraditional careers in the military and those who had supported their husband's careers as dependent military wives.

Women's rights advocates argued that women should be included with men in mandatory registration of eighteen-year-olds for a potential military draft, saying that this went to the heart of stereotypes about "women's place" in society. They maintained that women do not want a protected role because that translates into secondary status, especially for those in uniform who are barred from jobs leading to combat. Schlafly, who had tried to intervene in the draft registration suit, maintained that women were and wanted to remain a "protected" class," kept from war to bear and care for children (Schlafly

1981). Many men agreed. The chief of the York, Pennsylvania Human Relations Commission, Theodore P. Jefferson, Jr., speaking against women being drafted, said, "In all society you will find that animals are first concerned about preventing harm to their breeding stock."

In a five to four ruling on *Rostker* v. *Goldberg* the Supreme Court agreed that Congress had the right to exclude women from the draft registration. In writing for the majority, Justice Rehnquist said Congress was not required to "engage in gestures of superficial equality." But in a minority opinion, Justice Marshall warned that the court was placing its "imprimatur on one of the most potent remaining expressions of ancient canards about the proper role of women."

The next day the Court dealt a blow to traditional women, wives of military men, ruling they have no right to share the pensions their husbands accumulate. In the *McCarty* v. *McCarty* ruling, the Court said a wife's eighteen-year marriage to an army officer did not give her any right to the pension as part of their joint community property when they divorced. The pension was his alone, a "personal entitlement."

The Court also left intact an Illinois ruling that "separate but equal" athletic teams in contact sports are valid when Justice Stevens refused a petition from an eleven-year-old sixth grade girl to try out for the sixth grade boys' basketball team where she apparently would have been a strong contender. The school and its athletic association insisted she play with the sixth grade girls' team, although she clearly was beyond their athletic level and therefore was denied competition with her equals. Stevens said, "Without a gender-based classification in competitive contact sports, there would be a substantial risk that boys would dominate the girls' programs and deny them an equal opportunity to compete in interscholastic events." New Right conservatives have made prohibition of boys and girls competing together in sports a major priority, including it in their proposed family protection act.

In another key case, the Supreme Court upheld a Utah law that required a physician to notify parents of a minor seeking an abortion, rejecting claims this would endanger the health of the fifteen-year-old unmarried girl, still living at home, saying the state had the right to strengthen parental rights. Again, "parental rights" has become a rallying cry for conservatives.

As antiabortion legislation moved through the United States Senate, state action on this controversy was mixed. The Pennsylvania legislature defeated a national model antiabortion bill drafted by Americans United for Life of Chicago. The Massachusetts Legislature ruled that conscientious objection to abortion could not be a basis for job dismissal or refusal to promote. In Michigan, Juvenile Court Judge Donald Halstead of Kalamazoo came under national attention for refusing to permit an abortion for an eleven-year-old girl made pregnant by her mother's boyfriend. The judge, whose antiabortion views were well known, delayed action on the girl's request, and then ruled it was too late to terminate her pregnancy.

In other major cases the Supreme Court:

Struck down a Louisiana law giving husbands total control over community property, which had led to the sale of a jointly owned homestead to pay for debts a wife did not know her estranged husband had accumulated.

Let stand a California law that gender distinction was valid in permitting prosecution of a minor male for rape or sexual intercourse with a female who also was a minor, on grounds the state had a "strong interest" in preventing pregnancies.

Reversed a Texas ruling and said employers had discretion to choose among "equally qualified candidates" with no obligation to promote a woman who was no better qualified than two male applicants.

Let stand a New York move striking down a law that outlawed sodomy between consenting adults, bringing to twenty-five the states that have removed such laws from their books.

Pay Equity and Comparable Worth. Pay equity issues clearly were among the most significant on the legal horizon, with the related comparable worth argument posing potential for changes of earthshaking proportions in women's role in today's work environment.

The Supreme Court removed a major roadblock from pursuit of pay equity issues with a five to four decision that women can sue on allegations that their pay is discriminatory even if they are not comparing their jobs with those of men. The court in *County of Washington, Oregon* v. *Gunther,* agreed with four women jail guards that they should be able to sue for sex bias even though they were not alleging they should receive equal pay for equal work. Their jobs differed from those of male guards but they said sex bias accounted for at least some of the 25 percent pay disparity. In effect, the Court said the equal pay act did not preclude persons from suing for damages under the far broader Title VII of the 1964 civil rights act when pay bias can be proved without a direct comparison of men's and women's work.

Two major federal studies illustrated the dimensions of the pay equity dilemma. A three-year, $210,000 study of comparable worth issues by the National Research Council of the National Academy of Sciences concluded that persistent discrimination keeps women's pay 40 percent lower than men's, despite decades of struggle for equity. Reflecting the changed political climate, no new federal policy to remedy the problem was recommended. In early 1982 the Bureau of Labor Statistics in the Department of Labor found that even in the same occupations women earn far less than their male counterparts. Hospital health technicians, for instance, earned an average of $273 if they were women and $324 if they were men; women elementary school teachers averaged $68 a week less than men; women bookkeepers earned $98 a week less than men doing the same work; and male computer systems analysts earned $546 a week compared to $420 for women.

Two trend-setting decisions in Georgia and California in 1981 provided new leverage to remedy the continuing pattern of pay inequities. Federal judges held that a woman's salary at her previous job could not be the sole basis for start-up wages at a new job because this perpetuated societal patterns of discrimination in which women were valued less than men for the same work. The Georgia judge struck down a rapid-transit pay scale where, based simply on her past wages, a woman was paid less than a man doing the same job. In Sacramento, a judge ordered Allstate Insurance Co. to pay sales agents equally who were training for the same positions, nullifying the company's system in which a woman trainee drew a stipend of $825 a month compared to $1,000 for male trainees in the same class—again, based on her previous salary.

Women also used union muscle to gain breakthroughs on the controversial comparable worth issue. Two thousand city employees in San Jose, California, represented by the American Federation of State, County, and Municipal Employees (AFSCME) held a nine-day strike after a study found that jobs dominated by women paid between 2 percent and 10 percent below the city average, but jobs dominated by men averaged 8 percent to 15 percent above the city average. A librarian earned $5,746 less than a senior chemist at the sewage plant. The mayor's secretary earned 47 percent less than a senior air conditioning mechanic.

The strike produced a pledge that San Jose would spend $1.45 million in the next two years to equalize salaries of city workers. Later in the year, the state of California followed suit, starting in January 1982 to determine salaries based on the value of work for women-dominated jobs. Annual reports were due to be made to the legislature and to the unions bargaining for state workers. Hawaii subsequently passed a resolution urging all employers to adopt the concept of equal pay for work of comparable value. Studies were begun in other states. The Kentucky Commission on Human Rights found the pay gap in its state was widening between women and men from $1,836 in 1976 to $3,466 in 1980.

In some areas, unions have taken the lead in helping eliminate pay inequities, such as the International Union of Electrical Workers and AFSCME, which, after the California successes, made pay equity a priority in negotiations in Connecticut and Florida. In others, unions themselves have been the barrier, and courts were finding them equally at fault with employers. The Teamsters were ordered to pay damages for intentionally discriminating against women by maintaining separate all-male and all-female bargaining units at a food wholesaler in Pennsylvania, with women earning only 65 percent of the men's salaries for comparable work.

In some situations men argued that women were paid less because they could not do the heavy lifting or operate the heavy machines as they did. In one notable sex bias trial in 1981, a woman janitor demonstrated to a Chicago judge that she could indeed handle the heavy floor-scrubbing equipment, refuting the men's arguments that women were paid $113 a month less because they had to clean with mops. In that case fifty-one women janitors for the city of Chicago won $450,000 in back pay and an increase in their monthly pay.

New Frontiers. Women continued to make gains in the still heavily male-dominated field of law enforcement. Courts in 1981 ordered the United States Border Patrol to review its physical examinations and retest all women who failed the test between 1975 and 1980; the United States Forest Service was ordered to pay $1.5 million to Pacific Southwest women employeess who proved a lack of promotion for women generally; and North Carolina agreed to set aside 25 percent of training slots for state troopers toward an ultimate goal of 41 percent women (compared to the current status of one woman out of 1,150 positions). In other rulings women gained admittance to jobs as dispatchers in sheriffs' departments and to police and firefighter jobs. An Elmwood Park, New Jersey, woman was reinstated to the firefighting squad after settling a sex bias charge that included harassment by wives of other firemen. One wife had offered to pay $5 to any pitcher at the department's summer baseball meet who would hit the woman firefighter in the head with the baseball.

In a significant victory, seventy-seven women officers won $902,857 in back pay from the Baltimore police department. The police chief had testified he did not think women could be police officers because God had created them as "little bits of fluff." One woman officer in Baltimore was awarded $57,010 after being terminated when the department could not find shoes or a uniform in her size.

As women formed their own associations in construction, mining, and other nontraditional jobs and as they increasingly won court suits challenging male-only barriers, individual women sought out transfers on their own to higher-paying blue-collar jobs within their city or private company. A city hall receptionist in Burlington, Iowa, for instance, filed suit after being turned down in her request to drive a dump truck for the city. She had driven school buses, pick-up trucks, and farm tractors; the man who got the job had four years' less seniority—and had occasionally driven a garbage truck.

Women continued to make inroads at high-salary plants where they had been excluded partly because employers contended they might face damage to their reproductive organs due to hazardous products under production. Federal and circuit courts have given mixed readings on whether employers can exclude all women from such jobs or whether applicants should be able to apply if they want to face possible health risks in exchange for the high wages. Men rarely are screened for potential risks to their reproductive organs. Hawaii and Connecticut legislatures voted in 1981 to require employers to inform workers of health risks from hazardous products, and Connecticut prohibited employers from requiring a woman to be sterilized to keep her job.

Courts also strengthened the legal rights of women in the nontraditional fields of top management. A federal circuit court said Wynn Oil Co. could bypass a woman for a more qualified male applicant for a job working with foreign customers, but it cannot refuse to promote her if the motive is fear that overseas customers would balk at dealing with a woman. In another case a federal court upheld the dismissal of a surly employee who was refusing to perform up to required standards out of resentment from having a woman boss. The New York Supreme Court upheld a record individual award of $219,000 to a former woman executive at Burlington Mills who proved she and other women had systematically been excluded from or underused in jobs leading to top executive posts.

Sexual Harassment and Rape. As women took jobs in mostly male surroundings they faced opposition from their colleagues that sometimes escalated to verifiable cases of sexual harassment. Suits multiplied. Although New Right activists argued that this pattern justified keeping women from these jobs, courts and the general public increasingly sided with the women in demanding that the abuse stop.

A federal judge in the District of Columbia ruled a woman does not have to prove economic loss to sue for damages from sexual harassment. A woman on a Ford assembly line and her husband won $32,000 after they sued the plant's foreman and supervisor, saying she had been a target of harassment. In Tacoma, Washington, a policewoman won $150,000 after proving damage from rumors that she had had sexual relations with thirty-six officers and that male coworkers implied her job would be easier if she complied.

The public also became more supportive of women's rights activists and of prosecutors seeking penalties against rapists and calling for ouster of public officials who clung to sexual stereotypes about rape victims. A furor arose in Wisconsin after a judge called a five-year-old rape victim "obviously promiscuous." Women's rights activists attempted to remove the head of a rape squad at the Spokane, Washington, police department who wore a T-shirt at a police party with the quote "Lay Back and Enjoy It."

Single-Sex Private Clubs. One area in which the administration has done a clear reversal is in lifting the psychological and peer pressure applied to high government officials who belong to discriminatory private clubs that bar women or members of minority or religious groups.

Several cabinet secretaries in the Carter administration had resigned their memberships under fire from women's groups and with encouragement from the president himself. In the Reagan administration, members of the exclusive all-male clubs include not only the president, Vice President Bush, Secretary of State Haig, and Attorney General William French Smith, but other lesser ranked officials. They scoffed at suggestions they resign. Haig said, when asked at a confirmation hearing, that he did not think the United States had come to the point where it would no longer support Boy Scouts or Girl Scouts but insisted on "unisex" scouts.

The Reagan administration also revoked the so-called country club regulation passed in the final days of the Carter administration that would have prohibited federal contractors from paying dues for its employees to discriminatory clubs. This had been projected as one more form of pocketbook leverage to persuade the clubs to change their membership policies.

In California, the all-male Bohemian Club (whose members include Reagan) was found guilty of illegal discrimination against women who wanted to work for the club but had been barred because members said it would embarrass them to have women around on their casual, occasionally nude retreats. Court rulings on the continuing fight by women to win admission to the U.S. Jaycees were mixed in 1981, with the Minnesota Supreme Court saying they must be admitted because the 320,000 membership national service group is a public accommodation and therefore cannot discriminate. The same argument was turned down in the District of Columbia, however. The issue is pending before highest State courts in Alaska and Massachusetts and before the Eighth Circuit Court of Appeals in Minnesota. Meanwhile, local Jaycee chapters began withholding their dues from the national organization in protest of the vote to continue to bar women. Similar fights were occurring on the local levels of other national service clubs such as the Rotary and Lions.

The New Right and Politics

The New Right is an umbrella term for dozens of very conservative and often radical groups. They range from "old right" crusaders from the 1950s anti-communist witch-hunts such as Phyllis Schlafly and her husband, to the newer Religious Right television evangelicals including Moral Majority leader Jerry Falwell who brings in $1 million a week on his *Old-Time Gospel Hour* television show seen on 392 stations.

Although some of these persons have been active in conservative causes for decades (Indiana's Moral Majority chief Greg Dixon led his state's opposition to John F. Kennedy's presidential campaign and to the ERA in the 1970s), they rarely have been so well financed and so well equipped with national communications facilities to mount their attacks against such forces as feminism, civil rights, liberals, or Democrats.

They take credit for registering millions of previously inactive voters in 1980 on behalf of Ronald Reagan, and have attempted to exercise a major role in his administration: If not appointments for themselves, then veto power over who is named; if not the policy they might like, then some say in what course is followed. They were far more influential in social welfare issues in the first year of the Reagan administration than in any other areas, and pressure was applied on the White House from a growing bloc of New Right senators and congressmen who were swept into office in 1980.

Their hit list included women who work; affirmative action; abortion; sex education (Schlafly calls it "classroom pornography"); family planning centers; laws on child abuse or domestic violence (Greg Dixon says child-abuse laws will create "gestapo agencies"); the ERA; gun controls; child-care centers; shelters for battered wives; federal judges (the Religious Roundtable called them "born-again ayatollahs of paganism"); birth control distribution; teaching of evolution and many fiction classics.

Their agenda for action was broadened considerably in 1981. Schlafly began a national book censorship campaign, calling feminists "ruthless, Gestapo-type censors" and accusing schools of teaching "secular humanism" (a New Right code phrase for many evils). Using the national grass-roots network created during her anti-ERA fight, she began a crusade to pressure librarians to buy "books that are conservative, pro family, patriotic . . .and pro-private enterprise" (Schlafly 1981). By the end of 1981, national library associations said book censorship had increased 500 percent during that year alone.

The New Right took on other fights as well. The Moral Majority succeeded in its national campaign to persuade Congress to overrule the District of Columbia City Council on a bill to modernize criminal laws on rape and sexual relations among minors and consenting adults. It fought child abuse laws in a variety of states, defending parents' rights to whip their children. A group calling itself the Family Protection Lobby persuaded Baltimore television station WJZ-TV to pull a federally produced message that urged children who had been beaten by their parents to "talk to a teacher, friend or minister." The Liberty Lobby condemned the message, saying it encouraged "children . . . to 'rat' on their parents" (*Bulletin* 1981).

Other goals: To change tax and Social Security laws to promote a woman's dependency on her husband; to end federal funding for Planned Parenthood's family planning center and require that parents be notified if minors are given birth control advice or devices; to repeal federal guidelines banning workplace sexual harassment; to repeal laws prohibiting sex discrimination such as Title IX in education; to dismantle federal structures that had promoted sex equity and helped break down job and educational barriers for women and minorities; to raise barriers again to women in non-traditional jobs; to stop the mingling of sexes in school sports; to reduce recruitment of women for the military; and to enact constitutional bans on busing, affirmative action, and abortion.

One vehicle for much of this was the family protection act. Sponsors said it would end federal intrusion in the family, such as interference in child abuse or domestic violence. It would repeal Title IX and other sex equity laws, would let states "limit or prohibit" sex intermingling in sports, would restrict the Supreme Court's jurisdiction in such controversial areas as busing, school prayer, and abortion. It would also prohibit federal funding for textbooks that "do not reflect a balance between the status role of men and women, do not reflect different ways in which men and women live and do not contribute to the American way of life as it has been historically understood" (text of the proposed bill).

They did not talk about it much openly but one core dynamic of the New Right movement was restricting modern women's options and returning society to the days when they were submissive and dependent. The Rev. Tim LaHaye, one of five national board members of the Moral Majority who with his wife has begun a nationally telecast family life program, quotes scripture that says, "Wives submit yourselves to your own husbands, as unto the Lord, in everything. . . . " The newly formed National Christian Action Coalition objected to O'Connor's selection for the Supreme Court not because of her views on abortion, but because of her sex, with coalition leader William Billings saying God will punish America for disobeying the order that women "not be placed in positions of authority over men, or to sit in a seat of judgment over men."

George Gilder, author of *Wealth and poverty,* which Reagan called required reading for his cabinet, said the government's emphasis on ending poverty must be on strengthening the man's role, not giving job skills or more support payments to women, who head more than 90 percent of welfare families. He restated the historic cliché that men perform best when women and children depend on them: "Women have long horizons within their very bodies, glimpses of eternity within their wombs. Civilized society is dependent upon the submission of the short-term sexuality of young men to the extended maternal horizon of women. This is what happens in monogamous marriage: the man disciplines his sexuality and extends it into the future through the womb of a woman . . . The woman gives him a unique link to the future and a vision of it. He gives her faithfulness and a commitment to a lifetime of hard work."

Schlafly, herself quoting Gilder, gave an even more explicit view of what the New Right coalition had in mind. She opposed separate Social Security benefits for housewives, saying, "The dependent wife and mother—who cares for her own children in her own home—performs the most socially necessary and useful role in our society. . . . It would be a tragic mistake for Congress ever to adopt any public or tax policy which encourages mothers to assign child care to others and enter the labor force."

Teaching her six children to read at home by keeping them out of first grade, she used McGuffey Readers that taught "the time-honored virtues—love of God, patriotism, thrift, honesty, respect for elders, where there's a will there's a way, the Golden Rule, true courage, manliness, kindness to the less fortunate, obedience to parents, the value of prayer, the consequences of idleness and truancy, crime doesn't pay and why virtue and love are worth more than material riches. . . . We'd all be better off if we just gave the Hay-Wingo phonics books to every parent with a five-year-old and said 'teach your child yourself.'"

She further says, "Sexual harassment on the job is not a problem for the virtuous woman except in the rarest of cases. When a woman walks across the room, she speaks with a universal body language that most men intuitively understand. Men hardly ever ask sexual favors of women from whom the certain answer is 'no.' . . . In those rare cases where a virtuous woman finds that sexual harassment is a condition of her employment, the social injustice is real—but as a subject of congressional concern it is totally dwarfed by the injustice of sexual harassment or intimidation of women in the armed services who do not have the freedom to resign. . . . "

She said affirmative action is a cruel "harassment by feminists and their federal government allies against the role of motherhood and the role of the dependent wife. The feminist goal is to induce all wives and mothers out of the home and into the work force. This goal would eliminate the role of motherhood and make child care a responsibility and probably a function of government. The military, the courts and the federal bureaucracy have capitulated to feminist demands and ordered the hiring of women in work situations where putting men and women together is likely to result in fornication, adultery, divorce or illegitimate births. Such orders are based on the notion that we must close our eyes to the immoral consequences and push women into every nontraditional job, even if it destroys families."

Finally, she called on Congress to reject demands to change the so-called marriage tax or to increase child-care tax deductions, both of which benefit working couples, saying these in effect "harass, disadvantage or discourage the role of motherhood and its essential complement, the role of male provider. Congress should reject all proposals which include financial inducements to wives to enter the labor force or to mothers to assign care of their children to institutions."

Equal Rights Amendment

Conservative forces won a major victory on the ERA in 1981 when Federal District Judge Marion Callister ruled that Idaho and four other states had the constitutional right to rescind their previous approval of the ERA. He also said Congress had ruled illegally in extending the time deadline until June 30, 1982. Pro-ERA forces had tried unsuccessfully to remove Callister from the case because of his activism in the upper echelons of the Mormon Church, which has been one of the major opponents of the amendment.

The National Organization for Women (NOW) appealed the Callister ruling, urging the Supreme Court to review the case promptly before the time ran out. Initially, the Justice Department said it was joining NOW in its petition for swift review. Within hours of an outraged protest from New Right crusaders against the ERA, the department dropped its request for a "speedy" review. The Supreme Court agreed to review the case—in due course. At the very least, NOW contended, this cleared the legal air for states to act on the ERA during the spring and early summer of 1982.

Despite a vigorous grass-roots campaign and a $15 million media drive, pro-ERA forces failed to win a single new state in 1981, leaving them with scant chance of approval by the deadline. Most of the year was spent mustering support in the fifteen states that had not ratified, with the major effort occurring in six. The only vote was in Nevada, where it was defeated handily on a voice vote. In early 1982 votes fell short of ratification in Oklahoma, Georgia, Virginia, and Missouri.

Sixteen states have put ERAs into their constitutions. The American Law Review, in a 1979 study of the impact, concluded that many laws that previously had favored women had been altered to be sex-neutral. The NOW Legal, Defense, and Education Fund, in a 1981 review contended that major changes in the laws had occurred that mostly opened up options for women. It said few judges, attorneys, or women seemed to know that the state ERAs existed in some states.

Polls and Elections

A gender gap emerged separating women and men's ratings of President Reagan that was unprecedented in polling history. By the year's end the difference had widened to 16 percent in some polls. Women of all ages and educational levels gave him dramatically lower approval ratings than did men. Political scientist Everett Carll Ladd, writing in *Public Opinion,* rebuffed skeptics who said the gender gap was comprised mostly of feminists or younger working women, saying, "Reagan gets a lower rating among women than men, consistently and systematically." He found no comparable gap in polls dating back to Eisenhower.

Women were far more pessimistic about Reagan's handling of the economy, about prospects for better times ahead, about the chances he may lead the country into war. They also chose the Democratic Party over Reagan's Republican Party in far greater numbers than men.

Republicans and some Democrats explained the gender gap away by saying it reflected women's traditional pacifist inclinations. Women's rights groups insisted otherwise, maintaining that the polls reflect antipathy toward Reagan because of his opposition to the ERA and abortion and his reversal on many equity issues. They noted that the ERA is at an historic approval rating of 63 percent (Gallup poll, summer of 1981) and they point to an ABC/Washington Post poll last June that showed 66 percent support for steps to strengthen and change the status of women.

The gender gap against Reagan dates back to the closing months of the 1980 campaign, after the publicity given Republicans for abandoning their forty-year support of the ERA and their endorsement of a platform plank that called for selection of judges with antiabortion views. On election day an Associated Press/NBC poll found that men backed Reagan by a 56 percent to 36 percent margin but women split their votes 47 percent to 45 percent. Polling director Evans Witt concluded that "Reagan has a woman problem," finding that the war-monger image was one factor but that "the issue of women's rights was more significant" (Witt 1981).

Although GOP pollsters persisted in calling women "lagging" indicators who ultimately would fall in line behind men (who were "leading" indicators), that apparently did not happen in the Virginia governorship race in November of 1981. Polls the week before the election by the Washington Post showed pro-ERA Democrat Charles Robb with an overall margin of 7 percent over his Reagan-backed opponent, Marshall Coleman. His margin among women was far greater: 56 percent to 39 percent. Robb said afterward that the women's vote had been a significant factor in his easy victory, together with a massive turnout of black voters.

The 1982 elections will provide more clues as to whether there is a gender gap against Reagan and whether politicians consider it to be formidable. In the elections held in 1981 women proved themselves serious contenders. Former congresswoman Elizabeth Holtzman, who lost a narrow race in 1980 to be senator from New York, once again challenged the entire Democratic political establishment and was elected district attorney in Brooklyn. In the booming Sun Belt, city controller Kathy Whitmire upended a field of fifteen to become mayor of Houston (Table 3). Whitmire, who was widowed in her late 20s, had honed her speaking skills by campaigning for the ERA on behalf of the Texas Women's Political Caucus. She turned the corner in the final weeks of the runoff when she challenged the burly, conservative old-time sheriff to a debate. He had been grumbling privately about how such a young, petite, blonde woman could possibly cope with rough-and-tough Houston. When he refused her debate offer, Whitmire showed her sense of humor and political daring by demanding: "Why won't he come out and fight like a man?"

Beyond Reagan: On to 1982

The fear of more budget cuts and policy reversals and the prospect that the New Right may strengthen its support in Congress has prompted major rethinking among women's rights groups. Reagan has helped many groups focus their priorities, resolve internal troubles, and either go out of business or mount a strong resistance. For some, he became a major catalyst for increasing membership and raising money. This was true of the National Organization for Women, for instance, whose members increased from 120,000 at the end of 1980 to 160,000 at the end of 1981. Also, NOW broke into the ranks of successful direct-mail fundraisers, scoring its first million-dollar month in February of 1982. Another group raising considerable money as a result of the Reagan scare was the National Abortion Rights Action League (NARAL), which began pilot projects in more than a dozen states to rally support for prochoice positions in anticipation of a constitutional amendment on abortion going from Congress to the states in 1982 or soon afterward.

Another major group, the National Women's Political Caucus, celebrated its tenth anniversary, elected a Republican feminist (Kathy Wilson) as chair, and made its 1980s priority the election of many more women to state legislatures, where they now are 12 percent of the total. The National Women's Education Fund launched a two-year effort in ten regions of the country to teach women how to gain access to the public policy process. The goal was to reach minority women who have been virtually disenfranchised from the political process in most areas.

The Congresswomen's Caucus decided in 1981 to get serious about strengthening its ability to support a staff to write speeches, do research, and

Table 3.
Women Mayors in Cities With Population Over 100,000

Mayor	City	Population
Jane M. Byrne	Chicago, Ill.	3,005,072
Kathryn Whitmire	Houston, Tex.	1,594,086
Margaret Hance	Phoenix, Ariz.	764,911
Eileen Anderson	Honolulu, Hawaii	717,852
Dianne Feinstein	San Francisco, Calif.	678,974
Janet Gray Hayes	San Jose, Calif.	636,550
Patience S. Latting	Oklahoma City, Okla.	403,213
Eunice Sato	Long Beach, Calif.	361,334
Carole K. McClellan	Austin, Tex.	345,496
Corrine Freeman	St. Petersburg, Fla.	236,893
Helen G. Boosalis	Lincoln, Neb.	171,932
Ruth Finley	Huntington Beach, Calif.	170,505
Sara J. Robertson	Worcester, Mass.	161,799
Jo E. Heckman	Pasadena, Calif.	119,374
Peggy Mensinger	Modesto, Calif.	106,105
Mary K. Shell	Bakersfield, Calif.	105,611
June V. Bulman	Concord, Calif.	103,251
Barbara Bennett	Reno, Nev.	100,756

Source: U.S. Conference of Mayors, 1982.

keep track of the mushrooming numbers of pieces of legislation affecting women. It assessed members $2,500 a year, similar to fees charged by other special-interest caucuses. Some congresswomen quit in protest, others retired or ran for other office. None of the five Republican women elected in 1980 joined. That left eleven congresswomen, including GOP Sen. Nancy Kassebaum of Kansas. In late 1981 they opened the caucus to men who also supported women's rights. By early 1982 there were seventy-six members (with the eleven women comprising the executive committee), and the name was changed to the Congressional Caucus on Women's Issues. (See Tables 4 and 5 for data on women in state and federal legislatures.)

The caucus took the lead in 1981 in holding hearings on Social Security and the impact on women; on sex bias in insurance; the impact on women of budget programs; the controversy on women in the military; the impact of federal layoffs on women and minorities; and on Title IX, the law banning bias in education. The caucus met with many cabinet members to question them about public policy issues in their area. In early 1982 the caucus cosponsored a symposium on affirmative action and the first extensive examination in eight years of women's economic status.

Some groups invited confrontation in 1981, such as Congressional Union, a newly formed nonviolent militant group working for the ERA. Early in 1982, with excommunicated Mormon Sonia Johnson as strategist, the group chained themselves to the White House fence and used rope ladders to vault over the fence before the eyes of astonished guards. Most pursued more conventional ways of adjusting to the new realities. Increasingly, they won grants from major corporations to expand their efforts, such as initiation of fourteen congressional fellowships for graduate students on public policy issues affecting women to be sponsored jointly by the Women's Research and Education Institute and the George Washington University's Women's Studies Program.

Women Employed of Chicago and the Women's Legal Defense Fund intensified their joint monitoring process of affirmative action and the government's activities on this issue. The Cleveland-based grass-roots group, Working Women, launched a national campaign in defense of the rights of women workers. Those groups, with the Congresswomen's Caucus and the National Women's Law Center, forged even stronger ties in 1981 to national civil rights groups to resist the threats.

Some organizations with long histories took on new projects to meet emergencies of the day. The Girls Club of America opened a national research center to dispel the "Cinderella" myth that a man will come along to rescue the girls from most of life's decisions. The American Association of University Women launched a two-year project to aid women in higher education with sex-bias lawsuits. The initial money would go to support five former faculty members who sued Cornell University.

One other innovative venture was founded in 1981: A Wonder Woman Foundation, funded by Warner Communications to "eliminate sex-based discrimination and stereotyping." It was named after the comic book heroine created in 1941 to give women and girls a model they could identify with, a "champion of strength and self-reliance." The foundation plans a film celebration and a $100,000 grant program for individual women over the age of forty.

Obviously, the reversals of 1981 dramatize the reality that the women's movement has encountered well-financed and formidable resistance. Society as a whole is still debating "women's place"—and so are many individual women. But if the business community believes the Reagan administration's erosion of affirmative action relieves them of any need to hire women, and if New Right conservatives believe women will agree to return to a submissive, dependent role, the array of new ventures undertaken in 1981 should given them pause.

Major 1981 Congressional Hearings

Printed transcripts of hearing records are available from the U.S. Government Printing Office.

Abortion

Senate Judiciary Subcommittee on the Separation of Powers, on S. 158, the Human Life Bill, by Sen. Jesse Helms (R-N.C.) to declare that life begins at conception and that therefore all abortions are banned. (This was reintroduced late in 1981 as S. 1841.)

Senate Judiciary Subcommittee on the Constitution, on S.J. Res. 10, the Human Life Federalism Amendment by Sen. Orrin Hatch (R-Utah) to give states and the Congress the power to ban abortions and to declare that abortion is not a right guaranteed by the Constitution, thus overruling the 1973 Supreme Court decision.

Family Planning

Senate Labor and Human Resources, on S. 288, and the House Energy and Commerce Subcommittee on Health and the Environment, on H.R. 2807, to reauthorize Title X of the Public Health Service Act, which contains the federal government's major family planning and adolescent health programs. These hearings, especially in the Senate, became the focus of attacks on Planned Parenthood and its abortion counseling.

Separate hearings were held by the Senate Education and Human Resources subcommittee on aging on S. 1090 by Sen. Jeremiah Denton (R-Ala.) on the chastity bill, the Adolescent Family Life Bill, which ultimately was wrapped into Title X as a $30 million teenage counseling program to give them alternatives to abortion.

Judiciary

Senate Judiciary Committee on the nomination of Sandra Day O'Connor to the Supreme Court, September 9-11, 1981.

Table 4.
Women in State Legislatures — 1981

	1981 Senates Total Women/Total Seats		1981 House/Assemblies Total Women/Total Seats		Percentage of Women State Legislators
Alabama	0	35	6	105	4.3
Alaska	2	20	4	40	10.0
Arizona	5	30	12	60	17.0
Arkansas	1	35	4	100	3.7
California	2	40	10	80	10.0
Colorado	4	35	19	65	23.0
Connecticut	8	36	32	151	21.4
Delaware	2	21	7	41	14.5
Florida	4	40	12	120	10.0
Georgia	2	56	15	180	7.2
Hawaii	4	25	10	51	18.4
Idaho	2	35	8	70	9.5
Illinois	4	59	28	177	13.6
Indiana	4	50	8	100	8.0
Iowa	2	50	16	100	12.0
Kansas	4	40	18	125	13.3
Kentucky	2	38	8	100	7.2

Louisiana	0	39	2	105	1.4
Maine	6	33	36	151	22.8
Maryland	3	47	25	141	14.9
Massachusetts	5	40	14	160	9.5
Michigan	0	38	16	110	10.8
Minnesota	5	67	19	134	11.9
Mississippi	0	52	2	122	1.1
Missouri	2	34	20	163	11.2
Montana	4	50	13	100	11.3
Nebraska	Unicameral Legislature		5	49	10.2
Nevada	2	20	5	40	11.7
New Hampshire	2	24	121	400	29.0
New Jersey	1	40	7	80	6.7
New Mexico	2	42	5	70	6.3
New York	4	60	14	150	8.6
North Carolina	3	50	19	120	12.9
North Dakota	3	50	15	100	12.0
Ohio	1	33	9	99	7.6
Oklahoma	1	48	11	101	8.1
Oregon	1	30	19	60	22.2
Pennsylvania	1	50	10	203	4.3
Rhode Island	5	50	10	100	10.0
South Carolina	2	46	9	124	6.5
South Dakota	3	35	8	70	10.5
Tennessee	1	33	5	99	4.5
Texas	1	31	11	150	6.6
Utah	1	29	6	75	6.7
Vermont	4	30	35	150	21.7
Virginia	1	40	8	100	6.4
Washington	8	49	27	98	23.8
West Virginia	2	34	14	100	11.9
Wisconsin	2	33	18	99	15.2
Wyoming	3	30	14	62	18.5
Totals	131	1932	770	5550	12.0

Source: The National Women's Political Caucus, 1981.

Women in the United States Congress and State Legislatures 1971-1981

CONGRESS	1971	1981	Change
Number of Women	11	20	+9
Total Number of Seats	535	535	0
Percentage	2	4	+2

STATE LEGISLATURES	1971	1981	Change
Number of Women	362	901	+539
Total Number of Seats	7603	7482	-121
Percentage	5	12	+7

Table 5.
Women Members of Congress

Name and House	Party and State
Sen. Nancy Landon Kassebaum	R-Kansas
Sen. Paula Hawkins	R-Florida
Rep. Lindy Boggs	D-Louisiana
Rep. Marilyn Lloyd Bouquard	D-Tennessee
Rep. Beverly B. Byron	D-Maryland
Rep. Shirley Chisholm	D-New York
Rep. Cardiss Collins	D-Illinois
Rep. Millicent Fenwick	R-New Jersey
Rep. Geraldine A. Ferraro	D-New York
Rep. Bobbi Fiedler	R-California
Rep. Margaret M. Heckler	R-Massachusetts
Rep. Marjorie S. Holt	R-Maryland
Rep. Barbara Kennelly*	D-Connecticut
Rep. Lynn Martin	R-Illinois
Rep. Barbara A. Mikulski	D-Maryland
Rep. Mary Rose Oakar	D-Ohio
Rep. Claudine Schneider	R-Rhode Island
Rep. Patricia Schroeder	D-Colorado
Rep. Virginia Smith	R-Nebraska
Rep. Olympia J. Snowe	R-Maine

*Kennelly took her seat in early 1982 after winning a special election to fill a vacancy.

Employment and Affirmative Action

Senate Labor and Human Resources oversight hearing on Women and Employment Problems, including the April hearings at which Phyllis Schlafly testified on sexual harassment.

Senate Judiciary Subcommittee on the Constitution, on S.J. Res. 41, the Equal Protection Amendment, by Sen. Orrin Hatch (R-Utah) to ban affirmative action.

Senate Labor and Human Resources, Enforcement of Fair Employment Laws and Policies, oversight on the Office of Federal Contract Compliance Programs in the Department of Labor, including Hatch's attacks on affirmative action as practiced by the OFCCP in its monitoring of the 350,000 federal contractors.

House Education and Labor Subcommittee on Employment Opportunities, Oversight Hearings on Equal Employment Opportunity and Affirmative Action hearings. July 15, September 23-24, and October 7 detailed in part the success of affirmative action.

Older Women

Senate Special Committee on Aging, oversight on impact of federal budget proposals on older Americans, including testimony by Laurie Shields of Older Women's League that 60 percent of elderly women rely entirely on federal aid.

House Aging Committee Task Force on Social Security and Women, oversight hearings on women and federal pensions, by Rep. Mary Rose Oakar (D-Ohio).

Women's Economic Equity Act

A package of more than a dozen bills was introduced as S. 888 and H.R. 3117. Hearings were held in 1981 on two proposals: pensions for military spouses and equity in insurance.

House Energy and Commerce Subcommittee on Commerce, Transportation and Tourism, on H.R. 100, providing for sex equity in health, disability, auto, life, and other forms of insurance.

House Armed Services Subcommittee on Military Pensions and Compensation and Senate Armed Services Subcommittee on Manpower and Personnel, on military pensions for spouses, with the primary legislation sponsored by Rep. Pat Schroeder (D-Colo.) and Sen. Roger W. Jepsen (R-Iowa).

Women in the Military

An all-day symposium October 21 was held on Recruitment, Utilization and Military Women, to examine the Reagan administration's reversal of recruitment of women. Sponsored by Rep. Pat Schroeder (D-Colo).

Women's Economic Status

On February 3, 1982 the House-Senate Joint Economic Committee held the first oversight hearing in eight years on women's economic status entitled The Economic Status of Women and Its Effect on Family Income. Includes testimony from economist Barbara Bergmann on impact of Reagan programs on lower-income women.

BIBLIOGRAPHY

Books

Badinter, Elisabeth. *Mother love: myth and reality*. New York: Macmillan, 1981. Translation from French best seller that critics equate with Betty

Friedan's *Feminine mystique* in argument that biology is not destiny and in defense of working mothers.

Brown, B. A.; Freedman, A. E.; Katz, H. N.; and Price, A. M. *Women's rights and the law.* New York: Praeger, 1977. Comprehensive assessment of the impact of the ERA on the legal system.

Bureau of Labor Statistics. *Perspectives on working woman: a databook.* Washington, D.C.: The Bureau, 1980. A general resource on women's role in the economy with more than 100 tables.

Center for Women Policy Studies. *Proceedings of the national symposium on harassment and discrimination of women in employment, July 7-9, 1981.* Washington, D.C. Culmination of three days of discussions at national symposium on grievance and counseling approaches, litigation, research, and employee and management training.

Davis, Angela Y. *Women, race and class.* New York: Random House, 1981. She warns that race and class can no longer be ignored if the women's movement is to be resurrected.

DuBois, Ellen Carol, ed. *Elizabeth Cady Stanton. Susan B. Anthony.* New York: Schocken, 1981. Comprehensive survey of historical contributions to feminist political demands for suffrage by Stanton and Anthony who argued that women must join together politically to control the impact of law and government on their lives.

Felsenthal, Carol. *The sweetheart of the silent majority: the biography of Phyllis Schlafly.* New York: Doubleday, 1981. An unauthorized but friendly biography of the woman who takes credit for stopping the ERA. Background on her early life, her early activism in conservative causes and politics, as well as details of her war on the ERA.

Friedan, Betty. *The second stage.* New York: Summit, 1981. A controversial major book by the woman whose *Feminine mystique* helped create the modern women's movement. She decries the crusade for change that "seemed to express a hate for men and a lack of reverence for childbearing that threatened" traditional women profoundly.

Gilder, George. *Wealth and poverty.* New York: Basic Books, 1980. A valued economist-theorist of the Reagan administration who argues that working mothers cannot do credible jobs because they are distracted by duties at home. Men are motivated to do well in the workplace and in monogamous marriages when the man "disciplines his sexuality and extends it into the future through the womb of a woman."

Heatherly, Charles L., ed. *Mandate for leadership: policy management in a conservative administration.* Washington, D.C.: The Heritage Foundation, 1981. Blueprint for Reagan's turn to the right by a conservative think tank.

Hull, Gloria T.; Scott, Patricia Bell; and Smith, Barbara, eds. *All the women are white, all the blacks are men, but some of us are brave.* Old Westbury, N.Y.: Feminist Press, 1980. Calls for recognition of the reality of sexual oppression as well as racial oppression in lives of black women.

Janssen-Jurreit, Marielouise. *Sexism: the male monopoly on history and thought.* New York: Farrar, Straus & Giroux, 1981. Translation of German bestseller that contends that reproduction, as an economic and social tool, can enable women to exert pressure on the male-dominated power structure.

Lansing, Marjorie, and Baxter, Sandra. *Women in politics: the invisible majority.* Old Westbury, N.Y.: Feminist Press, 1980. Contemporary study of women's struggles to break through stereotypes and political barriers to elected office.

Lee, Rex E. *A lawyer looks at the equal rights amendment.* Provo, Utah: Brigham Young University Press. 1980. The argument against the ERA by former law school dean at Brigham Young who is Reagan's Solicitor General with authority for arguing sex equity cases, among others, before the Supreme Court.

Mandel, Ruth B. *In the running: the new woman candidate.* New York and New Haven: Ticknor & Fields, 1981. Mandel, who directs the Center for the American Woman and Politics, tries to isolate how a woman's sex affects her candidacy and leadership. Also tries to analyze what helps and hinders a woman's drive forward in public life.

Oakley, Ann. *Subject women.* New York: Pantheon, 1981. Synthesis of legal changes in status of women, including their role in the work force, increased access to power and participation in politics, and the barriers to full equality.

Okin, S. M. *Women in western political thought.* Princeton, N.J.: Princeton University Press, 1979. A history of political philosophy focused on the work of Plato, Aristotle, Rousseau, and Mill, and analysis of the gap between formal and real equality for women.

Rogan, Helen. *Mixed company: women in the modern army.* New York: G. P. Putnam's Sons, 1981. Timely analysis of the performance by women in uniform, conflicting attitudes toward them, the incidence of sexual harassment, and policy issues facing the country about the future role of military women.

Rothman, Sheila M. *Women's proper place: a history of changing ideals and practices, 1970 to the present.* New York: Basic Books, 1978. Good chapters on the politics of protection, the imposition of protective labor laws in the 1920s, and their long-lasting consequences.

Smith, Ralph E., ed. *The subtle revolution: women at work.* Washington,

D.C.: Urban Institute, 1979. Looks at the vast changes of the past thirty years when women took and kept full-time jobs. Makes clear the biggest barrier to women's equality is occupational segregation.

Treiman, Donald J., and Hartmann, Heidi, eds. *Women, work and wages: equal pay for jobs of equal value.* Washington, D.C.: National Academy Press, 1981. A National Research Council report from the National Academy of Sciences on the continuing pervasive pattern of job segregation, where women do different work than men and where pay scales are lower the more the job category is dominated by women.

Weisberg, Kelly, ed. *Women and the law: the social historical perspective.* Cambridge: Schenkman, 1981. See especially the chapter by political scientist Susan J. Tolchin on patterns of exclusion that keep women out of the judicial selection process, including a theory by former attorney General Edward Levi that women were not represented among top law firms because they took five to ten years out to rear children.

Walshok, Mary Lindenstein. *Blue collar women: pioneers on the male frontier.* New York: Doubleday, 1981. The rewards of high pay and independence that may bring more happiness than comparably paying jobs in the white-collar world as many more occupations open up to women.

Warenski, Marilyn. *Patriarchs and politics: the plight of the Mormon woman.* New York: McGraw-Hill, 1980. A timely examination of women in the Mormon church from the nineteenth century to present, including the small but growing threat to the patriarchial system that restricts women's roles by such activists for the ERA as Sonia Johnson, who was excommunicated in 1980.

Journals, Magazines, and Pamphlets

Bergmann, Barbara R. "The shibboleth of the shrinking pie." *Perspectives: The Civil Rights Quarterly,* Summer-Fall 1981. Economist's conclusion that discrimination, not good or bad economic times, remains the barrier to good jobs for women and minorities.

Bergmann, Barbara R. "Women's economic condition in the 1980s: bad and getting worse." Joint Economic Committee of Congress, February 3, 1982.

Berkson, Larry; Carbon, Susan; and Houlden, Pauline. *Judicature,* December-January 1982. Special issue on the history of women on the bench, profiles of women judges at state and federal levels, and analysis of Justice Sandra Day O'Connor.

Bulletin. People for the American Way. A monthly newsletter on activities of the Religious Right. See October 1981 issue, p. 2, an attack against federal child abuse television spots.

Bureau of Labor Statistics. "Employment: a special issue." *Monthly Labor Review*, February 1981. Data on two-earner families, employment situation for military wives, and updated information on women workers.

Children's Defense Fund. "A children's defense budget: an analysis of the president's budget and children." February 1982. A 215-page overview of budget cut impact on poor families.

Collier, Ellen C. "Women in the armed forces." *Congressional Research Service,* Library of Congress. January 29, 1982. Overview of the policy questions involving an increase of women in uniform and criticisms of any increase as well as references to studies that justify the performance of women in the military.

Congressional Record, September 3, 1980, pp. 511807–511919. More than 100 pages of articles questioning the need and equity of affirmative action, put in the Record by Sen. Orrin G. Hatch (R-Utah), sponsor of a proposed constitutional amendment to ban it as both a sexist and racist idea. Good summary of conservative complaints about affirmative action.

Conservative Digest, "The pro-family movement," May-June 1980. Text and charts on key players in the new political movement that is so influential in the Reagan administration. Leaders date their emergence to coalitions against the ERA, abortion, lifestyle issues, and the crusade for tax-exempt rights for Christian schools.

Conservative Digest, "Which conservatives do you most admire?", pp 18-23, September 1981. Poll results from readers on leaders in and outside Congress. Good primer on who's who in the New Right crusades against the ERA, abortion, domestic violence bills, and federal aid to education including Title IX.

Decter, Midge. "The intelligent woman's guide to feminism." Heritage Foundation *Policy Review*, Spring 1981. Leading neoconservative attacks the women's movement, saying its view of women as victims amounts to hatred and contempt of women.

de Marcellus, Robert. "Fertility and national power." *Human Life Review,* Winter 1981. Criticizes $60 million in federal funds to family planning activities in a precursor of New Right attacks on Planned Parenthood. He says the main threat to the United States is its low fertility rate.

Engel, Randy. "Time to kill Title 10 and end the plague of Planned Parenthood." *Conservative Digest*, June 1981. Outline of New Right attack on federal funding of the nation's largest family planning umbrella group.

Equal Employment News. Betsy Hogan Associates, Brookline, Mass. A monthly digest of EEO court rulings, state and private actions, and federal regulatory changes and EEO trends.

Equal Employment Opportunity Commission. "Comparable worth: issues and alternatives." 1980. Discusses legal framework, job evaluation and concepts and practices of comparing unequal jobs.

Equal Employment Opportunity Commission. "Final amendment to guidelines in discrimination because of sex." *Federal Register*, November 10, 1980. Final guidelines on sexual harassment prohibitions that hold employers responsible for working conditions. The Reagan administration has held these up for probable change.

Equal Employment Opportunity Commission. Hearings on Job Segregation and Wage Discrimination, April 28-30, 1980, Washington, D.C. Overview of EEOC's emphasis on elimination of systematic patterns of discrimination as well as the view of job bias as seen by business, workers, and federal agencies.

Equal Employment Opportunity Commission. "Interpretive guidelines on employment discrimination and reproductive hazards." *Federal Register*, February 1, 1980. The Carter administration's proposal on legal limits on screening men and women for jobs that could pose reproductive hazards. These were withdrawn in early 1981 after Reagan's election.

ERA Impact Clearinghouse: Index and References. NOW Legal Defense and Education Fund and the Women's Law Project, 1980. Data bank of more than 250 cases brought under state ERAs in sixteen states, indexed by state and subject matter.

ERA Impact Project. NOW Legal Defense and Education Fund and the Women's Law Project, 1981. Report of two-year study of impact of legal changes resulting from the 16 state ERAs.

Freed, Dorris J., and Foster, Henry H. "Divorce in the 50 states: an overview as of August 1, 1981." *Family Law Reporter,* Bureau of National Affairs, October 20, 1981. A survey of the impact of the Supreme Court's ruling that military pensions are not required to be part of a divorce settlement, and analysis of new locator services for child-custody cases.

Galebach, Stephen H. "A human life statute." *Human Life Review*, Winter 1981. The legal strategy by antiabortion activists that they followed later in 1981 to push ahead a proposed law to declare "a simple likelihood that actual human life exists from conception." This would protect that "person" from abortion by extending constitutional guarantees under the fourteenth amendment to it.

Gatsis, Andrew J. "ERA would mean women in combat role, devastation of our fighting forces." *Conservative Digest*, October 1981. Attacks the increase of women in the military as a move by the women's movement to "unisex the society" and says women are hampering readiness and lowering morale by their presence.

Gertner, Nancy. "Bakke on affirmative action for women: pedestal or cage?" *Harvard Civil Rights/Civil Liberties Law Review*, no. 1 (Spring 1979):173–214. Questions different standards used by Supreme Court to evaluate racial cases versus sex discrimination cases.

Ginsburg, Ruth Bader. "Sexuality under the fourteenth and equality rights amendments." *Washington University Law Quarterly,* Winter 1979. Leading sex bias authority (now a federal judge) examines equal protection guarantees with those secured under ERA proposal.

Gladstone, Leslie. "Pregnancy as a discrimination issue." *Congressional Research Service*, Library of Congress, January 12, 1981. Update on continued challenges to laws prohibiting pregnancy discrimination and chronology of post-1963 laws.

Gruhl, John; Spohn, Cassia; and Welch, Susan. "Women as policymakers: the case of trial judges." *The American Journal of Political Science*, Midwest Political Science Association. They examine the convicting and sentencing behavior of men and women judges in more than 30,000 felony cases and find no marked differences, although women were more likely to sentence women defendants to prison than men judges were.

Hassman, Phillip E. "Construction and application of state equal rights amendment forbidding determination of rights based on sex." *American Law Reports*, volume 90, 1979. Analysis of impact so far on the sixteen state ERAs on changing rights of women in those states.

Holsti, Ole R., and Rosenau, James N. "The foreign policy beliefs of women in leadership positions." *The Journal of Politics,* Southern Political Science Association. More important than differences in sex were the occupations of the leaders studied.

Kandel, Thelma E. "Women can't bank on affirmative action." *Perspectives: The Civil Rights Quarterly*, Spring 1981. Contends women are seen but not heard in banks, with little movement upward since the first studies in the mid-1970s.

Kasun, Jacqueline. "The international politics of contraception." Heritage Foundation *Policy Review*, Winter 1981. An attack on U.S. foreign aid programs on family planning. Questions the core premise that there is a population explosion that should be curbed.

Keith, Robert E. "Resolution of paternity disputes by analysis of the blood." *The Family Law Reporter*, November 24, 1981. Bureau of National Affairs. With 16 percent of all births now occurring out of wedlock, blood analysis is being used more frequently to establish paternity claims so the parents rather than the government can bear costs of child-rearing.

Ladd, Everett Carll. "Reagan and women." American Enterprise Institute. *Public Opinion*, January 1982. Discusses the historic evolution of a "gender gap" for Reagan.

Levitan, Sar A., and Belous, Richard S. *Monthly Labor Review*, November 1981. They attack fallacies about working women, including any cause-and-effect tie between rising divorce rates and the number of working women, the difference a wife's earnings make in stabilizing a family income, and increasing number of female-headed families.

National Center on Women and Family Law. "NCOWFL to help battered women in rural areas." *Clearinghouse Review* 15, no. 1 (May 1981):68-70. Roundup on women's issues in legal services, women in the military, and child-snatching.

Nelson, Richard R. "State labor legislation enacted in 1981." *Monthly Labor Review*, January 1981. State-by-state survey of such actions as pregnancy job rights, the right of workers to be informed of reproductive hazards, and action on comparable worth issues of pay equity.

Noonan, John T., Jr. "In re the 'human life bill.' " *Human Life Review*, Summer 1981. Continued defense of concept that Congress itself can declare a fetus a human being but conceding that this would be only a first step toward the real goal of a constitutional amendment banning all abortions.

"Older women: the economics of aging." Women's Studies Program and Policy Center at George Washington University and the Women's Research and Education Institute, Congresswoman's Caucus, January 1981. Policy paper on issues affecting older women.

Phillips, Howard. "President's move to de-fund the left important part of his economic plan." *Conservative Digest*, April 1981. Elimination of more than forty individual federal social programs by combining them into block grants of uncommitted money for the states to use as they wished was a major part of New Right strategy to abolish federal programs on legal services, rat control, family planning, venereal disease, welfare rights, and fluoridation of water.

Rabinove, Samuel. "Private clubs under siege." *Perspectives: The Civil Rights Quarterly*, Fall-Winter 1981. Examines the power of all-white, all-male clubs and the legal and political pressures to force open the doors.

Real, Jere. "What Jerry Falwell *really* wants." *Inquiry*, August 3 and 24, 1981, pp. 13-18. The Bible, according to Falwell, says the ERA is wrong and women "are the weaker vessel" and must be kept under a husband's control.

Reed, Leonard. "Fairness runs amok: what's wrong with affirmative action." *Washington Monthly*, January 1981. Too many legalistic requirements and mandates for "equality of result" mar federal affirmative action efforts.

"Review of poverty law, 1979-1980." *Clearinghouse Review* 14, no. 10 (January 1981). Valuable chapters on employment and women that give overview of ferment in laws affecting poor women and on efforts to reduce sex stereotyping in the workplace.

Rothenberg, Randall. "The neoliberal club." *Esquire*, February 1982, pp. 37-46. The younger generation of Democrats break from the New Deal liberals and their social agenda including many "equality" issues.

Schlafly, Phyllis. The Phyllis Schlafly Report. November 1981. A roundup on her latest crusade against textbooks by feminists and humanists.

Schorr, Alvin L. "Single parents, women and public policy." *Journal*, Institute for Socioeconomic Studies, Winter 1981-1982. Policy options for single mothers who often are poorly trained and unlikely to hold jobs very long although they normally work full time in longer-than-average days. An overview of United States and Europe and aid to these single parents, and a conclusion that women's work at home has not declined nearly as much as their hours at paid work have increased.

Simpson, Peggy. "Target: working women." *Working Woman,* December, 1981. How Reagan's budget cuts and regulatory curtailments affect women, plus influence of the New Right on administration policies.

Sobran, Joseph. "Why conservatives should care about abortion." *Conservative Digest* 7, no. 11 (November 1981): 14-16. Contends that abortion "distorts the family ethic" as much as "welfare destroys the work ethic."

Sowell, Thomas. "Thoughts and details on poverty." Heritage Foundation *Policy Review*, Summer 1981. Conservative black economist argues that affirmative action has created an incentive not to hire from disadvantaged groups. Also says the real wage differences are between married women and everybody else because they are caring for children and husbands at home and this hampers their work.

U.S. Commission on Civil Rights. "Affirmative action in the 1980s: dismantling the process of discrimination." November 1981. Makes a case for affirmative action, including goals and timetables, to correct past and continuing patterns of bias against women and minorities.

U.S. Commission on Civil Rights. "Child care and equal opportunity for women." June 1981. Says the federal government can do more to expand and coordinate child-care policies to help extend equal rights to women, especially poor women.

U.S. Commission on Civil Rights. "Civil rights: a national, not a special interest." June 25, 1981. Traces civil rights progress since the Civil War and measures President Reagan's 1981 budget against that backdrop, concluding that another period of retrenchment may be starting.

U.S. Commission on Civil Rights. "Directory 1981." January 1981. A 549-page listing of private groups and government agencies whose primary concern is civil rights. Includes capsule summaries of major civil laws and executive orders. An update of the 1975 directory.

U.S. Commission on Civil Rights. "Equal opportunity in the foreign service." June 1981. Praises recent federal steps to increase women and minority options but says much more is needed, especially at middle and top-level positions.

U.S. Commission on Civil Rights. "The equal rights amendment: guaranteeing equal rights for women under the constitution." June 1981. A twenty-nine-page statement analyzing arguments against the ERA such as curbs on states' rights, impact on homemakers and the family, and liability for military service under a draft.

U.S. Commission on Civil Rights. "The federal response to domestic violence." January 1982. In-depth study of nineteen federal programs that did or could respond to needs of abused women, with analysis of what must be done.

U.S. Commission on Civil Rights. "Under the rule of thumb: battered women and the administration of justice." January 1982. A companion report that examines pattern of police and judicial treatment of spouse abuse, concluding this is too often treated as a family matter rather than as a crime and calling for more shelters for temporary refuge for victims.

U.S. Commission on Civil Rights. "Who is guarding the guardians?" October 1981. A report on police practices as they affect minorities and women, both in hiring patterns and in exercise of authority.

U.S. Commission on Civil Rights. "Women: still in poverty." July 1979. A valuable analysis of how poor women are affected by the welfare system, job training programs, and the availability of child care. Good background for evaluating the impact of Reagan policy and budget changes.

Witt, G. Evans. Opinion outlook, *National Journal*, March 9, 1981. Analyzes exit polls from 1980 elections and those taken in subsequent months to discuss Reagan's "woman's problem."

Women's Bureau. "Employment goals of the world plan of action: development and issues in the United States." Department of Labor, July 1980. The key paper prepared for the Copenhagen conference on the United Nations Decade for Women. Gives overview of changing role of workers and pending policy issues such as sexual harassment, comparable worth, pay equity, workplace hazards and reproductive capacity, and women's options in nontraditional jobs.

Women's Research and Education Institute of the Congresswomen's Caucus. "A director of selected women's research and policy centers." July 1981. Carried out with a corporation grant that mandated they "establish regular communication between researchers and policy-makers concerned with women's issues."

Women's Studies Program and Policy Center, George Washington University, and Women's Research and Education Institute of the Congresswomen's Caucus. "Older women: the economics of aging." January 1981. The vulnerability of older women who are largely dependent on Social Security, with few outside resources such as insurance or pensions.

Organizations

Center for the American Women and Politics, Eagleton Institute of Politics, Rutgers-The State University, New Brunswick, NJ 08901.

Center for Women Policy Studies, 2000 P Street NW, Suite 508, Washington, DC 20036.

Chicana Rights Project, Mexican-American Legal Defense and Education Fund, 517 Petroleum Commerce Building, 210 N. St. Mary's Street, San Antonio, TX 78205.

Children's Defense Fund, 1520 New Hampshire Avenue NW, Washington, DC 20036.

Congressional Caucus on Women's Issues (formerly the Congresswomen's Caucus), 2471 Rayburn House Office Building, Washington, DC, 22207.

ERAmerica, 1525 M Street NW, Suite 206, Washington, DC 20005.

Eagle Forum (Phyllis Schlafly's major group), P.O. Box 618, Alton, IL 62002; and 316 Pennsylvania Avenue SE, Suite 203, Washington, DC 20003.

The Federal Education Project, Lawyers Committee for Civil Rights Under Law, 733 15th Street NW, Suite 520, Washington, DC 20005.

Federally Employed Women, 1010 Vermont Avenue NW, Suite 821, Washington, DC 20005.

Federation of Organizations for Professional Women, 20000 P Street NW, Suite 403, Washington, DC 20036.

League of Women Voters Education Fund, 1730 M Street NW, Washington, DC 20036.

National Abortion Rights Action League, 1424 K Street NW, Second Floor, Washington, DC 20005.

National Center on Women and Family Law, 799 Broadway, Room 402, New York, NY 10003.

National Commission on Working Women, Center for Women and Work, 1211 Connecticut Avenue NW, Suite 310, Washington, DC 20036.

National Council of Negro Women, 815 2nd Avenue, Ninth Floor, New York, NY 10017.

National Organization for Women Inc., 425 13th Street NW, Suite 1048, Washington, DC 20004.

National Organization for Women, Legal Defense and Education Fund, 132 West 43rd Street, New York, NY 10036.

National Women's Education Fund, 1410 Q Street NW, Washington, DC 20009.

National Women's Law Center, 1751 N Street NW, Washington, DC 20036.

National Women's Political Caucus, 1411 K Street NW, Washington, DC 20005.

Older Women's League Educational Fund, 3800 Harrison Street, Oakland, CA 94611.

Planned Parenthood of America, 810 7th Avenue, New York, NY 10019; and its new national political lobbying arm, 1220 19th Street NW, Suite 303, Washington, DC 20036.

Project on Equal Educational Rights, 1112 13th Street NW, Washington, DC 20005.

Wider Opportunities for Women, Women Workforce Special Project, 1511 K Street NW, Washington, DC 20005.

Women's Campaign Fund, 1725 I Street NW, Suite 515, Washington, DC 20006.

Women's Equity Action League, 805 15th Street NW, Washington, DC 20005.

Women's Law Fund, 1621 Euclid Avenue, Cleveland, OH 44115.

Women's Legal Defense Fund, 2000 P Street NW, Suite 400, Washington, DC 20036.

Women's Research and Education Institute (data research arm of the Congresswomen's Caucus), 204 4th Street SE, Washington, DC 20003.

7 | Popular Culture

Michaele Weissman

Trivialization of Feminist Concepts

In television, mass market magazines, movies, and fiction one detects the presence of new ideas about women that originated in the women's movement. Often by the time these ideas have seeped down into the popular culture, they have been trivialized and debased.

The *Playboy* (1981) magazine article about Rita Jenrette, whose ex-husband John was convicted of taking a bribe from an undercover FBI man, was entitled "The liberation of a congressional wife" (April). The piece was cast as if the decision of this young woman to disclose the ignominious acts committed by her husband and herself was politically and socially significant. Jenrette confuses narcissism with self-expression, a confusion that is made clear in the article's first sentence, "I never looked like a Congressional wife."

Jenrette portrays herself as a courageous truth-teller set against the evil, cigar-chomping power brokers of Washington, although except to discuss her husband's bribe-taking, the only charge against male politicians that she makes is that they made passes at her when she wore clingy dresses. She describes posing for a *Playboy* photo spread as the rational choice of a determined woman commencing a new (singing) career:

> So I decided to give it a try. I'm sure my friends will be surprised
> at my revelations . . . I know that some will criticize me. But I no
> longer intend to live my life worried about what others will say.
> During five years as a Congressional wife, everyone else made
> much of my looks. Now it's my turn. (p. 204)

In this piece and in many like it liberation is a fast fix. The fact that real change requires struggle, fortitude, moral courage, and time is overlooked. Instead,

193

serious subjects are treated frivolously and frivolous subjects are presented as if they were serious. What Jenrette and writer Kathleen Maxa did in the *Playboy* piece was remove the language of feminism from its context. Words that describe change and struggle were applied to actions no more profound than the painting of a toenail.

This same separation of language from substance can be seen week after week in *People,* Time/Life's big money-maker, the most successful new magazine in a decade. Every week *People* runs virtually the same article about the "liberation" of a female movie star. The first three-quarters of the piece describes how messed up the actress used to be; toward the end we read how she has found health and happiness—a new life—through one or all of the following—pure food, psychotherapy, est, the Bahai religion, a new man, a new baby, a new manager. Usually the cure took place three weeks before the interview.

An August 24, 1981 profile of actress Margot Kidder (Lois Lane in *Superman I* and *II*) observed the requirements of the formula. First Kidder's drug and alcohol problems, her mental instability, her numerous love affairs, and her two failed marriages were trotted out for inspection. Then her new life was described:

> In Malibu Margot keeps active riding horses and going to dance and exercise classes. She also supports political candidates (she campaigned for John Anderson) as an ardent feminist who's angered by racism, the Moral Majority and not being able to live up to her artistic and moral standards. Analysis, she says, is currently helping her to cope. "I have a hard time watching myself on screen without wanting to vomit," she says. (p. 88)

Feminism. Racism. Moral Majority. The words are tossed around with the ease of kids throwing Frisbees; underneath, however, there is no structure on which they can rest. Using these words in this context cheapens them.

Further evidence of the trivialization of concepts from the women's movement abounds. One particularly insidious example was the novel published with a great deal of clamor this year by New American Library. The book written by Anne Tolstoi Wallach, who is described on the jacket as "vice president and creative director at a major New York agency," is called *Women's Work* and it details the struggle of a female vice president of a large, conservative advertising agency to be elevated to the post of senior vice president.

What is terrifying about this book, given the author's clear feminist identification, is the sheer unlikeability of her heroine, Domina Drexler, whose idea of female independence seems to begin with the purchase of one's own diamond earrings:

> Then get up, she told herself. Put on something terrific for extra courage. Your diamond stud earrings. They shine with success. Especially when you're going to face a man who knows you

bought them for yourself. A man who once joked: if you give a
woman a Christmas bonus, you can be sure she'll have new
jewelry the first working day after the holidays. The bastard. (p. 4)

Wallach certainly understands the hardships under which women labor in the
corporate fields. What she does not understand is that for women to be
feminists they must possess some humanizing vision that sets them apart.

Wallach deals with the crucial feminist issue—work—in a cheap and
exploitive way. Cheap and exploitive might be amusing. In this instance, they
are not. The world portrayed is too cold, too thin and mean-spirited to create
a book that is good to read. An underlying deprivation weighs the story
down. This feeling is most tangible in Wallach's description of Domina
Drexler's best friend, Maran Slade, a former model tormented by the loss of
her looks, who dies on the operating table while undergoing a facelift:

Almost everything bad that had ever happened to Maran had
been when she was lying down: sex, the birth of her daughter,
pneumonia, fainting in stuffy studios, sunburn, awful night
arguments. (p. 28)

That the environment the author describes is repulsive is a secret we seem to
know, but she has not learned. One wonders if the failure of this book to be
the blockbuster the publisher expected was the result of its unpleasantness or
the public's resistance to female senior vice presidents.

A similar lack of seriousness undermines three films about women:
Private Benjamin (which has also been made into a television series), *9 to 5*,
and *The Incredible Shrinking Woman*. These movies are the feminist
equivalent of black exploitation. In the guise of promoting liberation, they
present women in highly unflattering, curiously stereotypical ways. Also
distressing are the poor scripts and the lack of technical skill apparent in these
works. All three have a sloppy, slapdash feel, as if whoever made them didn't
care all that much about what they were doing.

Private Benjamin, directed by Howard Zieff, stars Goldie Hawn as Judy
Benjamin, a blond, spoiled, Jewish-American princess who joins the army
after her bridegroom drops dead. (He dies as Judy, still in her wedding dress,
commits a sexual act on him in the backseat of a car.)

In the first half of the movie we see Private Benjamin transformed from a
sniveling rich girl ("I want to wear my sandals. I want to go out to lunch") to a
gung-ho kind of soldier. By the use of what used to be called "feminine
wiles," Private Benjamin is responsible for her team's total victory during war
games—she rips apart a sister soldier's red bra, makes a phoney camp flag,
and lures the "enemy" into an ambush.

The second half of the picture is set overseas. Judy is in Brussels working
for NATO in the procurement division ("Finally I'm doing what I was born to
do—shop"). She becomes engaged to a rich French gynecologist who means
to marry and enslave her. As she is in danger of losing her new-found
independence, Judy's pals from basic training come to her rescue. In a

reversal of the famous wedding scene from *The Graduate,* she leaves him waiting at the altar.

Pauline Kael (1980) said about Private Benjamin (and her comments hold true for *9 to 5* as well): "This is the sort of feminist movie in which almost every man is an insensitive boor or fool, yet the heroine gets what she wants by manipulation and the shrewd use of sexual blackmail—which we're meant to find adorable" (*New Yorker,* November 11, 1980). This film has a new kind of double standard; unlike the old one, it is rigged in favor of women.

As skewered as its feminism is *Private Benjamin*'s attitude toward the military. The film is a blatant propaganda piece. An army camp comes across as just the place a girl should go to grow up, a kind of Outward Bound with pay. The social, political, and moral implications of a career in the war machine do not exist. Nor is any reference made to the change in public attitude toward the military since the Vietnam War. In this film, Vietnam never happened.

Nine to Five, directed by Colin Higgins, is a feminist revenge fantasy in which three office workers, the uptight, newly divorced housewife, Jane Fonda; the stalwart single parent, Lily Tomlin; and the office sexpot, Dolly Parton, kidnap their mean, dirty-minded boss whom they suspect of embezzlement. While the boss is in captivity the women transform their work-place into an environment fit for human habitation. Among the reforms are equal pay for equal work, flexible hours, hiring the handicapped, and day care for small children.

The director and screenwriter never really stay with their subject. Instead of making a movie about work and workers, they have made a second-rate caper comedy that traces the women's effort to unravel the plot in which their boss is embroiled. Much of the film's humor derives from the leather harness Fonda, Tomlin, and Parton rig up to keep him from straying, which creates unsavory sadomasochistic overtones. Equally disturbing, throughout the film Dolly Parton's large breasts are seen as a subject of hilarity—a rather peculiar attitude in a feminist film.

The Incredible Shrinking Woman directed by Joel Schumacher, stars Lily Tomlin as a housewife who wears pastel-colored polyester pants suits and lives in a pastel-colored suburban house. Tomlin develops an allergy to household products and begins to shrink, becoming so tiny that she is in danger of disappearing. She is saved at the point of oblivion when the shrinking process is spontaneously reversed.

Some of the early scenes have a sort of surrealistic wonder to them: A ten-inch-high Tomlin climbs into the kitchen sink to wash a six-inch-high head of lettuce and is almost ground up in the garbage disposal. As in *9 to 5,* the filmmakers did not have enough respect for their subject to stick with it. They felt compelled to graft onto their original premise a pointless mystery plot in which bad guys kidnap Tomlin to get hold of the substance that is making her shrink. The level of humor in this portion of the story can be deduced from the fact that a gorilla in the lab cage next to Tomlin's is responsible for freeing her.

What the producers and directors of these two films are saying is that movies cannot be made about such unimportant people as office workers and housewives. If this were not their underlying attitude they might have had the courage to end up with the movies they set out to make.

More evidence of the way feminist themes are trivialized in popular culture can be seen on television, particularly in its treatment of professional women. A disproportionate number are young and beautiful, earn their living as doctors, lawyers, and journalists, and are single.

The short-lived CBS series *Jessica Novak* starred Helen Shavers as an ambitious young television reporter and exemplifies the medium's depiction of career women. An advertisement for the series describes its heroine saying, "as a woman she's fighting to find her own life and someone to share it." One cannot imagine saying this for a series about a 30-year-old newsman. Instead, the advertisement would focus on his profession rather than on his personal life.

Jessica Novak and her female counterparts (Mary Richards on *The Mary Tyler Moore Show* was the original) are portrayed as professionals, but not as equals of men in their fields. Although they may be smart and dedicated, they are still journalistic ingenues. Being single adds to this image; after all, what's more girlish than going out on dates?

It all adds up to a presentation of female professionals as too young or too sexual to possess power or authority or to pose a threat to men. They may be portrayed as having glamorous and desirable work, but the traditional power structure—with men in control—remains absolutely intact. Where a professional woman is shown to have maturity and authority, as in the CBS series *Nurse* starring Michael Learned, she has been given a traditionally female job where she need not supervise or compete with men.

Trivializing feminist concerns is furthered by television's requirement that programming appeal to a mass, middle-of-the-road audience. Radical or difficult ideas are altered to make them less controversial; ideas that ought to be developed are ignored.

In the NBC program *Love, Sidney,* the first network series to have a homosexual as its main character, Sidney Schorr, played by Tony Randall, has a homosexual past but a nonsexual present, because NBC feared offending "middle America." This program is about an unconventional "family" that includes Sidney, a 50-year-old commercial artist; Laurie, an unmarried 25-year-old actress; and Patty, Laurie's child. In an up-to-date switch of role-playing, Sidney works at home and takes care of Patty; however, the impact of this series would have been far greater if NBC had not suppressed nearly all references to Sidney's homosexuality.

Television producers must possess double-think to present some of the programs they do. Take, for example, the movie starring Jaime Lee Curtis, *The Dorothy Stratton Story.* This special chronicled the rise to fame and the violent death of Dorothy Stratton, the beautiful, young, and gifted 1980 *Playboy* magazine playmate-of-the-year who was shot to death in a murder-suicide by her estranged husband, Paul Snider.

Coming through clearly in this film is Stratton's feeling that the men in her life—her possessive husband who "discovered" her in a small provincial town in Canada; Hugh Hefner, whose organization brought her to Hollywood; the legion of agents, lawyers, and advisors handling her career, and the lover she moves in with when she leaves the deranged Snider—were all in control of her life while she had no control at all. "Somebody else pulling the strings," is how Stratton bitterly describes leaving her husband for a new man.

On one hand, this film is more sophisticated than might have been expected: Rather than pin Stratton's death exclusively on her mentally ill husband, the director and screenwriter seem to be saying that it was Stratton's dependency, her feeling that others and not she "pulled the strings," that led her to be victimized. On the other hand, the filmmakers fail to take their own point to its logical conclusion. They refuse to indict the *Playboy* system that imports pretty young women to Hugh Hefner's Hollywood "hutch" to be shaped and packaged and turned into the latest luxury item. The program abdicates its responsibility. Hefner and company are presented as benign, idealistic men whose goal is to make the Dorothy Strattons of the world happy and rich. A lie such as this at its center invalidates the film.

Sexual Portrayal

The Dorothy Stratton Story exemplifies film's preoccupation with women as sexual victims. When the victimization comes in the form of murder, Hollywood prefers the objects of the assault to be, like Stratton, young and beautiful. Invariably the murder itself is preceded by a scene in which the woman writhes in terror, begging, as Stratton does, to be spared.

Scenes of murder and mayhem are evoked in *Looker* with attention to detail and coherence that the rest of director/screenwriter Michael Crichton's film simply does not possess. It concerns the murder of four female models ("They want us dead because we're too perfect") all of whom have recently undergone plastic surgery at the hands of a famous Los Angeles plastic surgeon, played by Albert Finney. The police want to pin the murders on Finney, who has to catch the real murderers who hide behind a multinational corporation. While the plot is never adequately explained, *Looker* has one thing to offer—the vision of a young woman screaming in terror and then, in slow motion, being tossed from a rooftoop and landing, splayed, with bone-shattering impact on the top of an automobile.

Ivan Passer's *Cutter's Way* (originally released as *Cutter & Bone*) has both murder and sex at the center of its plot. Richard Bone, a California pretty-boy and gigolo, witnesses a prominent Santa Barbara millionaire dump the body of a young woman in a back alley. Bone (Jeff Bridges) and his best friend, Alex Cutter (John Heard), a crippled, half-blind, alcoholic Vietnam veteran, set out either to trap or blackmail the murderer.

Lisa Eichorn plays Mo, Cutter's wife, also alcoholic, who is in love with Bone, and who is the only "sane" one of the three. Mo's sanity cannot save her life, however. She suffers, drinks, and cannot stop herself from wanting Bone even though she knows precisely what he is. When she finally is seduced by him, she weeps while they make love, afterwards telling him the last holdout of the Richard Bone fan club has succumbed. Mo dies in a fire, possibily arson, after Bone breaks his promise to stay with her for the night.

This is an apocalyptical film about American violence. Cutter is an instrument of violence. Women die in this film for only one reason—their paths cross those of violent men.

Another powerful film about violence is Martin Scorsese's *Raging Bull,* starring Robert De Niro as the prizefighter Jake La Motta. In this grim film, Scorsese captures the utterly consuming nature of male violence. La Motta turns on all those who are close to him, but his primary victim is his wife Vicki (played by Cathy Moriarty), who is a kind of Desdemona, accused by La Motta of imaginary transgressions. When the fighter has succeeded in driving away Vicki and all to whom he is attached, his violence does not abate. He turns his rage against himself—repeatedly smashing his head against the stone wall of a prison cell after he has been arrested.

Some sexual victims, like Tuesday Weld in the movie *Thief,* directed by Michael Mann, are tormented psychologically instead of physically. *Thief* is about a criminal, played by James Caan, who gets out of prison with a dream: To pull off a big job, buy a home, settle down, have kids, and be rich and normal forever. Weld, who plays a pretty, hard-luck woman whose life is repeatedly smashed apart by men, is the woman he marries. She can see that Caan is nothing but trouble, but when he sets out to woo her, she is won. When Caan's big dream starts falling apart (organized crime is crowding him) he gives her a small fortune in cash and sends her away. This woman is the toy of men and circumstances; she has no power to shape her own fate.

In Neil Simon's *Only When I Laugh,* Marsha Mason plays the central character—a forty-year-old cured alcoholic actress struggling to stay sober. She is hurt deeply by her much younger lover who throws her over for a much younger woman. Joan Hackett plays a former college beauty queen, a woman who works at being beautiful the way some people work at curing cancer, whose husband leaves her just days before her fortieth birthday.

The other side of the sexual victim is the sexual predator. In the past sexually eager females were usually schemers interested less in sex than in grabbing power from men. Nowadays, women are portrayed as being eager for sex, "horny" in a way only men used to be. The male objects of women's desires are now ambivalent.

In *Four Friends,* written by Steve Tesich and directed by Arthur Penn, the hero Danilo rejects the sexual advances of the high school girl with whom he and his two best friends are in love. The reason? Her approach is insufficiently romantic—she has come rapping on his bedroom window early in the morning. This scene, set in the early 1960s, feels a bit anachronistic; in those still repressive days not too many boys were turning down sexual invitations.

A timely scene, however, shows Sally Field's sexual overtures to Paul Newman in Sydney Pollack's movie, set in the present, *Absence of Malice.*

Newman plays a man with family ties to the underworld who is wrongly accused in the press of murdering a labor leader. Field is the overeager reporter who prints the story after it is leaked to her by a prosecutor. Newman comes calling on Field at her office to complain about this trial by newspaper. As they talk over their differences, Field says: "I'm thirty-four years old. I don't have to be courted." Newman turns her down, saying he prefers to be the one to do the asking. Later the two do get together, on Newman's terms. An exchange, which symbolically restates Newman's male prerogatives, occurs as they loll in bed. Field says, "I'm available Wednesday, Thursday, Friday, Saturday, Sunday, and Monday." "What about Tuesday?" Newman asks. "OK. Tuesday," she answers.

Another example of predatory female behavior can be seen in Blake Edward's cynical movie about Hollywood, *S.O.B.* The main character in the film is a movie director, played by Richard Mulligan, whose most recent picture has been a total flop. Failure sends him into a state of collapse, which may be why he does not pay much attention when his house is more or less invaded by a pair of pot-brained California good-time girls. These roller-skating beauties are young, sexy, and dressed in shorts, and make themselves useful answering the phone and opening the door. They are sexual predators, though, not prey. So sexually indulged are the Hollywood-Malibu denizens who visit Mulligan's house that the women have trouble finding takers.

The last scene of the thriller *Eyewitness*, directed by Peter Yates, precisely shows the altered relations between female and male. Sigourney Weaver, playing yet another aggressive television reporter, and William Hurt, a janitor, have just been rescued by the police. The murderer, who turns out to have been Weaver's elegant, educated fiance, has been taken away. Weaver and Hurt stare at each other across a distance. In a traditional movie he would have moved toward her for an embrace, and the film would have been over. Here a major reversal occurs. Hurt stands still and Weaver, the more forceful of the pair, moves toward him.

It is perhaps the disquiet this reversal provokes in men that has resulted in the glorification of a fifteen-year-old child as a sex symbol. The child in question is Brooke Shields, a tall, lanky veteran of eight films. The controversial movie in which she appeared in 1981 was *Endless Love,* based on the Scott Spencer novel of teenage sexual obsession and directed by Franco Zeffirelli.

Prior to its appearance feminists expressed outrage at the sexual exploitation of Shields; however, much of the furor died down after the film's release. Although sexual passion was undoubtedly intended, there was none in *Endless Love* and no apparent sexual exploitation of its star. Zeffirelli has admitted that to produce the effect of orgasm on Shields's face, he squeezed her large toe. During these ecstatic moments, Brooke Shields looks like a girl whose big toe is being squeezed.

The notable lack of sexuality in all of Shields's movie appearances raises a question. Could it be that this is what makes her so appealing as a sex symbol? Here is an exquisite face absolutely devoid of experience and emotion. Here is a teenager who carries her body as if it were the most delicate china; one feels she has not yet grown used to transporting so much height. She is a sexual cipher. One wonders if the men who have fantasized about her are eager to awaken her sexual desire or if the fantasy revolves around coercion. For many men, the fact that grown women no longer feign sexual indifference but are actually sexually eager has undercut their pleasure. There is no conquest when a partner is willing. Perhaps Brooke Shields's appeal is that in herself she is not sexual—she must be won, or, more ominously, she must be taken.

One sees evidence of the same phenomenon that makes Shields a sex symbol in the babydoll, be-ruffled, white pinafore, white T-straps, white ankle socks many women were sporting in the summer of 1981. One cannot help noticing that as women become more noticeable, more activist in real life, in fashion they are required to become smaller, thinner, younger, and more infantile. In 1981 a woman who objected to the babydoll look might have dressed in a jungle fatigue jumpsuit or in a business suit and tie. The high fashion choices seem to have been dress like an infant or dress like a man.

Blockbusters

Some television programs and movies in 1981 were greeted with so much acclaim or made so much money that an overview of women in popular culture cannot ignore them. Since these works were all enormously popular, the way they portray women carries the weight of popular approval.

Hill Street Blues is an NBC police drama that won eight Emmy awards in 1981, a record for a weekly series. The program, notable for its sharply drawn characterizations and its bunker humor, keeps tabs on a dozen or so main characters, all of them associated with the violent Hill Street police precinct.

Among the female characters who appear weekly are public defender Joyce Davenport, played by Veronica Hamel, whose lover is precinct captain Frank Furillo, and uniformed police officer Lucy Bates, played by Betty Thomas. Both of these women are grownups, not ingenues. They are professionally effective and at the same time capable of feeling.

The Davenport-Furillo relationship is full of dramatic and emotional possibilities because of the opposing nature of their work. In one episode, Furillo's undercover cops arrest a suspect in a series of vicious muggings of old people and Davenport gets the suspect, who is probably guilty, out of jail and has the charges thrown out on the grounds that he was illegally entrapped. Davenport's besting of Furillo does not cause a breach between them (each is doing a job) nor does it undercut the sense of sexual warmth and regard that flows between the two.

In the same episode, the scene is switched and Officer Bates is pursuing a suspect in a gang war killing. It is night; she closes in on the suspect and orders him to halt, but he turns on her and begins firing. She returns the fire and kills him instantly. Lucy looks at the body; she has killed a fourteen-year-old. Furillo arrives at the scene and assures Lucy that she has done what she had to do. A stunned Lucy moves towards the shadows with tears streaming down her face. Joyce is sitting in Furillo's car. "What happened?" she asks as he gets in and slams the door. "A fourteen-year-old kid shot a ten-year-old girl," Frank answers.

One feels a great deal of thought and care went into the creation of the characters of Joyce Davenport and Lucy Bates. Important questions were asked. Not only what would she do, but how does she think, and what would she feel? In many of the big movies in 1981, the male filmmakers seemed to be asking a different question about their female characters: Not, who is she, but who is she to me? More than television, movies are still about men and male myths.

An example of the second-handedness of women in film is *The French Lieutenant's Woman,* based on the John Fowles novel about an illicit romance set in the Victorian era, screenplay by Harold Pinter, directed by Karel Reisz, starring Meryl Streep as Sara Woodruff and Jeremy Irons as Charles Smithson. In Pinter's screenplay we know Sara Woodruff almost exclusively by the pain and torment she creates in her lover's life. She is allowed to have very little reality except insofar as she impinges on Charles and disrupts his respectable Victorian existence. She is more metaphor than human being.

Scenes in which Fowles illuminated what Sara felt are suppressed. The most crucial of these concerns the one sexual encounter between Charles and Sara. In the book, when the two finally go to bed, Charles prematurely ejaculates and the experience is a humiliating disappointment. Sara, who is reaching hungrily towards sexual fulfillment, seeking in it an avenue of self-expression, receives nothing. In the film this sexual moment is portrayed in golden, romantic terms, distorting the book and Sara's subsequent disappearance. The pseudofeminist ending Pinter has tacked onto the film, in which a tranquilized Sara returns to Charles, does not alter the fact that the entire movie objectifies its heroine, never asking how the world feels to her, asking only how she is perceived by Charles.

One of the year's major commercial hits was *Superman II,* directed by Richard Lester, starring Christopher Reeve as Superman and Margot Kidder as Lois Lane. It combines this same view of women with some of the ambivalence about female sexuality discussed earlier. The movie, which is technically quite dazzling, is a retelling of the Sampson and Delilah myth of the strong man who loses his powers after being seduced by a woman. In this latest version, Superman, after a forty-year courtship, finally marries Lois Lane. They have sex and Superman loses his magical powers. He can no longer leap tall buildings or deflect on-rushing trains. He has a fight with a tough and is beaten and humiliated. Only when he renounces his sexuality and his love of Lois Lane are his powers restored. Then he is once again available to serve as the protector of the free world and star in the coming epic, *Superman III.*

One wonders about the renewed popularity at this moment in history of male adventure stories such as *Superman.* Contained in these tales are potent fantasies, usually associated with the latency period in a boy's psychological development, of invincibility. Perhaps the political events of recent years, particularly the emergence of women's consciousness, have something to do with the return of this material.

Steven Spielberg's *Raiders of the Lost Ark,* a hyped-up adventure story made with an admirable and expensive attention to detail and locale, appeals to the same audience as *Superman II,* but its portrayal of women is very different. *Raiders,* starring Harrison Ford as Indiana Jones and Karen Allen as Marion Ravenwood, contains none of the incipient sexism of *Superman.* Superman is a chivalrous hero who must protect Lois Lane; Indiana Jones is an unchivalrous antihero who leaves Marion alone to take care of herself. From her first scene as the proprietor of a low-life bar in upper Nepal who must fight off a band of nasty thugs, we know she is equal to the task. The rough-and-tumble character of Marion brings new clout, new power, new stature, and new pow to the role of loyal sidekick.

In Warren Beatty's epic *Reds,* starring Beatty as Jack Reed and Diane Keaton as Louise Bryant, another variation, this one quite sophisticated, is enacted on the theme of tried and true companionship. Set in the decade following 1910, *Reds* tells the story of American journalist Reed, the only American to be buried inside the Kremlin, who played a major role in explaining the Russian Revolution to the rest of the world. Bryant, Reed's wife, was also a writer, although a far less accomplished one than he.

Much of the film focuses on the relationship between them. Keaton does a fine job illuminating the difficulties of a woman with unsatisfied ambitions of her own who is married to a productive, charismatic man. For a long time her professional jealousy of Reed makes her unable to write. Every good paragraph that pours from him makes her feel smaller and weaker and makes her fight even harder against the help Reed offers her. With half her energy Bryant is wedded to Jack Reed—and she does love him—and with the other half she assails him because his presence makes her feel diminished.

Only by evolving as a self-sustaining being can Bryant resolve this conflict. The psychological resolution of the problem occurs when they go to Russia during the Revolution. Bryant experiences a breakthrough in her work and the two share a thrilling historical adventure as partners. Moreover, when they return to the United States, she is able to strike out on her own. While

Reed writes *Ten Days that Shook the World,* Bryant departs on a lecture tour describing what she saw and experienced. She has found her voice and her maturity.

Fiction

The confusion created by changing sexual roles, which is very much an issue in *Reds* and in other works discussed here, has become an overriding consideration in contemporary fiction. An exploration of the meaning of women's and men's roles and of the emotions that surround these roles is underway; some deal with the the nature of sexual identity itself. This is being carried out by authors of both sexes, as domestic and sexual issues that in the past were viewed as the exclusive domain of women writers are now likely to be sensitively treated by either sex.

It ought to be noted that 1981 was not a very distinguished year for fiction. One is hopeful, however, that the exploration of female and male experience that has begun will lead in the future to important books.

The impact of feminist ideas and agitation on men is apparent from the first sequence of Leonard Michaels's novel (1981), *The men's club,* published by Farrar, Strauss & Giroux: "Women wanted to talk about anger, identity, politics, etc. I saw posters in Berkeley urging them to join groups. I saw their leaders on TV. Strong articulate faces. So when Cavanaugh phoned and invited me to join a men's club, I laughed."

But the narrator, a college professor at Berkeley, does join the club and in this short, terrifying novel he describes the violent regression that occurs when seven professional men in early middle age gather to talk about themselves.

They talk about sex. What comes through is the inability of these over-gratified men to feel satisfied. The host takes out his collection of photographs of the 622 women he has slept with. To the narrator they all look alike. The host reveals he and his wife have an "understanding" about his infidelities. Another club member, Solly Berliner, reveals he and his wife also have an "understanding":

> Cavanaugh . . . bent toward Berliner. "Solly aren't you jealous when your wife is making it with another guy?"
> "Jealous?"
> "Yeah, jealous."
> "No, man. I'm liberated."
> "What the hell does that mean?" I said.
> Berliner said, as if it were obvious, "I don't feel anything."
> "Liberated means you don't feel anything?"
> "Yeah, I'm liberated."

Talking is followed by an orgy of eating and drinking during which the men consume all the food the host's wife has prepared for her meeting the next evening: "The preparations for the women's group would feed our club. The idea of delicious food, taken this way, was thrilling." The feast on stolen food is an act of rage and revenge against women.

The group degenerates into a violent gang and begins to destroy the house: "Knives were chasing each other across the dining room, booming, bashing against the door, rarely sticking . . . The door seemed torn by monstrous fangs." The seven go outdoors and howl like wolves. When the host's wife returns and finds her house destroyed her husband turns to her and says, "I guess you're like angry."

For a feminist, reading *The men's club* feels like a glimpse into the heart of the beast. Here, finally exposed, are the fear and loathing and violence men feel towards women—extreme feelings the women's movement has exacerbated. Here, too, is a map that describes the ways in which men in groups are allowed to regress, returning not to boyhood but to an infancy in which every impulse must be gratified. *The men's club* deals with the relations between the sexes at their most extreme, at the far point on the spectrum at which men and women really do not like one another.

Surviving sisters, by Gail Pass (1981), published by Atheneum, is almost as violent. It is about the anger of two sisters trapped in a patriarchal family ruled by their uncle, Constantine Lampros.

This story has the outline of a Greek tragedy: Two brothers have died, one a soldier in Vietnam, the other a war resister in Canada. Their uncle and guardian refuses to bury the latter. Alexandra, their sister, who is powerful and angry, goes on a hunger strike to force Constantine to bury her brother. She dies accidentally, and Irena, the surviving sister who has always been afraid of her uncle, must avenge all three siblings.

After Alexandra's death Irena fantasizes that she has taken Alex's anger into herself and it has made her strong enough to fight Constantine. She becomes an avenging angel, bearing witness to his crimes: "She turned her head so he could see her eyes. I'll hate you forever for what you've done. You'll always see hatred in my eyes. I will never let you forget this."

In the course of the book Irena frees herself from her uncle and from all men—"When would it stop? Always some man was laying claim to her, grasping, brutalizing"—by becoming a lesbian.

What makes *Surviving sisters* notable is the violence of its emotions. Pass explores its female manifestations, and in a way that is related, she appropriates the sexual mastery associated with men through their power to penetrate, transposing the act of "entering" into a female activity:

> Unquestioning, he lay back and let her pull off his clothes. Her slip and pants followed as he kicked away the blankets to stretch full length in the middle of the bed. When she braced herself over him, his arms went around her neck; again she entered him, and the surge of power made her hips gyrate with excitement . . .

This anatomically curious passage can be viewed as a refusal by the author to cede any portion of sexual or emotional expression exclusively to men.

In *Dad,* by William Wharton (1981), published by Knopf, the protagonist John Tremont is a man who tries very hard to outwoman a woman by being even more nurturing, more virtuous, more self-sacrificing than a woman could be. Tremont is an American painter who lives in Paris. When the book begins he has just returned home to California to visit his ailing parents. During his visit his mother dies and Tremont's father suffers a disabling stroke. Most of the book describes Tremont's exhausting effort to care for his father. He spends his days cooking, cleaning, nursing, and shopping, and still his father's condition deteriorates drastically. Wharton focuses on the close-ups searching for the truth about his relationship to his father in the lunch he cooks or the filth he cleans. What is interesting is that a male author has devoted an entire book to describing a man's effort to master household and nurturing tasks.

Books about growing up used to focus on characters no older than eighteen or twenty. Since feminism lifted the lid off female identity and revealed great depths of dependency and immaturity hidden within women in their 20s, 30s, and 40s, scores of novels have explored their painful efforts to grow up.

One of these is Anne Bernays's *The school book* (1980), published by Harper & Row, describing one year in the life of Sally Cooper, a flute player in her 40s who lives in Cambridge. The issues in this book are basic—work and love, to take oneself seriously in work, to commit oneself to a relationship. Bernays gives us some witty dialogue on these subjects. Sally Cooper is talking on the telephone to her lover, Lou, after having received an invitation to join a major chamber group:

> I used her invitation as an excuse to call Lou. We hadn't spoken for nearly a week; I was starved.
> "Why didn't you say yes right away?"
> "Scared, maybe."
> "Scared?" He seemed to think I was nuts. "What are you afraid of?"
> "Success?"
> "Bullshit," he told me.
> "It's not," I said. "Haven't you heard of fear of success?"
> "Another fad," he said. "It's gotta go the way of biofeedback. And I suppose women are more frightened of it than men?"
> "Yes."

Sally Cooper agrees to join the chamber group. She also decides to make a commitment to Lou.

Another novel that ends with the female protagonist, Daphne Mathiesson, making a commitment to a man is Alice Adams's novel, *Rich rewards* (1980), published by Knopf. Like Sally Cooper, Daphne is a divorced woman in her 40s, who until the beginning of the novel has failed to make a commitment to work—she describes herself as "a decorator, of sorts"—or to a man. Like Sally, Daphne has great wit and good deal of insight:

Like many people of my generation and my sort of education . . .
my friends and I did a lot of emotional temperature taking, so to
speak. We were always very interested in how we were . . . other
friends and I used certain key phrases in regard to ourselves and
others—phrases dull enough in themselves but for us significant.
"In bad shape" meant terrible, nearly suicidal, probably; and so on
upward through various intimately known gradations, until we
arrived at "better," an ideal state. *I really think I'm better* indicated
true happiness: not euphoria—we all knew the dangers in
that—but warm contentment, our goal. We were certain too that
happiness meant some good balance of love and work and
probably some money.

Mary Gordon's novel *The company of women* (1980) is less well crafted. The
entire middle section of the book loses its tone and credibility, but hidden
within the first and last segments is beautiful writing about the bonds that tie
women together, tie mothers and daughters to each other, and tie all of us to
our past.

Gordon's main character is Felicitas Maria Taylor who "was called after
the one virgin martyr whose name contained some hope of ordinary human
happiness." Felicitas was brought up in Brooklyn by her widowed mother,
Charlotte, by three adoring godmothers, and by Father Cyprian Leonard, a
priest so orthodox that "when his brothers wrote to him of his mother's death,
he did not answer. He had written in reply to the letter saying she was dying,
'Has she had the last sacraments?'"

Felicitas, as Father Cyprian says, "is our only hope," the only child in a
community of adults. She is attached to adults in ways that separate her from
other children. "How could she say to her friends that the deepest pleasure of
her life was riding to the six o'clock mass alone with Father Cyprian in the
front of his red pickup truck?"

As a student at Barnard in 1969, Felicitas has a love affair with a political
science professor. She becomes pregnant and finds herself unable to undergo
an abortion. Her decision to bear the child thrusts her out of the secular world
she has just entered as a college student and returns her to the company of
women. "I now see that my pregnancy . . . my illegitimate motherhood, was
the only thing that could have kept me near him [Cyprian], near to all of them
in fact."

Gordon's book raises the possibility that women and men are not free to
create themselves in a moment—that each person is a product of a past that
continues to exert a powerful influence long after one is adult, that efforts to
liberate oneself undertaken naively, may end in failure. Her book defies contemporary ideas about what constitutes an independent life. Not through
flight, but through taking her place in the line of women, Felicitas achieves a
kind of "liberation."

At the end of *The company of women*, Felicitas, her daughter, her
mother, the godmothers, and Father Cyprian are living in upstate New York.
Felicitas is planning to marry the man who runs the local hardware store:

"And I go on, the daughter of my mother. The mother of my daughter, care-taker of the property, soon to be a man's wife. My life is isolated, difficult and formal. It is, perhaps, not the life I would have chosen, but it is a serious life. I do less harm than good."

Gordon takes women's lives and the relationships that shape them, to use her word, "seriously." One feels relief encountering an author for whom human connections still resonate, still contain deep meanings worthy of exploration. Throughout popular culture one feels that the content of relationships between the sexes has been diminished and reduced. When rage is removed, often little of emotional significance remains. Even authors of obvious talent such as Bernays and Adams suffer from a diminution of vision; their books move from point A to point B, but no further. What is missing is a vision that would synthesize old and new ideas about women and men.

Instead of a vision, what one detects is the lingering shock produced by the alteration of sexual politics. Fifteen years after the appearance of the women's movement, a stunned, emotionless quality continues to pervade much fiction and film dealing with sexual issues. In *The men's club* and in films such as *Raging Bull, Thief, Cutter's Way*, and even *Four Friends*, which contains a father-daughter murder-suicide, violence, more often than not, sexual violence, has replaced emotion. Leonard Michaels, author of *The men's club*, raises the possibility that underneath the violence no feeling remains. This fear is also expressed in Wally Shawn's quirky screenplay, *My Dinner with Andre*, directed by Louis Malle, when Andre Gregory predicts that ten years from now men will pay ten thousand dollars to be castrated so that they may feel something, anything.

Artists have not yet imagined what men and women do feel or will feel in a world altered to make room for both sexes. What some artists have succeeded in doing, however, is moving back from the precipice of sexual rage. They have begun to use the light of feminist perspective to illuminate relationships between women, between men, between women and men. This is what Mary Gordon has done in *The company of women*. Her attitude of respect is an antidote, in fact, to Solly Berliner's declaration that liberation is the absence of feeling.

REFERENCES

Jenrette, Rita, and Maxa, Kathleen. The liberation of a congressional wife. *Playboy,* April, 1981, p. 117.

People August 24, 1981.

Tolstoi, Anne Wallach. *Women's work*. New York: New American Library, 1981.

Kael, Pauline. The current cinema. *New Yorker*, November 11, 1980.

Michaels, Leonard. *The men's club*. New York: Farrar, Strauss & Giroux, 1981.

Pass, Gail. *Surviving sisters.* New York: Atheneum, 1981.

Wharton, William. *Dad.* New York: Knopf, 1981.

Bernays, Anne. *The school book.* New York: Harper & Row, 1980.

Adams, Alice. *Rich rewards.* New York: Knopf, 1980.

Gordon, Mary. *The company of women.* New York: Random House, 1980.

MOVIES

Absence of Malice, screenplay by Kurt Luedtke, directed by Sydney Pollack, with Sally Field and Paul Newman.

Cutter's Way, screenplay by Jeffrey Alan Fiskin, directed by Ivan Passer with Jeff Bridges, John Heard, and Lisa Eichorn.

Endless Love, based on the novel by Scott Spencer, screenplay by Judith Rascoe, directed by Franco Zeffirelli, starring Brooke Shields.

Eyewitness, screenplay by Steve Tesich, directed by Peter Yates, with Sigourney Weaver and William Hurt.

Four Friends, screenplay by Steve Tesich, directed by Arthur Penn, with Craig Wasson and Jodi Thelen.

The French Lieutenant's Woman, based on the novel by John Fowles, screenplay by Harold Pinter, directed by Karel Reisz, starring Meryl Streep and Jeremy Irons.

The Incredible Shrinking Womam, screenplay by Jane Wagner, directed by Joel Schumacher, with Lily Tomlin and Charles Grodin.

Looker, written and directed by Michael Crichton, with Albert Finney.

My Dinner with Andre, screenplay by Wally Shawn, directed by Louis Malle, with Wally Shawn and Andre Gregory.

9 to 5, screenplay by Colin Higgins and Patricia Resnick, directed by Colin Higgins, with Jane Fonda, Dolly Parton, and Lily Tomlin.

Only When I Laugh, screenplay by Neil Simon, directed by Glenn Jordon, with Marsha Mason, Joan Hackett, James Coco, and Kristy McNichol.

Private Benjamin, written by Nancy Meyers, Charles Shyer, and Harvey Miller, directed by Howard Zieff, with Goldie Hawn.

Raging Bull, written and directed by Martin Scorsese, with Robert De Niro and Cathy Moriarty.

Raiders of the Lost Ark, written by Lawrence Kasdan, directed by Steven Spielberg, with Harrison Ford and Karen Allen.

Reds, written and directed by Warren Beatty, with Warren Beatty and Diane Keaton.

S.O.B., written and directed by Blake Edwards, with Richard Mulligan, William Holden, and Julie Andrews.

Superman II, written by Mario Puzo, directed by Richard Lester, with Christopher Reeve and Margot Kidder.

Thief, written and directed by Michael Mann, with James Caan and Tuesday Weld.

TELEVISION

The Dorothy Stratton Story, NBC, aired November 1, 1981, with Jaime Lee Curtis.

Hill Street Blues, NBC, with Daniel J. Travanti and Veronica Hamel.

Jessica Novak, CBS, with Helen Shavers.

Love, Sidney, NBC, with Tony Randall.

Nurse, CBS, with Michael Learned.

Additional Books of Note

Fielding, Joy. *Kiss Mommy Goodbye.* New York: Doubleday, 1981. An angry book about a custody fight and subsequent "legal kidnapping" of two children by their father.

Lowery, Beverly. *Daddy's Girl.* New York: Viking, 1981. An amusing recounting of the attempt by a country singer/songwriter to free herself from her emotionally consuming father.

Maynard, Joyce. *Baby Love.* New York: Knopf, 1981. An examination of the lives of the teenage mothers who hang out at the laundromat in a small New England town.

Morrison, Toni. *Tar Baby.* New York: Knopf, 1981. A parable about race and sex, which has at its center acts of child abuse committed by a white beauty queen mother against her son that were hidden for thirty years by her black servants.

Rebeta-Burditt, Joyce. *Triplets.* New York: Delacorte Press/Seymour Lawrence, 1981. A comic novel about the quest for identity of a Los Angeles television executive who is one of triplets.

Whedon, Julia. *A Good Sport.* New York: Doubleday, 1981. An amusing novel about a woman who leaves her sportscaster husband for a fling with a professional basketball player.

Additional Films of Note

The Four Seasons, written and directed by Alan Alda, with Alan Alda, Carol Burnet, Rita Moreno, and Jack Weston. This film describes the effect on three couples—best friends—when one couple breaks up and the husband marries a much younger woman.

Mommie Dearest, screenplay by Frank Yablans, Frank Perry, Tracy Hotchner, and Robert Getchell, directed by Frank Perry, with Faye Dunaway. Dunaway plays Joan Crawford in a film based on the book by Christina Crawford, daughter of the film star, who says her mother was a child-abuser.

Rich and Famous, a remake of the 1940s film, *Old Acquaintance*, directed by George Cukor with Jacqueline Bisset and Candace Bergen.

Psychology of Women: Feminist Therapy

8

Virginia K. Donovan *
and
Ronnie Littenberg

Feminist therapy in 1981 grew, though its growth was disorderly and diverse. There was no center, no leading exponent, no single theory, and few articles or books. In part this has to do with the origins of feminist therapy. Born in the women's movement, it retains much of the quality of a social movement, and is better defined by the political awareness and social commitment on the part of the therapist than by the particular set of techniques she uses. Therefore, it is important to describe the history and politics of feminist therapy.

The critical examination of therapy (and psychological theory) by the women's movement of the 1960s was inevitable both because of the nature of therapy and because of its use as an ideological weapon against women. On one hand, therapy concerned itself with those areas of experience assigned to and "carried" by women in our culture—primarily relationships and feelings (Miller 1976). On the other hand, psychological theories about women's nature were used to justify women's place in the home and their "appropriate" roles in relation to men and children. Therapists treated women for their failure to adjust to a world of increasing contradictions for women.

Historical Background

Since World War II women's lives have been changing rapidly. Women were drawn into the work force at record levels during the war, when they assumed

---

*Both authors contributed equally to this paper. Order of authorship was determined by a flip of the coin.

211

jobs previously reserved for men. They were later pushed out of these jobs by returning soldiers. Women's participation in the work force never returned to prewar levels and a powerful ideology emerged (or reemerged in new forms) (Ehrenreich and English 1978) that helped justify their return to the home and acceptance of work at low pay. Psychology, advanced as a neutral, objective science of behavior, was central to this ideological effort. Behavioral scientists joined child-rearing experts in promoting the theory of maternal instinct; women would fulfill themselves by caring for their children. Less than total mothering would lead to deprived children; children needed constant attention by one caretaker or they became apathetic and hopeless. Penis envy and its resultant rejection of femininity was considered the cause of women's desire for other kinds of fulfillment. Similarly, female masochism was offered as an explanation of why self-abnegation was really gratification. Perhaps most cruelly, women were blamed for any problems with their children (mothers must have been overprotective or rejecting or both) (Ehrenreich and English 1978) and with their own inability to find contentment (they were neurotic).

Women who were full-time housewives found themselves increasingly isolated, sometimes from the extended families and communities they had moved away from expressly to benefit the children. In general these women were isolated from adult company, especially from other women, and from the social relations that being part of the work force promotes. Housework was devalued (domestic skills bought in the marketplace yielded very low wages), invisible, repetitive, lonely, without boundaries, and often empty. Women who felt forced to sacrifice their own needs by an ideology that taught that serving others was their only legitimate role logically felt an increasing loss of self-hood.

Other changes in women's lives increased the tension between idealized domestic life and actual possibilities. Women's lives could not make up for the contradictions in the whole society between human needs and the social inequalities of race, class, and sex. They continued to enter the labor force (in 1960, 40 percent of all American women held jobs), and more of those who did were married with children. They juggled the demands of work and home without the support of day care, flexible work arrangements, or collectivized (or even shared) household responsibilities. They were likely to continue to look for jobs that were part-time, flexible, and easy to enter and exit, that is, low-paying jobs. At the same time, larger numbers of women were graduating from college than ever before and facing the choice of pure domesticity or women's low-paid work, since college degrees often brought them no gain in the job market.

Betty Friedan (1963) named the barrage of propaganda that blamed women for their unhappiness in the face of these increasing contradictions and changing expectations, "the feminine mystique." A general critique of women's relationship to society emerged and was consolidated in the formation of the National Organization for Women in 1964. Militant middle-class feminists revived liberal feminism and demanded equality for women. Although this movement did not challenge the larger social structure, it did push beyond the demand for formal equality in civil and political spheres to recognition of women's oppression in the "private" areas of life — including sexuality and reproduction.

At the same time, a political movement was growing that did begin to question capitalism. The civil rights movement of the early 1960s exposed the underside of the prosperous 1950s: racism and poverty. The rise of black consciousness at home and of Third World liberation movements abroad expanded ideas of freedom and liberation. The Vietnam War brought home an awareness of the workings of the United States political economic system overseas. These movements helped clarify how, in this economic system, many people paid a high price so that some fewer members could make a profit.

In the social movements accompanying these events women worked side by side with men, expanding their analysis of the oppression of others, and gradually recognized the direct impact of oppression on their own lives. A women's liberation movement burst forth in the late 1960s that went further than any had before, both in its social criticism and in its understanding of the penetration of capitalism into personal life. Women discovered that their intimate oppression forced a redefinition of political and personal life and captured this insight in the phrase, "the personal is political."

Consciousness raising was a main method women used to break through previous perceptions of the world and themselves. Central to this process were the connections drawn between personal experiences and feelings and social reality; the recognition that many problems formerly seen as purely personal were now seen as shared by many women and thus were part of their social experience.

As women questioned all aspects of personal life, attention necessarily turned to psychological theories and therapy. Therapy was one area outside the home that dealt with private life — the world of family relationships and feelings. With exploration of people's intimate experiences in the family, a route was provided to understand how social reality is internalized. For example, therapy reveals how society's relations of domination and submission are reproduced by a hierarchical family (men are heads of household) in which children first learn to accept inequality as natural and are socialized into sex roles and relations of power.

Women took some of the lessons of consciousness raising and tried to refashion therapy so it would be more useful and less oppressive. Therapy could be, it was hoped, a place for a more thorough exploration of one's situation as a woman, focusing on the particular ways women learned about human relations and themselves and examining their (often hidden) needs and desires. Therapy could also be a method of changing the sometimes indirect or self-defeating ways women tried to get their needs met (directness by women in trying to meet their own needs had always been accompanied by the threat of isolation). To do this, however, certain aspects of therapy had to be changed.

Feminist Therapy Defined

Szasz (1961), Chesler (1972), Tennov (1976), Johnson (1980), and others have written of how traditional psychotherapy has been used as a means of social control and as such is harmful to women and other oppressed groups. Among the criticisms made by feminists are that the structure of the therapeutic relationships is based on authoritarian, patriarchal roles and reinforces women's sense of dependency and inadequacy; that a medical model treats unhappiness as pathology or as an illness; that the goal of treatment becomes adjustment not change; and that social problems are often treated as though they were the responsibility of the individual.

During the past decade several books and papers on feminist therapy have been published (Mandler and Rush 1974; du Bois 1976; Williams 1976; Rawlings and Carter 1977; Brodsky 1980; Gilbert 1980; Kaschak 1981; Ernst and Goodison 1981). These describe therapists' attempts to reconceptualize the goals of therapy and the nature and function of the therapeutic process, and how to adjust the role of the therapist to be more compatible with newly developed theory on the psychology of women as well as with the overall goals of the women's movement. Beyond agreement that feminist therapy is not based on a particular theory of psychological development or on specific therapeutic techniques, definitions differ widely. In fact, a recent paper by Kaschak (1981) provides a detailed comparison *among* feminist therapies. She divides them into radical grassroots, radical professional, and liberal professional approaches and compares these to nonsexist and traditional psychoanalytic therapy.

This discussion does not attempt to review all that is currently being said or written, but rather describes one approach or way of thinking about women and therapy, and identifies some of the major issues being addressed by therapists of similar orientation.

To begin, feminist therapy must be distinguished from other kinds of services or experiences often provided by feminist organizations (even though some of these may have a therapeutic effect or be used in conjunction with therapy), and from nonsexist therapy. Therapy is a voluntary consulting or counseling relationship in which the therapist has formal training or acquired skills in the helper or facilitator role. The problems to be worked on are defined by the client and, at least initially, perceived by her to be partly personal in nature. Usually the client is also seeking relief from some kind of subjectively experienced psychic discomfort or pain. Therapy as described here is not a counseling relationship characterized as primarily educational or information-sharing (job counseling, referral networks, etc.), or which only teaches a particular skill (assertiveness training, relaxation techniques, etc.), or which is a leaderless activity (consciousness raising, support, or self-help groups).

A therapist who is not overtly authoritarian or oppressive and who espouses egalitarian values with respect to sex roles is not necessarily a feminist therapist, although she may share values and attitudes with feminist therapists (Rawlings and Carter 1977; Kaschak 1981). With a nonsexist, humanistic approach sex-role behaviors are not prescribed and may even be openly questioned. A client is assumed to be a person with strengths; these are identified and allied with by the therapist to promote the client's development as a competent and autonomous person. The therapy relationship is characterized by trust, mutuality, and respect.

Feminist therapy becomes distinct from nonsexist therapy in the therapist's analysis of the forms of social, economic, and political oppression that affect women individually as well as a group. This analysis informs the therapist's understanding of how women develop and function in our society, and of how change may occur. (Without this analysis a therapist is not a feminist therapist even if she identifies herself as one.) The feminist therapist's belief that the personal is political, that for fundamental changes to occur in the emotional lives of women basic social structures must change, has two direct implications for her work. The first is that she actively struggles with the manifestation of sexism, racism, and class oppression that affect her own attitudes and values. She believes that therapy is *not* value free and that she must understand her own values and make them explicit. The second is that she believes that there are no individual solutions for social, moral, and political problems; however, she recognizes that joining with others to work for change can be a major source of validation and empowerment.

Concretely, these implications mean that a feminist therapist cannot be working in an isolated way. She must be informed of and involved in working with women and other groups for social change. She must be aware of the social and political work going on in her community so that she is able to share her understanding and resources with her clients.

A crucial aspect of her work is in helping her clients to distinguish the things in their lives or situations for which they are personally responsible, to identify self-defeating behaviors, and to differentiate both from attitudes and circumstances that reflect broader social problems. With respect to the former, the therapist helps her clients set goals and develop skills so they are able to make effective and appropriate changes in behavior. With respect to the latter she tries to validate the clients' experiences of frustration or powerlessness, and encourages them to meet and join with others who have similar problems.

Feminist Critiques of Theory

Since feminist therapy is not grounded in a separate coherent theory of psychological development and change, feminist therapists have examined traditional theories for their usefulness in conceptualization and practice of therapy. These examinations take different forms depending on the nature of the theory. In the case of family therapy, recent focus has been on integrating feminist therapy principles with a family systems approach. Feminist therapists have assessed gestalt, encounter, and humanist therapies and described techniques they found useful. They have tried to deepen, revise, and reformulate psychoanalytic theory according to feminist insights. Current thinking in each of these areas is briefly described.

Family Systems Therapy

The practice of family therapy usually involves techniques based on major concepts about family systems (Chasin and Grunebaum 1980). These concepts are sometimes organized into particular systems approaches (structural theory, communications theory, Bowen theory), but writers have also tried to integrate these approaches or provide transcendent concepts (Framo 1972; Chasin and Grunebaum 1980). The most general theme is that the unit of understanding or treatment is the family or the system. Family therapists believe that individual behavior can best be understood as part of an interacting system. In a family or closely related unit, members "reciprocally carry part of each other's psychology and form a feedback system which in turn regulates and patterns their individual behaviors" (Framo 1972, p. 271).

Many therapists are drawn to family systems therapy as an effective and realistic approach that helps people deal with interpersonal relationships. It allows therapists to work with all members of a system, for example, children and parents, without becoming an advocate for either (as was often the case in traditional child-guidance clinics); they can work with both people in a couple or with an extended family.

Family therapy theory includes a number of underlying assumptions attractive to many therapists. It emphasizes the importance of social context in determining behavior, viewing symptoms as manifestations of system difficulties. It moves away from victim-blaming and medical models of individual pathology; all behavior is seen as adaptive in its context, and thus traditional concepts of etiology and diagnosis are eschewed.

Although many family therapists would describe themselves as adherents of equality between men and women, there has been a stunning absence of discussion of sexism and feminism in the literature. This makes it likely that most family therapists in fact hold unexamined values and biases about women's role in the family (Hare-Mustin 1978), about definitions of power and reality in the family, and about what constitutes mental health for women (Broverman et al. 1970; American Psychological Association 1975). Without consciousness-raising about sexism, therapists are unaware of ways they may subtly (or not so subtly) reinforce traditional roles and behaviors that are damaging to women. Only very recently have writings appeared about family systems approaches and feminism (Hare-Mustin 1978; Gurman and Klein 1980; Caust, Libow, and Raskin 1981; Libow et al. 1981).

They have pointed to cases in which the model of family therapy is biased against women, as in the Bowen model that explicitly values intellectual processes over emotional processes, and the Boszormenyi-Nagy model that supports sex-stereotyped roles (Hare-Mustin 1978). Even when the model is thought to be value-free, sexism often exists in the therapist's assumptions about what behavior is expected from each. For example, family therapists may see themselves as models for appropriate sex-role behavior and sex-role relations in which men dominate. Hare-Mustin (1978) points out how "Minuchin sees himself as modeling the male executive functions, forming alliances, most typically with the father, and through competition, rule-setting, and direction, demanding that the father assume control of the family and exert leadership, much as Minuchin leads and controls the session" (p. 184). Similarly, women therapists are often taught to use their feminine traits of warmth and wisdom (parallel to women's traditional roles in the family) to appeal to the masculine instincts of male clients (Hare-Mustin 1978).

Accompanying a lack of analysis of sexism, family therapists often adopt a morally neutral stance that can lead to their defining behavior only as a "couples interaction," even when the behavior may assault a woman's sense of reality or, in some cases, actually physically harm her. In contrast, feminists believe that some behavior is wrong and unacceptable (such as physical abuse) and disagree with the tendency in a systems approach to see oppression as a "mutually regulated dance."

Marriage is viewed as a closed system by family therapy models, with little attention given to members' relationships with the outside world (Gurman and Klein 1980). This conceptualization results in tremendous distortion of power relationships within the family by ignoring women's lack of power, limited economic opportunities, and experiences of sexism in the rest of the world. The power aspects of sex roles in the family are largely ignored by family therapists unless it is the women who appear to have power. Then the power (real or apparent) is seen as the basis for psychological dysfunction (Hare-Mustin 1978).

In the closed-model system a woman is defined primarily in relational terms and implicitly expected to derive her identity and satsifactions within the family unit (Gurman and Klein 1980). This reproduces the way in which women are defined in our culture and allows little space for the kind of self-exploration so often denied to women and so much needed by them. Although some family therapy models stress the need for a balance between separation and closeness, for a woman to balance out a lifetime of living through and for others, she may need the context of individual or group therapy to begin to see herself as a separate person.

Libow and associates (1981) describe how issues of power and insight are the major sources of differences in approach between family and feminist therapy. In their structural approach, family therapists rely on "expert" power, power based on the knowledge and skills of the therapist as owned by her and needed by the family. The expert role is strategic, and is used to exert pressure to effect change. She may use a variety of techniques that are active, directive, and whose purposes are not necessarily made explicit to the family. Insight is not a goal in itself.

In contrast, feminist therapists rely on "referent power," based on using the self as a point of identification and emphasizing the commonality of women's experience. The feminist therapist is seen as a partner in a collaborative venture; she stresses respect in the relationship between client and therapist in order to move away from the paternalistic models of expert doctor and dependent patient, and to respect the client's capacity for self-knowledge and self-direction. She thus tries to demystify the therapy process, and stresses open and direct communication between herself and her client. Insight, consciousness-raising, and education are viewed as necessary to an understanding of one's personal history and social and political realities.

Family and feminist therapy differ as well in their approach to sex, class, and ethnic differences. Some family therapists feel that ethnic and class characteristics must be noted to understand the family, but not necessarily challenged (Pearce 1980; Libow et al. 1981). They argue that to do so might drive families away. Feminist therapists directly explore and confront sex-role-related stereotyped behavior as well as the influence of class and ethnic behavior. They believe that in a society that is sexist, racist, and stratified by class, it is impossible to know who you are and where you stand without understanding how those stratifications affect your history and possibilities. Not to explore these dimensions is to return women's problems to the realm of being "only internal."

Not all feminist family therapists agree that power and insight must be handled differently. (This is partly the result of different schools of family therapy.) Hare-Mustin (1978) argues that it is possible for a family therapist to equalize the relationship by demystifying therapy and by using consciousness-raising, education, and insight. She also provides examples of how issues such as sex, race, and class could be explored in the context of family therapy.

Family systems theory and practice have been developed on a model of the heterosexual nuclear family. Although theorists would claim that this approach can be applied to any system, for example lesbian couples or single-mother families, this has yet to be demonstrated. Examination of family therapy by feminists is only beginning. To what extent it can be used with nontraditional families or in nonsexist ways, or integrated with principles of feminism is still controversial. Discussion is tentative, and much more is needed: on the different kinds of family therapy and their relationship to feminist therapy; on description of the populations, problems, and goals brought to therapy; and on the sexual politics of family therapy.

Human Potential Movement or Growth Movement Therapy

Very little has been written by feminist therapists on the human potential movement (sometimes called third-force psychology or growth movement therapy). Human potential therapies emphasize the importance and validity of feelings and individual entitlement. They consist of strategies to help people bypass some defenses and resistances against directly experiencing feelings. Ideally, this is attempted in a context in which the client feels safe and trusting.

In their book, *In our own hands: a woman's book of self-help therapy*, Ernst and Goodison (1981) describe why they and other feminists might be drawn to this approach. Growth movement therapies promote self-awareness, self-assertiveness, and acceptance of one's feelings and one's body. As with some other therapies, to emphasize feelings is to enter and validate the realm of experience assigned to women. However, growth movement therapies make a public credo out of knowing and attending to one's own feelings. For women, this has a liberating aspect. By training, women are more likely to recognize others' needs than their own. They are also more likely to be punished if they try to meet their own needs in direct or open ways (Miller 1976). Growth movement therapies provide techniques that help identify feelings, and that give permission for the expression of taboo or unacceptable feelings. For example, gestalt techniques aid in the discovery of feelings that have been denied by examining projections of one's own feelings onto parts of dreams and onto behaviors and attitudes disliked in other people, or by uncovering unconscious conflicts between needs and obligations.

These therapies also encourage and train people in the direct expression of their feelings. Female socialization usually prohibits women from being directly angry, competitive, or even dependent (dependency is both sanctioned and condemned). Encounter techniques permit and teach more direct assertive behaviors to substitute for the indirect and sometimes manipulative ones on which women have learned to depend.

Feminist therapists have found the growth movement's emphasis on body awareness and acceptance to be useful. Women have been kept ignorant of their bodies' workings, taught to be scared or disgusted by their bodies' sexual and other physical functions, and alienated from their bodies by mass media stereotypes of beauty (Barbach 1975; Orbach 1978; Ernst and Goodison 1981). Growth movement techniques include direct work with the body to loosen blocks against feelings (Reichian therapy) and strategies for becoming aware of feelings and attitudes about one's body.

The liberating aspect of this focus on feelings and entitlement is accompanied by a philosophy (and often practice) that is deeply oppressive to women as well. This approach implicitly and explicitly emphasizes feelings to the exclusion of intellect and values and fails to take into account the individual's social context. Feminist writers (Ehrenreich and English 1978; Ernst and Goodison 1981) have criticized the human potential movement for its lack of analysis of sexism and the social conditions that affect and constrain experience and opportunity. Without such an analysis the human potential movement disregards the sources of pain, suffering, and oppression that exist in society and shape contemporary life.

By positing unlimited potential for individual transformation and growth, the human potential movement assumes an isolated human being, free to restructure her life situation. This atomized person has within her her own reality, which is largely independent of social structures and interpersonal relations. In this view something is real only if it is felt to be real. This promise of total control may be particularly seductive at a time when a woman is experiencing less control over her life and less possibility for fulfillment.

The human potential movement's ideal individuals are completely self-centered and free to seek their own gain at whatever cost to others. It leaves out consideration of social embeddedness and the process through which needs are satisfied in a social context. Human bonds and responsibility are also denied by this model that both encourages women to practice an aggressive individualistic male model of living and perpetuates their sense of aloneness.

Self-awareness is emphasized to the exclusion of other types of awareness. The lack of race, class, and sex analysis allows participants to forget these "troublesome" aspects of life. Women are offered a false egalitarianism that denies the discrimination and unequal treatment they actually receive in daily life. These more universal values such as racial, sexual, and social equality are ignored, since human potential therapies consider values to be excess baggage that detract from individual achievement.

Without an understanding of sexism, in practice these therapies reproduce sexist and authoritarian modes within the therapeutic relationship (Ernst and Goodison 1981). Issues of leadership are rarely addressed. In some instances cult leaders and showmen such as Fritz Perls and Werner Erhard offer a patriarchal model of domination as they refuse to deal with power and authority in the therapy relationship. In other forms of growth movement therapy the therapist may identify himself as a humanist and claim that therapy can be without any power relationship. (Feminists believe therapy always involves a power relationship that should be recognized and explored.)

Instant trust and uncritical openness, which are particularly difficult for women, are often goals of human potential therapies. While no one should be expected to offer such blind faith, women often have been pressured to do so even though this repeats their unquestioning submission to men. Women simply do not have the freedom to be openly angry and assertive and, in fact, male society would not accept this kind of intimacy coming from women's own perspectives and initiatives. In general, values concerning desirable behavior are formulated without regard to their particular meaning to women. Physical touching, for example, is uncritically encouraged without consideration of its associations for women with sexual possession and male exertions of power.

The same blindness to sexism is manifested in humanistic psychology's blindness to racism and class stratification. By not even trying to grasp these central structures of society, humanists reinforce their own variant of the status quo. Thus they do not question capitalism or patriarchy, and they tailor techniques to contain and manage discontent. For example, they run sensitivity groups for large corporations, conduct transactional analysis groups in prisons, and operate encounter sessions between police and ghetto residents (Ehrenreich and English 1978).

Feminist therapists have taken from the human potential movement techniques for uncovering feelings, and have applied them in settings that can become safe places for women to share feelings and values (Ernst and Goodison 1981). They have rejected the underlying assumptions of the human potential movement that individual improvement and liberation are possible or sufficient.

Psychoanalysis

Psychoanalysis is both a theory of development, of society, and of civilization, and a form of therapy. Both exist within Freud, but the tension between them is complex and often contradicted. The pressure on the individual practitioner to focus on the individual and attempt to help find particular solutions to her problems has led to revisions in theory that continue to be disputed (Schneider 1975; Jacoby 1975). The relationship between psychoanalytic theory and psychoanalytic therapy has not been clarified by feminists who criticized Freud's theory of female development for its male supremacist view; that is, acceptance of the authority of patriarchal society, of the biological inferiority of women, and of the superiority of vaginal orgasm. They have also criticized his cultural theory that transforms historical phenomena into universal, biological instincts and they have documented Freudian concepts never substantiated by research (Millett 1970; Chesler 1972; Brown 1973; Schneider 1975; Rohrbaugh 1981). Recently, some feminists have attempted to use the psychoanalytic methodology to develop new insights on female psychology (Chodorow 1978; Miller 1976). These attempts will be described briefly. Our focus, however, is primarily on feminist *therapy*, not theories of development or the psychology of women.

Very little has been written by feminists on psychoanalytic treatment and still less on the relationship of theory to practice. Ernst and Goodison (1981) describe how psychoanalysts' training, because it is expensive and selection is highly controlled, tends to eliminate all but financially well-off white men. Training is hierarchical and conservative, discouraging questioning and alternative points of view. Treatment is costly, further removing analysts from contact with anyone unlike themselves. Psychoanalysts bring to the therapy situation the values and attitudes of the dominant patriarchal society, and although they may examine the way their feelings affect the therapy (countertransference), they are less likely to examine the way their values do. Transference in therapy involves a power relationship within which the client ("patient" in psychoanalytic terms) is encouraged to reexperience childhood feelings. New emotional experiences with authority figures may be constructive, but if the reality of the relationship is denied and not explored they can also be harmful. Psychoanalysis locates the source of current feelings in early childhood experiences and this is similarly double-edged. It may be helpful to recognize the origins of assumptions about interpersonal relationships and to find earlier bases for feelings, but this can also invalidate a woman's sense of her objective social and economic realities if these are not also identified.

Despite these problems and dangers, many feminist therapists incorporate some concepts from psychoanalysis into a psychodynamic approach. These include concepts of the unconscious, transference, conflict, and a general understanding developed by Freud of how social reality takes root in personality through early childhood experiences. While there are some articles written from a feminist perspective by psychoanalysts or with a psychoanalytic approach (Miller 1973; Strouse 1974), we have seen nothing by feminist therapists explicitly about the usefulness of psychoanalysis as a therapy.

Two recent books by feminists working within the psychoanalytic tradition have attempted to comment on, use, and revise psychoanalytic theory toward new understandings of female development. Jean Baker Miller, in *Toward a new psychology of women* (1976), offers a fascinating account of how a shift in perspective from a male point of view to a feminist one alters our understanding of female psychological dynamics. Beginning with an analysis of women's subordinate status to men, she examines how this social role defines the personality characteristics that women develop and determines their activities, roles, and emotional experiences. Men (or dominants, as she calls them, thus extending the analysis to power relationships among other groups as well) hold power and create social structures and ideology that justify their power and "scientifically" demonstrate how *their* nature is *human* nature. Women are assigned to parts of human experience and human nature that are unacknowledged and denied by men, such as feelings of "vulnerability, weakness, helplessness, dependency, and the basic emotional connections between an individual and other people" (p. 22). Issues women deal with—human development and human ends (how to care for people, how to organize society to serve people)—concern basic questions of our culture and need to be reintegrated into the whole society to be solved. Miller's analysis generates new understandings of women's strengths and weaknesses and of their search for creativity and affiliation. She argues that psychoanalysis has been mainly concerned with these crucial areas of experience, but at the same time she shows how a perspective that begins with an analysis of social roles allows and requires reformulations of psychoanalytic concepts, psychological terminology, and theories of development and female nature.

Nancy Chodorow, in *The reproduction of mothering* (1978), uses object relations theory to explain how women's role as primary, and at times exclusive, child-rearer creates sex differences and leads to the social organization of gender inequality. Chodorow offers the most elaborate view to date of the mother-daughter relationship and how it affects our sense of ourselves as independent persons and our relationships to others. Unlike Miller's book, however, sexuality and early emotional experiences are emphasized over social and historical factors, and some feminists believe that psychoanalytic assumptions previously challenged by feminists as invalid, remain (Rich 1980; Rohrbaugh 1981). Rohrbaugh (1981) argues that Chodorow accepts Freud's theory of penis envy and castration anxiety despite the fact that these have not been verified in research, that she assumes all women are heterosexual, and that she uses sexuality as an explanation for mothers' differential treatment of boys and girls, but leaves out social explanations, in effect blaming women for female oppression. Rohrbaugh points out how Chodorow maintains that women define themselves in relational terms as a result of emotional and personal experience rather than as part of a social role.

The resurgence of interest in psychoanalysis has been noted by many feminist therapists. At the 1981 conference of the Association for Women in Psychology (AWP), papers on this topic drew overflowing crowds. Because feminist therapy has not grown from a theoretical base in psychological theory and because its development is still in the early stages, feminists are drawn to possible sources of new insight and theory. Whether or not psychoanalysis can provide them remains highly controversial.

Problems Addressed by Feminist Therapists

A feminist perspective has enabled therapists to "see" problems that previously have been ignored, thought to be insignificant, or have been looked at incorrectly. Some of the issues recently addressed have been: violence toward women—rape, battering, incest, and sexual harassment; substance abuse—alcohol and drug addiction, compulsive eating and dieting; and sexuality.

Although these issues influence the lives of most women, they have been avoided by therapists (including women) for several reasons. First, most therapists have been trained in traditional (male) psychological theory, which as Naomi Weisstein (1971) put it ". . . has nothing to say about what women are really like, what they need and what they want . . ." (p. 209).

Second, therapists have had to struggle with personal reluctance to involve themselves with problems that may evoke their own deep fears (a common reaction to battering and incest), that arouse feelings of contempt or revulsion toward their clients' unacceptable, non-sex-role stereotypic behavior (e.g., the alcoholic mother who neglects her children), or that make them feel frustrated and angry at their clients' powerlessness and victimization.

Third, many women clients experience a deep sense of shame and guilt about their problems, blaming themselves and perceiving (often accurately) that they will also be blamed by others. Out of a sense of self-protection they often deny, minimize, or communicate only indirectly the existence of their "unacceptable" problems.

In response to these three obstacles, feminists have tried to educate themselves and the general public by documenting the existence, incidence, and manifestations of problems affecting women, their causal factors and psychological consequences. They have also worked to develop treatment and support services and to coordinate their work with other community (often nonprofessional) groups.

Violence Toward Women

Feminists writing about violence toward women (Brownmiller 1975; Walker 1979, 1980; Herman 1981; Leidig 1981) have attempted to dispel several popular myths: namely, that victims of violence "asked for it" or provoked it, that violence typically occurs between two disturbed individuals, or that violence occurs mainly among nonwhite or poor people. Whether it takes the form of rape, battering, incest, sexual harassment, or pornography, a feminist analysis holds that violence against women is pervasive and is the product of a patriarchal culture in which men control the form of social institutions and women's bodies.

The *threat* of violence affects all women and benefits all men, and as such is a potent source of social control that keeps women isolated, frightened, subservient, and dependent. Typically, when women do report incidents they are disbelieved or blamed. The greater the intimacy between perpetrator and victim the less the incidence of reporting and the greater the tendency to blame the victim (Leidig 1981). Thus acts such as marital or date rape, spouse battering, or incest are often kept hidden and many times are not identified by the victim as violent.

Walker (1979), writing about battered wives, and Herman (1981), about father-daughter incest, report that victims of domestic violence often feel confused about whether they identify themselves as victims and that this confusion in part reflects guilt or shame about their experiencing feelings of pleasure, closeness, or power in the relationship with the abusive man. A similar confusion is often experienced by victims of sexual harassment (e.g., the young female worker being pressured to be sexually involved with a male boss) or rape (e.g., forcible sex occurring after a date or when the woman has been drinking, or sex between therapist and client).

While media coverage, educational campaigns, and the establishment of local hotlines, crisis centers, and shelters have helped to break down the isolation of some women victims, many others continue to live with a sense of deep shame and guilt, holding themselves responsible for what has been done to them. Feminist therapists have attempted to deal with this problem by learning about the form and consequences of violence, particularly domestic violence, so they can recognize symptoms and indirect clues that violence has occurred and help their clients to share their painful secrets.

While traditional psychotherapeutic approaches might use a model of intrapsychic pathology (e.g., the woman is masochistic, the man psychopathic) or a family systems perspective of shared responsibility (each party has responsibility for the events between them), a feminist approach would emphasize labeling events for what they are: sex under circumstances of coercion is rape, pushing and hitting even if no medical attention is needed is battering, any form of secret sexual contact between a parent or parent figure and a child is incest, and so forth. The therapist would share her belief that although the victim is not to blame, she might need to take major steps to protect herself in the future. The therapist would also work to educate her client about healthy intimacy and sexuality, since many women have had little experience with sexual relationships that are caring and mutually satisfying.

A feminist therapist assumes that a working therapeutic alliance is not possible if a woman's health and safety are in danger and may involve herself in some kind of direct legal intervention or in helping her client get money and shelter; in any case, the therapist works concretely with the woman to develop escape or conditions of safety for herself and her children. The assumption that the client's safety is primary also determines the form of therapy. For example, Walker (1979, 1980) concluded that it is almost impossible to make couple therapy safe for a battered woman—that a woman's need to please combined with her fear of the batterer massively interferes with her being able openly to express her feelings in therapy. Walker therefore recommends individual or group treatment for the woman and separate treatment for the man. Herman (1981), in contrast, reports that some family therapy programs for victims of father-daughter incest have been effective, but she notes that in these programs the offenders have been ordered by the courts to participate and that nonparticipation would mean jail sentences.

Because the privacy of the individual therapy relationship may in effect reinforce a woman's isolation and need for secrecy, most feminist therapists at some point encourage clients who are victims of violence to involve themselves in community-based programs or groups. In most major cities there are networks of shelters and hotlines for rape victims and battered women. Typically, these provide shelter, legal, economic, and medical advocacy, and some kind of counseling. Individual and group counseling for rape victims emphasizes women giving comfort and support to each other about the trauma experienced with its accompanying fear, rage, and sense of powerlessness and invasion.

Assertiveness training and gestalt techniques are often used in counseling programs for battered women; the former to teach appropriate, effective ways of expressing their needs and protecting themselves; the latter to help evoke, in a safe setting, feelings (particularly those of anger) that previously have been expressed only indirectly or repressed altogether. Counseling usually takes place in a group and often the counselors themselves are former victims. This structure provides a direct way for women who have been isolated, dependent, and powerless to see that they can support and protect each other and together find effective ways of confronting their oppression and reconstructing their lives.

In many areas groups for incest victims have been formed, some led by therapists, some by other victims, and some established on a leaderless self-help basis. These groups provide a supportive context for victims to share their secret, to express the feelings of rage and sadness felt toward parents for abusing or failing to protect them, and usually to plan some kind of direct steps to confront or to share with other family members what has occurred. The breakdown of secrecy both within the group and within the family helps free victims from the paralyzing sense of shame and guilt with which most of them have lived for many years.

Substance Abuse

Although addiction to drugs and alcohol tends to be more profoundly disruptive to women's lives and functioning than compulsive eating and dieting, feminist analyses have shown that women with these problems have much in common. Feminists interpret women's addictions as being both a symbolic protest against the pressures and demands placed on them in our society and as attempts to reconcile or escape these pressures. Up to a point, use of alcohol or drugs or concern with dieting and thinness is culturally supported: women must strive to be sexier, funnier, calmer, and more beautiful for men. Furthermore, several billion-dollar industries are involved—the drug industry, the medical establishment, food, entertainment, and clothing industries. When women's involvement with food or drugs gets out of control, that is, when they can no longer fulfill their caretaking, nurturing, and sexual functions, they are judged harshly as being repulsive, weak, self-destructive, and crazy. It is with both the widespread existence of addictions and the condemnation of women who "go public" with their problem that feminists have concerned themselves.

Drug and Alcohol Addiction.　From one-third to one-half of the alcoholics in this country are women, making a conservative figure of 3.3 million women with serious drinking problems (Sandmaier 1980). Sixty to eighty percent of psychotropic drugs prescribed (depending on classification as tranquilizer, sedative, or stimulant) are prescribed to women (Nellis 1980). An estimated one to two million women have prescribed-drug dependencies and many are cross-addicted to alcohol (Fidell 1981). Addictions cross class, race, and ethnic lines. Despite these statistics, drug and alcohol addiction are generally viewed as male or lower-class phenomena; research and treatment efforts have been almost exclusively directed toward men (Nellis 1980; Sandmaier 1980; Gomberg 1981; Fidell 1981).

As with violence against women, the erroneous view of addictions as sex-linked or class-linked partially reflects how women hide the problems out of shame and guilt. This distortion also serves a function in our sexist society. The double standard where men's excessive drinking is tolerated but women's is not maintains male power by punishing and condemning women for deviating from the "true" female role. This serves as a warning to other women to hide or deny their commonality with the "fallen woman" (Sandmaier 1980). When drugs are involved (since for women most drugs are legally obtained by prescription) pressure to hide the scope of the problem is strong, for to not do so would implicate the government, drug companies, and the medical profession (Nellis 1980).

Most drug and alcohol treatment programs and techniques have been developed for men and have been singularly ineffective for women. First, these programs almost never accommodate the realities of women's lives—that most are poor or economically dependent and have almost exclusive responsibility for raising their children. Unless a program can help free a woman from at least some of her work and family responsibilities, she cannot participate in treatment *at all*. Programs developed by women for addicted women have begun to incorporate child care and job training components but progress has been slow due to lack of funding and nonsupportive social attitudes. (For the women who have already lost their families and homes—the "bag ladies"—there are seldom available shelters or legal or medical help that they need to survive.)

Many male-oriented drug and alcohol programs use aggressive confrontation techniques to challenge the men's perceptions of control, power, and self-sufficiency. These are highly inappropriate for women and serve to reinforce their already low self-esteem, sense of powerlessness, and dependency. Even supportive self-help treatment approaches (such as Alcoholics Anonymous) are often male-dominated and as such encourage women to give up their addiction so that they may return to their homes and their nurturing roles as wives and mothers, thus reinforcing their guilt that they have failed as women (Nellis 1980; Sandmaier 1980).

Feminists and therapists try to intervene in the cycle of powerlessness, anger, and guilt by providing (usually in a group context) support and analysis that the women's "failures" as wives, mothers, and women reflect their attempts to live up to impossible societal standards, and that their guilt and self-hatred only compound the problems. Practical needs are addressed and self-control is urged. Typically, the focus is on here-and-now aspects of the women's lives; they are encouraged to develop friendships and to learn to advocate for and support each other in times of stress and crisis.

Recognizing the high rate of alcoholism in the lesbian and gay communities (several studies show an incidence of about 35 percent) (Sandmaier 1980) and the heavily heterosexual orientation of most traditional treatment programs and self-help groups, feminist therapists have begun to do outreach and develop services to meet the special needs of these clients. These therapists interpret the high rate of alcoholism as a function of gay bars being the *only* safe and available social context in which lesbians can socialize. Also, living in society where they are so openly feared and hated creates tremendous pressure and many lesbians turn to alcohol and drugs to anesthetize their feelings of anger, guilt, and self-hate. Through lesbian alcoholic groups, education in the gay community, sponsorship of drug and alcohol-free coffee houses and cultural events, and through support groups for friends and lovers of alcoholics, progress has been made in providing support and encouragement for lesbian women to gain better control over their drinking and drug use.

Eating Disorders. Societal preoccupation with thinness is the basis of several major industries: fashion, health clubs, diet books and foods, drugs, weight loss programs, and so on, and these are aimed at and paid for primarily by women. Weight and dieting are the foci of many women's lives no matter how little their actual weight deviates from population norms, for there is the widespread belief that being thin makes you beautiful, happy, and desirable to men.

Bruch (1973), in her pioneering work, notes that many people misuse eating functions in an effort to solve or hide problems of living. She views eating disorders as being on a continuum with the extremes of obesity and anorexia nervosa having much in common: the experience of not owning one's sensations and body, distorted and unrealistic body images, and the misperception of body functions so that food intake becomes associated with power and control. She says that an essential aspect of anorexia nervosa is a pervasive sense of ineffectiveness. "The main issue is a struggle for control, for a sense of identity, competence, and effectiveness" (p. 25).

Bruch locates the source of eating disorders in a culture that overemphasizes thinness and in disturbed family interactions. Feminists, however, have taken her analysis a step further by pointing out that the central features of anorexia nervosa—the sense of powerlessness and the symbolic attempts to gain control—describe the conditions of life *for most women*. Chronic patterns of misusing food and dieting are seen as both a symptom of women's sense of futility in trying to cope with contradictory role demands, and as problems in and of themselves (Boskind-Lodhal 1976; Orbach 1978; Wooley and Wooley 1980).

As with other issues addressed by feminist therapists, the treatment of choice for eating disorders is group therapy. Early groups for compulsive eaters and dieters emphasized fat and overweight (Orbach 1978). Therapists discovered, however, that more and more women attending groups were not overweight but showed other symptoms: anorexics—women who had dieted to the point of starvation; "fat thin people"—women who maintained a normal weight level only through constant dietary vigilance; and bulimics— women who compulsively and regularly binge and then purge food by vomiting or using laxatives. What these women had in common with overweight women were distorted body images, guilt, and self-hate about their eating behaviors, and unrealistic ideas about what food and weight control would give to them. Accordingly, the focus of feminists' treatment groups broadened to include those women.

Orbach (1978) in her work with compulsive eaters and Boskind-Lodhal and Sirhan (1977) in their work with bulimics describe similar approaches to therapy groups. They use a combination of behavioral and gestalt techniques to help members explore meanings attributed to fat and thin to understand ways they use eating or dieting to avoid anxiety-provoking situations, to develop greater body and sensory awareness, and to reclaim aspects of themselves previously denied or attributed to weight, for example, competence, power, anger. Emphasis is not on weight or dieting but on members relearning to recognize hunger and to use food to satisfy that need. At the same time, they examine how their socialization as women has contributed to their conflicts and problems, and discuss how in their daily lives they may begin to assume more autonomy and control.

Sexuality

In the consciousness-raising groups of the late 1960s and early 1970s, as women shared with each other their most personal and intimate experiences they came to realize that as long as men took an active, dominant, autonomous role, and women a passive, receptive, reactive role, sexual relations became another area of male dominance and control. Following the principle that the personal is political, feminists developed an analysis of sexuality that held that major support for male dominance and patriarchy lay in men's control over the reproductive and sexual uses of women's bodies. Women do not have reproductive freedom; they lack control over contraception, abortion, sterilization, childbirth, and child care, and the sexual division of labor places the burden and responsibility for child rearing solely on women. Neither do women have freedom of sexual expression—the right to control the choice of a partner and to determine when sexual relations are to take place. There is the cultural requirement that legitimate female sexual expression be only within heterosexual marriage; women who fail to abide by this standard are denied the financial and political protection of men. Feminists concluded that there can be no sexual liberation without women's liberation—that until women had control over their bodies and access to the political, social, and economic privileges allowed men, the so-called sexual liberation movement served only men.

A feminist analysis of sexuality has had a major impact on the work of therapists. Most sex research and psychological theories assume a patriarchal male model sexuality with an emphasis on activity, autonomy, and achievement of orgasm and dissociated from the interpersonal and emotional aspects of relationships (Miller and Fowlkes 1980; Person 1980). Feminists believe the forms of expression of sexuality are not innate but reflect political and cultural institutions that affect the conditions of one's life and one's consciousness (Rich 1980). A feminist therapist would not assume heterosexuality or hold it to be the only standard of health, but rather would believe that other forms of sexual expression (lesbian relationships, celibacy, and having and raising children outside of marriage and the nuclear family) are not the only valid but may be the only viable options for some women. Sexuality would not be considered to be a matter of lifestyle or limited to what happens in bed. The feminist therapist would move the focus away from genital sexuality to issues of identity, expression of intimacy, and the capacity for the experience of sensual pleasure.

Lesbians and Therapy. Many lesbians seek therapy from feminist therapists or lesbian feminist therapists. Most lesbians are not in therapy because of problems with sexuality per se, but because of the stresses of living in a society that assumes heterosexuality and severely sanctions homosexuality. Abbott and Love (1971) state, "Lesbianism is the one response to male domination that is unforgiveable" (p. 610). The lesbian suffers the oppression of all women and, in addition, is denied the benefits of a sexist system: financial security, protection, and the reflected status and power of men.

Some of the particular problems dealt with in therapy are social isolation and feelings of shame and guilt about being lesbian. In addition, lesbian adolescents, mothers, and couples have special problems and are particularly vulnerable to legal and political harassment. Much of the shame and guilt experienced by lesbians derives from the discrepancy between the societal and family values with which they were raised, and their choice to be openly lesbian (Litwok et al. 1979). The feminist therapist can help her lesbian clients by emphasizing and validating the affirming, strengthening aspects of a woman's decision to live independently of men.

Since a major problem of many lesbians seeking therapy is isolation, a feminist therapist *at a minimum* must be familiar with the activities, problems, and resources of the lesbian and gay community to help her client join and get support from that community (Sang 1977; Litwok et al. 1978). Escamilla-Mondanaro (1977) argues that only a lesbian therapist is equipped to help a lesbian client. While others do not feel this is absolutely necessary for good therapy, it is clear than an important factor is the extent to which the therapist can serve as a role model and the setting of therapy validates and affirms a lesbian and gay lifestyle.

Inhibition of Sexuality. Person (1980) writes that traditionally the two problematic areas of female sexuality have been those of masochism and inhibition of sexuality: problems of assertion in the interpersonal context, inhibition of sex per se (that is, desire, arousal, or orgasm), and low sex drive. The problem of female masochism has long been reinterpreted as being about power relationships in a patriarchal culture (Horney 1967; Person 1974; Miller 1976). Women's "low sex drive" is regarded by feminists to reflect both differences in male and female socialization and male sexual expression being held to be the norm of health (Person 1980; Miller and Fowkes 1980; Tiefer 1981).

Assuming, then, that a woman has adequate information about physiology, anatomy, and arousal, problems of sexuality may lie in the interpersonal realm, for example, not insisting on adequate stimulation, faking orgasms, attending to her partner's needs at the expense of her own; or they may reflect psychological fears or conflicts so that she is not able to experience desire, arousal, or orgasm. While a feminist therapist may work with a client individually to help her sort out in which areas her perceived sexual problems lie, an increasingly popular and effective form of treatment has been time-limited groups modeled on those described by Barbach (1975) for preorgasmic women.

Preorgasmic groups differ from traditional approaches to sex therapy in that the emphasis is on the woman's own needs, a partner is not necessary, and the approach and techniques are not limited to heterosexual women. The structure of the groups is typically six to eight members who meet twice a week with two coleaders for a period of about five weeks. In addition, members do one hour daily homework exercises that emphasize getting in touch with their bodies and sexual feelings and learning how consistently to achieve orgasm alone. Group discussions are combinations of education about physiology and anatomy and members' sharing experiences and using each other as sources of validation, permission, and support. As with so many other forms of group treatment for women, members usually experience a sense of relief and strength in sharing with other women both their pain and despair and their sense of exhilaration and liberation at being able to feel more autonomous and in control of their lives.

Clinical Practice of Feminist Therapists

One outcome of the women's movement in the 1970s was the development of alternative feminist services that would be responsive to the needs of women: crisis centers, hotlines, shelters, counseling centers, women's schools, and therapy collectives. Many feminist therapists have chosen to work in these settings. From an analysis of the oppressive aspects of a hierarchical work structure and professionalism (Tennov 1976), from community organizing and political work, and from their personal experience in consciousness-raising groups of sharing resources, power, and responsibility (Kravetz 1980), some feminists have organized their service agencies on collective decision making, authority, and financial bases. Decision making is by discussion and consensus, tasks and leadership roles are shared or rotated, and salary levels are based on need or the principle of equal pay for equal work rather than on the therapist's degree or level of advanced training. Although therapists must often sacrifice the status, pay, and security of jobs in mainstream mental health settings, working in collectives gives them far greater control over their working conditions and a way to integrate their feminist analysis, social and political activism, and practice on a day-to-day basis.

Feminist therapists who cannot or have chosen not to work in alternative settings have focused on educating and organizing around sexism in their workplaces. This may take the form of identifying institutional policies that support or encourage sexism or other forms of oppressive social relations, demanding and running different treatment services for women, confronting sexist or racist attitudes among colleagues, and organizing staff training and education programs. Schultz (1977) gives a good personal description of working to combat sexism and racism in a drug-treatment program.

Through participation in professional organizations and coalitions, feminist therapists, regardless of work setting, come together to share and coordinate resources. Training, supervision, and study groups allow them to raise consciousness about biases in their attitude and work, to keep abreast of theory development and research on the psychology of women, and to develop ways of incorporating these insights and new information into clinical practice.

Future Directions

For the most part, feminist therapy has been oriented to women in their 20s, 30s, and 40s. The different needs of adolescents, older women, women in institutions (mental hospitals or prisons), and of the physically disabled need to be acknowledged and taken into account.

Although most feminist therapists have been in consciousness-raising and political groups and found the group experience itself to be invaluable to their personal and political development, little has been written on all-women therapy groups: how they develop and function, what concepts and techniques from traditional theory and research might be useful (or harmful), and when group or individual therapy is indicated. These topics need to be considered and explored.

While some feminist criticisms of therapy and psychological theory have noted heterosexist biases (Rich 1980; Rohrbaugh 1981), in feminist therapists' revisions this critical point has been for the most part ignored. Similarly, although feminists stress the importance of awareness of race and class, their importance in the practice of feminist therapy is virtually never discussed in published papers. These issues need to be integrated at the level of theory development for the implications they have on how therapy is practiced.

Feminist therapy is more developed in practice than in theory. Earlier we said this is because of its origins in social movement and its vital continuing connections with the reality of women's lives today. Feminists need to construct theory that maintains the dialectic between the individual and society (in contrast to most psychological theories of development that attend primarily to the individual), and that can bridge the gap.

REFERENCES

Abbott, S., and Love, B. 1971. Is women's liberation a lesbian plot? In *Woman in sexist society*, eds. V. Garnick and B. K. Moran, pp. 601–21. New York: Basic Books.

American Psychological Association. 1975. Report of the task force on sex bias and sex-role stereotyping in therapeutic practice. *American Psychologist* 30:1169-75.

Barbach, L. 1975. *For yourself: the fulfillment of female sexuality.* New York: Doubleday.

Boskind-Lodahl, M. 1976. Cinderella's stepsisters: a feminist perspective on anorexia nervosa and bulimia. *Signs: Journal of Women in Culture and Society* 2(1976):341-56.

Boskind-Lodahl, M., and Sirhan, J. 1977. The gorging-purging syndrome. *Psychology Today* 10, no. 10:50-52.

Brodsky, A. M. 1980. A decade of feminist influence on psychotherapy. *Psychology of Women Quarterly* 4:331-44.

Broverman, I. K.; Broverman, D. M.; Clarkson, F. E.; Rosenkrantz, P. S.; and Vogel, S. R. 1970. Sex role stereotypes and clinical judgments of mental health. *Journal of Consulting and Clinical Psychology* 34:1-7.

Brown, P. 1973. *Radical psychology.* New York: Harper Colophon Books.

Brownmiller, S. 1975. *Against our will.* New York: Simon & Schuster.

Bruch, H. 1973. *Eating disorders.* New York: Basic Books.

Caust, B. L.; Libow, J. A.; and Raskin, P. A. 1981. Challenges and promises of training women as family systems therapists. *Family Process* 20:439-47.

Chasin, R., and Grunebaum, H. 1980. A brief synopsis of current concepts and practices in family therapy. In *Family therapy*, eds. J. Pearce and L. Friedman, pp. 1-15. New York: Grune & Stratton.

Chesler, P. 1972. *Women and madness.* Garden City, N.Y.: Doubleday.

Chodorow, N. 1978. *The reproduction of mothering: psychoanalysis and the sociology of gender.* Berkeley: University of California Press.

Chodorow, N. 1981. Oedipal asymmetries and heterosexual knots. In *Female psychology: the emerging self*, ed. S. Cox, pp. 228-47. New York: St. Martin's.

du Bois, B. R. 1976. Feminist perspectives on psychotherapy and the psychology of women: an exploratory study in the development of clinical theory. Unpublished doctoral dissertation, Harvard University.

Ehrenreich, B., and English D. 1978. *For her own good: 150 years of the experts' advice to women.* Garden City, N.Y.: Anchor.

Ernst, S., and Goodison, L. 1981. *In our own hands.* Los Angeles: J. T. Parcher. Distributed by Houghton Mifflin, Boston.

Escamilla-Mondanaro, J. 1977. Lesbians and therapy. In *Psychotherapy for women*, eds. E. I. Rawlings and D. K. Carter, pp. 256-65. Springfield, Ill.: Charles C Thomas.

Fidell, L. S. 1981. Sex differences in psychotropic drug use. *Professional Psychology* 12:156-62.

Framo, J. L. 1972. Symptoms from a family transactional viewpoint. In *Progress in group and family therapy*, eds. C. Sager and H. S. Kaplan, pp. 271-308. New York: Brunner/Mazel.

Friedan, B. 1963. *The feminine mystique.* New York: Norton.

Gilbert, L. A. 1980. Feminist therapy. In *Women and psychotherapy*, eds. A. M. Brodsky and R. T. Hare-Mustin, pp. 245-65. New York: Guilford.

Gomberg, E. S. 1981. Women, sex roles and alcohol problems. *Professional Psychology* 12:146-55.

Gurman, A. S., and Klein, M. H. 1980. Marital and family conflicts. In *Women and psychotherapy*, eds. A. M. Brodsky and R. T. Hare-Mustin, pp. 159-84. New York: Guilford.

Hare-Mustin, R. T. 1978. A feminist approach to family therapy. *Family Process* 17:181-94.

Herman, J. L. 1981. *Father-daughter incest*. Cambridge: Harvard University Press.

Horney, K. 1967. *Feminine psychology*. New York: Norton.

Jacoby, R. 1975. *Social amnesia*. Boston: Beacon.

Johnson, M. 1980. Mental illness and psychiatric treatment among women: a response. *Psychology of Women Quarterly* 4:363-71.

Kaschak, E. 1981. Feminist psychotherapy: the first decade. In *Female psychology: the emerging self*, ed. S. Cox, pp. 387-401. New York: St. Martin's.

Kravetz, D. 1980. Consciousness-raising and self-help. In *Women and psychotherapy*, eds. A. M. Brodsky and R. T. Hare-Mustin, pp. 267-83. New York: Guilford.

Leidig, M. W. 1981. Violence against women: a feminist-psychological analysis. In *Female psychology: the emerging self*, ed. S. Cox, pp. 190-205. New York: St. Martin's.

Libow, J. A.; Raskin, P. A.; Caust, B. L.; and Ferree, E. F. 1981. Feminist therapy and family systems therapy: reconcilable or irreconcilable differences? Submitted for publication.

Litwok, E.; Weber, R.; Ruox, J.; DeForest, J.; and Davies, R. 1979. *Considerations in therapy with lesbian clients*. Philadelphia: Women's Resources.

Mandler, A. V., and Rush, A. K. 1974. *Feminism as therapy*. New York: Random House.

Miller, J. B. 1973. *Psychoanalysis and women*. New York: Brunner/Mazel.

Miller, J. B. 1976. *Toward a new psychology of women*. Boston: Beacon.

Miller, P. Y., and Fowlkes, M. R. 1980. Social and behavioral constructions of female sexuality. *Signs: Journal of Women in Culture and Society* 5:783-800.

Millett, K. 1970. *Sexual politics*. Garden City, N.Y.: Doubleday.

Nellis, M. 1980. *The female fix*. Boston: Houghton Mifflin.

Orbach, S. 1978. *Fat is a feminist issue*. New York: Berkeley Medallion.

Pearce, J. K. 1980. Ethnicity and family therapy: an introduction. In *Family therapy: combining psychodynamic and family systems approaches*, eds. J. K. Pearce and L. J. Friedman, pp. 93-116. New York: Grune & Stratton.

Person, E. S. 1974. Some new observations on the origins of femininity. In *Women and analysis*, ed. J. Strouse, pp. 289-302. New York: Grossman.

Person, E. S. 1980. Sexuality as the mainstay of identity: psychoanalytic perspectives. *Signs: Journal of Women in Culture and Society* 5:605-30.

Rawlings, E. I., and Carter, D. K. 1977. *Psychotherapy for women*. Springfield, Ill.: Charles C Thomas.

Rich, A. 1980. Compulsory heterosexuality and lesbian existence. *Signs: Journal of Women in Culture and Society* 5:631-60.

Rohrbaugh, J. B. 1981. The psychology of women, 1980. In *The women's annual, 1980—The year in review*, ed. B. Haber, pp. 200-230. Boston: G. K. Hall & Co.

Sandmaier, M. 1980. *The invisible alcoholics: women and alcohol abuse in America.* New York: McGraw-Hill.

Sang, B. E. 1977. Psychotherapy with lesbians: some observations and tentative generalizations. In *Psychotherapy for women*, eds. E. I. Rawlings and D. K. Carter, pp. 266-78. Springfield, Ill.: Charles C Thomas.

Schneider, M. 1975. *Neurosis and civilization.* New York: Seabury.

Schultz, A. P. 1977. Radical feminism: a treatment modality for addicted women. In *Psychotherapy for women*, eds. E. I. Rawlings and D. K. Carter, pp. 350-69. Springfield, Ill.: Charles C Thomas.

Strouse, J. 1974. *Women and analysis: dialogues on psychoanalytic views of femininity.* New York: Dell.

Szasz, T. 1961. *The myth of mental illness.* New York: Harper & Row.

Tennov, D. 1976. *Psychotherapy: the hazardous cure.* Garden City, N.Y.: Anchor/ Doubleday.

Tiefer, L. 1981. Contemporary sex research. In *Female psychology*, ed. S. Cox, pp. 23-41. New York: St. Martin's.

Walker, L. E. 1979. *The battered woman.* New York: Harper & Row.

Walker, L. E. 1980. Battered women. In *Women and psychotherapy*, eds. A. M. Brodsky and R. T. Hare-Mustin, pp. 339-63. New York: Guilford.

Williams, E. F. 1976. *Notes of a feminist therapist.* New York: Praeger.

Weisstein, N. 1971. Psychology constructs the female. In *Woman in sexist society*, eds. V. Gornick and B. K. Moran, pp. 207-24. New York: Basic Books.

Wooley, S. C., and Wooley, O. W. 1980. Eating disorders: obesity and anorexia. In *Women and psychotherapy*, eds. A. M. Brodsky and R. T. Hare-Mustin, pp. 135-58. New York: Guilford.

9 | Women and Religion

PART ONE: FEMINIST SCHOLARSHIP IN THEOLOGY

Constance H. Buchanan

The emerging field of women's studies in religion is shaped further each year by new research and theoretical work coming out of its various disciplines— theology, psychology and sociology of religion, ethics, history, scripture, and comparative religions. In some years, the appearance of major works by leading figures has moved feminist religious thinking in radically new directions or has substantially developed approaches to central theoretical problems in the field. No such literature was published in 1981.

Among the books that did appear, however, were a number that contribute in important ways to the growth of the field. These illustrate some of the established directions in which feminist religious thinking has been moving. In doing so, they address and further refine questions at the heart of this debate: What is the nature of women's distinctive religious experience and perspectives? To what extent has religion operated as an oppressive or liberating force in women's lives? Do religious and intellectual symbol systems constructed by men provide resources for interpreting and shaping women's contemporary experience? What commonalities and differences arise in women's religious experience when the variables of culture, race, and class are taken into account?

As feminist theory in religion has developed over what is now more than a decade, the predominant conversation has been among feminist scholars. It has grown increasingly complex and sophisticated as participants have explored the ways in which gender and assumptions about it have shaped both religious systems of belief and institutions. Male theologians have for the most part, although with important exceptions, paid scant attention to the critical and constructive work of feminists. Many have thought it illegitimate scholarship motivated by the "ideology" of the feminist movement in society. (At the same time, these have maintained that traditional scholarship in theology is free of political ideology.)

For this reason and because it has been seen as not dealing with the "real" theological problems of today, that is, problems defined by men, feminist theology commonly has been ignored and often dismissed as a fad. Mainstream male theologians have for the most part steadfastly avoided serious consideration of the challenges and proposals in feminist thinking, continuing to pursue their own directions of thought. At best, those who have read to any extent in the growing body of feminist theology have responded by remarking in passing on its significance, but have failed to come to grips, even in the context of their own subject matter, with the implications of its analysis.

In light of this lack of substantial engagement with feminist thinking it is both interesting and important that 1981 saw the publication of a small volume entitled God as Father? (Metz and Schillebeeckx). Two prominent European male theologians have collected a number of articles, over half of which are by other men in this field, on the topic of the image of God as father. The book is significant because it brings together male and feminist investigation of what feminists identify as the central problem on the contemporary theological agenda. It is extremely useful as well for the ways in which it reveals the state of the conversation between male and feminist theologians.

As the editors themselves point out in the foreword, this conversation is just beginning. That is clear from the content and approach of the chapters contributed by men. Many display a remarkable lack of familiarity with the substance of the feminist critique, demonstrating that it is still conceivable for some male theologians to address the topic of God as father without reference to feminist thought. Even more remarkable, especially in essays written by men who have given some consideration at least to Daly's Beyond God the Father (1973), is failure to come squarely to grips with the issue of women's oppression. It is, of course, this issue that feminists link directly to the traditional concept of God as father, and which gives rise to their fundamental critique of that concept. Yet this book makes it clear that from the perspective of many white and black male theologians it is still possible to give a male-centered analysis of the meaning and the social and cultural implications of the image of God the father in Christian doctrine.

It is intriguing, although also annoying in the view of Dorothee Sölle (1981), a female contributor to the volume, to read this analysis. Several essays see the problem as Christianity having lost its ability to comprehend the reality of God the father. Like feminists, they see religious symbolism as influenced by social structures, but move in a far different direction. They argue that it is society's loss of the powerful father figure that has thrown the image of God as father into question. Loss of the mystery and authority of human fatherhood has weakened our capacity for experiencing the mystery and authority of the divine father. One author uses this analysis to explain the link between family and religious symbolism. Another, in an article entitled "Pater absconditus," dramatically decries the loss of the powerful father, concluding, ". . . when the father is lacking so too is the principle that provides the foundation of society" (Metz and Schillebeeckx 1981, p. 26). This school of thought represents in theology the equivalent of the focus on "father absence" that was dominant in social scientific research on the family almost a decade ago.

A second position, which represents a more central line of argument, is most effectively presented in Jurgen Moltmann's chapter "The motherly Father," which makes the case that has widespread support among Catholic and Protestant male theologians and biblical scholars. He says he will not defend the traditional patriarchal concept of God that establishes a patriarchal pattern for human life in which ". . . family, political, and religious pyramids all point to the highest power in heaven, from whom they all receive their authority—to the Lord God, the Father of All" (Metz and Schillebeeckx 1981, p. 52). He argues instead for a new interpretation of God as parent in which divinity is identified with liberating love and not with the power and omnipotence that were characteristics of God the authoritarian, universal father. Here the concept of father emerges from God's relationship with Christ the Son. Based on what is referred to as the "Abba experience" of Jesus, God is understood not as one who demands of his children ultimate obedience, but rather as one who out of suffering love gives them freedom to realize their full humanity. This concept allows us to see that Christianity ". . . is not in fact a father-religion, but a 'son's religion' " (Metz and Schillebeeckx 1981, p. 55). Further, Moltmann claims, the notion of God as loving father includes the "feminine element" in two senses: "a father who both begets and gives birth to his son is no mere male father. He is a motherly father" (p. 53). Second, he identifies the feminine with the quality of suffering that characterizes a fatherly God in his grief over the death of his Son. The significance of this reinterpretation of God as "Daddy" rather than patriarch is, according to Moltmann, the resulting conception of human beings as children of God who are all free and equal members of a human family. In such a family there can be no dynamic of privilege and subordination that on the basis of sex or class sets one child over another.

The complexity of the theological conversation about liberation into which Moltmann enters with this thesis is illustrated not only by feminist perspectives but also by black and Latin American perspectives. In his article "The meaning of God in the black spirituals," black theologian James Cone argues that any interpretation of God as Liberator must be consistent with black people's religious experience. He demonstrates that the view of God as liberating love is not new to the oppressed. Black slaves understood the biblical message to be about a mighty God who acts in history to deliver the weak from their slavery to the strong, the lowly from their bondage to the powerful. He agrees on the basis of black experience that God creates people to be his children and so wills the dignity and personhood of all. As presented by Cone, however, the oppressed do not allow God's liberating love to be separated from his ultimate power. From the perspective of the black slave, divinity necessarily brings the two inextricably together:

> For enslaved Blacks believed that there was an omnipotent, omni-present, and omniscient power at work in the world, and that he was on the side of the oppressed and the downtrodden. (Metz and Schillebeeckx 1981, p. 54)

When the historical experience of oppression is taken into account, in other words, attempts to dissociate God's power from his liberating love are thrown into question.

When feminist voices enter this conversation, as they do particularly in chapters by theologians Dorothee Sölle and Rosemary Ruether, the inade-quacies of both white and black male theology become vividly clear. Both women agree with the need to reject the concept of God as patriarch in favor of one that identifies as divine not the power of subjection but of liberation. However, they press the fundamental critique that the concept of divine power as domination is inextricably bound up with the concept of God as male. Sölle claims that in light of women's experience of traditional religion, it is not possible simply to reject a God of patriarchal power, as Moltmann does, and maintain the symbol of father. Because the two are integrally related historically, exclusively male symbolism for God must be rejected at the same time or women will remain subordinate. A caring, gentle father is still a father. Ruether presses the point further. Her argument that the hallmark of patriarchy is assignment of a secondary and mediating role to the feminine in a male-dominated doctrine of God is well illustrated by Moltmann's proposed concept of God the motherly Father. In her view, theologians must probe more deeply, questioning whether the very concepts of masculine and feminine are not themselves patriarchal creations.

Out of this feminist critique, which on the basis of women's experience of oppression cuts to the heart of patriarchal thinking, there emerges a distinctive contribution to discussion of new concepts of God. Both Sölle and Ruether propose that rejection of the patriarchal image ought to entail rejec-tion of the image of human beings as children. In their view, the divine ought to be understood as representing full, responsible personhood for both women and men. They are uncomfortable with maintaining in any way an exclusively or even dominantly parental concept of God. In Ruether's words, ". . . even the Parent image must be recognised as a limited analogy for God(ess), often reinforcing patterns of permanent spiritual infantilism and cutting off moral maturity and responsibility. God(ess) as creator must be seen as the Ground of the full personhood of men and women equally" (Metz and Schillebeeckx 1981, p. 65).

In Christianity, another central theological problem identified by feminists is Jesus Christ, the Son of God and the Messiah. Rosemary Ruether (1981) poses this problem directly in "Christology and feminism: can a male savior save women," a chapter in her book *To change the world: christology and cultural criticism.* Traditional interpretations of Jesus' meaning in Christianity have made him the focal point of the androcentrism and sexism of the tradition's theology and institutional life. Male theologians have claimed that the incarnation of God in male form in the historical figure of Jesus was not accidental but necessary. For them Jesus has symbolized the reality that, in Ruether's words:

> The male represents wholeness of human nature, both in himself
> and as head of the woman. He is the fullness of the image of
> God, whereas woman by herself does not represent the image of
> God and does not possess wholeness of humanity. (p. 45)

No wonder that feminists have questioned whether Christ could ever symbolize liberation and full humanity for women. Those who have come to reject Christianity do so in large part because they conclude that the savior it proclaims is a symbol that cannot transcend patriarchy. Other feminists, like Ruether, have argued that the symbolic meaning of Christ can and must be reinterpreted, freed of the patriarchal presuppositions that have imprisoned it. The essays in *To change the world* move in this direction, exemplifying in their approach to christology the theoretical framework that characterizes her feminist theology. Ruether treats the question of the meaning of Jesus for women in the context of its relationship to his meaning for the poor, the Third World, anti-Judaism and religious intolerance, and exploitation of the environment. In her view, traditional interpretations of his life and ministry have been used to "perpetuate political detachment, religious bigotry, sexism and negation of nature" (p. 4). Her fundamental point is that the sociopolitical meaning of the messianic idea, of the promise of salvation represented by Christ, has been lost in Christian theology and must be recovered. She argues that Jesus symbolizes most profoundly the prophetic call for a transformed social order; that his life and ministry addressed social patterns of oppression as well as the individual dimension of sin. Specifically, it addressed the notion of hierarchy itself, the fundamental dualism of privilege and unprivilege, which lies at the heart of all these patterns. A reconstructed view of Christ as iconoclast understands him historically and in terms of our contemporary world as opposed to this core dualism,

> . . . as critic rather than vindicator of the present hierarchical
> social order. The meaning of Christ is located in a new future
> order still to come that transcends the power structures of
> historical societies, including those erected in the Christian era in
> "Christ's name." (p. 55)

Consistent with her theoretical position that sexism is historically the original expression of this pattern of domination and subordination, Ruether argues that in his ministry Jesus spoke especially to outcast women ". . . because they are at the bottom of this network of oppression" (p. 56).

Whether they are working within or outside established traditions, feminists in religion who are seeking to construct female interpretations of God, self, and the world are coming to grips with the question of whether male symbolic systems offer useful resources for this task. Several of the works published in 1981 reflect feminist attempts critically to appropriate these systems in philosophical theology and psychology, and make a significant contribution to clarifying and refining the issues.

Feminism and process thought (Davaney 1981) contains essays exploring the possibilities for mutually enriching dialogue between these two theoretical approaches to defining reality. The essays are based on papers first presented at a symposium on the topic held at Harvard Divinity School in 1978. Their authors understand feminism and process thought to share important common ground in their criticism of traditional Western ways of thinking about self, world, and God, and in their fundamental assertions and presuppositions:

> Both assert that Western humanity has primarily understood the
> world dualistically and patterned reality hierarchically. Being,
> within this traditional vision, has been elevated over becoming,
> static over dynamic activity, independence and self-completeness
> over interdependence and relatedness. Further, primary differenti-
> ations have been made between God and the world, men and
> women, humanity and nature. In each instance, one side of the
> dualistic model has been understood as subject, with intrinsic value
> and power, while the other has been an object valued solely in
> relation to the subject. (Davaney 1981, p. 2)

This analysis points to what feminists in religion have identified as their major theoretical task: developing a mode of thinking about reality that overcomes the subject-object dichotomy that has for centuries structured Western thought. Contributors to the book propose that feminists share this task with proponents of process philosophy. Together, feminism and process philosophy may arrive at new insights important for constructing a nonhierarchical, nondualistic world view. Through this collaboration feminism would gain a highly developed metaphysical framework useful for understanding and setting forth women's experiences; that framework, constructed primarily by men, would be enlarged and further developed in light of women's experience.

What makes process philosophy, unlike most philosophical systems constructed by men, appear congenial to feminist thought is its fundamental conception of the "rhythm of process" as the basic structure of reality. In her chapter "Androgynous life: a feminist appropriation of process thought," theologian Valerie Saiving (Davaney 1981) demonstrates the fruitfulness of bringing process thinking to bear in resolving the problem of androgyny in feminist thought. It provides a model for envisioning a new understanding that does away with the primarily male-defined vision of the complementarity of stereotyped "masculine" and "feminine" natures and the pattern of dominance and subordination inherent in them. In "Becoming human: a contextual approach to decisions about pregnancy and abortion," theologian Jean Lambert (Davaney 1981) uses process philosophy concepts to help construct a feminist vision of human becoming based on women's experience of continuing or terminating pregnancy. Other chapters in the collection are less successful, illustrating reservations about this enterprise held by feminists who insist that the proper starting point for building feminist theory must be the actual individual and collective historical experience of women, not a metaphysical system.[1]

Freudian and Jungian psychology are further examples of male theoretical frameworks that have been appropriated by some scholars. Several works published in 1981 illustrate the varying ways in which they are used to interpret women's experience and explore their spirituality. Among these are *Receiving woman: studies in the psychology and theology of the feminine* by Ann Belford Ulanov, and *The Goddess: mythological images of the feminine* by Christine Downing. The latter seeks to contribute to the efforts of feminists who reject established religions as irredeemably patriarchal to discover outside of these traditions images of female divinity, of the Goddess. In the author's words:

> . . . in recent years many women have rediscovered how much
> we need the goddess in a culture that tears us from woman, from
> women, and from ourselves. To be fed only male images of the
> divine is to be badly malnourished. We are starved for images
> which recognize the sacredness of the feminine and the
> complexity, richness, and nurturing power of female energy.
> (p. 4)

Downing agrees with those who understand gods and goddesses not as external beings but as human projections of internal psychological forces that transcend the personal and historical. While critical of the male bias in Jung, she uses his theory to examine the goddesses of Greek mythology, believing they have living power as representatives of archetypal dimensions of women's experience. In her view, knowledge of these dimensions is valuable for freeing women of patriarchal stereotypes of the feminine, deepening their self-understanding, and opening up new visions of female possibility. The mythic patterns represented by goddesses such as Persephone, Ariadne, Hera, Gaia, Athena, Artemis, and Aphrodite help women ". . . to see who we are and what we might become" (p. 2).

[1]For an important response to this volume and detailed discussion of central issues in the development of feminist method, see the review by Beverly Harrison in *Signs* (Winter 1982).

Downing brings into focus a major tenet of feminist scholarship in religion: concepts of the feminine and masculine expressed in myth powerfully shape our personal, social, and cultural experience. She believes they do so primarily through the individual and collective unconscious. While she is aware that the concept of the feminine in classical mythology is patriarchal, nonetheless she maintains that women can discover in these goddesses dimensions of what Jung called the eternal feminine and, further, that we can recover much about the goddesses in prepatriarchal traditions.

Others, who see it as a major task of feminist scholarship not to confuse male-defined notions of the feminine with women, would be distinctly uncomfortable with this approach. Rejecting any notion of the feminine or masculine as eternal, they view both as socially constructed concepts and creations of patriarchal culture. For this reason they also reject as a feminist ideal (and as a concept of God) of androgyny understood as the uniting of masculine and feminine characteristics in one being. Ruether states this position well. Calling for the more radical criticism of basic assumptions necessary for arriving at a nonpatriarchal view of reality, she is critical of those content to surface and elevate the suppressed feminine within or outside of established religious traditions:

> Both assume that the recovery of the female as icon of the divine means the vindication of the "feminine." Neither ask the more fundamental question of whether the concept of the feminine itself is not a patriarchal creation. Thus the vindication of the "feminine," as we have inherited that concept from patriarchy, will always be set within a dualistic scheme of complementary principles that segregate women on one side and men on the other. Even if this scheme is given a reversed valuation, the same dualism remains. (Metz and Schillebeeckx 1981, p. 65)

A further criticism of the psychological approach to exploring women's spirituality represented here by Downing is given by ethicist Beverly Harrison (1981b). She takes issue with a focus on women's experience that emphasizes being and neglects doing. According to Harrison, ". . . we can never make sense of what is deepest, 'wholiest,' most powerfully sacred, in the lives of women if we identify women only with the more static metaphor of being, neglecting the centrality of praxis as basic to women's experience" (p. 46). Her argument raises central questions in the debate about the nature of female spirituality and feminist theology, the most important of which concerns the moral and social dimension of women's religious experience and vision. Any attempt to come to a genuine understanding of both, in her view, must recognize ". . . the very real historical power of women to be architects of what is most authentically human . . . [to be] the chief builders of whatever human dignity and community has come to expression" (p. 47).

With the attempt to construct feminist theology, whether that means radical reinterpretation of the symbol systems of established traditions or the creation of new traditions, another major focus is recovery of the lost history of women's religious experience, which has been a subject of debate among feminists. Some, who feel there can be no place for women in patriarchal traditions such as Christianity and Judaism, see little value in historical research. In their view, it only serves to uncover further evidence of religion's oppression of women and of women's own spirituality profoundly distorted by patriarchal religious beliefs. Believing women must create new religious alternatives for themselves, they try to discover a distinctly female spirituality in the experience of contemporary women.

Others are not willing to accept as adequate interpretations of the past interpretations written by centuries of male scholars. They want to know the history of religion in women's lives and of women in religion that has so far been systematically ignored. They believe this history is not one of oppression only and that it is usable in two major ways: First, it has major implications for revising our understanding of the past; second, it provides insight into the nature of women's spirituality that is a crucial resource for developing feminist theology.

Several works published in 1981 extend our knowledge in this area. Two of these (Ruether and Keller 1981; Wilson-Kastner et al. 1981) are pioneering works in that they present primary source materials by and about women heretofore unavailable or unknown.

The dramatic character of women's history is well illustrated by *A lost tradition,* which presents the theological writings of the four early Christian women whose works are extant. Two of these women were known previously to have existed because we had fragments of their writings. The other two have been unknown and never before translated into a modern language. As the editors claim, this is "the first volume of Mothers of the Early Church." Reading here the words of Perpetua, Proba, Egeria, and Eudokia for the first time, one is confronted with the stark reality that women have simply not existed in our awareness and study of what is known as the Patristic Era, the era of theologians called the Church Fathers. We have been led to believe, as male scholars have assumed and said, that there were no early Christian women writers. Now we know better and wonder whether any more will be discovered.

The writings of these women are significant for several reasons, primarily because they change and enlarge our picture of the early Church. Adding to the scarce evidence for the roles and position of women in early Christianity, they further nuance our understanding of how both changed in the beginning centuries of the tradition. The increasing data on the lives of women who were virgins, widows, prophets, wives, deaconesses, and martyrs strengthen knowledge about women that is independent of the attitudes toward them expressed in the writings of the patristics. While we do not have here a female theologian who rivals the learning and influence of leading Church Fathers, we do have "literate and literary women with a variety of concerns" (Wilson-Kastner et al. 1981, p. xxiv). Perpetua's account of events leading to her martyrdom, Proba's theological poetry, Egeria's diary of her pilgrimage, and

Eudokia's varied writings show us that, "The early church is more than the theologians and controversies" (p. xxiv). They move us in a way the significance of which is only beginning to be explored beyond a focus on theology, priests, and men. For women readers especially, they provide the intriguing and powerful experience of hearing for the first time distant female voices commenting on their faith.

The study of women and religion in American history continues to be one of the most exciting and rapidly deepening areas of scholarship in women's studies. It is an area being developed simultaneously by feminist scholars in the field of religion and of American social history. Recognition of its importance for the study of women in American history and of the powerful interconnectedness of women's religious and social experience led before 1981 to a number of foundational books in women's studies (Cott; Douglas; James; Porterfield; Sklar; Scott).

In 1981 Ruether and Keller contributed to this growing scholarship with publication of the first volume in their three-volume documentary history project on women and religion in America. The book focuses on recovering what has been the unknown history of women's participation in the "formative" nineteenth century in Christianity and Judaism in this country, particularly their leadership roles. Specifically, it addresses seven major topics: women and revivalism, women in utopian movements, the leadership of nuns in immigrant Catholicism, the Jewish woman's encounter with American culture, the struggle for the right to preach, lay women in the Protestant tradition, and women in social reform movements. For each topic there is a section made up of primary source materials introduced by an interpretative essay. Together the essays and documents bring to light recovered parts of the religious history of American women long ignored and mostly unknown. To read them is to experience one's sense of the history of women and of religion in this country changing. There are new worlds to see here and new voices to hear that we have not seen or heard before.

A central question in the historical as in the contemporary debate on the impact of religion on women's lives and social roles is the extent to which religion operated as an oppressive or liberating force. This book makes the case that for black and white women of diverse traditions in nineteenth-century America it did both. While religion reinforced women's subordination and helped to socialize them to accept the domestic maternal role, it also provided them with the spiritual resources to envision new roles for themselves in the world outside their traditional sphere. On the whole, according to Ruether and Keller, evidence supports the view that this liberating power of religion, not its repressive power, predominated. Identified by the Victorian doctrine of womanhood as naturally pious and spiritual, large numbers of women found in religion not only a field in which they could use their talents, but also a rationale encouraging a new view of themselves in the world. For if as it was thought women were possessed of a higher degree of spirituality than men, it was clear they had not only a special duty but also a call to take up roles outside the home in which they might work to redeem humanity. Such thinking was a central force motivating and legitimizing women's service in new ways to church and society:

> Throughout every movement considered in *Women and religion in America,* one sees religion as an infinitely variable instrument for "enlarging women's sphere" through utopian movements, evangelism, ordination, missionary work, and social reform. (p. x)

Of course, within religion the rapidly expanding activities of women raised the question of their proper role in church and synagogue. In mainline Protestantism this provoked a full-scale debate over the ordination of women that is remarkable in its similarity to the contemporary debate.

The third historical work, *Women in new worlds: historical perspectives on the Wesleyan tradition* (Thomas and Keller 1981), is the first of two volumes of papers from a historic conference held in 1980. This conference was the first held on women in a major American denomination and the first sponsored by the historical agency of a mainline Protestant church, the United Methodist Church. Bringing into focus the history of Methodist women within and outside of their church, these papers demonstrate in the context of one denomination how in the last century religion has played a central role in the establishment of a public life for themselves by American women.

The opening address by Kathryn Kish Sklar relates the development of scholarship in the history of women in Methodism to that in the history of American women and religion in general. She identifies a fourth stage in that development, exemplified by this volume, in which the effects on women's religious and social experience of class, community, ethnicity, and race are examined. Of particular interest is her discussion of the importance of religious sources for understanding the history and meaning of women's lives in America. Sklar identifies three main areas illuminated by them:

> . . . women's interior lives—that is, their consciousness about and attitudes toward the world and their own experience of it; women's social status relative to men, as measured by their comparative access to leadership and authority within the church; and women's participation in social movements, so often inspired by religious beliefs and so closely related to their religious associations. (Thomas and Keller 1981, p. 64)

Finally, 1981 saw the publication of two works by black women and women of color that have particular significance for feminist thinking in religion. These are *The sanctified church* by Zora Neale Hurston, which contains previously unpublished materials on Black Holiness and Pentecostal religious traditions in which women play a prominent role; and *This bridge called my back: writings by radical women of color,* edited by Cherrie Moraga and Gloria Anzaldua. This is a collection of imaginative pieces and essays that shed vivid light on the perspectives of Third World women in the United States. Several, especially Audre Lorde's "Open letter to Mary Daly" and Gloria Anzaldua's "O.K. Momma, who the hell am I?" are powerful criticisms of white feminist theology.

Lorde points out the inherent racism of feminist religious thinking that has not moved beyond "a patriarchal western-european frame of reference," thus dismissing as a source the powerful spiritual heritage of Third World women. Such feminist thinking not only fails to achieve an adequate analysis of patriarchy, but also distorts the similarities and differences in the experience of white women and women of color by assuming "that all women suffer the same oppression simply because we are women" (Moraga and Anzaldua 1981, p. 95).

Anzaldua's interview with spiritualist Luisah Teish illustrates that along with basic differences there are major commonalities in the spiritual experience of women of color and white women. Like some white feminists, Teish sees the reemergence of feminism as an expression of Goddess energy and sees black women's spirituality as providing the vision and inner strength for their liberation in society. Locating the origins of black feminism in women's reaction to the sexism of the black power movement, she also identifies the sexual and racial oppression of women of color as fundamentally spiritual: "The basic problem that we have had was believing somebody else's story about us—what we can and cannot do, who we can and cannot be" (Moraga and Anzaldua 1981, p. 230).

The works discussed here reflect the lines along which feminist conversation continued to deepen and grow in 1981 and represent the theoretical dimension of the on-going development in the field. Particular works, such as Ruether and Keller's and Thomas and Keller's, have provided new insight that allows us to see this contemporary development in the historical context of women and religion in America. A major distinctive characteristic of this contemporary development is precisely the rapidly growing size and significance of this theoretical dimension. Feminist theology continues to be stimulated by and to shape the religious activities of women inside and outside established traditions. It continues to show that, contrary to a common belief, religion has not ceased to be a powerful force in the life of individuals and society.

PART TWO: THE LEADERSHIP AND EMPOWERMENT OF WOMEN

Sandra Hughes Boyd

Women's Issues and Ordination

Most religious feminists recognize the inherent dangers in focusing on the ordination of women as the only and major concern for women. The ordination of women has, however, provided a forum and focus for articulating and examining issues facing women in many of the religious traditions. Women in denominations that have ordained women for decades find it difficult to bring to consciousness the variety of issues they face in the church. Such efforts in these institutions are often met with the argument, "We ordain women—what's the problem?" The most creative work around women's issues in the Episcopal church, for example, was accomplished during its intense struggle for the ordination of women in the early and mid-1970s. The most insightful and exciting exchanges and writing about a broad range of women's issues in religion are now taking place in context of debates in the Roman Catholic church about ordination of women.

The history of attempts by Roman Catholic women to speak with bishops about their issues illustrates the importance of ordination as a focus. Beginning in the spring of 1976, they began demonstrating publicly at meetings of the National Conference of Catholic Bishops (NCCB) to raise the issue of justice for women in the church. In November of that year a group of more than twenty national and local organizations calling themselves the Women of the Church Coalition began attempts to find an avenue for dialogue with and input into the NCCB. It was two years later, following the involvement of more than 2,000 women in the Second International Conference on the Ordination of Women, that a committee of the NCCB first met with representatives of the Women's Ordination Conference (WOC) to investigate the idea of and plan a dialogue about women's issues.

That took place over the next two years, concluding in December of 1981. While the final report is expected in the spring of 1982, an interim report was released in May 1981 indicating several conclusions agreed on by the participants. The report referred to a bishops' synod document of 1971, which said that while the church was witnessing to others about justice in the world, it recognized that it needed itself to be an agent of justice in its own corporate life. Participants acknowledged, "The church seems to invite reflection on its own internal life and structures to ensure that there is a sense of equality in the treatment of men and women" (Dialogue 1981, p. 90). One of several specific aspects of the church's life that was addressed was complementary roles between men and women. The women and bishops agreed, "The concept of complementarity is not an appropriate model for accepting women as members of the church, because it too often implies a 'separate but equal' notion that is in fact not equal" (p. 90).

The interim report articulated several points of disagreement between the women and the bishops. A central theme was the different "mind sets" out of which various views arise. Bishops in general were said to approach issues out of a traditional view that "Christ founded a church in which he vested authority in Peter and the Twelve who handed it down to their successors . . . [and in which] the pope and the bishops constitute the magisterium . . . the official arbiter of orthodoxy" (p. 90). The women disagreed with this and described their operative view of church structure this way: "The present official leadership structures of the church that are both hierarchical and patriarchal were not explicitly instituted or intended by Christ; they are historically developed in relation to culture over a long period of time and are therefore mutable" (p. 90).

Despite these different approaches to church structures and acknowledgment that the official magisterium (teaching office) of the church had already studied and restated the tradition that excluded women from ordained priesthood, the participants agreed that "the full promotion of full participation of women in the church is a matter that requires extensive study and development in the Catholic tradition" (p. 91).

Further evidence of carefully stated challenge to the magisterium came from well-known and highly respected Roman Catholic theologian Karl Rahner (1981). He called into question certain kinds of statements put forth by the magisterium as official and binding. Citing Paul VI's *Humanae vitae* (on contraception) and the Vatican's declaration against the ordination of women, Rahner said, "I do not see either in the arguments used or in the formal teaching authority of the Church as actually asserted a convincing or conclusive reason for assenting to the(ir) controversial teaching" (p. 10).

Pastoral Letters

Three pastoral letters about women in the church and ministry were issued by Roman Catholic bishops in 1981. A letter prepared by the diocesan priests' senate but endorsed and issued by Bishop John S. Cummins (1981) of Oakland, California, charges that the clergy must "actively recruit women to serve on parish councils (and other parish committees)," continue to ask women "to serve in the visible ministries of readers, eucharistic ministers and cantors," and "give equal consideration to men and women whenever hiring" (p. 332).

A second letter was issued by Bishops Victor Balke and Raymond Lucker of Crookston and New Ulm, Minnesota respectively. It said, "Sexism is a moral and social evil . . . it is not the truth of the biological or psychologial sciences, nor is it the truth of the Gospel . . . sexism is a lie." Pointing out that "the psychological costs of sexism are indeed extremely high," the letter says that "the only adequate response to this evil is Christian feminism" (p. 344).

A third pastoral letter, however, might better be characterized as a "pacifier." Issued by Archbishop Peter Gerety (1981) of Newark, it acknowledged that "women have been and are still being denied their rightful place in society and the church," and that "the church should be a model of what the human community is meant to be and can be under the Gospel," and that "we must . . . put our own household of the faith in order!" (p. 583). It develops, however, that the main themes for women are obedience, complementarity, and proper roles. Gerety quotes a Vatican statement that "woman must fulfill herself as woman!" and for man and woman "one complements the other." Gerety clearly does not wish to do away with women's participation in the church. They are strongly urged to continue to commit themselves to full-time church ministry, but the vocations to which they should respond are those "permitted by the church" (p. 586).

The Position of Women as Reflected in the New Canon Law

The first new Code of Canon Law for the Roman Catholic church since 1917 is expected to be made public Pentecost Sunday 1982. Its intention is to reflect the spirit of the Second Vatican Council and it has been in development for a number of years. Drafts have been circulating and continually subject to criticism by canon lawyers and theologians over the period of revision. Among the critiques that express concern for women's status are technical ones by Thomas J. Green (1979, 1980) and a popular treatise by Richard J. McBrien (1981).

One of the principles for the revision of the code called for "the articulation of a common legal status for all believers adequately reflecting fundamental Christian equality . . . while admitting the legitimacy of functional differentiations rooted in sacred orders" (Green 1980, p. 268). The new code, however, reflects a clear preference for a hierarchial model of the church (McBrien 1981, p. 433) and is vague in the manner in which it reflects the sacramental grounding of fundamental rights and obligations (Green 1981, p. 634). This is indicated in a number of specific ways.

The Vatican II emphasis on collegiality between the pope and the bishops is largely ignored by the code's "failure to structure the papal-episcopal relationship in . . . balanced terms" (Green 1979, p. 649). The bishops are perceived as "helpers of the pope rather than as fellow bishops and collaborators in the governance of the church" (McBrien 1981, p. 433). The Roman Curia (administrative and bureaucratic structure of the Vatican) is placed at the service of the pope without explicit reference to the College of Bishops, a violation of the Vatican's decree that the Curia "perform its duties not only in the name of the pope, but also 'for the good of the churches and in the service of the sacred pastors' " (McBrien 1981, p. 434; Green 1979, p. 650).

Although Roman Catholic documents beginning with Vatican II exhibit little direct discriminatory content and, in general, forbid sex discrimination in relation to basic Christian rights and obligations, there are several areas that reflect the inferior legal status of women (quite apart from the issue of their ordination). There is no provision for participation of women religious in the Synod of Bishops, although members of clerical religious institutes may attend (Green 1979, p. 634; 1980, pp. 278–279; McBrien 1981, p. 433). Women are excluded from service as papal legates, although the basic duties of this position require neither office nor jurisdiction (Green 1979, p. 634; McBrien 1981, p. 433). Women are precluded from being formally installed as lay ministers, although as laypeople their participation is de facto provided for in another canon, and ordination is not an issue (Green 1979, p. 634; 1980, p. 279; McBrien 1981, p. 433). Green and McBrien agree that such restrictions on the participation of women contradict a basic principle of canonical reform " 'that the law should not readily bar individuals from exercising ecclesial (church) ministries unless it is an extremely serious matter of ecclesiastical discipline affecting the common good' " (Green 1979, p. 636; McBrien 1981, p. 433).

Ordination and Women in Seminaries

While one denomination celebrated twenty-five years of having fully recognized clergywomen, another approved the admittance of women as ministers. The United Methodists celebrated their long history of women evangelists and preachers with an April conference at Garrett-Evangelical Theological Seminary. The General Synod of the Reformed Church of America approved an amendment to its *Book of church order,* which allowed ordination of women as ministers of the Word. At the same time, however, a "conscience clause" allowed dissenters to refuse to participate in such ordinations (Reformed Synod 1981).

Two denominations reported that one-half or more of their master of divinity degree candidates were women. The Unitarian Universalists have exactly 50 percent women, and in the United Church of Christ women constitute 52 percent of its seminary contingent (Women seminarians 1981).

A survey of women in seminaries conducted by the Women's Ordination Conference of the Roman Catholic Church (Swidler 1982) showed that the number of women faculty and students in divinity programs had just about doubled in the past five years in the reporting seminaries.

A very different study of seminaries has been ordered by the Vatican Congregation for Catholic Education. The first of its kind in the United States, it was announced in a September letter by Archbishop John Roach (1981), president of the National Conference of Catholic Bishops. The review "is based on a desire to assist [the seminaries] in their ongoing process of renewal" and expresses "concern about the best use of personnel and resources," the letter said. Its overseer was to be a bishop from the United States, but the letter was explicit in stating that he was to be "ultimately responsible in this matter to the Holy See" (p. 264).

Most concern about the review was expressed quietly in seminary communities, and seminary Rectors were cautious in their public response. While one said the idea of the study was " 'not as alarming as it may seem,' " another was willing to admit that the women's issue was on the agenda of the study (Swidler 1982, p. 1).

Others were stronger in their opinions, as reported in the *National Catholic Reporter* (Neilsen 1981). David Thomas of Regis College in Denver, is quoted as follows: " 'One of the areas of likely concern would be moral theology and sexual ethics . . . particularly . . . in how *Humanae vitae* (on contraception) is being taught . . . when it is being fully supported, given lip service or openly criticized in the seminaries.' " Another priest and former seminary teacher said " 'I think the real target is women in seminaries. . . . Rome is concerned about the presence of women in the same program as seminarians, women as teachers and spiritual directors, and women in the same living situations as seminarians' " (Neilsen 1981, p. 25).

The Women's Ordination Conference survey indicated that many of the seminary administrators strongly supported the presence of women in seminaries. One indicated that he " 'would strenuously argue against any move to eliminate women from any of the seminary's programs' "; another said " 'seminaries will have rather serious deficiencies in their overall priestly formation programs if women are not part of the administration, faculty and spiritual formation teams' " (Swidler 1982, p. 1).

The preliminary results of a study of protestant women clergy sponsored by the Ford Foundation were reported by the Center for Social and Religious Research at Hartford Seminary. The study showed that: Clergywomen were four times more likely than clergymen to report difficulty in being ordained; clergywomen in denominations such as Episcopal were very pessimistic about support for their career moves by their superiors (often because a "conscience clause" allows superiors to refuse to accept women); laypeople were reluctant to advocate employment of women clergy in contradiction of the general perception that women are equally effective as men; and while the difference in the percentage of women paid less than $10,000 between the entire sample and those with five years or less experience is only 1 percent, men in the same categories improved by 6 percent. Nevertheless, the study's director said, "The difficulties (women) are encountering . . . in balance appear no more onerous than (the difficulties) men are facing as parish ministers . . . clergywomen have arrived" (Briggs 1981, p. 32). The final report of the study is expected to be published in late 1982 under the title *Women of the cloth: a new opportunity for the churches* (Carroll 1982).

World Council of Churches Consultation

The culmination of a four-year study program of the World Council of Churches (WCC) came at a consultation meeting in Sheffield, England in July. The 250-person delegation heard Archbishop of Canterbury Robert Runcie as honorary speaker warn in the opening worship service against "an over-concentration on the issues involved in the ordination of women," which may, he said, "reinforce a clericalist view of the church" (Weidman 1981, p. 821). Most were aware that Runcie himself opposes ordination of women in his own denomination. If there was any doubt about his point of view, it was dispelled when Runcie quoted a remark of Luther about women having big hips to sit on and stay home, while he paid tribute to women's "other" (than ordained) ministries (Jones 1981, p. 18).

Dr. Phillip Potter, General Secretary of the WCC, without naming Runcie, nevertheless provided a rebuttal when he decried the "impotence of our male-dominated churches to see, to hear, to feel, to decide and to act." He continued, "We have systematically, *systematically* left aside the central nature of God's revelation and taken up all the things that strengthen and confirm our attitudes of domination and authority and hierarchy (p. 18).

Several recommendations were forwarded from the consultation to the WCC and its member churches including: A call for the WCC to evaluate its own programs and procedures in regard to sexism, racism, and classism; that 50 percent of the 1983 world assembly speakers be women; that three of the six WCC presidents be women; that language in all WCC publications be inclusive; that "there be a careful inquiry into the significance of the representation and symbolism of Christ in the ordained ministry"; and that persons in local churches "become aware of their own unconscious pre-suppositions as they approach the Bible" (Jones 1981, p. 18).

No more Women Readers in Catholic Diocese

Bishop Glennon P. Flavin of Lincoln, Nebraska issued a directive that bans the reading of Scripture by any other than "instituted lectors" in Catholic parishes of his diocese. Only males can serve as instituted lectors. The Rev. Robert Vasa, conductor of the diocesan training programs for readers and alter servers, said, "In order to emphasize the importance, dignity and seriousness of the role of reading the word of God, bishop has decided that as of January 1, 1984, only instituted lectors will be permitted to read the Scripture in the mass and other sacred celebrations" (Catlin 1981, pp. 1, 24). This left the unmistakable impression on many that women serving in such roles are somehow an impediment to the "importance, dignity, and serious-ness" of worship.

Women's Proper Roles in the Southern Baptist Denomination

The Southern Baptist Convention, held in Los Angeles, brought good news and bad news for women. Girl pages were allowed at the convention this year for the first time. But former Convention President Adrian Rogers said in a sermon that wives should be submissive to their husbands, that "the Bible is against she-men and he-women,'" that "'a woman doesn't think with her head,'" and told a joke about a woman who has a "'Supreme Court figure: no appeal'" (Lyles 1981). The Convention elected a woman as its first vice president. She is Christine Gregory, who has just completed a six-year term as president of the Women's Missionary Union where she traveled 150,000 miles a year to raise $62 million for missions in the last year alone. It was reported that she "graciously [denied] being a figure of power and influence in Baptisdom"; her election, she said, was not a referendum on feminism, but "'an affirmation of missions'" (Lyles 1981, p. 695).

Abortion

It is exceedingly difficult and even perilous to attempt to survey or summarize arguments in the abortion dispute. There are several reasons, however, why it is important to examine and seek to understand the underlying issues in this debate. The justifications that receive the most publicity on both sides of the dispute appear to be extremely simple and straightforward; however, they are most often *presented* as simple and straightforward, and leave the essential historical context and rationale unpresented or unclear. Those unpresented or underrepresented issues clearly demonstrate that the issue is *not* simple — that it is, in fact, terribly complex.

What follows is a description of the political status of the abortion debate, particularly in relation to the participation of religious groups in the dispute. Then comes a summary of several recent contributions to an understanding of the issue from the perspectives of theology, ethics/moral theology, and the sociology of religion.

The Political Situation

A major development in the antiabortion battle in 1981 was endorsement of the Hatch human life federalism amendment by Archbishop John P. Roach, president of the National Conference of Catholic Bishops, and Terence Cardinal Cooke, chair of the Bishops' Conference for Prolife Activity. (The Hatch amendment says, "A right to abortion is not secured by this Constitution. The Congress and several States have the concurrent right to restrict and prohibit abortions: Provided, that a law of a State which is more restrictive than a law of Congress shall govern.") This was the first time that the Roman Catholic bishops had endorsed specific legislation to ban abortion. Speaking for the bishops, Roach told a Senate subcommittee on the Constitution: "We are committed to full legal recognition of the right to life of the unborn child and will not rest in our efforts until society respects the inherent worth and dignity of every member of the human race" (Bishops 1981, p. 359).

The bishops and other supporters of the amendment felt that it would have a better chance of passage than the previously proposed Constitutional amendment, which would have explicitly extended the protection of the fifth and fourteenth amendments to the unborn. The Hatch amendment would help create a climate in which abortion would become less socially acceptable by establishing that a right to abortion is not secured by the Constitution. Eventually, enough support would be gathered to pass a second Constitutional amendment that would outlaw abortion throughout the country.

An internal battle over political strategy between factions of the antiabortion forces was highlighted when several bishops objected to not having been consulted about the decision to support the Hatch amendment. They thought that it fell short of the bishops' goal of a total ban. For them, only a Constitutional amendment explicitly outlawing abortion was permissible. They said that under the Hatch amendment some states would impose a ban but others would allow it for any reason.

Other objection to the Hatch amendment came from supporters of the human life bill (HLB), a congressional bill that would define the term "person" in the fourteenth amendment to include the fetus from the moment of conception. Supporters of the HLB charged that trade-offs for tuition tax credit legislation were being made in return for the bishops' support of the Hatch amendment. They claimed that the necessary two-thirds vote for any constitutional amendment on this issue could not yet be secured, whereas a simple majority and President Reagan's signature for the HLB were already obtainable. They said that the HLB would force the Supreme Court to take another look at its 1973 decision making abortion legal under certain circumstances.

Others argued that if Congress passed the HLB, either the Supreme Court would strike it down or it would be open to amendment by future congresses. It was noted that legal history did not support the proposition that Congress could overrule or alter the Supreme Court's interpretation of basic constitutional concepts.

A number of religious groups stood fast in opposing constitutional amendments or congressional action to prohibit abortion. The Executive Council of the Episcopal Church unanimously opposed a constitutional amendment on "human life" and stated its "'unequivocal' opposition to legislation which would 'abridge or deny the right of individuals to reach informed decision in the matter of abortion'" (Executive Council 1981, p. 17). The Right Rev. George N. Hunt, newly elected Bishop of Rhode Island, asked Episcopalians to oppose attempts to define the beginning of life and efforts to ban abortion because, he said, "If we allow someone else to legislate a moral posture for us, we have given up our God-given duty to make responsible choices" (*Christian Challenge* 1981, p. 20).

The National Women's Division of the American Jewish Congress in March sponsored a human life amendment teach-in. Rabbi Henry Siegman, Executive Director of the American Jewish Congress, testifying before a Senate Subcommittee on Separation of Powers, said, "The proper role of government in a free society is to allow the different religious traditions to inculcate their own beliefs with respect to the appropriateness of abortion, and to leave that final decision to the women, answering to God and conscience" (Daum 1981, p. 16).

The general synod of the Reformed Church in America, meeting in Hamilton, Ontario, engaged in heated debate over the issue and denied an overture calling for support of a human life amendment to the Constitution. Instead, they reaffirmed the position previously adopted by the denomination that emphasized the sanctity of human life, but added "that sometimes a choice must be made between two evils" (Reformed Synod 1981 p. 760).

Ruth Daugherty, president of the Women's Division, Board of the Global Ministries of the United Methodist Church, said that "'many United Methodists have worked vigorously to maintain this right [abortion] and to oppose the enactment or implementation of legislation that would restrict or prohibit this legal right'" (Pro-Lifers 1981, p. 160). She promised that the church "'will continue to oppose efforts to amend the United States Constitution to make abortion and some forms of birth control illegal'" (p. 160).

Theological Issues

Several theological issues are implicit in the abortion debates. One very basic one is whether the proper focus for discussion is scientific or religious. There has been considerable effort expended by antiabortion religious factions to convince people that the issue is merely a scientific one. Roman Catholic Archbishop Roach, during his testimony in support of the Hatch amendment, said that the question of "human life" was one that science had already settled: "The scientific data fully support the common-sense claim that each human individual comes into existence at conception, and all subsequent states of development are simply that— phases of growth and development in the life cycle of an individual already in existence" (Bishops 1981, p. 359).

(In light of the largely successful efforts by proponents of this approach to convince the public of its truth, it is significant that the Supreme Court of Arkansas in early 1982 was clear in its decision that "creation science" was not science but religion, and that its teaching therefore violated the Constitution's guarantees of separation of church and state [Stuart 1982, p. 1].)

Paul D. Simmons (1981), in an article entitled "The 'Human' as a problem in bioethics," warned against the tendency to focus on biological factors to define what is "human." This approach assumes that an answer to the question of what makes a fetus a human being can be found "in a more or less quantifiable factor," which is then established as a criterion for determining what constitutes a human being (p. 97). There are two possible results from this method, he says. Both the fetus and the pregnant woman are seen in terms of their genetic codes and this defines them as having equal moral value; or the fetus is seen as *becoming* a human being at some particular biological stage in its development. The definition as to exactly which stage is the crucial one is open to considerable difference of opinion in the scientific community (pp. 98-99).

The question is not whether the fetus is human, Simmons says. The fetus belongs to the human species. The issue is more properly what is a *person*. He concludes, "It is not logical to say that the fetus (or conceptus) out of which a person will develop is identical with a person and is, like a person, a living human being" (pp. 99-100). The debate as to what constitutes a person is not, then, merely a scientific issue, but one that needs to be carried out both by theologians and scientists who, in the process, provide important correctives for each other (p. 105).

Another theological issued raised by the abortion debates is the classic Christian concept of original sin. Two writers had similar opinions about the way this might affect people's attitudes toward abortion. Bill J. Leonard (1982) wondered, "Are the rights of unborn innocents more easily defended than those of born sinners? Do some view the born as 'tainted' by original sin once they move from the womb to the fallen world? Does that factor, knowingly or unknowingly, affect the way some prolife folk respond to rights for the born?" Does this lead persons to believe that women who become pregnant outside marriage or who cannot support their children properly must bear complete responsibility and even punishment for their actions?, he asks (p. 8).

Rabbi David M. Feldman (1981), speaking at a symposium on the theology of prochoice in the abortion decision, referred to the concept of original sin as playing an important, if usually unspoken, part in the abortion arguments. Because of the belief that sin was inherited through the process of generation, it would be consistent that a fetus be saved rather than the mother, he said. The mother presumably had been baptized and would thus go to heaven at her death. Every effort would be made to see that the fetus was brought to term so that it could be baptized and cleansed from its original sin (p. 48). Also operative here, Feldman said, is an assumption that when one "chooses life" in the classic otherworldly Roman Catholic sense, one understands that to be life in the next world, rather than in this world (p. 49).

Feldman noted that the Jewish approach is very different. There are several possible moments when the soul enters the fetus and the Talmud says that the matter is one of the "secrets of God." When Jewish people "choose life" they understand that to mean life on *this* earth. "The Sabbath or even Yom Kippur are to be violated to avoid a threat to life or health," he said. Looking at abortion in this light, Jewish belief is that the fetus has "a right to be born, but that right is relative; it is secondary to the absolute right of the mother to her life, to her health, to her essential welfare" (p. 52).

Beverly Wildung Harrison (1981a), also speaking at the symposium, noted that in the history of Christian theology, "The central metaphor for understanding all life is as a *gift* of God." In such a context it follows that pro-creation itself easily becomes a primary metaphor for the divine blessing of human life. She noted also that it has been only in the last century that any question has been specifically raised about the appropriateness of this "unqualified sacralization of procreation" in Christian theology (p. 11).

Ethical Issues

Harrison describes the moral absolutism that she sees operative in the abortion debates. Most persons who maintain a right-to-life position are absolutists in two ways. They admit only one principle to the process of moral reasoning and only one possible meaning or application of that principle. Such a restriction means that a range of other moral values is slighted. There are often several principles relevant to any one decision; and there are many ways to relate a given principle to a situation. The moral absolutism involved in respect for human life is one, she says, "that should be honored by all." It must also be recognized, however, that this principle often comes into conflict with other valid ones in the process of making real-world decisions (Harrison 1981 p. 16; 1981d p. 19).

She also charged that many Christian thinkers do not seem to understand women's right to bodily integrity: "They seem to think that such talk is a disguise for women to plead self-indulgence." Her analysis is that this misunderstanding arises out of the Christian tradition's "spiritualizing neglect of respect for the physical body." There is no precedent in Christian thinking that "starts with body-space, or body-right, as a basic condition of moral relations" (1981d, p. 20).

Harrison warns that the claim to bodily integrity is not to be confused with mere liberties. "To claim that we have a moral right to procreative choice does not mean that we believe that women can exercise that right free of all moral claims from the community." Girls need to be taught that childbearing is not a capricious, individualistic matter, nor is having as many children as one wishes necessarily beneficial to the whole of human society (1981d, p. 20).

Sociological Issues

Pope John Paul II probably unwittingly highlighted some key issues for women during two recent speeches. In an address to Italian physicians and surgeons quoted in a December 1981 United States bishops' pastoral letter on health and health care (1981), he referred to recent technological advances made in medicine. The pope made the point that such development suffers from a fundamental ambivalence: "While on the one hand it enables men and women to take in hand their own destiny, it exposes them on the other hand to the temptation of going beyond the limits of a reasonable dominion over nature, jeopardizing the very survival and integrity of the human person" (U.S. Bishops 1981, p. 400). The second speech was given from his balcony in May shortly before Italians were to vote on two abortion measures. He said, "The church considers any legislation favorable to procured abortion a most serious offense against the primary rights of man and the divine commandment . . ." (On file 1981, p. 2). The key phrases to a feminist are "going beyond the limits of a reasonable dominion over nature" and "against the primary rights of man."

B.W. Harrison (1981c) claims that it is no accident that a warning phrase such as the first of those quoted is often sounded when abortion is under discussion. She notes the irony that "Christian theology everywhere else celebrates the power of human freedom to shape and determine the quality of human life except when the issue of abortion arises" (p. 15). The pope may have been intending that the word "man" be understood in a generic sense in the second phase, but feminists believe the fact that abortion is seen as a threat to the power of males to be a major, if largely unspoken, factor in the virulent campaign against freedom of choice.

Harrison maintains that the power of males radically to shape creation has never seriously been challenged. "When one stops to consider the awesome power over nature which males take for granted and celebrate, including the power to alter the conditions of human life in myriad ways, the suspicion dawns that the near hysteria that prevails about the immorality of women's right to choose abortion derives its force from misogyny rather than from any passion for the sacredness of human life" (1981c, pp. 15-16). The emphasis on procreation as a metaphor for God's gift "takes on special meaning when expressed within a *patriarchal* society in which it is the *male's power* which is enhanced by this 'divine gift.'" She continues, "Many of the efforts at social control of procreation-including church teaching on the subject of contraception and abortion . . . [are] part of a *system of control* over women's power to procreate" (1981a, pp. 11-12). This attitude treats abortion as an abstractable act (1981c, p. 14) and ignores the desperate struggle by women to gain some control over nature's profligacy in conception. Harrison says that women's lack of social power in all of recorded history "has made this struggle to control procreation a life-bending, often life-destroying one" (1981c, p. 17).

She also charges that men, especially celibate men, "romanticize the total and uncompromising dependency of the newly born infant upon the already existing human community" (1981c, p. 17). This dependency is even greater in a fragmented, centralized, urban, industrial modern culture than in a rural culture.

Harrison also notes that opponents of a prochoice stance who demand that early fetal life be tendered full human standing are often the same people who opposed the equal rights amendment. "We have every right to be enraged," she says, at the situation in which the society and movement which proclaims a zygote at the moment of conception to be a person with the same rights as a citizen is the same society that "denies full social and political rights to women" (1981a, p. 14). Those who deny that women deserve to control procreative power say they do this out of "moral sensibility," in the name of the "sanctity of human life." Harrison concludes: "We have a long way to go before the sanctity of human life will include genuine regard for every female already born, and no social policy which obscures that fact deserves to be called 'moral'" (1981c, p. 14).

Language, Imagery, and Titles

On the ecumenical scene and in various religious groups, language continues to provoke controversy and endless discussion. What is increasingly clear, however, is that language is not the only issue. Numerous commentators have addressed issues of theology, psychology, and sociology in the context of the language discussion. After looking briefly at some of the events taking place in various religious groups, we will investigate the deeper implications of the issues.

Ecumenical Groups and Individual Denominations

In 1981 the concerted campaign against attempts by the National Council of Churches (NCC) to provide an inclusive-language lectionary, or selection of scripture passages for public worship (Boyd 1981, p. 254), was focused in a nationally distributed statement from the conservative evangelical Religious Roundtable. Its letter called the NCC lectionary "'a very anti-Christian Bible'" and an attack "'on God Himself'" that had been undertaken to "'tamper with the Word of God in order to please the radical feminists and other anti-God groups.'" The statement charged that sexually neutral language would undermine traditional American family life. Objections to the Roundtable's letter were registered by Methodists in the *United Methodist Reporter* and by the presiding bishop of the Episcopal Church who called the attack on the NCC "'unwarranted and inaccurate'" and suggested that "'Episcopalians disregard it'" (*Christian Challenge* 1981a, 1981b).

The Consultation on Church Union sponsored a November conference on language and liturgy at Scarritt College in Nashville. More than 100 participants gathered for a program that ranged from highly theoretical lectures to nonsexist hymn-sings.

A great deal of controversy was aroused over a liturgy prepared for the World Day of Prayer by Church Women United, a worldwide ecumenical group. The liturgy was written by seven Christian women of native American descent and based on a creation theme that stressed the place of nature within God's plan. God was referred to as "Creator God" and the "Great Spirit," the earth as "Mother Earth," the wind likened to the Holy Spirit, and the sun to the knowledge of Christ. Several objections charged that the service tended toward "'heathen-naturalistic faith'"; included a "'pantheism quite remote from the New Testament'"; did not express the "'uniqueness

[of] the Lord and his dealing with our sin'"; and that it was "'sub-Christian'" (Critics 1981; Sparks fly 1981, p. 8).

Participants in the 1981 general synod of the United Church of Christ used a new paperback supplementary hymnal *Everflowing streams* (Duck 1981). It contains inclusive language versions of traditional hymns and avoids usage of the words Lord, king, thee, and thou, warlike and bride-of-Christ imagery, and masculine pronouns for Christ.

Episcopalians in eastern Massachusetts have been reading in their diocesan newspaper an ongoing dialogue over what to call women priests, two of whom began by arguing that as male priests are called "Father," they would like to be called "Mother" (Gatta and McLaughlin 1981). Responding to this, other women priests and laypeople objected that the church fosters and supports dependency and hierarchical tendencies by the use of either or both titles (Letters 1981).

Theological, Sociological, and Psychological Issues

There is increasing recognition in many quarters of the depth of the issues implied in a discussion of language, imagery, and titles. Roman Catholic bishops and women participating in a dialogue on women's issues acknowledged that the reason many women reject the idea that terms such as men, brothers, or sons refer to both men and women is that this language is "a cultural expression of the view that women are subordinate persons who can only be represented by the male and *cannot represent themselves in their own name*" (Dialogue 1981) (my emphasis). The dialogue also recognized that the eucharist (or Holy Communion) itself has become problematic for many women because the refusal of the church to allow women to serve as priests leads them to the conclusion that "women are incapable of imaging Christ" (Dialogue 1981, p. 89).

Three articles published in 1981 addressed a variety of the concerns involved in this question. They were written by Rita M. Gross, Jewish theologian and professor of comparative religions at the University of Wisconsin-Eau Claire; Dorothee Sölle, German feminist theologian who teaches at Union Theological Seminary in New York City; and Diane Tennis, staff member of the General Assembly Mission Board of the Presbyterian Church in the United States.

Gross acknowledged that all religious language is by nature analogous and metaphorical. Yet because the concept "of a personal Ultimate is at the living heart of the Jewish symbol system," Jewish theology and practice will necessarily continue to use anthropomorphisms to describe God (1981 p. 185). She warned, however, that to ignore the analogous and metaphorical nature of religious language by allowing oneself to think that there is a real correspondence between one's limited images of God and God is to be "unrealistic, self-aggrandizing, and fundamentally idolatrous" (1981 p. 184).

Gross noted that not only are masculine pronouns always used by traditionalists to refer to God, they are also used by atheists and philosophical critics of anthropomorphism. At the same time there is an "automatic and very strong prejudice" against using feminine pronouns and images (1981 p. 184). In examining this phenomenon Gross speculated that although language about God does not really tell about God, it *does* tell "a great deal about those who create and use the God-language." She charged that this God-language "mirrors and legitimates the profoundly androcentric character of . . . the religious dimensions of being Jewish" and expresses a "profound and long-standing alienation between women or femaleness and the central values of Jewish religious tradition" (1981 p. 185).

Although feminist critics may question whether the Christian religious tradition has ever seriously valued women or femaleness, they would certainly agree to the existence of a "profound and long-standing alienation" between women/femaleness and Christianity itself. Most of the components of and reasons for the alienation appear to be the same in the two religious traditions.

Tennis and Gross looked at the sociological and psychological aspects of autonomy, limits, and finitude. Tennis (1981) charged that patriarchy feels the need to hold onto its myth of male autonomy: "When men keep hold of the self-sufficient, unilateral Father, they incorrectly presume the Creator's self-sufficiency . . . and also their own as the male mirror of the male God" (p. 164).

Gross developed the theme by offering the explanation that the experience of limits, particularly related to birth and death, is closely connected with sexuality. We fear and reject our own embodied condition and thus reject sexuality as an acceptable religious symbol. Most people see the traditional male images of deity—God the Father, the God of our fathers—as nonsexual symbols. Because the male deity is sexless, God is exalted above sexuality, a sexuality that belongs to the female (1981, pp. 191–192).

Images of the divine feminine for Gross, however, are the ones that contain all opposites and thus have greater ability to communicate an acceptance of limits and finitude. She put it this way: "The Goddess gives and She takes away, not out of transcendent power but because that is the way things are . . . limits, endpoints, death are not punishments from an external transcendent deity but simply part of reality and neither positive or negative" (1981, p. 190).

From a psychological standpoint, looking at the issue of dependency, Tennis said, "The reality is that men are not autonomous, independent, in charge and in control" and that they are, in fact, "dependent upon women for a kind of perpetual 'mothering' in a culture and religion that values male transcendence" (1981, p. 165). Some dependent men, she continued, fear the displacement of God as father but "do not want either to acknowledge mother control, which is enraging to them, or to accept mothering responsibility." Such men "need a controlling King of Heaven and a continuity to traditional power arrangements on earth, even while resenting the control and harboring its deep resentments." One of the powerful attractions of the religious radical right, she concluded, is its "rhetorical maintenance of immature power relationships." This serves not only to keep women in their places but also to keep both men and women in dependency (1981, p. 166).

Sölle elaborated on the theological dimensions of such power relationships. She wondered why we should "honor a God whose most important quality is power, whose interest is subjection, whose fear is inequality." A relationship with such a divinity "destroys our ability to act, our truthfulness, our understanding." She concluded that "if this is God's chief interest . . . then there is absolutely no reason for a woman to honor, love or pay attention to such a being" (1981, p. 182).

REFERENCES

Balke, V., and Lucker, R. 1981. Male and female God created them. *Origins* 11 (November 5):333–38.

Bishops support Hatch amendment. 1981. *Origins* 11, no. 23 (November 19):357–59.

Boyd, S. H. 1981. Status of women in organized religion. In *The women's annual: 1980 — The year in review*, ed. Barbara Haber. Boston: G.K. Hall & Co., pp. 243–56.

Briggs. K. A. 1981. Women in clergy show more gains. *New York Times*, November 15.

Carroll, J. W. et al. 1982. *Women of the cloth: a new opportunity for the churches*. San Francisco: Harper & Row.

Catlin, R. 1981. Bishop "dignifies" scripture readings by banning women. *National Catholic Reporter* 17, no. 44 (October 16):1, 24.

Christian Challenge 1981a. 20, no. 5 (May):18.

Christian Challenge 1981b. 20, no. 6 (June):22.

Christian Challenge 1981c. 20, no. 11 (December):20.

Critics take to war path over Indian prayer ritual. 1981.*Christianity Today* 25, no. 7 (April 16):64.

Cummins, J. S. 1981. Oakland statement on women in ministry. *Origins* 11 (November 5):331–33.

Daly, M. 1973. *Beyond God the Father: toward a philosophy of women's liberation*. Boston: Beacon.

Daum, A. 1981. The Jewish stake in abortion rights. *Lilith*, no. 8:12–17.

Davaney, S. G., ed. 1981. *Feminism and process thought: the Harvard Divinity School/Claremont center for process studies symposium papers*. New York: Edwin Mellen Press.

Dialogue on women in the church: interim report. 1981. *Origins* 11, no. 6 (June 25): 81-91. (Also *New Women/New Church* 4, no. 3 (May 1981):3-6.)

Downing, C. 1981. *The Goddess: mythological images of the feminine.* New York: Crossroad.

Duck, R. 1981. *Everflowing streams: songs for worship.* New York: Pilgrim Press.

Executive council: good reports. 1981. *Episcopalian* 146, no. 4 (April):17.

Feldman, D. M. 1981. Is abortion murder or not? *Church and Society* 71, no. 4 (March-April):46-53.

Gatta, J., and McLaughlin, E. 1981. What do you call a women priest? *Episcopal Times* 6 (October):4.

Gerety, P. 1981. Women in the church. *Origins* 10, no. 37 (February 26):582-88.

Green, T. J. 1979. The revision of canon law: theological implications. *Theological Studies* 40, no. 4 (December):593-679.

Green, T. J. 1980. Critical reflections on the schema of the people of God. *Studia Canonica* 14, no. 2:235-322.

Gross, R. M. 1981. Steps toward feminine imagery of deity in Jewish theology. *Judaism* 30 (Spring):183-93.

Harrison, B. W. 1981a. Free choice: a feminist perspective. *Church and Society* 71, no. 4 (March-April):6-21.

Harrison, B. W. 1981b. The power of anger in the work of love. *Union Seminary Quarterly Review* 36 (Suppl):41-57.

Harrison, B. W. 1981c. Theology of pro-choice: a feminist perspective, part I. *Witness* 64, no. 7 (July):14-18.

Harrison, B. W. 1981d. Theology of pro-choice: a feminist perspective, part II. *Witness* 64, no. 9 (September):18-21.

Hurston, Z. N. 1981. *The sanctified church.* Berkeley, Calif.: Turtle Island.

Jones, A. 1981. "Sexist" church attacked as WCC ends conference. *National Catholic Reporter* 17, no. 36 (July 31):1, 18-19.

Leonard, B. J. 1982. The rights of the "born." *Christian Century* 99, no. 1 (January 6-13):8.

Letters. 1981. *Episcopal Times* 6 (December):10-11.

Lyles, J. C. 1981. Southern Baptist detente. *Christian Century* 98, no. 22 (July 1-8): 694-95.

McBrien, R. J. 1981. A theologian's view of the new code. *Origins* 11, no. 27 (December 17):430-36.

Metz, J. B. and Schillebeeckx, E., eds. 1981. *God as father?* New York: Seabury Press.

Moraga, C., and Anzaldua, G., eds. 1981. *This bridge called my back: writings by radical women of color.* Watertown, Mass.: Persephone Press.

Neilsen, M. 1981. Vatican seminary study to force women out? *National Catholic Reporter* 17, no. 42 (October 2):25.

On file. 1981. *Origins* 11, no. 1 (May 21): 2.

Pro-lifers demand action. 1981. *Christian Century* 98, no. 5 (February 18):159-60.

Rahner, K. 1981. *Concern for the church.* New York: Crossroad.

Reformed synod. 1981. *Christian Century* 98, no. 4 (July 29-August 5):760.

Roach, J. 1981. Study of U.S. seminaries launched. *Origins* 11, no. 17 (October 8): 263-64.

Ruether, R. R. 1981. *To change the world: christology and cultural criticism.* New York: Crossroad.

Ruether, R. R., and Keller, R. S., eds. 1981. *Women and religion in America.* Vol. 1, *The nineteenth century.* San Francisco. Harper & Row.

Simmons, P. D. 1981. The "human" as a problem in bioethics. *Review and Expositor* 78, no. 1 (Winter):91-108.

Sölle, D. 1981. Mysticism, liberation and the names of God. *Christianity and Crisis* 41, no. 11 (June 22):179-85.

Sparks fly over world day of prayer service. 1981. *Canadian Churchman* 107, no. 4 (April):1, 8.

Stuart, R. 1982. Judge overturns Arkansas law on creationism. *New York Times,* January 6.

Swidler, A. 1982. WOC conducts seminary study. *New Women/New Church* 5, no. 1 (January):1.

Tennis, D. 1981. The loss of the Father God: why women rage and grieve. *Christianity and Crisis* 41, no. 10 (June 8):164-70.

Thomas, H. F., and Keller, R. S., eds. 1981. *Women in new worlds: historical perspectives on the Wesleyan tradition.* Nashville: Abingdon Press.

U.S. bishops' pastoral letter on health and health care. 1981. *Origins* 11, no. 25 (December 3):400.

Ulanov, A. B. 1981. *Receiving woman: studies in the psychology and theology of the feminine.* Philadelphia: Westminster Press.

Weidman, J. 1981. A community of mutuality. *Christian Century* 98, no. 26 (August 26-September 2):820-22.

Wilson-Kastner, P. et al. 1981. *A lost tradition: women writers of the early church.* Lanham, Md.: University Press of America.

Women seminarians in majority. 1982. *National Catholic Reporter* 18, no. 14 (February 5):4.

BIBLIOGRAPHY

Theology

Davaney, Sheila Greeve, ed. *Feminism and Process Thought: The Harvard Divinity School/Claremont Center for Process Studies Symposium Papers.* New York: Edwin Mellen Press, 1981. A collection of papers interesting for their illumination of the nature of feminist thought in the attempt to examine its affinities with Whitehead's philosophy.

Harrison, Beverly Wildung. "The Power of Anger in the Work of Love: Christian Ethics for Women and Other Strangers." *Union Seminary Quarterly Review* 36 (Suppl. 1981):41–57. Explores from an ethical perspective the implications of women's historical lives for developing feminist theology and understanding female spirituality.

Metz, Johannes-Baptist, and Schillebeeckx, Edward, eds. *God as Father?* (Concilium Series, 143) New York: Seabury Press, 1981. A collection of articles by European, South American, and American theologians gives a good indication of the state of the discussion between feminist and male theologians.

Ruether, Rosemary Radford. *To Change the World: Christology and Cultural Criticism.* New York: Crossroad, 1981. This important contribution by a leading feminist theologian illustrates how the figure of Jesus might be reinterpreted.

Ulanov, Ann Belford. *Receiving Woman: Studies in the Psychology and Theology of the Feminine.* Philadelphia: Westminster Press, 1981. A Jungian approach to identifying what is distinctive in feminine psychology and theology.

History

Johnson, Sonia. *From Housewife to Heretic.* Garden City, N.Y.: Doubleday, 1981. Mormon woman excommunicated by her church for publicly protesting its highly organized political activity against the ERA tells the story of her journey toward activism.

Nunally-Cox, Janice. *Foremothers: Women of the Bible.* New York: Seabury Press, 1981. Intended as a beginning consciousness-raising tool for adult discussion groups, the author surveys the role of women in the Bible from Old Testament times to the early church.

Ochshorn, Judith. *The Female Experience and the Nature of the Divine.* Bloomington: Indiana University Press, 1981. Comparing the generally positive attitudes toward women exhibited in ancient near eastern polytheistic texts with negative ones found in biblical texts, Ochshorn raises an important question about the relation of the development of monotheistic religion to the spread of misogyny in Western culture.

Ruether, Rosemary Radford, and Keller, Rosemary Skinner, eds. *Women and Religion in America. Vol. 1: The Nineteenth Century.* San Francisco: Harper & Row, 1981. In this first of three projected volumes, Ruether and Keller provide introductions to and primary documents on the religious history of American women in the nineteenth century. The work is an excellent survey of the subject.

Thomas, Hilah F., and Keller, Rosemary Skinner, eds. *Women in New Worlds: Historical Perspectives on the Wesleyan Tradition*. Nashville: Abingdon Press, 1981. Despite the limitations implicit in the title, the essays are significant for the general study of women in American religion. They range from Kathryn Kish Sklar's fine analysis of historical writing about women and religion to a variety of descriptive pieces on the movement of women into fuller participation in the church's life.

Wilson-Kastner, Patricia, et al. *A Lost Tradition: Women Writers of the Early Church*. Lanham, Md.: University Press of America, 1981. Contains important religious writings of women in early Christianity not previously available in published form.

Jewish Women

Greenburg, Blu. *On Women and Judaism: A View from Tradition*. Philadelphia: Jewish Publication Society, 1981. Orthodox Jewish woman tells the story of her struggle to reconcile a growing feminist consciousness with loyalty to her religious tradition and beliefs. Parts of the book are excerpted in the Spring/Summer 1982 issue of *Lilith: The Jewish Women's Magazine*.

Mazow, Julia Wolf, ed. *The Woman Who Lost Her Names: Selected Writings by American Jewish Women*. San Francisco: Harper & Row, 1980. Fine anthology of short stories, memoirs and excerpts from novels explores the American Jewish woman's relationship to herself, her family, her tradition, and to other women.

Roiphe, Anne. *Generation Without Memory: A Jewish Journey in Christian America*. New York: Linden Press, 1981. This combined autobiography and essay reflects the search into the meaning of her Jewish heritage which Roiphe undertook at the age of forty-four. When she looks at the inferior state in which women are kept in traditional Judaism, she wonders if a truly nonpatriarchal Judaism is possible.

Sexuality

Church and Society 71, no. 4 (March-April 1981):6-21. Special issue of this Presbyterian bimonthly publication includes presentations made at a Symposium on the Theology of Abortion sponsored by the Religious Coalition for Abortion Rights and Religious Leaders for Free Choice, a study guide, and bibliography.

Harrison, Beverly Wildung. "Theology of Pro-Choice: A Feminist Perspective, Part I." *Witness* 64, no. 7 (July 1981):14-18; Part II. *Witness* 64, no. 9 (September 1981):18-21. These two articles present important ethical and theological issues not commonly addressed in the usual clamor of the abortion debate.

Black Women

Moraga, Cherrie, and Anzaldua, Gloria, eds. *This Bridge Called My Back: Writings By Radical Women of Color.* Watertown, Mass.: Persephone Press, 1981. A rich collection, extremely useful for its presentation of the diversity of perspectives belonging to women of color.

Hurston, Zora Neale. *The Sanctified Church.* Berkeley, Calif.: Turtle Island, 1981. The daughter of a black Baptist minister has provided an anthology of materials on the black church, many of which have never before been published.

Women in Ministry

Weidman, Judith L., ed. *Women Ministers.* San Francisco: Harper & Row, 1981. Essays covering topics such as church administration, preaching, counseling, social ministry, and clergy couples range from purely descriptive treatments to fine analytical essays on "A Ministry of Presence" by Brita Gill and "Social Ministry" by Lora Gross.

Russell, Letty M. *Growth in Partnership.* Philadelphia: Westminster Press, 1981. Charting the necessary steps toward partnership between women and men and between human beings and God, Russell's hopeful and optimistic approach recommends the book for adult Christian study groups.

Mythology, Language, and Worship

Clark, Linda, et al. *Image Breaking/Image Building: A Handbook for Creative Worship with Women of Christian Tradition.* New York: Pilgrim Press, 1981. The result of a seminar that explored "the implications of feminism for styles and structures of Christian worship," the book provides exercises for increasing the awareness of one's own religious depths, theoretical articles, personal reflections, sample worship services, poems, prayers, and bibliography.

Downing, Christine. *The Goddess: Mythological Images of the Feminine.* New York: Crossroad, 1981. Downing's thesis is that familiarity with female imagery of the divine frees women from patriarchal stereotypes, deepens their understanding, and creates new visions of female possibility.

Duck, Ruth. *Bread for the Journey* and *Everflowing Streams: Songs for Worship.* New York: Pilgrim Press, 1981. The first is an anthology of resources for creating worship services in nonsexist language, and the second is a book of traditional hymns rewritten into inclusive language.

Gross, Rita M. "Steps Toward Feminine Imagery of Deity in Jewish Theology." *Judaism* 30 (Spring 1981):183-93. Gross addresses a range of issues from the metaphorical nature of religious language to the experience of limits and its relation to sexuality as theologically expressed.

Watkins, Keith. *Faithful and Fair: Transcending Sexist Language in Worship.* Nashville: Abingdon Press, 1981. Believing that Christian public worship is indeed "dominated by the metaphors of masculinity," Watkins provides commentary on the issues, practical guidelines for addressing the problems, and a collection of sample psalm adaptations.

ORGANIZATIONS

This is a very selective list from the many groups that concern themselves specifically with women's issues in the religious traditions.

Catholics Act for ERA
3311 Chauncey Place, #303
Mt. Ranier, MD 20822

Catholics for a Free Choice
2008 17th Street NW
Washington, DC 20009

National Women's Division
American Jewish Congress
15 E. 84th Street
New York, NY 10028

Priests for Equality
P.O. Box 651
Hyattsville, MD 20782

Religious Coalition for Abortion Rights
100 Maryland Avenue NE
Washington, DC 20002

Religious Committee for the ERA
475 Riverside Drive, Room 830A
New York, NY 10115

Women's Ordination Conference
34 Monica Street
Rochester, NY 14619

10 | Violence Against Women

Freada Klein

For more than a decade popular media have devoted considerable attention to the changing status of women. They cite achievements in removing barriers to employment and education, and the increasing diversity of family patterns. The sobering topic of violence against women is rarely raised in assessing women's changing status; yet incidence of this violence is one very telling measure of the status of all women in this society.

In assessing the responses to various forms of violence against women, it becomes apparent that professionals and activists are operating in two very distinct spheres. Feminist activists, who are on the front lines in assisting women's escapes and recovery, use language marked by passion and involvement in their analyses of the dynamics of violence. Rapists and batterers are described as the "shock troops" and the "home guard of male supremacy." On the other hand, researchers by definition are supposed to operate with detachment as they tabulate statistics and present papers on "spouse abuse," "domestic violence," and "sex offenders." The contrasts in language reflect different world views, which are based on different sets of experiences.

Much of the research reviewed in this chapter indicates the impressive accuracy with which feminists analyzed the causes and dynamics of each form of violence against women; however, analyses preceded the research, in some cases by more than ten years. The absence of significant collaboration between academics and activists has resulted in serious losses—to the advancement of knowledge on the issues and to the victims.

The first section of this chapter examines the conditions that barely a decade ago provided the impetus for activists to unearth issues buried by silence and tacit approval. Subsequent sections review recent research findings relevant to each form of violence: rape, woman-battering, sexual harassment, child sexual assault, and pornography and sexual violence in the

270

media. Findings published within the last two years are included because of their impact on developments in 1981. Emphasis is placed on new research topics and designs and studies that tested premises articulated by feminist activists. The final section reviews and compares the efforts of individuals and groups with regard to services, funding cuts, innovative legislation and legal battles, and forms of resistance to sexual violence.

History

Rape crisis centers emerged in many United States cities in the early 1970s, generally without knowledge of each other's existence. Their simultaneous development gives rise to a major question: what specific historical events and cultural forces merged to focus reexamination of a social condition shrouded in silence and obscured by myths for centuries?

The focus on violence grew out of the consciousness-raising groups of the women's liberation branch of the contemporary movement.[1] Women who had been active in the civil rights and antiwar movements became discontent with their status within those movements and their opportunities in society at large. They used their skills and analytic frameworks to create autonomous women's groups and caucuses in existing organizations. The consciousness-raising format, in which participants discussed their shared experiences as women, was widely used. Within the safety of these small groups, three themes emerged that gave rise to the contemporary movement against violence against women: (1) the commonality of their victimization; (2) the insensitive responses of institutions, families, and friends; (3) and the impact of sexual violence in restricting their aspirations and mobility.

These discussions included reexamination of the so-called sexual revolution, one feature of which was the separation of sexuality from reproduction. As women lost the power to exchange sexuality for economic security, they also lost societal approval for refusing sexual advances. The problems of rape and coercion emerged for discussion.

Rape crisis centers and public speak-outs on this issue were direct outgrowths of consciousness raising. Early centers had three components: direct service, institutional reform, and community education. As they uncovered the realities of rape—that it is likely to be committed by a normal man who is known to the victim—it became possible to look at the more subtle, entrenched forms of violence. Public discussion of rape by dates, neighbors, and acquaintances led to evaluation of "normal" heterosexual relationships. This combined with the notion that what happens to individual women in the course of their lives reflects the values and structures of the whole society (summarized in the slogan, "the personal is political") made it possible to examine violence in other spheres in women's lives. The family, once viewed as the sanctuary from the harshness of urban, industrialized life, was exposed as the most violent unit in contemporary society. Wife abuse became the next major issue. Shortly thereafter, sexual harassment on the job and on campus was brought to public attention. Here the efforts of people working on issues of violence combined with those working for improved conditions for women's employment to create a climate receptive to this concern.

Throughout the 1970s groups formed across the United States to address specific forms of violence. The phenomenon of simultaneous identification of issues continued. As each type of violence was exposed, an array of cultural practices and attitudes was scrutinized. Links between acts of sexual violence and the socialization process of girls and boys were hypothesized. Violent images and sexual objectification in media, advertising, and pornography were examined as contributing factors.

By the mid-1970s the term "violence against women" emerged to encompass many issues: sterilization abuse, child sexual assault and incest, sexual abuse by physicians and therapists, as well as rape, battering, and sexual harassment. In fact, one of the first conferences on violence against women, held in 1975 in San Francisco, included workshops on nearly thirty specific forms.

The first two years of the 1980s witnessed continuing collaboration among groups devoted to combatting specific forms of violence against women. The search continues to uncover the commonalities—in the causes, in the effects on victims, and in strategies to eliminate them from all women's lives.

Rape

By 1972 at least eight rape crisis centers had opened—in Detroit, Berkeley, Washington, D.C., Ann Arbor, Philadelphia, Hartford, and Boston. Four years later the number was at least 400, and by 1979, there were 1,000 programs offering some assistance to rape victims.

Since 1974, forty-nine states have revised their rape laws with the aim of making it easier for victims to report the crimes and obtain convictions. The lone hold-out is Mississippi. Tens of thousands of rape victims have received emotional support, information, and advocacy, impressive accomplishments that are largely due to the efforts of feminist activists.

Yet basic questions remained unanswered. Perhaps the most striking is the lack of accurate incidence data, due in part to an array of methodological problems, especially under-reporting and differing definitions. The resultant data gap is handled differently, depending on the ideological bent of the presenter. For instance, FBI Uniform Crime Report Data is sometimes presented as is, and sometimes multiplied by a factor of ten to compensate for under-reporting. The estimate that one in every three women in the United States will be raped during her lifetime appears frequently, attributed to a study by the Los Angeles Commission on Assaults Against Women, or to statistical calculations combining the FBI figures as modified with a projection of rising rape rates through the year 2000, using the increase in reported rapes from 1960 to 1975 as a base.

Although recent research has not contributed to more accurate information about the incidence of rape, a great deal has been reported on other aspects of the issue in the last two years. This section briefly summarizes the literature that tests feminist analyses of causality and addresses questions about prevention, attitudes toward rape, and victims' service needs. The findings have direct implications for both policymakers and activists.

Research on the feminist assertion that rape is attributable to cultural forces concluded that it is indeed cultural rather than biological, and that "rape in tribal societies is part of a cultural configuration that includes interpersonal violence, male dominance, and sexual separation" (Sanday 1981, p. 25). Researchers also studied a correlate of the cultural determinism: that in societies with attitudes and practices conducive to rapes, all men are potential rapists. This view stands in sharp contrast to literature predating the antirape movement, which assumed rape to be a product of individual psychopaths. It was found that among male college students, 25 percent indicated that they definitely would commit rape if they were assured of not being caught (Malamuth 1981); that more than one-half of young men studied indicated some likelihood that they themselves would rape if assured of avoiding punishment (Malamuth, Haber, and Feshbach 1980); that nearly one-third of men in a university population report some degree of sexual aggressiveness, and more than one-half of the women report some degree of sexual victimization (Koss and Oros 1980b).

Attitudes toward rape and attribution of causality were frequent topics of investigation. A random sample of 598 adults revealed acceptance of myths associated with sex role stereotyping, adversarial sex beliefs, and acceptance of interpersonal violence (Burt 1980). Males are more likely to blame the victim (Anonymous 1981; Kanekar and Kolsawalla 1980; Thornton, Robbins, and Johnson 1981); and women who are raped by men they know do not define their experience as rape (Koss and Oros 1980a). Criminal justice personnel are likely to attribute rape to individual men's and women's characteristics, to doubt approximately one-half of the complaints brought before them, and to see prevention as best brought about by women changing their behaviors. Social service personnel hold different views; they attribute rape to differential socialization processes, believe nearly three-quarters of the women who bring their cases to them, and believe that the modification of social norms would reduce rape (Feldman-Summers and Palmer 1980). Potential jurors' attitudes toward rape and women are more similar to those held by police than those of rape crisis counselors or convicted rapists (Feild and Bienen 1980). Whereas potential jurors and police are most likely to believe victim-blaming myths, rape crisis counselors and rapists hold more accurate information. An encouraging note is that physicians and counselors previously untrained in rape crisis intervention are likely to change their attitudes over time, growing less likely both to see victims as inviting attack and rape as motivated by sexual desire (Calhoun 1980).

Rape research, and to a lesser although significant extent, rape services, have perpetuated racism by ignoring the history of rape and racism in America.[2] Although very little research during this period focused on these dynamics, important exceptions deserve to be noted. The Sexual Assault Crisis Service in Hartford, Conn., examined the factors contributing to an overwhelmingly white population of service users in a city with roughly equal black, Hispanic, and white populations. Methods of outreach and the race of staff members were significant barriers to minorities who knew about and were willing to use the service.[*] Another study found that black women were less likely to have their rape cases come to trial and to result in conviction than white women (LaFree 1980a). Furthermore, the racial composition of the victim/defendant dyad seems to be more important than the race of either individual in determining the outcome of legal cases (with black men accused of assaulting white women receiving the most serious charges and the longest sentences) (LaFree 1980b; Feild 1980). When a black woman was the victim, black and white rapists were not differentially treated (Feild 1980). The one study that considered the impact of rape on Hispanic women concluded that values within Hispanic cultures lead to resolution without intervention from existing institutions, and that the threat of rape leads these families to constrain the mobility of their female members (Quinones-Sierra 1980).

Research on reporting of rape found that the degree of force used and prior knowledge of the assailant were significant determinants (Skelton and Burkhart 1980); white women report rape significantly more often than do black, Hispanic, or Asian women, especially to the police and rape crisis centers. The expected outcome of reporting, which varied somewhat by racial group, was found to be a less accurate predictor of intention to report a rape than a woman's expectation of social support (Feldman-Summers and Ashworth 1981).

Studies that addressed the question of whether women confronted with an assailant should resist or submit, found that in general, women who actively resist by fighting back, running away, or screaming are more successful at avoiding rape than those who passively resist by crying, pleading, or appealing to the humanity of the assailant. Women who used physical force quickly were most likely to escape (McIntyre, J. 1981; Barth 1981a). Further comparisons of victims with avoiders indicate that the likelihood of being raped is associated with knowing the assailant, using only passive resistance, being assaulted in one's home, being concerned with avoiding death or mutilation, and the presence of a weapon or threat of death. In contrast, the likelihood of avoiding rape was associated with assault by

[*] Donna Landerman, personal communication, 1980.

strangers, employing active and passive resistance techniques, being assaulted outside, and focusing one's concern on not being raped (Bart 1981b). Fighting back, whether or not it deters assault, may aid a victim's self-esteem and her emotional resolution of the incident (Sanders 1980).

There was a recent test of the feminist assertion that the threat and reality of rape restrict women's independence and mobility. Women report significantly more fear than men do, which curtails their daily activities. The most fearful are the elderly, the poor, and members of racial or ethnic minorities; this fear often results in adopting either a strategy of isolation or of using street-wise techniques (Riger and Gordon 1981).

Two studies conclude that criminal justice system practices have not changed significantly despite legislative reform. One study points to the important symbolic and educative value of such reforms (Loh 1981), while the other recommends incorporating rape into existing statutes of aggravated and violent assault (Schwartz and Clear 1980).

Rape crisis counseling can be improved using guidelines from recent research. The three stages of the rape trauma syndrome (Burgess and Holmstrom 1974) have been expanded to five stages of victim response: initial crisis, denial, symptom formation, anger, and resolution (Forman 1980). Follow-up studies reveal that at one year postassault, victims experience more depression and less pleasure in day-to-day activities than matched nonvictim controls (Ellis, Atkeson, and Calhoun 1981), and exhibit continuing fear and anxiety (Kilpatrick, Resick, and Veronen 1981). One center determined that its limits stemmed from its hospital location and its disproportionate focus on the collection of legal evidence relative to the small number of women who chose to report to police (Ruch and Chandler 1980). One effective treatment program, on the other hand, attributed its success to supportive counseling that maintained power and control in the hands of the victim rather than those of the counselor (Ledray and Chaignot 1980). Based on a national survey, victims are indeed receiving crisis intervention and supportive services, but centers are deficient in providing long-term counseling and follow-up (King and Webb 1981).

Marital Rape

Explorations of marital rape are noticeably absent from the literature. While it is occasionally included as a form of wife abuse, it has not yet received specific attention. Concern about the incidence and effects of marital rape has come from activists whose focus has centered on three themes: (1) removing the marital exemption from existing statutes or enacting new legislation (see Activism section for further discussion); (2) sensitizing direct-service providers, especially those within battered women's shelters, to the emotional consequences and appropriate intervention strategies for victims; and (3) expanding the concept of violence against women.

Woman-Battering

In 1974 Women's House, the first United States refuge for battered women and their children, opened in St. Paul, Minnesota. By 1976 a sufficient number of resources existed to publish a national directory, *Working on wife abuse*. Current estimates suggest the existence of 1,000 hotlines, shelters, and programs for battered women.

The National Coalition Against Domestic Violence launched in 1977 now attracts over 600 service providers and activists to its conferences. Parallel coalitions of service groups exist in more than thirty-five states; forty-nine states have now revised their statutes covering battering; thirty-six of these specifically include protective orders for victims. This time the hold-out is South Dakota, where the governor vetoed protective legislation.

These achievements are again directly attributable to feminist analysis, spirit, and concerted effort. Most writers on the subject credit the women's movement in general and the specific work of the antirape movement for creating a climate receptive to shattering the silence surrounding battering, and challenging the acceptance of a husband's right to control his wife through violence.

Battered-women's advocates have had to confront and correct myths of victim-blaming and of individual psychopathology as did their predecessors working against rape. Responding to the needs of these women and their children has also meant tackling traditional, idealized notions of the sanctity of the nuclear family and the priority of maintaining it intact.

Incidence figures for battering are nearly as muddled as those for rape, and the disparity between reported and unreported figures is at least as great. Every eighteen seconds a woman in the United States is beaten by her husband, according to a popular statistic credited to the FBI. Others have projected that battering occurs in anywhere from one-quarter to one-half of all marriages or male/female cohabiting relationships (Jones 1981; National Clearinghouse on Domestic Violence 1980).

Research reported in academic journals in 1980 and 1981 by and large supported feminist rejection of the commonly held notions that battering only occurs in "problem" families, that alcohol overuse leads to battering, and that women must be masochistic to stay in violent relationships.

The overall level of violence and the sexist structure of the family and of society have been identified as the social causes of wife-beating. Earlier work pointed to the history of women's subordination, especially in the family, as the major factor (Dobash and Dobash 1979). One study, applying small group theory to couples, concluded that male violence is high where power imbalances exist and is lowest with couples whose power is distributed equally (Dutton 1980). Consistent with this power theme, a study of battered women in a Denver safe house found that women remained in their relationships because of economic dependence. More than half had children and depended on their husbands for financial support (Browne 1980). Additional evidence comes from a study whose focus was not battered women. In investigating abuse and neglect of the elderly, it was found that victims are usually females over sixty-five who lack the physical and financial resources for independence (Rathbone-McCuan 1980).

Following the lead of research conducted in the early 1970s, especially Gelles's *The violent home* published in 1974, current studies emphasize the intergenerational cycle of violence.[3] One found that 70 percent of battered women were psychologically or physically abused as children (Browne 1980). Other findings show that wife abuse and child abuse are likely to occur in the same families (Dietz and Craft 1980). A cross-cultural study of forty-six societies demonstrated that where wife beating is frequent, physical punishment of children is also frequent (Levinson 1981). An investigation of black families found violence to be tied to cultural and economic forces: Afro-American rates of violence, although consistent with overall American statistics, were significantly higher than in African societies (Staples 1980).

Alcohol use was found to be highly correlated with battering, but as feminists learned from their direct service experience, its use was to excuse the violence or to make the assaults seem temporary (Frieze and Knoble 1980).

The unresponsiveness of certain professionals has also been the subject of scholarly attention. Four reasons were identified to explain the ineffectiveness of the legal system: limitations of both civil remedies and criminal action, reluctance to become involved in battering cases, and inadequate police response (Constantino 1981; Loving and Farmer 1980). Four deficiencies on the part of social workers were also delineated: emphasis on preservation of the family unit; fear and lack of training in dealing with violent situations; inappropriate use of psychodynamic interpretation; and lack of case integration (Constantino 1981).

Specific service models were described and evaluated in a few reports. A detailed evaluation of twenty-six family violence programs funded by the Law Enforcement Assistance Administration concluded that the most effective intervention for battered women was the combination of feminist-run shelters with protective orders from the criminal justice system.[*] Minnesota has adopted a comprehensive statewide approach including shelters, an education program, voluntary therapy for batterers, and mandatory reporting requirement for all medical, law enforcement, and social service agencies (Oberg and Pence 1980).

After surveying 163 programs for battered women, and conducting eight site visits, one researcher concluded that shelter was the most critically needed service. Additional recommendations include studying programs within community contexts, involving women at all levels of program administration, and recognizing the importance of community education to long-range solutions.

[*] Jeffrey Tagan, personal communication, 1981.

Sexual Harassment

In 1976 two organizations were addressing the subject of sexual harassment on the job. Working Women's Institute in New York focused on sexual harassment within the context of working women's concerns, while the Alliance Against Sexual Coercion initially approached the problem as a form of violence against women.

That same year, *Redbook* magazine captured national attention when it reported that 88 percent of the 9,000 women responding to their survey had received unwanted sexual attention on the job (Safran 1976). One year later a suit against Yale University brought by students charging sexual harassment and a survey at the University of California at Berkeley brought awareness of the existence of harassment in higher education.

The Equal Employment Opportunity Commission (EEOC) issued guidelines in 1980 declaring sexual harassment in employment to be a form of sex discrimination, barred by Title VII of the 1964 Civil Rights Act. In 1981 the Office of Civil Rights (OCR) of the U.S. Department of Education made clear through a policy statement that sexual harassment of students is similarly covered under Title IX of the Educational Amendments of 1972.

Although barely a dozen separate organizations exist offering counseling and advocacy services to victims, countless committees and task forces have been formed within workplaces, unions, academic institutions, and women's organizations.

Feminist analysis and effort can certainly be credited with the identification of this problem. Thousands of workplaces have adopted personnel policies and grievance procedures, and hundreds have conducted training programs for segments of their work force. To date, their effectiveness in terms of prevention or fair resolution of disputes is unknown.

Published research on incidence or dynamics of sexual harassment is scarce. Campuses and firms that conduct their own surveys do not as a rule widely disseminate the findings. The bulk of professional literature on the subject in the last two years indicates that the American working world is coming to terms with the existence of the problem and the matter of legal liability (Clutterbuck 1981; Driscoll 1981; Zemke 1981; Carey 1981; Renick 1980; Breed 1980; Tillar 1980).

Perhaps the single most important piece of research completed is the random sample survey of 20,000 federal workers. Conducted under the auspices of the Merit Systems Protection Board (MSPB) and mandated by Congress, this study alternately confirms and challenges feminist perspectives on situations in which sexual harassment is most likely to occur. A detailed report of their findings, "Sexual harassment in the federal workplace: is it a problem?", was published in March 1981.

Confirmation of several key points included that sexual harassment was indeed found to be rampant. Forty-two percent of women working for the federal government between May of 1978 and May of 1980 experienced some form of harassment ranging from subtle, nonverbal behaviors to rape. Thirty percent of all surveyed had experienced a severe form (actual or attempted rape or assault; deliberate touching, pinching, or cornering; the receipt of letters, phone calls, or materials of a sexual nature). Not only bosses are in a position to harass. In fact, the majority of incidents reported in the survey were between coworkers.

Challenges to feminist analyses centered on the most likely targets of sexual harassment. Extending the basic framework that it is an abuse of the power that men hold over women, feminists have identified specific vulnerable populations. These include women in low-paying, low-status positions, women of color harassed by white men, new entrants or those reentering the labor force after a prolonged absence, single heads of households, and those pursuing nontraditional occupations (Klein 1981). Federal data confirm only these last two assertions, however. Women in professional/technical or administrative/management positions were slightly more likely to experience harassment than those in office/clerical or blue-collar jobs. Women of color did not experience more harassment than did white women, nor was it predominantly interracial. Both of these findings raise questions of awareness and definitions. Women in lower-paying positions may be resigned to accepting certain behaviors as part of the job, while women in higher status positions expect a work environment free from harassment. Women of color may define their experiences of interracial harassment as racial rather than sexual. Although women new to the labor force were disproportionately victims, the critical variable seems to be age rather than length of time in employment (Merit Systems Protection Board 1981).

Barbara Gutek has conducted four studies on sexual harassment in employment: three surveys of Los Angeles area workers, and one experimental study (Gutek, Nakamura, Gahart, Handschumacher, and Russell 1980; Gutek and Nakamura 1982; Gutek 1981a). A summary of her findings includes:

1. 10 percent to 15 percent of women have quit a job because of sexual harassment.
2. Approximately one-third of all working women have suffered some negative behavioral consequences of sexual harassment.
3. Women experience sexual harassment regardless of education, income, age, or attractiveness. Married women experience less.
4. Men find sexual overtures from women at work flattering, but women are not flattered by sexual overtures from men (Gutek 1981b).

The theme of differing male and female perceptions was echoed in the findings of a survey of executives jointly conducted by *Redbook* and the *Harvard Business Review*. Executives of both sexes are in agreement that one-directional, blatant sexual harassment is wrong. They disagree, however, both on what constitutes harassment and on the extent of the problem (Collins and Blodgett 1981).

Sexual harassment in education was exclusively addressed by a report whose purpose was to convince policymakers that this is a serious problem. Based on descriptive anecdotes solicited from college and university students nationally, the publication covers definitions, coping strategies of students, legal options, and institutional liability (Till 1980).

Other publications of note include those written by individuals who intervene. Mary Rowe's successful approach to informal resolution was developed while handling cases at Massachusetts Institute of Technology (1981). A description of subtle forms of sexual harassment (e.g., by coworkers, customers, and clients; during job interviews; office romances) and their effects on women workers is the subject of a publication based on client data from the Working Women's Institute (Crull and Cohen 1981). Sexual harassment in comprehensive and vocational high schools is covered in a guide produced in Massachusetts. Included are descriptions of peer-to-peer sexual harassment, background on the issue, strategies and sample policies for guidance counselors and administrators, and a curriculum to be incorporated into high school classes (Klein and Wilber 1981).

Child Sexual Assault

Ninety percent of child sexual assault victims are female (Price and Valdiserri 1981). By the age of eighteen, 25 percent of girls will have experienced some sexual abuse (Sanford 1980). Between 80 percent and 90 percent of child sexual assailants are known to their victims; in fact, they are usually a family member (Children's Hosptial National Medical Center, 1980). Father-daughter incest occurs in 1.5 percent of the general population (Finkelhor and Straus 1980). Most sexual abuse goes on for a long period of time, averaging about two and one-half years. (Adams-Tucker 1981; Peretti and Banks 1980).

Only recently has the sexual abuse of children received attention by feminist researchers and activists. Unlike the case with rape, battering, and sexual harassment, their task has not been to expose a previously ignored topic. Rather, their challenge has been to evaluate the assumptions that underlie the current extensive literature describing child sexual assault and the treatment modes that follow from it. Specifically, a fuller understanding has been achieved by shifting the line of inquiry from probing intrafamilial psychodynamics to exploring the relationship between traditional power dynamics within the family and within society.

Of particular importance is the publication of the first book to combine a feminist analysis with a clinical study. In *Father-daughter incest,* Judith Lewis Herman (1981a, 1981b), a feminist psychiatrist, provides a scholarly discussion of the theories that have served to disguise and dismiss not only incest, but the larger domain of child sexual assault. Her study revolves around three myths: incest is rare, it is usually harmless, and the father is not to blame. Herman begins with Freud's rejection and reinterpretation of the evidence of incest in his caseload. Explanations of the incest taboo by anthropologists and of the origins of fathers' power in the family are reviewed, followed by a discussion of the "seductive daughter" and "collusive mother" constructs, commonly seen as the "causes" of incest.

Findings from interviews with forty adult white women who had had incestuous relationships with their fathers are presented in some detail; twenty cases of seductive father-daughter relationships are also presented. Comparisons between the two situations reveal striking similarity not only to each other but to typical families as well. Characteristics include an ordinary family appearance, negative attitudes towards sex, the existence of traditional sex roles with fathers unquestionably the heads of households, and mothers submissive to fathers. Dynamics that distinguish incestuous families include mothers in poor health, large numbers of children, and problem drinking.

Herman also discusses treatment models for victims, families, and abusers, and the effects of criminal justice system intervention. A concluding chapter on prevention of sexual abuse distinguishes between short-term and long-term measures. The former include consciousness raising among potential victims and sex education for children and parents. She is unequivocal about a long-term solution:

> For the locus of the problem is ultimately in the structure of the
> family. As long as fathers rule but do not nurture, as long as
> mothers nurture but do not rule, the conditions favoring the
> development of father-daughter incest will prevail. Only a basic
> change in the power relations of mothers and fathers can prevent
> the sexual exploitation of children. (1981b, p. 206)

Much of the current professional literature stands in sharp contrast to Herman's sensitive work. The need to move from clinical approaches to an examination of "the broader social ills" was a theme at the recent international meetings on child abuse and neglect (Besharov 1981). Four types of literature were found: (1) studies of incidence and dynamics of child sexual assault; (2) clinical studies; (3) analysis of long-term effects of sexual abuse; and (4) suggestions for improvement in the professional handling of cases.

Incidence and dynamic studies confirm that sexual abuse, especially of girls, is widespread and is committed by males known to the victims (Adams-Tucker 1981; Cline 1980; Johnson 1980; Tilelli, Turek, and Jaffee 1980; Finkelhor 1980a; Finkelhor and Straus 1980). In a study of sibling sex, females reported more experiences and were more likely to have been exploited and to feel badly about them than males (Finkelhor 1980b). The amount of sexual abuse suffered by either or both parents was greater than average (Goodwin, McCarthy, and DiVasto 1981; Price and Valdiserri 1981). The imposition of the mothering role on the daughter in incestuous families was also noted (Herman 1981a; Jiles 1980; Price and Valdiserri 1981). One study identified several high-risk factors for girls, including living with a stepfather and the absence of mother (Finkelhor 1980b).

Clinical studies generally minimize the harmfulness of sexual assault on a child (LaBarbera, Martin, and Dozier 1980), or more often, blame the daughter or mother for the assault (Cline 1980; Nadelson and Rosenfeld 1980; Arndt 1981; Costell 1980).

Investigation of long-term effects on the adult life of a victim of child sexual assault indicated a variety of adjustment problems (Peretti and Banks 1980; Meiselman 1980; Star 1981), especially depending on the degree of force used (Finkelhor and Straus 1980) and on the individual's interpretation of the situation (Courtois and Watts 1980).

Steps to increase the responsiveness of various professionals included recommendations for human service workers (McIntyre, K. 1981: Rubinelli 1980; Conte, Berliner, and Nolan 1980; Johnson 1980; Delson and Clark 1981; Courtois and Watts 1980; Jiles 1980; Gruber 1981), for school personnel (Jiles 1980), for hospital emergency room staff (Tilelli, Turek, and Jaffee 1980; Jiles 1980), and components of the criminal justice system (Jiles 1980; Conte, Berliner, and Nolan 1980; Anderson 1981; Oklahoma Supreme Court 1980).

Four articles cited social forces as the root of child sexual assault and identified social change strategies. Three articles specifically named patriarchal institutions and sexist attitudes as being at fault and requiring major societal transformation (McIntyre, K. 1981; Herman 1981a; Rush 1980). The fourth pointed to the need for sex education and the strengthening of parent-child relationships as steps toward prevention of the sexual abuse of children (Children's Hospital National Medical Center 1980).

Pornography and Sexual Violence in the Media

Pornography is a $7-billion-a-year industry; if it were unified into one corporation it would rank fortieth on the Fortune 500. Two to three million people a week patronize X-rated movies. The ten best-selling pornographic magazines sell 16 million copies a month, which is 20 percent to 30 percent of total newsstand sales (Langelan 1981); the combined readership of *Playboy* and *Hustler* tops the combined readership of *Time* and *Newsweek*. More than 300,000 children under sixteen years of age are involved in child pornography (Women Against Pornography 1981).

The central question in the debate concerning strategy is who is victimized by pornography. The easing of censorship laws in the early 1970s was justified by the 1971 ten-volume *Technical reports of the commission on obscenity and pornography*. The Commission found the effects of pornography to be harmless. Recent articles have convincingly criticized the Commission's research assumptions and methodology (Bart and Jozsa 1980; Diamond 1980; Russell 1980). New research using a variety of methodologies that differ from those of the Commission has consistently found that exposure to sexually violent media increases men's aggression and hostility to women, and increases their acceptance of violence against women. In summarizing the data, one of the researchers stated:

> Everyone finds the same results, no matter what measures they use. There are no discrepant data here at all. (Donnerstein 1980)

The evidence of links between viewing or reading sexual violence and physical acts of sexual violence would be troubling enough if confined to hard-core pornography. Yet feminists have pointed out for several years and scholarly analyses now confirm, that the depiction of sexual violence in soft-core media and advertising is rapidly increasing (Malamuth and Check 1981; Malamuth and Spinner 1980; Langelan 1981; Donnerstein 1980; Bart and Jozsa 1980).

Neil Malamuth and James Check, in the most recent published research:

> . . . directly test the feminist contention that mass media exposures that portray violence against women as having favorable consequences contribute to greater acceptance of sexual and non-sexual violence against women. (1981, p. 2)

Their study constitutes the first nonlaboratory experiment; the research subjects were 271 male and female college students:

> The results indicated that exposure to films portraying violent sexuality increased male subjects' acceptance of interpersonal violence against women. (p. 2)

Trends also indicated that exposure to sexually violent films increased males' acceptance of rape myths, yet decreased females' acceptance. These results were obtained using films shown on national television, whose primary themes were not sexual violence.

A review of three studies confirms that under varying conditions, after viewing an "aggressive-erotic" film, men displayed aggressive behavior toward women but not necessarily toward other men (Donnerstein 1980).

During 1981 two books on pornography by feminists were published. In *Pornography and silence: culture's revenge against nature,* Susan Griffin argues:

> Pornography is an expression not of human erotic feeling and desire, and not of a love of the life of the body, but of a fear of bodily knowledge, and a desire to silence eros. (p. 1)

Andrea Dworkin's approach in *Pornography: men possessing women* is more direct:

> This is a book about the meaning of pornography and the system of power in which pornography exists. Its particular theme is the power of men in pornography. (Preface)

Both works describe the recurring messages of misogyny that characterize pornography, and the impact of pornographic and other media on women's psyches. Considerable attention is also devoted by both authors to the frequency with which pornography combines sexual violence with racism and anti-Semitism.

Sexualized media violence is the first form of violence against women to come to public attention that is more acceptable to condone than oppose. After a decade of analyzing and responding to each form of sexual violence separately, pornography provides an impetus for understanding the commonalities. Evidence of the detrimental effects of exposure to pornography serves as a reminder that tolerance of, and propensity to commit, acts of violence against women are generalized behaviors and attitudes. The rapist, the batterer, the harasser, and the child sexual abuser are expressing similar views of women.

Activism

For more than a decade activists have struggled to develop organizations and public education strategies through which effectively to address the various forms of violence against women. While the focus of this section is on the significant activist trends and events of 1981, historical conditions that shed light on the current situation are also discussed.

Activists' responses to specific forms of violence against women have varied, in part according to the nature of the violence itself. They have ranged from individual acts of civil disobedience, to major class action suits, to the establishment of on-going organizations. Yet important parallels can be identified. Early activists on each issue began with the premise that all women are affected by sexual violence, whether or not they are the direct victims of any particular form. In an effort to catch the public ear, most issues were launched with speak-outs where those who had been victimized described their experiences, their feelings, and the attitudes and institutional responses they encountered. The organizations or groups that have formed to address each issue have taken on many tasks, including providing services to victims, gathering incidence data, educating the public, urging legislative and institutional reform, and developing an analysis of the social forces that perpetuate violence.

Services to Victims

While generally part of a broad-based movement against violence to women, services have grown independently of one another, resulting in great creativity in program development and structure. While some groups provided services as part of a social change strategy, others were exclusively service-oriented. The former were generally the first organizations established to address each issue. Activities were chosen for their consonance with the long-range vision of equalizing power relationships, and the predominant model of counseling was self-help. Similarly, nonhierarchical structures were established, characterized by collective decision-making, rotating responsibilities, and encouraging the development of leadership abilities in all participants. The benefits of this format include sustained commitment and enthusiasm for the organization, and significant support and development of skills for individuals. Many obstacles to maintaining this structure were encountered. Collectivity can be quite time-consuming. Furthermore, it works best when members have similar values and educational levels. Collectives, therefore, tend to have homogeneous rather than diverse membership, a fact often in conflict with ideology. In addition, operating on a largely volunteer basis can make it difficult to meet objectives.

Groups that are hierarchically structured often receive adequate funding and community support, which means that more services are consistently provided. With narrower job descriptions though, workers frequently burn out on the day-to-day demands of supporting women in crisis; options for rotating positions are often nonexistent. Hierarchical structures usually demand prior expertise, making it less likely that former clients will be hired, and this prevents the development of leadership and other skills among the groups' members.

In 1981 the loss of funding, experienced or anticipated, resulted in modification of many services. Some rape crisis centers and battered women's shelters closed. Some merged with other violence-against-women groups or with human service agencies. Many have limited direct services — which are the most expensive and time-consuming to maintain — in favor of monitoring the institutions theoretically responsible for intervening. Educational efforts and prevention campaigns become tied to fund-raising efforts. In addition, funds supporting regional networking and skill-sharing have been cut. The Domestic Violence Technical Assistance programs, formerly ACTION-funded, are no longer in operation. Similarly, *RESPONSE Newsletter,* formerly funded by the Law Enforcement Assistance Administration and the Department of Health and Human Services, is no longer distributed without cost.

Coalitions and Networks

The National Coalition Against Sexual Assault (NCASA) and the National Coalition Against Domestic Violence (NCADV) are among the national, regional, and state coalitions formed by service groups. Although specific coalitions have not formed on other issues, national information clearinghouses and networks do exist. Commonalities of purpose include skill-sharing, strategy and program development, fund raising for member groups, reducing isolation, and combatting burn-out.

Achievements of coalitions and networks, generally unattainable by smaller units, are numerous. For example, NCASA's intense lobbying campaign during 1981 resulted in a portion of block grant funds to be earmarked specifically for services to rape victims in each state. NCADV's Women of Color Task Force recently received a $40,000 planning grant to design model programs to meet the employment and training needs of battered women, particularly members of racial minorities.

State groups have been instrumental in lobbying for funds for shelters and, in some instances, in helping to establish the criteria by which monies are distributed.

Legal Arena

While recognizing the importance of reforming the criminal justice system, feminist activists point out that it is far from a solution. Racial and class biases at each stage of enforcement have been well documented with respect to all crimes. Activists have therefore had to work for even-handed legislation and persevere to minimize prejudiced application and outcome. Due in large part to the groundwork done by activists, three doctors were convicted of raping a nurse in Boston this year.

Revisions of rape and battering statutes in forty-nine states represent a major accomplishment. Civil suits against rapists and batterers are becoming increasingly common.

Perhaps the most creative use of legislation has been that of fourteen states imposing taxes whose revenues are earmarked to fund services. Most states have taxed marriage licenses and divorce filings, but noteworthy exceptions exist. Texas taxes liquor, Pennsylvania fines those convicted of violent crimes, and Wisconsin fines violators of their domestic violence law.

Legislative reform alone does not usually mean immediate changes in daily practices. *Bruno* v. *Codd,* a class action suit, was filed on behalf of all battered women against the New York City police and family court for failure to uphold the law. Since then at least five other suits have been filed: Cleveland, Ohio; Weslaco, Texas; Oakland, California; Los Angeles, California; and in southern Illinois (National Center on Women and Family Law 1981b).

Within the last two years marital rape laws and sexual harassment court decisions (case law) have brought the complexities of male/female power relationships into the public arena. By mid-1981 five states treated marital rape the same as rape by a stranger. An additional 36 states permit marital rape charges under some circumstances, with various limits. Thirteen states, however, extended the "right" of marital rape to unmarried cohabitants (National Center on Women and Family Law, 1981a).

In January 1981 a U.S. Court of Appeals, in reversing an earlier decision, made clear its opinion that sexual harassment in and of itself is considered illegal under existing federal employment discrimination law (Title VII), and one need not prove economic consequences. This decision, *Bundy* v. *Jackson,* expands the right of working women to protest harassment not directly tied to job security.

A dangerous precedent was established in Pennsylvania in 1981: the right to legal confidentiality of the rape victim/rape counselor relationship was denied. Specific legislation permitting confidentiality is pending.

Law reforms have been met with some backlash. In eight states the constitutionality of recent legislation to assist battered women has been challenged on grounds of due process and equal protection of husbands. The marriage license tax has been challenged as a threat to the earnings of a wedding chapel. Battered-women's legislation has been upheld to date, but defense of legislation diverts resources from other activities.

Two suits against universities in Massachusetts for tacitly condoning sexual harassment through the absence of policies and grievance procedures received widespread attention in 1981. A class action against the University of Massachusetts at Boston involves allegations against a sex therapist by work-study students. At Clark University, the chair of the Sociology Department has been charged with sexual harassment by women students and faculty. He has initiated a suit for defamation of character totalling $23 million against five women who testified against him in a university hearing; the women had been told their testimony was confidential.

Resistance to Sexual Violence

The anger and frustration activists feel from living in a society with rampant violence against women are often transformed into inspiring public actions and events. Ranging from marches through city streets to organizing defense committees for individual women who fight back, these events keep issues in the public eye.

Women who focus on pornography and media violence have been innovative in breaking the silence. Exploitative billboards, window displays, and advertising campaigns have been confronted publicly and at times exposed for what they are. Women's groups led tours of pornography shops and peep-shows. Pickets and boycotts have been organized against plays (*Lolita* in New York), movies (*Dressed to Kill* nationally), and record companies and stores that promote images of sexual violence against women and children.

Acts of civil disobedience are growing. The Praying Mantis Women's Brigade in California urged the destruction of pornographic magazines on newsstands. Pornography theatre windows in Berkeley were smashed. "A woman was raped here" has been spray-painted on sidewalks throughout the country, and announcements of early curfews for men on facsimiles of police letterhead have been distributed in numerous communities.

Conclusion

The progress made in the past decade in identifying, intervening in, and resisting forms of violence against women represents a major achievement for women and a substantial challenge for the society. Previously, each form of violence was kept private and hidden. The true dimensions of each problem were unknown, yet dismissed as rare. Victims were blamed and assailants were deemed not responsible for their actions, and legal institutions and scholarly tradition reinforced these notions. Cultural imagery reflected and deepened the confusion between sexuality and violence. All of these practices have been exposed, and some significantly modified.

The distance yet to go is still monumental. In this culture, women's primary defining characteristic is still sexuality, and the boundaries between sexuality and violence are quite blurred for most men. Within this context, all forms of violence against women are sexual violence. To define rape, battering, sexual harassment, or child sexual assault only as acts of violence ignores the fact that violence itself has become eroticized. Until women are allowed to be more than sexual beings, until sexuality and violence are separated, and until violence is no longer used to maintain power differentials between races or sexes, our alarming rates of violence against women will be with us. Its eradication is only possible when the whole society says it is unacceptable.

NOTES

[1] Histories of the contemporary women's movement distinguish between the rights branch and the liberation branch. The former is associated with efforts at analyzing the status of women in contemporary society and reforming legal and institutional practices. Commissions on the status of women and the formation of NOW are examples of these organizations. By contrast, the liberation branch grew out of other political movements—civil rights, antiwar, and students'—and called for transformation of the whole society. Most of its early organizations were local women's centers, health collectives, and alternative media. (See *Personal politics, Rebirth of feminism,* and *They should have served that cup of coffee.*)

[2] *Aegis: A Magazine on Ending Violence Against Women* has consistently sought to point out the importance of multiracial definitions of forms of violence and multiracial service models and organizing strategies. An article by Deb Friedman, "Rape, racism, and reality," has been widely circulated.

[3] It is important to note that feminists have been critical of this intergenerational model. Kathleen Barry, in *Female sexual slavery,* points out that this notion of a self-perpetuating cycle creates hopelessness about eradicating the violence and obscures the role of social institutions in condoning male violence. The Massachusetts Coalition of Battered Women's Service Groups points out two additional deficiencies of this analysis in their training manual, *For shelter and beyond.* First, this theory ignores findings that indicate the significant number of batterers and battered women whose families of origin were nonviolent. Second, it has sometimes developed a pecking order of violence, erroneously blaming battered women for the high rates of child abuse.

REFERENCES

Adams-Tucker, C. 1981. A socioclinical overview of 28 sex-abused children. *Child Abuse and Neglect* 5:361-67.

Andersen, J. H. 1981. Iowa's inadequate protection against child molesting. *Iowa Law Review* 66 (March):623-37.

Anonymous. 1981. Rape and responsibility: how and how much is the victim blamed? *Sex Roles: A Journal of Research* 7:547-59.

Arndt, W. B. 1981. Sibling incest aversion as an index of oedipal conflict. *Journal of Personality Assessment* 45:52-58.

Bart, P. 1981a. *Avoiding rape: a study of victims and avoiders.* Washington, D.C.: National Center for the Prevention and Control of Rape.

Bart, P. 1981b. A study of women who both were raped and avoided rape. *Journal of Social Issues* 37:123-37.

Bart, P. B., and Jozsa, M. 1980. Dirty books, dirty films and dirty data. In *Take back the night: women on pornography*, ed. L. Lederer, pp. 218-38. New York: Morrow.

Besharov, D. J. 1981. The third international congress on child abuse and neglect: congress highlights. *Child Abuse and Neglect* 5:211-15.

Breed, A. F. 1980. Women in correctional employment. *Proceedings of the one hundred and ninth annual congress of correction*, pp. 247-54. College Park, Md.: American Correctional Association.

Browne, S. F. 1980.*In sickness and in health—analysis of a battered women population.* Denver: Denver Anti-Crime Council.

Burgess, A. W., and Holmstrom, L. L. 1974. *Rape: victims of crisis.* Bowie, Md.: Robert J. Brady.

Burt, M. 1980. Cultural myths and supports for rape. *Journal of Personality and Social Psychology* 38:217-30.

Calhoun, L. G. 1980. Interpreting rape: differences among professionals and non-professional resources. Paper presented at the Annual Convention of the American Psychological Association, Montreal.

Carey, S. H. 1981. Sexual harassment: a management issue. *Human Resource Management Journal.* Reprint. New York: Working Women's Institute.

Children's Hospital National Medical Center. 1980. *Public concern and personal action: child sexual abuse.* Washington, D.C.: Children's Hospital National Medical Center.

Cline, F. 1980. Dealing with sexual abuse of children. *Nurse Practitioner* 5:52-54.

Clutterbuck, D. 1981. When sex harassment becomes more than a bawdy office joke. *International Management.* Reprint. New York: Working Women's Institute.

Collins, E. G. C., and Blodgett, T. B. 1981. Sexual harassment . . . some see it . . . some won't. *Harvard Business Review.* Reprint. New York: Working Women's Institute.

Constantino, C. 1981. Intervention with battered women: the lawyer-social worker team. *Journal of the National Association of Social Workers* 26:456.

Conte, J. R.; Berliner, L.; and Nolan, D. 1980. Police and social worker cooperation: a key in child sexual assault cases. *FBI Law Enforcement Bulletin* 49:7-10.

Costell, R. M. 1980. The nature and treatment of male sex offenders. In *Sexual abuse of children: selected readings*, eds. K. MacFarlane, B. M. Jones, and L. L. Jenstrom, pp. 29-30. Washington, D.C.: National Center on Child Abuse and Neglect.

Courtois, C. A., and Watts, D. 1980. Women who experienced childhood incest: research findings and therapeutic strategies. Paper presented at the Annual Convention of the American Psychological Association, Montreal.

Crull, P., and Cohen, M. 1981. Expanding the definition of sexual harassment on the job. Research series no. 4. New York: Working Women's Institute.

Delson, N., and Clark, M. 1981. Group therapy with sexually molested children. *Child Welfare* 60:175-82.

Diamond, I. 1980. Pornography and repression: a reconsideration of 'who' and 'what.' In *Take back the night: women on pornography*, ed. L. Lederer, pp. 187-203. New York: Morrow.

Dietz, C. A., and Craft, J. L. 1980. Family dynamics of incest: a new perspective. *Social Casework* 61:602-609.

Dobash, R. E., and Dobash, R. 1980. *Violence against wives*. New York: Free Press.

Donnerstein, E. 1980. Pornography and violence against women: experimental studies. Unpublished paper. Washington, D.C.: National Institute of Mental Health.

Driscoll, J. 1981. Sexual attraction and harassment: management's new problems. *Personnel Journal* 60:33-36, 56.

Dutton, D. G. 1980. Social-psychological research and relevant speculation on the issue of domestic violence. In *Female offender*, eds. C. T. Griffiths and M. Nance, pp. 81-91. Burnaby, Canada: Simon Fraser University Criminology Research Centre.

Dworkin, A. 1981. *Pornography: men possessing women*. New York: Perigee.

Ellis, E. M.; Atkeson, B. M.; and Calhoun, K. S. 1981. An assessment of long-term reaction to rape. *Journal of Abnormal Psychology* 90:263-66.

Feild, H. S. 1980. Rape trials and jurors' decisions—a psychological analysis of the effects of victim, defendant, and case characteristics. *Law and Human Behavior* 3:261-84.

Feild, H. S., and Bienen, L. B. 1980. *Jurors and rape—a study in psychology and law*. Lexington, Mass.: Heath.

Feldman-Summers, S., and Ashworth, C. D. 1981. Factors related to intentions to report a rape. *Journal of Social Issues* 37:53-70.

Feldman-Summers, S., and Palmer, G. C. 1980. Rape as viewed by judges, prosecutors, and police officers. *Criminal Justice and Behavior* 7:19-40.

Finkelhor, D. 1980a. Sex among siblings: a survey on prevalence, variety, and effects. *Archives of Sexual Behavior* 9:171-94.

Finkelhor, D. 1980b. Risk factors in the sexual victimization of children. *Child Abuse and Neglect* 4:267-73.

Finkelhor, D., and Straus, M. A. 1980. Incest and family sexual abuse. Durham, N.H.: University of New Hampshire Family Violence Program.

Forman, B. D. 1980. Psychotherapy with rape victims. *Psychotherapy: Theory, Research and Practice* 17:304-11.

Frieze, I. H. and Knoble, J. 1980. The effects of alcohol on marital violence. Paper presented at the Annual Convention of the American Psychological Association, Montreal.

Goodwin, J.; McCarthy, T.; and DiVasto, P. 1981. Prior incest in mothers of abused children. *Child Abuse and Neglect* 5:87-95.

Griffin, S. 1981. *Pornography and silence: culture's revenge against nature.* New York: Harper & Row.

Gruber, K. J. 1981. The child victim's role in sexual assault by adults. *Child Welfare* 60:305-11.

Gutek, B. A. 1981a. A psychological examination of sexual harassment: disentangling sexual harassment from sexual interest. Paper presented at a conference at the Institute of Industrial Relations, Los Angeles.

Gutek, B. A. 1981b. Sexual harassment: results from a program of research. Unpublished paper, University of California, Los Angeles.

Gutek, B. A., and Nakamura, C. Y. 1982. Gender roles and sexuality in the world of work. In *Gender roles and sexual behavior: changing boundaries*, eds. E. R. Allgeier and N. B. McCormick, Palo Alto, Calif.: Mayfield.

Gutek, B. A.; Nakamura, C. Y.; Gahart, M.; Handschumacher, I.; and Russell, D. 1980. Sexuality and the workplace. *Basic and Applied Social Psychology* 1:255-65.

Herman, J. L. 1981a. Father-daughter incest. *Professional Psychology* 12:76-80.

Herman, J. L. 1981b. *Father-daughter incest.* Cambridge: Harvard University Press.

Jiles, D. 1980. Problems in the assessment of sexual abuse referrals. In *Sexual abuse of children: implications for treatment*, ed. W. Holder, pp. 59-64. Denver: American Humane Association.

Johnson, C. L. 1980. Child sexual abuse case handling through public social agencies in the southeast. Athens, Ga.: Regional Institute of Social Welfare Research.

Jones, A. 1981. *Women who kill.* New York: Fawcell Columbine.

Kanekar, S., and Kolsawalla, M. B. 1980. Responsiblity of a rape victim in relation to her respectability, attractiveness, and provocativeness. *Journal of Social Psychology* 112:153-54.

Kilpatrick, D. G.; Resick, P.; and Veronen, L. 1981. Effects of a rape experience: a longitudinal study. *Journal of Social Issues* 37:105-22.

King, H. E., and Webb, C. 1981. Rape crisis centers: progress and problems. *Journal of Social Issues* 37:93-104.

Klein, F. R. 1981. Sexual harassment in employment: a critical look at policy recommendations. Unpublished paper, Brandeis University.

Klein, F. R., and Wilber, N. 1981. *Who's hurt and who's liable: sexual harassment in Massachusetts schools.* Boston: Commonwealth of Massachusetts Department of Education.

Koss, M. P., and Oros, C. J. 1980a. The "unacknowledged" rape victim. Paper presented at the Annual Convention of the Psychological Association, Montreal.

Koss, M. P., and Oros, C. J. 1980b. Hidden rape—a survey of the incidence of sexual aggression and victimization on a university campus. Paper presented at Midwestern Psychological Association, St. Louis.

LaBarbera, J. D., and Dozier, J. E. 1980. Hysterical seizures: the role of sexual exploitation. *Psychosomatics* 21:897-903.

LaBarbera, J. D.; Martin, J. E.; and Dozier, J. E. 1980. Child psychiatrists' view of father-daughter incest. *Child Abuse and Neglect* 4:147-51.

LaFree, G. D. 1980a. Variables affecting guilty pleas and convictions in rape cases—toward a social theory of rape processing. *Social Forces* 58:833-50.

LaFree, G. D. 1980b. Effect of sexual stratification by race on official reactions to rape. *American Sociological Review* 45:842-54.

Langelan, M. 1981. The political economy of pornography: marketing misogyny at $7 billion a year. *Aegis: Magazine on Ending Violence Against Women* 32:5-17.

Lederer, L., ed. 1980. *Take back the night: women on pornography.* New York: Morrow.

Ledray, L., and Chaignot, M. J. 1980. Services to sexual assault victims in Hennepin county. *Evaluation and Change* Special issue:131-34.

Levinson, D. 1981. Physical punishment of children and wifebeating in cross-cultural perspective. *Child Abuse and Neglect* 5:193-95.

Loh, W. D. 1981. What has reform of rape legislation wrought? *Journal of Social Issues* 37:28-52.

Loving, N., and Farmer, M. T. 1980. *Responding to spouse abuse and wife beating—a guide for police.* Washington, D.C.: Police Executive Research Forum.

Malamuth, N. M. 1981. Rape proclivity among males. *Journal of Social Issues* 37:138-57.

Malamuth, N. M., and Check, J. P. 1981. The effects of mass media exposure on acceptance of violence against women: a field experiment. *Journal of Research in Personality.*

Malamuth, N. M., and Spinner, B. 1980. A longitudinal content analysis of sexual violence in the best-selling erotic magazines. *Journal of Sex Research* 16:226-37.

Malamuth, N. M.; Haber, S.; and Feshbach, S. 1980. Testing hypotheses regarding rape: exposure to sexual violence, sex differences, and the "normality" of rapists. *Journal of Research in Personality* 14:121-37.

McIntyre, J. 1981. Victim response to rape: alternative outcomes. Washington, D.C.: National Institute of Mental Health.

McIntyre, K. 1981. Role of mothers in father-daughter incest: a feminist analysis. *Journal of the National Association of Social Workers* 26:462.

Meiselman, K. C. 1980. Personality characteristics of incest history psychotherapy patients: a research note. *Archives of Sexual Behavior* 9:195-97.

Merit Systems Protection Board. 1981. *Sexual harassment in the federal workplace: is it a problem?* Washington, D.C.: U.S. Government Printing Office.

Nadelson, C. C., and Rosenfeld, A. A. 1980. Sexual misuse of children. In *Child psychiatry and the law*, eds. D. H. Schetky and E. P. Benedek, pp. 86-106. New York: Brunner/Mazel.

National Center on Women and Family Law. 1981a. Battered women—litigation packet. New York: The Center.

National Center on Women and Family Law. 1981b. Marital rape exemption packet. New York: The Center.

National Clearinghouse on Domestic Violence. 1980. Battered women—a national concern. Rockville, Md.: National Clearinghouse on Domestic Violence.

Oberg, S., and Pence, E. 1980. Responding to battered women. In *Perspectives on crime victims*, eds. B. Galaway and J. Hudson, pp. 385-91. St. Louis: Mosby.

Oklahoma Supreme Court. 1980. *Stewart v. Stewart*.

Peretti, P. O., and Banks, D. 1980. Negative psychological effects on the incestuous daughter of sexual relations with her father. *Panminerva Medica* 22:27-30.

Price, J. M., and Valdiserri, E. V. 1981. Childhood sexual abuse: a recent review of the literature. *Journal of the American Medical Women's Association* 36:232-34.

Quinones-Sierra, S. 1980. Rape within the Hispanic family unit. Unpublished paper.

Rathbone-McCuan, E. 1980. Elderly victims of family violence and neglect. *Social Casework* 61:296-304.

Renick, J. C. 1980. Sexual harassment at work: why it happens, what to do about it. *Personnel Journal* 59:658-62.

Riger, S., and Gordon, M. 1981. The fear of rape: a study in social control. *Journal of Social Issues* 37:71-92.

Rowe, M. 1981. Dealing with sexual harassment. *Harvard Business Review* 59:42-46.

Rubinelli, J. 1980. Incest: it's time we face reality. *Journal of Psychiatric Nursing and Mental Health Services* 18:17-18.

Ruch, L. O., and Chandler, S. M. 1980. Evaluation of a center for sexual assault victims—issues and problem areas. *Women and Health* 5:45-63.

Rush, F. 1980. *Best kept secret—sexual abuse of children*. Englewood Cliffs, N.J.: Prentice-Hall.

Russell, D. E. H. 1980. Pornography and violence: what does the new research say? In *Take back the night: women on pornography*, ed. L. Lederer, pp. 218-38. New York: Morrow.

Safran, C. 1976. What men do to women on the job. *Redbook* 149:217-23.

Sanday, P. R. The socio-cultural context of rape: a cross-cultural study. *Journal of Social Issues* 37:5-27.

Sanders, W. B. 1980. Rape and woman's identity. Beverly Hills: Sage.

Sanford, L. T. 1980. *Silent children—a book for parents about the prevention of child sexual abuse*. Garden City, N.Y.: Anchor/Doubleday.

Schwartz, M. D., and Clear, T. R. 1980. Toward a new law on rape. *Crime and Delinquency* 26:129-51.

Skelton, C. A., and Burkhart, B. R. 1980. Sexual assault—determinants of victim disclosure. *Criminal Justice and Behavior* 7:229-36.

Staples, R. 1980. Race, stress and family violence. In *Stress and crime*, ed. M. J. Molof, pp. 73-85. Washington, D.C.: National Criminal Justice Research Service.

Star, B. 1981. The short and long-term effects of sexual child abuse on the victims. Research in progress.

Thornton, B.; Robbins, M. A.; and Johnson, J. A. 1981. Social perception of the rape victim's culpability: the influence of respondents' personal-environmental causal attribution tendencies. *Human relations* 34:225-37.

Tilelli, J. A.; Turek, D.; and Jaffee, A. C. 1980. Sexual abuse of children—clinical findings and implications for management. *New England Journal of Medicine* 302:319-23.

Till, F. J. 1980. Sexual harassment: a report on the sexual harassment of students. Washington, D.C.: U.S. Department of Education.

Tillar, D. L. 1980. Sexual harassment in employment: legal perspectives for university administrators. Center for the Study of Higher Education, School of Education, Charlottesville, Va.

Women Against Pornography. 1981. Pornography fact sheet. New York: Women Against Pornography.

Zemke, R. 1981. Sexual harassment: is training the key? *Training Magazine* February, pp. 22-28.

RESOURCES

Listed here are organizations and print and nonprint materials that pertain to each form of violence against women. The emphasis is on practical materials, identified by those working in each field.

Violence Against Women — General

Aegis: A Magazine on Ending Violence Against Women. Feminist Alliance Against Rape, P.O. Box 21033, Washington, DC 20009. Subscriptions: $10.50 per year individuals, $25.00 institutions. An excellent quarterly publication that includes analytical articles on all forms of violence against women, discussions of strategies, and practical information and resources for organizers and direct-service providers. It consistently includes articles on racism and violence against women, such as building multiracial organizations and evaluation of racial biases in institutional practices and research.

Barry, Kathleen. *Female sexual slavery.* Englewood Cliffs, N.J.: Prentice-Hall, 1979. In this powerful work, the concept of female sexual slavery is used to cover ". . . ALL situations where women or girls cannot change the immediate conditions of their existence; where . . . they cannot get out; and where they are subject to sexual violence and exploitation" (p. 40). Cross-cultural evidence documents the international slave trade connected to prostitution, genital mutilation, rape, battering, incest, and pornography.

Boston Women's Health Book Collective. *Our bodies, ourselves.* New York: Simon & Schuster, 1976 and forthcoming. In the forthcoming edition of this now-classic book on women's health, a chapter will be devoted entirely to issues of violence against women.

Delacoste, Frederique, and Felice Newman, eds. *Fight back! feminist resistance to male violence.* Minneapolis: Cleis Press, 1981. P.O. Box 8281, Minneapolis, MN 55408. An inspiring compendium of analyses of trends in the movement against violence against women, the interconnections of racism and sexual violence, stories of individuals who fought back, and descriptions of group actions to challenge images and practices of sexual violence. A lengthy state-by-state directory of rape crisis centers, battered women's shelters, and women's political organizations is also included.

off our backs! 1841 Columbia Road, Washington, DC 20009. Subscriptions: $8.00 per year individuals; $20.00 institutions. This women's news journal has provided extensive coverage of violence against women in its monthly issues for over ten years. It is one of the best sources for current information on strategies and resources nationally and internationally. In addition to analytical feature stories, it reviews research findings, books, films, and other resources; conference announcements and federal policy changes are also reported.

Sanford, Linda Tschirhart, and Ann Fetter. *In defense of ourselves, a rape prevention book for women.* New York: Doubleday, 1979. A good, concise examination of cultural phenomena that promote women's victimization and unpreparedness for self-protection. Includes detailed descriptions and photographs of practical self-defense techniques, and a guide for using the book with different racial and age groups.

Rape

Bienen, Leigh. "Rape III" and "Rape IV," *Women's Rights Law Reporter*, 6(3) and supplement. Newark: Rutgers-Newark School of Law, 1981. These articles provide a detailed description of the state-by-state laws defining sex offenses.

Cambridge Documentary Films. P.O. Box 385, Cambridge, MA 02139. *Rape culture*, a 33-minute color film, uses excerpts from popular Hollywood movies, and interviews with feminists and convicted rapists to illustrate the role of societal forces in promoting rape. Produced in 1975, some of the media pieces are dated, but it is still widely used.

Columbus Women Against Rape. P.O. Box 02084, Columbus, OH 43202. With funding from NIMH, this organization investigated primary rape prevention strategies. Several publications are available including "Freeing our lives" which discusses short-term and long-term prevention strategies ($1.00); "Fighting back," covering practical safety tips ($.50);

296 | Freada Klein
and "Rape prevention workshops: a leader's guide," designed to teach individuals and organizations how to present workshops on rape prevention ($10.00).

Community Program Against Sexual Assault (CPASA). 100 Warren St., Roxbury, MA 02119. One of the too few rape crisis centers run by women of color to provide services to victims and community education and prevention programs primarily for black and Hispanic women. This group has been active in articulating the links between rape and racism. Recently they sponsored a Latin Women's Conference addressing, among other topics, violence against Latinas. Write for more information.

National Center for the Prevention and Control of Rape. National Institutes of Mental Health No. 13A-44 Park Lawn Building, 5600 Fishers Lane, Rockville, MD 20857. Since the mid-1970s the Center has funded a range of research and demonstration projects on rape. Bibliographies, monographs, and final reports are available at various prices.

National Coalition Against Sexual Assault (NCASA). Sharon Sayles, President, Minnesota Program for Victims of Sexual Assault, 430 Metro Building, Minneapolis, MN 55105. A national membership organization, NCASA sponsors annual conferences and publishes a newsletter. Regional representatives facilitate the exchange of information and resources. Standing committees function on certain topics. Annual dues: $15.00 individuals; $25.00 organizations.

ODN Productions, Inc. 74 Varick St., Room 304, New York, NY 10013; and 1454 Sixth Street, Berkeley, CA 94710. The *Acquaintance rape prevention* film series has been widely used and well received. It consists of four short films aimed at high school and college audiences; extensive guides for teachers and workshop leaders accompany the films. The focus is date rape. A version for the hearing-impaired is also available.

Rape Crisis Center of Syracuse, Inc. 423 West Onondaga St., Syracuse, NY 13204. This center has produced brief brochures on rape aimed at women of different ages. They have also published *Rape: awareness and prevention for educators*, a comprehensive resource book ($5.50); *Sometimes I need to say 'no'*, a play focusing on a child's right to bodily privacy ($3.00); and *Rape resource book*, a counseling and informational guide ($5.00).

Washington, D.C. Rape Crisis Center. P.O. Box 21005, Washington, DC 20009. As one of the first rape crisis centers in the United States, this center played an important role in fostering communications between projects. They recently sponsored the first national conference on Third World Women and Violence, and publish *How to start a rape crisis center*, an excellent resource for new programs ($5.00).

Woman-battering

Domestic Violence Technical Assistance Project (DVTAP). Casa Myrna Vasquez, P.O. Box 18019, Boston, MA 02118. A project of a battered women's shelter, DVTAP has developed materials, a newsletter, and sponsored conferences for service providers. Although recently defunded, "Outreach strategies to third world women" is still available; it is a particularly useful pamphlet for shelters and other service groups who seek to have their staff and clients represent the ethnic and racial diversity of the communities they serve.

Emerge. 25 Huntington Ave., Room 324, Boston, MA 02116. As the first men's group working with batterers, this organization's efforts have provided battered-women's shelters with an important referrral and useful information on the dynamics of battering. They have written a monograph, *Working with men who batter*, and in 1981 produced a film, *To have and to hold*, which features interviews with men who have been Emerge's counselors and clients.

Massachusetts Coalition of Battered Women's Service Groups (MCBWSG). 25 West Street, Boston, MA 02116. The MCBWSG has functioned as a strong source of information and technical assistance to services in the state. They published *For shelter and beyond—an educational manual for working with women who are battered* in 1981 ($5.00). It provides practical information on counseling and advocacy, and covers a range of issues that confront service providers in shelters: alcohol and drug use; women in severe crisis; and working with racial, class, and sexual preference differences. An annotated bibliography is included.

National Center on Women and Family Law. 799 Broadway, Room 402, New York, NY 10003. Funded through Legal Services Corporation, this center provides technical assistance on issues affecting battered women such as suits against criminal justice agencies for failure to enforce domestic violence legislation, and defending challenges to legislation; other priorities are marital rape legislation and cases, and civil suits against rapists and batterers. A variety of resource lists and packets are available on the topics of battering, marital rape, and child custody. Write for order forms and for Service Request Policy if seeking legal assistance.

National Coalition Against Domestic Violence (NCADV). 728 N St. NW, Washington, DC 20036. The NCADV has provided a powerful voice in the development of the battered-women's shelter movement through its production of technical assistance materials and sponsorship of conferences. *State domestic violence laws and how to pass them, a manual for lobbyists* is now available. Regional caucuses and the issues committee promote information sharing. The Women of Color Task

Force is planning model employment programs for former battered women.

ODN Productions, Inc. 74 Varick St., Room 304, New York, NY 10013; and 1454 Sixth Street, Berkeley, CA 94710. Three short films and a guidebook comprise the "Spouse abuse prevention" series, focusing on men who batter, the effects of their actions, and alternatives to violence. *In need of special attention* is a 17-minute color film, with training manual, designed to assist emergency room staff in establishing protocol for battered women.

Rape and Violence End Now (RAVEN). P.O. Box 24159, St. Louis, MO 63130. A men's group working to end violence against women, RAVEN primarily counsels batterers. In addition, they publish a quarterly newsletter, *Network news*, aimed at other men's groups, have produced a handbook on strategies for men working to end violence against women ($5.00), are planning the first national conference for men working against violence against women in 1982, and have a national mailing list of other men's organizations available.

Schechter, Susan. *Women and male violence: the struggles of the battered women's movement.* Boston: South End Press, forthcoming 1982. A description of the origins and evolution of the contemporary movement to help battered women, and a critical analysis of major developments. This book will be particularly useful to organizations and coalitions in designing future strategies.

Transition House Films, 25 West St., Boston, MA 02116. *We will not be beaten* features interviews with staff and residents of a shelter. It is a powerful analysis of the dynamics of battering, institutional response, and the role of shelters. In black and white, it is available in two versions of different lengths on film or video.

Warrior, Betsy. *Working on wife abuse.* 46 Pleasant St. Cambridge, MA 02139. Since the mid-1970s this directory, continually updated, is an extensive resource list of organizations and individuals working against battering. Other practical materials, such as sample forms and policies of shelters, are also included.

Marital Rape

National Clearinghouse on Marital Rape (NCOMR). Women's History Research Center, Inc., 2325 Oak St., Berkeley, CA 94708. The clearinghouse has published a pamphlet on the Greta Rideout case in Oregon ($1.00), and a brochure on marital rape. Send a self-addressed, stamped envelope for materials and for information about membership in the clearinghouse.

See National Center on Women and Family Law for their marital rape materials.

Sexual Harassment

Alliance Against Sexual Coercion (AASC). P.O. Box 1, Cambridge, MA 02139. The first organization in the United States to provide a comprehensive approach to the problem of sexual harassment has several publications available: *Sexual harassment: an annotated bibliography* ($7.00); *Sexual harassment and the law* ($5.00); *University grievance procedures, Title IX and sexual harassment on campus* ($4.00); *Fighting sexual harassment: an advocacy handbook* ($3.50). Send for descriptions of these and other materials.

Association of American Colleges, Project on the Status and Education of Women. 1818 R St. NW, Washington, DC 20009. Since 1971, the Project has provided a wealth of information on women in higher education. Their quarterly newsletter, *On Campus with Women*, consistently covers sexual harassment in education, including individual cases and law suits and federal and local policy changes, and reviews print and nonprint resources. A packet of articles on rape and sexual harassment is available. Send self-addressed stamped envelope for order form.

Backhouse, Constance, and Leah Cohen. *Sexual harassment on the job.* Englewood Cliffs, N.J.: Prentice-Hall, 1981. Originally published in Canada in 1978, this book is an excellent, quite readable overview of the issue. Case studies, history, analysis of the problem, and action plans for management and unions are covered.

Capital University Law Review. *Symposium on sexual harassment.* Vol. 10, 1981. As Catherine MacKinnon states in her introduction, "This volume documents and reflects the success, incompleteness and potential limits on this attempt to embody women's point of view in the law of sex equality." Articles discuss legal theory, the political dilemmas of trial strategy, the racist application of sexual harassment laws, and activities needed to accompany legislative change.

Clark Communications. 943 Howard St., San Francisco, CA 94103. *The workplace hustle*, a 30-minute color film, provides an introduction to sexual harassment on the job. Narrated by Ed Asner, it features interviews with Lin Farley, women who have experienced harassment, and groups of men and women discussing the topic. It does not include women in nontraditional occupations.

Goodmeasure, Inc. Media Dept., 330 Broadway, Cambridge, MA 02139. *A tale of O* is an amusing depiction of what happens when one O joins a work group of Xs who have never had an O in their group before. Highlights aspects of sex and race discrimination in nonthreatening ways. Available as a slide tape or videotape.

Farley, Lin. *Sexual shakedown: the sexual harassment of women on the job.* New York: McGraw-Hill, 1978. An analysis of the origins of sexual harassment in the economic system and in women's subordinate status within society. Includes case histories.

MacKinnon, Catherine. *Sexual harassment of working women: a case of sex discrimination.* New Haven: Yale University Press, 1978. A sophisticated legal and theoretical analysis of sexual harassment as a form of sex discrimination. Victims' experiences, patterns of women's participation in the work force, and an analysis of two theories of sex discrimination (as sex differences and as sex inequality) are explored.

Working Women's Institute. 593 Park Ave., New York, NY 10021. The Institute provides direct service and education, and operates a Legal Backup Center for sexual harassment cases and a Research Clearinghouse. Numerous original publications and reprints are available; included is a bibliography, research reports, law review articles, general information, and case load analyses of sexually harassed clients. Send a self-addressed stamped envelope for publication lists.

Child Sexual Assault

Child Assault Prevention Project. Columbus Women Against Rape, P.O. Box 02084, Columbus, OH 43202. A variety of literature with a focus on prevention is available. Classroom workshops for grades K through 8 include role plays; adult workshops aimed at identifying children in crisis have been developed.

Child Protection Center. Children's Hospital National Medical Center, 111 Michigan Ave. NW, Washington, DC 20010. Under previous funding from the Law Enforcement Assistance Administration, this center investigated different models of cooperative agency intervention and therapeutic techniques in working with victims. An informative slide show and research reports have been produced.

Child Sexual Abuse Prevention Project. Office of the County Attorney, 2000-C Hennepin Government Center, Minneapolis, MN 55487. Prevention programs for children have been designed and used in a variety of settings. Write for more information.

National Center on Child Abuse and Neglect. U.S. Department of Health and Human Services, Washington, DC 20013. The Center has funded research and has volumes of reports and literature available, including bibliographies. Especially recommended is Kee MacFarle et al., *Sexual abuse of children: selected readings*, publication #OHDS 78-30161, November 1980.

Parents United. Sexual Abuse Treatment Program, 840 Guadelupe Parkway, San Jose, CA 95110. One of the first human service programs working with incestuous families, this program claims a 90 percent success rate. Research reports and description of program model available.

Rape and Abuse Crisis Center. Fargo, ND 58102. Innovative materials have been developed for use with children in the classroom. Write for information on two publications in particular, *Red flag/green flag* and *One fly was a little bit frightened*.

Rush, Florence. *The best kept secret: sexual abuse of children*. Englewood Cliffs, N.J.: Prentice-Hall, 1980. Rush documents the history of the sexual abuse of children by reviewing the Bible, myths, fairy tales, and popular literature. She looks at the role of legal institutions, psychology, and "kiddie porn" in perpetuating the victimization of children.

Sexual Assault Center. Harborview Medical Center, 325 Ninth Ave., Seattle, WA 98104. Growing out of a local rape crisis center, this project has worked with sexually abused children since the mid-1970s. Much of their work has focused on preparing children to be effective witnesses in court proceedings without traumatizing them. Available materials include research reports and monographs.

See Rape Crisis Center of Syracuse for their materials on child sexual assault.

Pornography and Sexual Violence in the Media

National Film Board of Canada, 1251 Avenue of the Americas, New York, NY 10010. *Not a love story* is an excellent film about the concept of pornography and its relationship to physical acts of violence. Released in 1981, it has already received glowing praise from groups all over North America.

Odyssey Institute. 656 Avenue of the Americas, New York, NY 10010. The Institute has produced a slide show on child pornography, available for sale.

Women Against Pornography (WAP). 358 West 47th St., New York, NY 10036. They initiated touring pornography shops to encourage women to understand the messages conveyed by books, films, and peep-shows. A membership organization, WAP produces a bimonthly newsletter, *Newsreport*. Their slide show in adult or high school versions is available for purchase or rental. Write for membership and slide show information, and to request their educational fliers.

Women Against Violence Against Women (WAVAW). 543 North Fairfax Ave., Los Angeles, CA 90036. WAVAW began in 1975 to protest the sexual violence in record album advertising. Their boycott of record companies has in some instances brought about changes in company policy. They are a national membership organization with chapters across the country. Over the years WAVAW's slide show has been broadened to cover other forms of media violence. Write for the address of a local chapter and information on their newsletter, slide show, and other materials.

Women Against Violence in Pornography and Media (WAVPM). P.O. Box 14635, San Francisco, CA 94114. The group sponsors tours of pornography shops, pickets of abusive films, and other public events. Their monthly newsletter, *Newspage*, has featured bibliographies, an international directory of groups working against media violence, and numerous other topics. They have produced a slide show and *Write back! fight back*, a media protest packet ($3.50). Write for order form and price list.

11 | Women and Work

Sara Garrigan Burr

The major trend in 1981 affecting women in the work force was the ascendance of a conservative ideology of "women's work" in national politics. The view promoted by conservative political leaders seems at first glance to be archaic and unsuited to solving contemporary economic problems. Best articulated by Heatherly (1980) and George Gilder (1981), the New Right philosophy is built on sentimental nostalgia for patriarchal families, religion, and minimal governmental regulation. It is also linked to a military mentality that defines government's main responsibility as defense.

Changes in women's status in the work force between 1980 and 1981 were less remarkable than the polarization of attitudes toward their economic roles. Allied with the presidency of Ronald Reagan and a Republican-dominated Senate, the New Right's influence on national legislation became explicit in 1981. Women continued to organize around a variety of issues from equal training and pay to social security and pensions, and to study technological changes affecting them. Confrontation with the New Right organizational, legal, and legislative agenda, however, absorbed women's groups in a rear-guard action that although debilitating, was essential. The sense of momentum and progress that characterized the previous year for working women's associations was dissipated in 1981 by a series of attacks on the legislative framework that had been carefully constructed over seventeen years to produce a policy of equal economic opportunity.

The Women's Movement and Working Women

A foreboding that the ERA would not be ratified by the 1982 deadline fueled deep concern among feminist leaders, particularly as hard-won legal principles and social programs were threatened by conservative decision makers in the judiciary, congressional, and executive branches of government. A fierce

303

kind of political hardball typified the game plan to unravel women's economic rights. As that plan was steadily implemented, crystallizing in the Reagan budget, the "right to work" ideology prevailing in government clearly resisted women's progress beyond their traditional sphere (Data Center 1980; McIntyre 1979; Shanker 1982).

Although the National Advisory Council on Women's Educational Programs reported to Congress the positive impacts of Title IX (1981) in expanding women's educational and training participation, the current administration proceeded nevertheless to limit its commitment to affirmative action and related sex-equity policies. A patriarchal philosophy that saw all women as marginal in the work force, and that glorified the male head of household as the rightful breadwinner attempted to blame growing white male unemployment on women's competition for jobs (Schipper 1982; Fishman, Katz, and Fuller 1981). Department of Labor statistics, however, demonstrated the persistence of chronic, structural segregation by sex in the work force. Women's research on housework similarly revealed an ingrained social pattern of working women assuming primary responsibility for housekeeping. The rise of male, blue-collar unemployment in the steel, auto, and housing construction industries was not due to female competition, but to the reduction in net jobs in these sectors. Technological obsolescence, lack of managerial productivity, or the high cost of money over the past several years had depressed these areas of the economy. Economist Barbara Reagan (1981), commenting on the fact that men's unemployment rate exceeded women's in 1981 for the first time in twenty years, attributed the cause to occupational sex segregation. Those industries most resistant to female labor were hardest hit by the 1981 recession, while service industries such as insurance, banking, and health, which employ large numbers of women, were not damaged this year, and some, like insurance, experienced growth.

Sources of information about the New Right's economic theories and its connections to large corporate interests, religious groups, and churches are collected in an essay "Unraveling the right wing opposition to women's equality" (Fishman, Katz, and Fuller 1981). Among the wealth of magazine articles on the subject, *Ms.* published a roundtable scholarly discussion that places the New Right in the context of feminist philosophies and goals (Wohl 1981). The *Women's Political Times* and *National NOW Times* monitored New Right activities and leadership on a regular basis during 1981. Financial sources of neoconservative opposition to women's economic equity are detailed in these reports, and corporate influence through organizations such as the Equal Employment Advisory Council is analyzed. Originally formed to oppose affirmative action, this group consists of members from companies like Sears, Exxon, General Electric, and General Motors. Its current priority is to halt efforts to develop the law of comparable worth in equal pay. Richard Mellon Scaife is one individual who is profiled in this literature, which defines his role in funding groups such as the Heritage Foundation and the Mountain States Legal Foundation (which challenged the ERA extension in Judge Marion Callister's Ninth Federal Circuit Court in Idaho) (Rothmyer 1981). Scaife is perceived as a key financier of New Right organizations, although the Adolph Coors Foundation is most well known as one of their resources.

The argument was made years ago that the ERA and pay equity reforms would be so costly to big business that the largest corporations have become the most determined opponents of women's rights (Langer 1976). The roles of the Mormon Church, fundamentalist religious leaders, and politicians were more particularly detailed in the popular and newsletter press for working women in 1981, and in meetings and journals of women's studies (National Women's Studies Association 1981). The composition, lifestyle, biographies, and bank accounts of the elites associated with the Republican administration were widely discussed through the extensive communications network among union, white-collar, academic, elderly, and minority women. Comparison of the class-stratified trappings of Reaganomics with the large numbers of women affected by Reagan's budget cuts described what working women's associations commonly term an antiwoman administration (Simpson 1981).

The Status of Women in the Work Force

The primary source of statistics about women in the civilian and (to a much lesser extent) military labor forces is *Employment and earnings* (Bureau of Labor Statistics 1982), charting monthly activity in the labor force.

In 1981 there were 97.2 million persons in the United States labor force. "Over the year, however, the labor force was up 1.5 million, with white women accounting for three-fourths of the growth" (Bureau of Labor Statistics 1982). The total female labor force consisted of 52.3 percent of all women age 16 and over (51.7% in 1980). Nationally, the average unemployment rate among women reached 7.9 percent in December 1981. Among minority women aged 20 years and over, unemployment was 13.3 percent (15.1% among minority men). Median weekly earnings among women—"craft and other kindred workers"—increased 2.8 percent (constant dollars) or 13.8 percent in current dollars, from $209 to $238 per week. The number of women in the crafts and trades decreased from 603,000 in 1980 to 569,000 in 1981. There were more than twice as many women clerical workers than women working in any other occupation (11,099,000 compared with 5,297,000 professional and technical workers, the next largest category). The fact that the numbers of domestic houseworkers decreased during the year may be due to better job opportunities or to a lack of income available among middle-class households for domestic service wages (Grossman 1981).

Both men and women sales workers achieved increases in median weekly earnings over 1980 (men in 1981 current dollars rose 11.3%, or in constant dollars 0.4%; women in sales increased their earnings by 10.9% in current dollars, 0.1% in constant dollars). Male sales workers averaged $371 per week while women earned $194 per week. This gap is explained by the predominance of men in durable goods and women in nondurable goods sales (Stasz 1982). On the average, only women in professional and technical work achieved weekly earnings of more than $300. Women transport equipment operatives actually earned less per week than in 1980, dropping from $244 to $239, while their numbers increased from 126,000 to 159,000. Men in the same general occupation experienced only a 6.7 percent median weekly earnings increase, amounting to a 3.7 percent loss in constant dollars at $315 per week.

There are 3,160,000 employed females aged eighteen to nineteen years, the largest percentages of whom are semi-skilled or unskilled clerical workers and food service workers. Of all females age 16 to 19, 48.6 percent are in the labor force. For women 20 to 24 years, the participation rate is 69 percent, and 66.1 percent for women 25 to 54 years of age. Within the latter group, women between thirty-five and forty-four years of age have a labor force participation rate of 68.1 percent. Minority women in this age range have the highest rate of 72 percent.

According to the Endicott Report (Placement Center 1982), the greatest demand for June 1982 college graduates from the private sector will be in accounting, engineering, business administration, sales, marketing, and computer science. Engineers with bachelor's degrees can expect to earn an average annual salary of $25,428. Business and industry demand for college graduates in 1981 was 22,609, which is expected to increase 11 percent in 1982 (25,074) (*Industry Week* 1982). The proportion of women in accounting, personnel management, and labor relations has grown, and in computer science women's earnings are approaching men's. In the health fields, women's wages have shown improvement thanks to the militancy of nurses' associations and unions representing health technicians (the only jobs where men and women are equally paid) (Stasz 1981).

Issues: 1981

The Omnibus Budget Reconciliation Act of 1981

In the economics of public policy, the key issue area among working women was the Omnibus Budget Reconciliation Act of 1981 (H.R. 3982). Analyzed from the perspective of economic development, particularly at a community level, the budget impairs social services to women and families while failing to generate jobs. Budgeting for a weakened infrastructure (housing and public transportation) in combination with a tax plan many observers believe will concentrate wealth, and in conjunction with "fiscal federalism," will effectively impoverish central cities in the north and midwest where large numbers of the poor, most of whom are women, now subsist (Evans 1982; Shanker 1982).

In terms of specific development resources, the Omnibus Act:

1. Authorized a reduction to $290 million for the Department of Commerce's Economic Development Administration (created in 1965 to provide economic and community development aid to depressed areas).

2. Authorized a reduction to $14 million for low-interest loans and technical assistance, and $17 million for market rate loans for the National Consumer Cooperative Bank.

3. Increased interest rates for Small Business Administration loans and decreased its direct loan pool, instituting other tight money guidelines as well and limiting its women's business enterprise initiatives.

4. Eliminated public service jobs from CETA.

5. Substantially reduced Aid to Families with Dependent Children, especially affecting employed mothers who receive benefits.

6. Substantially reduced the food stamp program, particularly for the working poor and new participants (spending limits for the program are not expected to be sufficient to meet the claims of eligible persons even under the new regulations, unless inflation and unemployment fall as rapidly as is predicted by administration economists).

7. Reduced Medicaid benefits by $2 billion.

8. Reduced legal services, particularly for divorce cases.

9. Reduced family planning services by 25 percent.

10. Reduced the Women's Bureau staff by one-third, while trimming other Department of Labor activities by only 6 percent (*Congressional Quarterly Weekly Report* 1981).

The National Women's Conference Committee, established at the National Women's Conference in Houston in 1977, compared the Reagan budget unfavorably to its 1977 National Plan of Action. As analyzed by Catherine East and Kathryn Clarenbach of the National Committee, the services reduced by the Omnibus Act (in the interests of a balanced budget) are those of which women are the majority users: Of households receiving AFDC, 80 percent are headed by women, 61 percent of medicaid recipients are women; 150,000 women will lose CETA-funded job experience. Significantly, because many of the public CETA jobs were located in nonprofit centers for child care, rape victims, victims of domestic violence, senior citizens, and Headstart, these services will be reduced because of staff cutbacks. (The irony of the trickle down theory becomes quite apparent to feminist analysts looking at such connections.) Reduction of publicly funded legal services, 67 percent of whose clients are women, will hamper poor women's ability to divorce or otherwise protect themselves from civil and criminal injustice. Women-headed families occupy two-thirds of subsidized housing, which the Department of Housing and Urban Development will decrease by two-thirds (for new construction) under the new budget. Most food stamp users are women (69 percent), and women make up close to 100 percent of clients using family planning services (Rix and Stone 1981).

The Committee analysis of these impacts on women is put in the context of administrative guidelines and appointments to key posts under President Reagan. For example, the Committee points to Rex Lee, named Solicitor General, who opposes the ERA (for background on the Mormon stance on the ERA, see *Ms.,* November 1981). The Surgeon General, C. Everett Koop, opposes family planning and has had no previous experience in public health. The chairman of the Equal Employment Opportunity Commission, William Bell, has had no significant experience in civil rights law or in large organization administration. The removal of Arthur Fleming and Stephen Horn from the Civil Rights Commission also indicated a disregard for issues of women's civil and economic equity (National Women's Conference Committee 1982).

In terms of the regional impact of the new budget, urban planners concur that the distressed areas of the Frost Belt (northeast and midwest) will face serious problems, while cities in the Sun Belt will be unprepared to provide services to the poor migrating for jobs. The tax benefits (stepped-up depreciation schedules for physical plant and equipment) built into the Reagan economic plan will encourage new construction (most likely in the south and southwest) while discouraging rehabilitation of existing facilities that the northern cities need. While the poor are squeezed by reduction in services, there is no plan to assist them in relocating to new jobs. Nevertheless, the unskilled are following the work, causing concern to planners such as Norman Standefer of Broward County, Florida, who says the Fort Lauderdale area is already experiencing difficulty providing adequate sewers, roads, and buses for its increasing population, many of whom are unskilled workers and refugees (Lewis 1981). There is debate among administration officials and planners as to whether the Reagan administration has an urban policy at all. "Some contend that this stance—economy first, cities second—indicates the total lack of an urban policy, and they say that the nation's cities will suffer while such a policy is being fashioned. Others say that an explicit urban policy is evident, but not on one piece of paper" (Lewis 1981, p.18).

According to the United States Conference of Mayors, the bulk of Reagan's budget cuts come from urban programs, and mayors are worried about the effects of cutbacks in funds for economic development, mass transit, and housing. The Northeast-Midwest Coalition, composed of 213 members of the House of Representatives from eighteen Frost Belt states, argues that this region will suffer the most, as it previously received the largest proportion of funds for these purposes (Economic Development Administration, Urban Development Action Grants, Urban Mass Transit Administration). (For a discussion of the economic development framework existing at the end of the Carter administration, see Burr 1981.)

The analysis of the Omnibus Act prepared by the National Women's Conference Committee highlights the national budget's impact on women's economic development. The agenda exemplified in the International Women's Year *Plan* consists of health services including family planning, housing, child care, skilled employment and training, old age security and employment, transportation, low-cost capital, and business and technical education. These concerns were common to rural and urban women, and were the subject of model projects described in the American Planning Association's 1980 competition, "Planning to meet the changing needs of women." Yet programs implementing women's development policies were commonly perceived as "wasteful" or "corrupt" (Donnelly 1981). Government action induces women into the labor force by denying them social support systems for their households. At the same time, limited family planning and reproductive health care appears to be an incentive for reproduction. Inflation and male unemployment (the major forces moving women into the labor market), combined with governmental budget and tax actions, cause feminists to observe not that there is a total lack of a women's economic policy, but that the Republican party policy actively promotes economic inequality between women and men.

This male-female polarization over the politics of women's work is stated clearly in the proposed (1981) Family Protection Act, which retrieves a simplistic image of the male-headed family wherein woman's work is wholly defined by her reproductive capacity (*Christian Science Monitor* 1981; Lavine 1981).

Today, however, "Half of all wage-earning women are the sole support of themselves and others" (Stasz 1982; see also Swan 1981). This is the sort of fact that prompts women's development efforts and brings them so completely into conflict with Reaganomics. By December 1981 unemployment among female heads of household reached 10.7 percent, compared to a near record-setting national average (since World War II) of 8.9 percent of the entire civilian labor force. The wage gap between full-time, year-round male and female employees remained unchanged (men earned $1.00 for every $.59 earned by women). Although women increased their educational range and achievement, their entry into a wider variety of employments was not remarkable. Although women are now 25 percent of the work force in managerial job categories, they are statistically grouped in lower-paying levels of organizations. (Only 6 percent of women classified by the Department of Labor in managerial occupations earn more than $16,200 per year.) Research on attitudes surrounding women in management reflected a mixed cultural response to the influx of women into this area (Baron and Witte 1980).

Affirmative Action

Feminist commentators view the Reagan administration's approach (Dole 1981) to affirmative action as consistently acting "to weaken enforcement" (National Women's Conference Committee 1982; Simpson 1981; Stasz 1981). They cite administrators such as Assistant Attorney General William B. Reynolds, who has rejected class action sex discrimination suits in favor of processing individual cases. A reorientation of Department of Labor contract compliance policy is also viewed as "less enforcement." For example, currently all contractors receiving $50,000 worth of federal contracts must submit an affirmative action plan. The department, however, is now soliciting public comment on a proposal for only federal contracts of $1 million or more to require such plans. With respect to research contracts with universities, the proposed regulation would restrict the affirmative action requirement to the department or program receiving the contract, rather than the institution as a whole. Also under this proposal, contractors with an aggregate of $1 million would not be required to submit these plans. According to the Women's Equity Action League, the regulation would not cover most colleges and universities, since "81 percent of contracts awarded colleges and universities are for less than $1 million" (National Women's Conference Committee 1982). Women's employment among tenured faculty ranks has not increased substantially since 1972 (National Advisory Council on Women's Educational Programs 1981). Therefore women's advocates are concerned about any decrease of affirmative action hiring and promotion policies on campuses.

The Department of Labor is also considering eliminating the penalty of back pay awards, and has administratively reduced the authority of investigators. The resulting large backlog in the Department's Office of Federal Contract Compliance (OFCC) sparked the National Women's Law Center to file a contempt motion on June 24 challenging the backlog (Simpson 1981). At the same time, the Department has shifted away from a policy of challenging systemic sex discrimination in key industries such as insurance, banking, coal, and high technology. Similarly, Secretary of Labor Donovan opposes the Women in Construction program set up to monitor a 6.9 percent hiring goal in federally financed construction begun in 1978, consistent with his rejection of quotas and hiring goals. Donovan seems to have greater concern for reverse discrimination than sympathy for federal efforts to address institutional sexism.

A perspective on the role of assertively administered affirmative action policies can be gained by examining its impact in the coal industry. In 1973 there were no women working underground as coal miners (at least as statistically reported); by July 1981 there were 3,812. Women are served by advocacy groups such as the Coal Employment Project in Oak Ridge, Tennessee and the Western Kentucky Coal Mining Women's Support Team (Graff 1981; National Commission for Employment Policy 1981).

Sex Equity in Education and Pay

The half full, half empty glass, a report to Congress from the National Advisory Council on Women's Educational Programs (1981) on the effect of prohibiting sex discrimination in federally funded education programs, describes educational progress among women since passage in 1972 of Title IX of the Education Act amendments. The percentage of women enrolled in traditionally male vocational courses rose from 5 percent to 11 percent between 1972 and 1978. The number of women students in four-year colleges increased from 42 percent to 49 percent (1972 to 1979), and in two-year institutions, female enrollments now exceed those of men, rising from 44 percent to 54 percent between 1972 and 1979. Susan Margaret Vance, chairwoman of the Commission, said Title IX has proved itself to be "an extraordinary catalyst for change," most visibly apparent in athletics ("women athletes are no longer a rarity") (*New York Times* 1981). Federal intervention had occurred in only 1 percent of the nation's schools under Title IX, according to Bernice Sandler, a Commission member. She believes Title IX to be "the backbone of change in education because it creates the climate for change" (*Milwaukee Journal* 1981; *Green Bay Press—Gazette* 1981). The lack of concomitant progress in educational employment is accompanied by wide wage gaps between men and women and a dearth of women in top administrative posts. The report called for a continuing federal role in Title IX, although Reagan officials have expressed interest in deemphasizing enforcement.

A solid review of affirmative action history was issued by the United States Commission on Civil Rights (1981). This statement reviews the problem of discrimination, civil rights law, and the remedy of affirmative action. Its appendix offers "Guidelines for effective affirmative action plans." At the state level, similar assessments of sex equity progress in vocational education occurred during 1980-1981 (Wisconsin Board of Vocational, Technical and Adult Education 1981).

Sex equity in education is part of a matched pair of economic strategies among working women, pay equity in the workplace being the other half. During 1981 the issue of pay equity reached the Supreme Court in a comparable worth case whose settlement has prompted the filings of the Equal Employment Opportunity Commission (EEOC) complaints by union lawyers against the states of Washington, Connecticut, and Wisconsin and the city of Los Angeles. *Gunther* v. *Washington County, Oregon* opened the door to an expanded interpretation of the Equal Pay Act. The court ruled the state was in violation of Title VII of the Civil Rights Act in paying four Oregon prison matrons 70 percent of male guards' wages for substantially the same work. The Gunther decision of June 8, 1981 immediately affected the city of San Jose, where city workers (AFSCME) went on strike to achieve comparable worth salary adjustments. In July 1981, Local 101 of the American Federation of State, County, and Municipal Employees settled on increases for workers in 62 job categories, which over two years will average 25.1 percent for 1600 employees.

In the state of Washington, the issue of comparing job worth has a seven-year history that has yet to result in a wage policy satisfactory to the union and the legislature in setting government salaries (Stasz 1981; Celarier 1981). (The Center for Women in Government has published *Preliminary memorandum on pay equity: achieving equal pay for work of comparable value*

[Perlman and Ennis 1980]. This report gives an overview of litigation, research, organizing and legislation, as well as a bibliography and list of contacts.)

Military Issues

During 1981 the military as an employer assumed a much clearer identity in the public mind and defined its policy toward women somewhat differently than before. In the context of high unemployment rates among civilian skilled blue-collar men, the potential exists for satisfying the military need for skilled labor voluntarily by marketing enlistment as employment. Further prestige can be attached to the military by limiting women's occupational roles within it (*Spokeswoman* 1981).

To strengthen its marketing capability, the Department of Defense is joining the National Occupational Information Coordinating Council in integrating military occupational information into civilian occupational systems to look at methods of "inclusion and linkage" of the two systems. The anticipated results are "a more comprehensive supply/demand picture, increase(d) awareness of the military as an employer, and . . . more effective inclusion of military occupational and training information in career information delivery systems" (Wisconsin Occupational Information Coordinating Council 1982).

The economic implications of the all-male draft registration were understood by feminists within this employment context, among others. Registration was upheld by the Supreme Court (*Rostker* v. *Goldberg,* June 25, 1981), based on the military regulation barring women from combat. The Rostker case argued deference to Congress on military matters (the Military Selective Service Act, in particular), but women's groups believed the combat issue was being used to deny women equal access to a major economic institution that in peacetime functions increasingly as an employer. The attitude of viewing military experience as employment has motivated the Reagan administration to propose cutting off unemployment benefits to persons leaving the service. Failure to reenlist, in this logic, is like a resignation rather than a lay-off, therefore precluding eligibility for unemployment compensation (Fessler 1981).

Other implications derive from the military budget, principally, the fact that it is the only one in government to be increased substantially. Three-fifths of its procurement dollars have been spent in the south and west. According to the Northeast-Midwest Coalition, the Department of Defense will spend $40 billion on goods and services next year, 75 percent of federal procurement dollars (Lewis 1981; Thom 1981).

Several other military issues were raised by women during the year. For example, a task force was convened by the Women's Division of the Vietnam Veterans of America to study the problems of women veterans. Such research concentrates on men, according to Lynda Van Devanter, Women's

Division President and convenor of the task force. The federal government has collected few data about women Vietnam veterans, and estimates of their numbers range wildly from 7,000 to 55,000. Van Devanter states her experience indicates that "employment, loss of jobs and readjustment are all big problems" for women veterans (National NOW Times 1981).

Division between spouses of military retirement pay as part of a property settlement in divorce cases was ruled against on June 26 by the Supreme Court. The California case (McCarty v. McCarty) caused the Court to state that military retirement pay is not "properly" divisible at divorce (Goldsmith 1981). The unpaid but regulated role of military wives over a man's service career was wholly disregarded by the ruling. Retirement compensation is normally a significant part of a military couple's assets in old age, but the system as it pertained to individual servicemen was justified as an incentive to attract enlistments.

Pensions and Retirement Programs

Major resource publications in this subject became available by the end of 1981. The first issue of Women and Pensions was published in the fall of 1981, combining brief articles on law, legislation, lists of resources, and references on pensions. Pension law reform is an important emerging issue on women's political agenda, spearheaded by the Older Women's League, the Women's Pension Project of the Pension Rights Center, the Women's Equity Action League, and groups such as Coal Power. The report of the House Select Committee on Aging (1981) details the effect on women of the various public and private retirement systems. Helene Benson (1981) describes problems women are experiencing as workers and wives, and recommends changes in private pension law. The relation between "Work patterns and pensions" is examined in an AFL-CIO publication (1980). This perspective is relevant to one-fifth of the work force whose work schedules involve flex time, compressed work weeks or work years, permanent part-time work, job-sharing, or work-sharing (Lloyd 1981). The Older Women's League Education Fund (1981) studied pension, retirement, and social security systems in both military and civilian institutions. The case for pension law reform is well made by the Women's Equity Action League (1980).

Social Security inequities have also been the focus of scrutiny by groups such as the Congresswomen's Caucus, the Women's Equity Action League, and the Social Security Administration itself. Two important documents for background on women and the social security system are Social Security and the changing roles of men and women (U.S. Department of Health, Education, and Welfare 1979) and Treatment of men and women under the Social Security program (U.S. House of Representatives Subcommittee on Social Security 1980). A popular overview of the topic was published by Ms. (Schneir 1981). This article traces the stereotypes about married women that are contained in the law, and shows how they affect women in varying circumstances (divorced, single-earner, and two-earner families). Coal Power, an organization of widows, wives, and pensioners in the coal industry, promoted pension benefits for women in union contracts. The United Mine Workers contract for 1981 secured benefits ($95 per month) for widows of miners who retired before the federal pension law took effect in 1976 *(Women and Pensions* 1981).

Technological Changes in the Workplace

Persistent concern about video terminals (VDTs, CRTs) was reflected in working women's publications during the year. Scientific research indicates low-level radiation problems associated with the use of VDTs (Zimmerman 1982); other hazards include eye strain, back and neck strain, anxiety, irritability, and depression. Some commentators believe the use of video display terminals can be facilitated by designing work spaces to diminish the effects of strain and by assigning schedules that do not extend the duration of work by any single operator. Clerical unions are beginning to take a more militant stance. Working Women, a Chicago-based advocacy group for clerical workers that formed District 925, a national union of office workers, this year has called for elimination of VDTs. Working Women stated, "Not only will the units eliminate many clerical jobs from the labor market . . . but the terminals add to the health hazards mounting in modern offices" *(National NOW Times* 1981). The effect of downgrading clerical jobs (from secretary to word-processor, or file clerk to data-entry technician) is one concern that is related to the associated reduction of salaries—the introduction of piece-work rates. Jan Zimmerman (1981) argues, however, that new office technologies can reduce repetitive retyping and boring filing chores to a technical efficiency that will release secretaries for more managerial functions such as programming, design, and overall information systems management. The debate over computerized office systems is shaped by concerns over health, career paths, downgraded redefinitions of jobs, and ultimately, income for clerical workers. At present, the federal government ranks the occupation of secretary as the second most stressful in the economy, and academic research confirms that the "job of secretary is among the most stressful" according to Professor Dale Masi, University of Maryland's School of Social Work *(National NOW Times* 1981).

The Arts

The film *9 to 5* dramatized the conditions of clerical employment, albeit comically, with stars in lead roles, and brought the topic to the general public. Jane Fonda, Dolly Parton, and Lily Tomlin characterized the frustrated secretaries who do their boss's work and devised a collective action that was silly in itself, but which demonstrated the bonds among working women in offices.

The rarity of women directing and producing films and television shows commercially is remarkable, given their concentration in the arts and humanities in college. A recent study by the Directors' Guild of America showed that women have directed less than two-tenths of one percent (0.2 percent) of prime-time television network hours since 1949 (115 hours out of a total of 65,000 hours). *Media report to women* (1972 to the present), published by the Women's Institute for Freedom of the Press, reports on recent studies of the portrayal of women, statistics of employment of women and minorities, and the extent and progress of women's media abroad and in the United States. Media businesses founded by women are covered regularly, including new papers, magazines, and journals; conferences, legal actions, negotiations, and new media reform groups are tracked. The Institute also publishes *Index/directory of women's media* (1972 to the present) "an invaluable resource for almost any feminist enterprise or individual women's studies researcher" *(Feminist Collections* 1981, p. 15).

Artistic portrayal of women's work from farming to politics is becoming the subject of important exhibitions and projects. The most noteworthy exhibition in 1981 was the extended showing of Judy Chicago's *The Dinner Party* in the city of Chicago. This magnificent work represents active women whose biographies form a chronology of women's history. In sculpture, ceramics, china painting, and needlework, a profound vision of their experience, work, and limits is created. Record numbers of visitors attended the fall showing, causing its sponsor, the Roslyn Group, to extend it until February from the original December end-date.

The Smithsonian's National Museum of American History planned and assembled "Perfect in her place," an art exhibit that explores the role of women's work in United States history. Deborah Warner and Deborah Bretzfelder, in designing and assembling the exhibit, profiled women such as Sarah Breedlow Walker, the first black woman millionaire, and Mary Keis, the first woman awarded a patent. Through state grants, the National Endowment for the Humanities funded local projects similar to the one supported by the Wisconsin Humanities Committee on Women in the Workplace. A slide-tape program and traveling photo exhibit were produced by Barbara Morford during this project, representing a diverse history of Wisconsin women's workplaces in country and city. Selections from the Lewis Wickes Hines Collection (George Eastman House International Museum of Photography) (Doherty 1981) depict the images of working women during the period 1907 to 1938.

The Workplace and the Home: Conclusions

Research on women's dual responsibilities as homemaker and income-producer shows the depth of cultural assumptions regarding women's work in the home. Heidi I. Hartmann studied housework as an example of family-defined status roles carried into the larger community (1981). Natalie J.

Sokoloff (1981), in "Motherwork and working mothers," focuses on the stress experienced as women function as primary parent while employed. White and Brinkerhoff (1981) reported from their research that "sex typing remains strong in children's work socialization." Household behaviors and attitudes between couples are most affected by the current employment status of the wife, although attitudes about traditional roles persist despite "temporary" adjustments to the wife's employment, and "married couples are remarkably resistant to changing household norms and behaviors" (Huber and Spitze 1981). Homework is women's work.

These cultural attitudes and habits do not diminish the need to prepare for and find employment, particularly work that pays a living wage. "Women have always worked!" is an old slogan in the women's movement. Legal, legislative, and cultural barriers to their economic opportunity, however, are currently being reinforced by an educational bias in research on women's biology. Because technical education is so important to economic opportunity in American society, mathematics is a pivotal subject. The social psychology of girls' and women's math avoidance has received some attention. In December 1980, *Science* published an article by C. Benbow and J. Stanley concluding that "it is hard to dissect out influences of societal expectation and attitudes on mathematical reasoning." They "favor the hypothesis that sex differences in aptitude and achievement result from superior male mathematical ability" (Tooney 1981). The idea that mathematics is a sex-specific, genetically transmitted ability has been broadly discussed in the media. The Johns Hopkins University researchers believe men's math ability is genetically superior to women's. Nevertheless, their studies actually were inconclusive in separating social and biological causes of math ability in seventh-grade and eighth-grade girls and boys. Tooney (1981) summarized Jane Armstrong's report, "A national assessment of achievement and participation of women in mathematics," which found that there were "three factors that had a positive correlation with achievement: A positive attitude toward math, a perceived need for math for career-training, and the influence of others, including parents and teachers."

An intellectual climate that supports claims of male biological superiority in abilities particularly lucrative in contemporary United States society feeds the "biology backlash" of the New Right against women. Some view the math gene controversy as symptomatic of the larger New Right syndrome to limit women's roles. The climate of opinion in which biology versus society is debated as the ultimate cause of human behavior is heated in part because political, educational, and economic decisions are made in the context of beliefs about human nature. If decision makers believe humans develop their abilities through learning and practice, then educational programs are important. If, on the other hand, it is believed that one race or sex has innate abilities that are biologically determined rather than learned, that differences between races or sexes are biologically "fixed," then occupational or educational segregation by race or sex may be promoted. The role of science in shaping the terms of this debate is significant because of the prestige science enjoys as an objective set of methods. Criticisms of the bias in research on sex and gender are summarized by Nancy Tooney (1981). She links the math gene theory to the history of deterministic thought and places it in the context of social science research, as well as research on women and science. She stresses the interdependence of biology and society as influences on individual development. As some women scientists have pointedly asked contemporary biologists, "Have only men evolved?" "The politics of right and left" is what Susan Leigh Starr called her discussion of "sex differences in hemispheric brain asymmetry," but her phrase describes the polarization of ideologies about women's work in 1981 as well (Hubbard, Henifin, and Fried 1979).

REFERENCES

AFL-CIO. 1980. *Ourself: women and unions.* Washington, D.C.: Food and Beverage Trades Dept.

AFT/AFL-CIO. 1982. Democrats establish labor council. *On Campus* 1, no. 5:2, 10.

Baron, A. S., and Witte, R. L. 1980. The new work dynamic: men and women in the work force. *Business Horizons*

Benbow, C. P., and Stanley, J.C. 1980. Sex differences in mathematical ability: fact or artifact? *Science* 210:1262-64.

Benson, H. 1981. Women and private pension plans. Washington, D.C.: U.S. Department of Labor, Pension and Welfare Benefits Program.

Bureau of Labor Statistics. 1982. *Employment and Earnings* 26 (January).

Burr, S. G. 1981. Women and work. In *The women's annual—1980: the year in review.* Boston: G. K. Hall.

Celarier, M. 1981. The paycheck challenge of the eighties—comparing job worth. *Ms.* 4:38-44.

Christian Science Monitor. 1981. Editorial, July 23, p. 24.

Congressional Quarterly Weekly Report. 1981. 39:1461-1520.

Data Center. 1980. *The new right: readings and commentary.* Vols. 1-4. Oakland, Calif.: Data Center.

Despite economy, '82 grads will get "oyster." 1982. *Industry Week.* 212:79-80.

Doherty, J. L., ed. 1981. *Women at work.* New York: Dover.

Dole, E. H. 1981. My side. *Working Women* 6:156.

Donnelly, H. 1981. CETA public service jobs programs reach end of the line. *Congressional Quarterly Weekly Report* 39:1469.

Evans, M. K. 1982. Thumbs down for fiscal federalism. *Industry Week* 212:68.

Fessler, P. 1981. Labor/social security. *Congressional Quarterly Weekly Report* 39:1469.

Fishman, W. K., and Fuller, G. E. 1981. *Unraveling the right wing opposition to women's equality.* Washington, D.C.: Interchange Resource Center, 1-9.

Gilder, G. 1981. *Wealth and poverty.* New York: Basic Books.

Goldsmith, J. 1981. Supreme Court gives one-two blow. *National NOW Times* 14:10.

Graff, A. 1981. *The tools of the trade: a blueprint for moving young women into nontraditional careers.* Document no. 999. Madison, Wisc.: CETA Resource Clearinghouse.

Grengg, D. A. 1981. *Sex equity in vocational education.* Madison, Wisc.: League of Women Voters Education Fund.

Grossman, A. S. 1981. *Women in domestic work: yesterday and today.* Document no. 1088. Madison, Wisc.: CETA Resource Clearinghouse.

Hartmann, H. I. 1981. The family as the locus of gender, class, and political struggle. *Signs* 6:266-94.

Heatherly, C. L., ed. 1981. *Mandate for leadership: policy management in a conservative administration.* Washington, D.C.: Heritage Foundation.

Hubbard, R.; Henifin, M.S.; and Fried, B., eds. 1979. *Women look at biology looking at women.* Cambridge: Schenkman.

Huber, J., and Spitze, G. 1981. Wife's employment, household behaviors, and sex-role attitudes. *Social Forces* 60:150-169.

In brief. 1981. *National NOW Times* 14:2.

Langer, E. 1976. Why big business is trying to defeat the ERA. *Ms.* 9.

Lavine, D. 1981. Congress mulls family fate. *National Law Journal* 3:1, 30-31.

Lewis, S. 1981. Urban policy on the cheap. *Planning* 47:12-18.

Lloyd, K. R. 1981. Editorial. *Working Women* 6:1.

Men still hold top jobs, government study says. 1981. *New York Times*, October 18.

McIntyre, T. J. 1979. *The fear brokers.* New York: Pilgrim.

National Advisory Council on Women's Educational Program. 1981. *Title IX: the half full, half empty glass.* Washington, D.C.: U.S. Government Printing Office.

National Commission for Employment Policy. 1981. *Increasing the earnings of disadvantaged women.* Document no. 1024. Madison, Wisc.: CETA Resource Clearinghouse.

National Women's Conference Committee. 1982. Statement of concern. Madison, Wisc.: Women's Education Resources, University of Wisconsin-Extension.

National Women's Studies Association. 1981. *Conference program May 31-June 4, 1981.* College Park, Md.: University of Maryland.

Older women and pensions: catch-22. 1981. Oakland, Calif.: Older Women's League Education Fund.

Parker, L., and Loeb, C., eds. 1981. Items of note. *Feminist collections: women's studies library resources in Wisconsin* 2:15.

Perlman, N.D., and Ennis, B. J. 1980. *Preliminary memorandum on pay equity: achieving equal pay for work of comparable value.* New York: SUNY Center for Women in Government.

Placement Center. *The Endicott Report.* 1982. Evanston, Ill.: Northwestern University.

Rix, S., and Stone, A. 1981. *Impact on women of the administration's proposed budget.* Document no. 1026. Madison, Wisc.: CETA Resource Clearinghouse.

Rothmyer, K. 1981. Citizen Scaife. *Columbia Journalism Review*, July-August, pp. 41-50.

Schipper, H. 1982. The truth will out—an interview with Phyllis Schlafly. *Ms.* 10:88-92.

Schneir, M. 1981. Everything you need to know about Social Security. *Ms.* 10:81-84.

Sex-bias law has helped. 1981. *Milwaukee Journal*, October 8.

Sexual equity improves. 1981. *Green Bay Press—Gazette*, October 18.

Shanker, A. 1982. A sharp look inside Reagan's tax plan. *On Campus* 1:7.

Simpson, P. 1981. Target: working women. *Working Women* 6:74-78.

Sokoloff, N. J. 1981. Motherwork and working mothers. *Quest* 5, no. 3:41-52.

Stasz, C. 1982. Room at the bottom. *Working papers for a new society* January-February, pp. 28-41.

Swan, C. 1981. Recent OECD meetings on the employment of women. *Resources for Feminist Research* 10:34.

Thom, M. 1981. How six feminists would solve the U.S. economic crisis: a *Ms.* roundtable. *Ms.* 10:52-58, 76.

Tooney, N. 1981. The "math gene" and other symptoms of the biology backlash. *Ms.* 10:56-59.

U.S. Commission on Civil Rights. 1981. *Affirmative action in the 1980s: dismantling the process of discrimination.* Clearinghouse publication 80. Washington, D.C.: The Commission.

U.S. Department of Health, Education and Welfare. 1979. *Social security and the changing roles of men and women.* Washington, D.C.: U.S. Government Printing Office.

U.S. House of Representative Select Committee on Aging. 1981. *Women and retirement income programs: current issues of equity and adequacy.* Washington, D.C.: U.S. Government Printing Office.

U.S. House of Representatives Subcommittee on Social Security. 1980. *Treatment of men and women under the social security program.* Washington, D.C.: U.S. Government Printing Office.

White, L. K., and Brinkerhoff, D. B. 1981. The sexual division of labor: evidence from childhood. *Social Forces* 60:170-81.

Wisconsin Board of Vocational, Technical and Adult Education. 1981. *Promoting sex equity in the Wisconsin VTAE system.* Madison, Wisc.: VTAE Board.

Wisconsin Occupational Information Coordinating Council. 1982. *Newsletter* 2:6.

Wohl, L. C. 1981. Holding our own against a conservative tide. *Ms.* 10:50-53, 86-89.

Women's Equity Action League. 1980. Pension reform: retirement security for women. Washington, D.C.: The League.

Zimmerman, J. 1981. How to control the new technology before it controls you. *Ms.* 9:81-83.

RESOURCES

Association of Women Geoscientists, Box 1005, Menlo Park, CA 94200.

Bay Area Women Entrepreneurs, A Central Place, Woodward Bldg., 477 15th Street, Oakland, CA 94612. Sponsors seminars and workshops for self-development.

Black Career Women, Inc., 706 Walnut Street, Suite 804, Cincinnati, OH 45202. Provides a newsletter; offers career counseling and seminars.

Black Women Entrepreneurs, Inc., 2200 Woodward Towers, Detroit, MI 48226. Monthly newsletter; sponsors quarterly conferences for women in business.

Congresswomen's Caucus, Cochairs Representatives Pat Schroeder (D-CO) and Margaret Heckler (R-MA), 2471 Rayburn House Office Bldg., Washington, D.C. 20515. Publishes *Update*, a biweekly report about proposed federal legislation, congressional hearings, and court decisions affecting women.

League of Black Women, 111 East Wacker Street, Suite 321, Chicago, IL 60601. Offers counseling for women in business, workshops, and job placement services.

Leigh Communications, 676 St. Clair, Suite 1800, Chicago, IL 60611. Sponsors career convention in various cities around the country; workshops and corporate booths.

Pension Rights Center, 1346 Connecticut Avenue NW, Room 1019, Washington, D.C. 20036. Operates a women's pension information clearinghouse; publishes *Pension Facts* (#1 and #2), *Women and Pensions* (a newsletter).

Women in Geophysics, c/o Society of Exploration Geophysicists, Box 3098, Tulsa, OK 94101.

Women's Institute for Freedom of the Press, 3306 Ross Place NW, Washington, D.C. 20008. Publishes excellent reference and resource works on women in the media.

YWCA Jobs Network, 610 Lexington Avenue, New York, NY 10022. Sponsors career-related courses, programs for displaced homemakers and disabled workers, and job placement service.

CONTRIBUTORS

Barbara Haber, editor for this volume, is curator of printed books at the Arthur and Elizabeth Schlesinger Library on the history of women in America and a Radcliffe Scholar. Educated at the University of Wisconsin, the University of Chicago, and Simmons College, she is advisory editor for G.K. Hall's Women's Studies publications and author of *Women in America: A Guide to Books, 1963-1975* (G.K. Hall, 1978), which has been updated and issued in paperback by University of Illinois Press (1981). She is director of the NEH-funded project "Women in the Community: Where Were They? Where Are They? Where Are They Going?," which will enable the library to work with public libraries throughout the country to prepare programs about women for local audiences.

Sandra Hughes Boyd, an Episcopal priest, is reference librarian at the Episcopal Divinity School/Weston School of Theology libraries and priest associate of Christ Church in Cambridge, Massachusetts. She is a regular contributor of book reviews to *Library Journal* and coauthor of a forthcoming G.K Hall bibliography on the religious experience of American women.

Constance H. Buchanan is a member of the faculty of Harvard Divinity School and director of the School's Women's Studies in Religion program. This unique program serves as an international center for development of research and teaching in women's studies in the various fields of religion.

Sara Garrigan Burr received the Ph.D. in political science in 1977 from the University of California-Riverside. She has taught American politics, comparative governments, and modern political theory at UCR and the University of Wisconsin-Parkside. Meeting director of the Wisconsin IWY State Meeting for Women in 1977, she joined the staff of the Madison Development Corporation in 1978, where she presently manages its Commercial Rehabilitation Loan program. She is an honorary fellow of the Women's Studies Research Center at the University of Wisconsin-Madison.

Patricia Hill Collins is the former director of the African American Center at Tufts University. She received the master's degree in education from Harvard University and is currently a doctoral condidate in sociology at Brandeis University and adjunct professor of sociology at Northern Kentucky University.

Ann C. Conway, an instructor at Assumption College, Worcester, Massachusetts, is a doctoral candidate in sociology at Brandeis University, where she is researching the relation of ethnicity to medical care and conducting research on self advocacy and the disabled. She is a former health advocate for elderly immigrant women.

Virginia K. Donovan has a Ph.D. in psychology and is a feminist therapist. Since 1971 she has been a member of the Women's Mental Health Collective, a private, non-profit clinic in Somerville, Massachusetts.

Naomi R. Gerstel is an assistant professor at the University of Massachusetts-Amherst. Her doctoral dissertation, written while she was at Columbia University, and a series of subsequent articles, focused on commuter marriage. She is currently working on a study comparing women's and men's experience of marital dissolution.

Polly Welts Kaufman, as coordinator of the library program of the Boston Public Schools, supervises and trains the paraprofessionals who staff the elementary- and middle-school libraries in the system. She is an adjunct lecturer in the Teacher Certification program at the University of Massachusetts in Boston and at the Experimental College at Tufts University. Kaufman holds the Ed.D. in educational leadership and American studies from Boston University, the M.A. in history from the University of Washington, and the A.B. in American civilization from Brown University. She is currently editing a group of letters written by women who left the Northeast to teach in the Missouri and Mississippi River valleys between 1848 and 1854.

Freada Klein has been working on issues of violence against women for over ten years. Until 1976 she worked locally and nationally with rape crisis centers. At that time, she cofounded the Alliance Against Sexual Coercion, the first organization to provide a comprehensive approach to sexual harassment. Freada currently travels throughout the United States conducting trainings on sexual harassment at workplaces, and lecturing on rape causality and prevention for college audiences. She is also working on a doctorate in social policy and research at Brandeis University.

Ronnie Littenberg has a Ph.D. in clinical psychology. She is a feminist therapist and founding member of the Women's Mental Health Collective, a private, not-for-profit clinic in Somerville, Massachusetts. She works with the Massachusetts Childbearing Rights Alliance.

Peggy Simpson is the Washington correspondent for the *Boston Herald-American*. A Neiman Fellow (1978-1979), she has served as a Congressional correspondent for Associated Press (1968-1978), president of the Washington Press Club (1975-1976) and was the Associated Press specialist covering the women's political movement since it began.

Esther Stineman, formerly the University of Wisconsin System Librarian for Women's Studies, is the author of *Women's Studies: A Recommended Core Bibliography* (1979) and *American Political Women* (1980). She is in the American Studies Ph.D. program at Yale University, and commutes between New Haven and her home in Colorado.

Michaele Weissman is a freelance writer who lives and works in New York City. She is the author with Carol Hymowitz of *A History of Women in America*, published by Bantam Books. She has written for numerous popular publications including the *New York Times, Cosmopolitan, Mademoiselle*, and *Fortune*. Before becoming a freelancer, she worked as a news editor and producer for WOR Radio in New York City. Ms. Weissman has a degree in European history from Brandeis University. She is a native of Belmont, Massachusetts.

INDEX

Abbott, S., 230
Abel, Elizabeth, 135
Absence of Malice (Pollack), 199-200
Adams, Alice, 206
Adams, John Quincy, 125
Adams, Louisa Johnson, 125
Administration for Children, Youth, and
    Families, 31
Aid to Families with Dependent Children,
    99, 155, 307
Ain't I a Woman (Hooks), 109
Alcoholics Anonymous, 227
Alcott, Abbie May, 125
Alcott, Louisa May, 125
Allen, Karen, 203
Alliance Against Sexual Coercion, 278
American Association of University
    Women, 177
American College of Nurse-Midwives, 62
American College of Obstetricians and
    Gynecologists, 62
American Cyanimid, 72
American Law Review, 173
American Planning Association, 309
America's White Working-Class
    (Kennedy), 119
Anarchist Women 1870-1920 (March),
    122
Anderson, Sherwood, 133
Angell, Marcia, 42
Angelou, Maya, 127
Anthony, Susan B., 117-18
Anzaldua, Gloria, 246-47
Appalachian Pathways Conference on
    Women and Health, 70-71
Aptheker, Bettina, 34

Armitage, Susan, 123
Armstrong, Jane, 316
Asian-American Women, 87, 89, 95,
    102, 107
Association for Women in Psychology,
    223
Association of Intercollegiate Athletics
    for Women, 37-38
Auerbach, Nina, 133
Austen, Jane, 133
AWARE, 31

Balke, Victor, 250
Bank Street College of Education, 31-32
Barbach, L., 231
Barnes, Djuna, 135
Barton, Annie, 134
Basic Education Opportunity Grants, 99
Baym, Nina, 134, 135
Beatty, Warren, 203
Beauvoir, Simone de, 127
Beecher, Catharine, 124
Beechers, The (Rugoff), 124
Bell, Terrel, 158
Bell, William, 308
Benbow, C., 30, 316
Benson, Helene, 313
Bergmann, Barbara R., 2, 154, 181
Bernays, Anne, 206
Bernikow, Louise, 135
Besant, Annie, 126
Beyond God the Father (Daly), 237, 238
Billings, Robert, 154
Billings, William, 172
Bishops' Conference for Prolife Activity,
    254

Black Macho and the Myth of the Superwoman (Wallace), 108
Black Sister (Stetson), 130
Blackwell, Henry, 127
Black women, 87–109, 134, 175, 247, 274, 277, 286, 315
Blais, Marie-Claire, 132
Blake, J., 13
Bohemian Club, 170
Bordin, Ruth, 121
Born of the Same Roots (Hsu), 123
Boskind-Lodhal, M., 228
Boston Collaborative Drug Surveillance Program, 60
Boston Self-Help Center, 70
Boston Women's Health Book Collective, 59, 66
Boyd, Sandra Hughes, 5, 248–69
Bradstreet, Anne, 130
Bradwell, Myra, 160
Brennan, William, 161
Bretzfelder, Deborah, 315
Bridges, Jeff, 198
Brinkerhoff, D. B., 316
Brown, Louise, 64
Bruch, H., 228
Bruno v. *Codd*, 286
Bryant, Louise, 203–4
Buchanan, Constance H., 5, 236–47
Bundy v. *Jackson*, 286
Bunker Hill Co., 72
Burger, William, 161
Burke, Carolyn, 132
Burr, Sara Garrigan, 1, 303-20
Bush, George, 157, 169
Butler, Josephine, 126

Caan, James, 199
Callister, Marion, 173
Cannibals of the Heart (Shepherd), 125
Cantrell, Dean, 34
Carter, Jimmy, 153, 158, 161, 164, 169
Cather, Willa, 133, 135
Center for Self-Reliant Education, 32
Changing Bodies, Changing Lives, 66
Check, James, 283
Chesnut, Mary Boykin, 125
Chicago, Judy, 315
Chodorow, Nancy, 222–23
Chronicle of Higher Education, 39
Church Women United, 260
Cixous, Helene, 132
Clarenbach, Kathryn, 307
Clean Air Act, 72

Clean Water Act, 72
Coal Employment Project, 310
Coal Power, 313, 314
Coalition on Women's Appointments, 153
Coleman, Marshall, 174
College Art Association, 131
Collins, Patricia Hill, 2, 87–116
Commission on Obscenity and Pornography, 282–83
Common Differences (Joseph and Lewis), 108–9
Company of Women, The (Gordon), 207–8
Conditions, 130
Cone, James, 238–39
Congressional Caucus on Women's Issues, 176
Congressional Union, 176
Congresswomen's Caucus, 175, 313
Conservative Digest, 158–59
Conway, Ann, 3, 56–86
Cooke, Terence, 254
Coors, Adolph, Foundation, 305
Council for Interracial Books, 28
Courtot, Martha, 130
Crichton, Michael, 198
Critical Inquiry, 132
Cummins, John S., 249
Curtis, Jaime Lee, 197
Cutter's Way (Passer), 198–99, 208

Dad (Wharton), 206
Daly, Mary, 237, 247
Daugherty, Ruth, 256
Davis, Barbara Hillyer, 34
Davis, Jefferson, 125
Decter, Midge, 152
Defense Advisory Committee on Women in the Services, 158
Del Pinal, J. H., 13
De Niro, Robert, 199
Denton, Jeremiah, 152, 178
Denver Quarterly, 129
Developmental Disabilities Act, 70
Devine, Donald, 154
Diary of Virginia Woolf, The, 133
Dickins, Hazel, 130
Dickinson, Emily, 34, 130, 135
Dinesen, Isak, 127
Dinner Party, The (Chicago), 315
Directors' Guild of America, 315
Displaced Homemakers Network, 36
Dixon, Greg, 170

Donovan, Raymond, 310
Donovan, Virginia K., 4, 211-35
Doolittle, Hilda, 128
Dorothy Stratton Story, The, 197-98
Downing, Christine, 242-43
Dressed to Kill, 287
Dupon de Nemours, E. I., and Co., 72
Dushin, Donna Kate, 107
Dworkin, Andrea, 283

East, Catherine, 307
Edith and Woodrow (Shachtman), 125
Edwards, Anne, 128
Edwards, Blake, 200
Eichorn, Lisa, 198
Eisenhower, Dwight, 153, 174
Eliot, George, 126
EMBERS, 28
Emerson, Lidian Jackson, 128
Emerson, Ralph Waldo, 128
Eminent Victorian Women (Longford),
    126
Employment and Earnings (BLS), 305
Endicott Report, 306
Endless Love (Zeffirelli), 200-201
Environmental Protection Agency, 72
Equal Employment Advisory Council,
    304
Equal Employment Opportunity Com-
    mission, 28, 156, 158, 278, 308, 311
Equal Rights Amendment, 5, 6, 8, 14,
    150, 153, 154, 170-71, 173-74, 176,
    303, 304-5, 308
Erhard, Werner, 220
Erkut, Sumru, 35
Ernst, S., 219, 221
Escamilla-Mondanaro, J., 231
Evans, David, 158
Everflowing Streams (Duck), 261
Exxon Corp., 304
Eyewitness (Yates), 200

Faderman, Lillian, 135
Falkland Road (Mark), 120
Falwell, Jerry, 8, 9, 10, 161, 170
Family Protection Act, 155, 309
Farm and Factory (Dublin), 120
Father-Daughter Incest (Herman),
    280-81
Feldman, David M., 257
Feminism and Process Thought
    (Davaney), 241-42
Feminist Press, 28, 34, 119
Feminist Studies, 132

Fennema, Elizabeth, 30
Field, Sally, 199-200
Fifth Berkshire Conference on the History
    of Women (Vassar), 40
Filipino-American women, 88
Finney, Albert, 198
FIPSE, 34
Fitzgerald, Frances, 8, 9
Flavin, Glennon P., 253
Fleming, Arthur, 308
Fonda, Jane, 196, 314
Ford, Harrison, 203
Forsythe, Louise, 132
Four Friends (Penn), 199, 208
Fowles, John, 202
Fox, Mary, 39
Freeman, D. S., 14
French Lieutenant's Woman, The (Reisz),
    202
French, Marilyn, 134
Freud, Sigmund, 128, 133, 221-22, 242
Friedan, Betty, 152, 212
Friedman, Susan, 128
Frontiers, 132
Fund for the Improvement of Post-
    Secondary Education, 32

Gardiner, Judith, 133-34
Gasper, JoAnn, 154
Gatsis, Andrew J., 158-59
Gelpi, Barbara Charlesworth, 136
General Electric Corp., 304
General Motors Corp., 72, 304
Gerety, Peter, 250
Gerin, Anne Winifred, 124
Gerstel, Naomi, 4, 6-23
Gilbert, Sandra, 132, 135
Gilder, George, 10, 172, 303
Gilman, Charlotte Perkins, 126
Ginzburg, Eugenia, 122
Glasgow, Ellen, 133
God as Father? (Metz and Schillebeeckx),
    237-39, 243
Goddess, The (Downing), 242-43
Goldman, Emma, 123
Goldreich, Gloria, 29
Goldwater, Barry, 161
Goodison, L., 219, 221
Goodrich, B. F., Corp., 72
Gordon, Mary, 207-8
Grand Domestic Revolution (Hayden),
    131
Grau, Shirley Ann, 133
Gray Panthers, 69

Green, Thomas J., 250-51
Gregory, Andre, 208
Gregory, Christine, 254
Griffin, Susan, 283
Gross, Rita M., 261-62
Guide to Prescription Drug Costs, 64
Gutek, Barbara, 279

Hacker, Marilyn, 129
Hackett, Joan, 199
Haig, Alexander, 169
Halstead, Donald, 165
Hamel, Veronica, 201
Hare-Mustin, R. T., 217, 218
Harjo, Joy, 130
Harrison, Beverly Wildung, 5, 242n,
   243, 258, 259-60
Hartmann, Heidi I., 315
Harvard Business Review, 279
Hatch, Orrin, Amendment, 2, 178, 180,
   254-56
Hayden, Delores, 131
Hawn, Goldie, 195
Health Advocate of the Year Awards, 71
Heard, John, 198
Heart of a Woman, The (Angelou), 127
Heckler, Margaret, 156
Hefner, Hugh, 198
Helms, Jesse, 160, 177
Heritage Foundation, 156, 304
Herman, J. L., 224, 225, 280-81
HER Story: 1620-1980, 33
Higgins, Colin, 196
"Hill Street Blues," 201-2
Hispanic women, 87, 88, 89-92, 95,
   97-102, 104, 106, 107, 134, 274
History of Woman Suffrage (Stanton),
   117
Hoge, James, 128
Holtzman, Elizabeth, 175
Hooks, Bell, 109
Horn, Stephen, 308
Human life amendment, 71, 255
Hunt, George N., 255
Hurston, Zora Neale, 133, 246
Hurt, William, 200
Hustler, 282
Hyde amendment, 57-58

Immigrant Women (Seller), 122
Incredible Shrinking Woman, The (Schu-
   macher), 195, 196-97
Index/Directory of Women's Media, 315
Indian Health Service, 71

In Our Own Hands (Ernst and
   Goodison), 219
International Year of Disabled Persons,
   69-70
Irons, Jeremy, 202

Jacker, Corinne, 129
Jacob's Room (Woolf), 133
Jefferson, Theodore P., Jr., 165
Jenrette, John, 193
Jenrette, Rita, 193 94
Jepsen, Roger W., 181
"Jessica Novak," 197
Jewett, Sarah Orne, 135
John Paul II, 258
Johnson, Sonia, 176
Jones, Anne R., 132
Jones, Gayl, 133
Jordan, June, 129
Joseph, Gloria, 108-9
Journal of Popular Culture, 132
Journey into the Whirlwind (Ginzburg),
   122
Jung, Carl, 242, 243

Kael, Pauline, 196
Kahn, Coppelia, 134
Kane, Karen, 130
Kaschak, E., 214
Kassebaum, Nancy, 176
Kaufman, Polly Welts, 2, 24-55
Keaton, Diane, 203
Keis, Mary, 315
Kennedy, John F., 170
Kern, Louis J., 119
Kidder, Margot, 194, 202
Kingston, Maxine Hong, 123
Kinnard, Cynthia, 34
Kirkpatrick, Jeane, 151, 153
Kissel, Susan, 135
Klein, Freada, 3, 270-302
Koolish, Lynda, 129
Koop, Everett, 154, 308
Korean-American women, 88

*Labor and Education for Women
   Workers* (Wertheimer), 119
Ladd, Everett Carll, 174
La Guardia Community College, 32
LaHaye, Tim, 171
Lambert, Jean, 242
La Motta, Jake, 199
La Motta, Vicki, 199
Lapidus, Jacqueline, 130

Law Enforcement Assistance Administration, 277, 285
Laxalt, Paul, 7
League of Women Voters, 27
Learned, Michael, 197
Lee, Rex, 154, 308
Lems, Kristen, 130
Leonard, Bill J., 257
Lerner, Gerda, 41, 136
Lester, Richard, 202
Letters from Africa 1914-1931 (Dinesen), 127
Lewis, Jill, 108
Libow, J. A., 217
Liszt, Franz, 128
Littenberg, Ronnie, 4, 211-35
Lolita (play), 287
Long, Lynette, 29
Longford, Elizabeth, 126
Longworth, Alice Roosevelt, 125-26
Looker (Crichton), 198
Lopiano, Donna, 38
Lorber, Judith, 42
Lorde, Audre, 129, 247
Los Angeles Commission on Assaults Against Women, 272
Lost Tradition, A (Wilson-Kastner et al.), 244-45
Love, B., 230
"Love, Sidney," 197
Lucker, Raymond, 250
Luther, Martin, 253

McBrien, Richard J., 250-51
McCarty v. McCarty, 165, 313
Malamuth, Neil, 283
Malle, Louis, 208
Mann, Michael, 199
Man's Estate (Kahn), 134
March for Life, 57
Marek, George, 128
Marshall, Thurgood, 161, 165
Masi, Dale, 314
Mason, Martha, 199
Maxa, Kathleen, 194
Mecklenberg, Marjory, 154
Media Report to Women, 315
Medicaid, 99, 155, 307
Men's Club, The (Michaels), 204-5, 208
Merit Systems Protection Board, 278
Merrell-National Laboratories, 63
Michaels, Leonard, 204, 208
Miller, Jean Baker, 222

Millington, June, 130
Mitchell, Lucy Sprague, 126
Moltmann, Jurgen, 238, 239
Monroe, Lilla Day, 123
Monsanto Co., 72
Moore, Marianne, 133
Moraga, Cherrie, 130, 246
Moral Majority, 152, 154, 170-71
Morford, Barbara, 315
Morgan, Robin, 121
Moriarty, Cathy, 199
"Motherlogues" (Rubin and Friedensohn), 123
Ms., 304, 308, 313
Mujeres, Las (Elassar et al.), 106, 123
Mulligan, Richard, 200
My Dinner with Andre (Malle), 208

National Abortion Rights Action League, 175
National Advisory Council on Women's Educational Programs, 26, 27, 310
National Catholic Reporter, 252
National Coalition Against Domestic Violence, 276, 285-86
National Coalition Against Sexual Assault, 285
National Congress of Neighborhood Women, 32
National Education Association, 28
National Health Service Corporations, 71
National Identification Program for Women Administrators, 40
National Institute of Education, 31
National NOW Times, 304
National Organization for Women, 28, 69, 173, 175, 213
National Women's Conference Committee, 307-8
National Women's Division, American Jewish Congress, 256
National Women's Education Fund, 175
National Women's Health Network, 57, 59, 60, 70-71
National Women's Law Center, 310
National Women's Political Caucus, 175
National Women's Studies Association, 33
Native American women, 87, 95, 101, 102, 104, 107, 260
Nestle Company, 62-63
New Feminist Essays on Virginia Woolf, (Marcus), 133

New French Feminism (Marks and de Courtivron), 131
Newman, Paul, 199-200
New Right, 4, 6-23, 71, 136, 150-52, 154, 155-56, 159-60, 161, 165, 170-72, 175, 177, 303-5, 316
New York Review of Books, 134
Nightingale, Florence, 126
Nin, Anais, 135
Nine to Five, 33
9 to 5 (Higgins), 195, 196, 314
Nixon, Richard, 6
North Haven Board of Education v. *Bell*, 25
"Nurse," 197
Nurses Association of ACOG, 62

Oakar, Mary Rose, 181
O'Brien, Edna, 133
O'Connor, John, 161
O'Connor, Sandra Day, 58, 150, 153, 160-64, 172, 178
Office of Federal Contract Compliance Program, 157
O'Keeffe, Georgia, 127
Older Women's League, 69, 181, 313
Omnibus Budget Reconciliation Act, 306-7
Only When I Laugh (Simon), 199
Oppenheimer, Valerie, 16
Orbach, S., 228
Ordered Love, An (Kern), 119-20
Organization of American Historians, 136
Our Bodies, Our Selves, 66

Parton, Dolly, 196, 314
Pass, Gail, 205
Passer, Ivan, 198
Paul, Mary, 120
Paul VI, 249
Penn, Arthur, 199
People, 194
"Perfect in Her Place" (Warner and Bretzfelder), 315
Perls, Fritz, 220
Persephone Press, 129
Peters, Charles, 152
Phillips, Kevin, 6
Pierce, Samuel R., Jr., 101
Pinter, Harold, 202
Pioneer Women (Stratton), 123
Planned parenthood, 154, 159, 171, 177-78, 307
Playboy, 193-94, 197-98, 282

Plays by American Women (Barlow), 129
Politics of Domesticity, The (Epstein), 121
Pollack, Sidney, 199
Pornography (Dworkin), 283
Pornography and Silence (Griffin), 283
Porter, Katherine Anne, 126
Potter, Phillip, 253
Praying Mantis Women's Brigade, 287
President in Love, A (Wilson), 125
Private Benjamin (Zieff), 195-96
Psyche Reborn (Friedman), 128
Public Citizen Health Research Groups, 63
Public Opinion, 174

Rabkin, Norman, 134
Radical Persuasion, 1890-1917, The (Kraditor), 122-23
Raging Bull (Scorsese), 199, 208
Rahner, Karl, 249
Raiders of the Lost Ark (Spielberg), 203
Randall, Tony, 197
Rat, 121
Reagan, Barbara, 304
Reagan, Ronald, 1-3, 17, 56-57, 63-64, 87, 99-102, 150-161, 164, 169-70, 172, 174-75, 181, 255, 303-5, 307-9, 311-12
Receiving Woman (Ulanov), 242
Redbook, 278, 279
Reds (Beatty), 203-4
Reed, Jack, 203-4
Reentry, 42
Reeve, Christopher, 202
Rehnquist, William, 161, 165
Reisz, Karel, 202
Reproduction of Mothering, The (Chodorow), 222
RESPONSE Newsletter, 285
Reynolds, William Bradford, 101-2, 156-57, 309
Rheinstein, Max, 16
Rhys, Jean, 133
Rich, Adrienne, 129, 130
Rich Rewards (Adams), 206-7
Right Woman, The, 154
Riley, Pamela, 29
Ristow, Juliet, 66
Ritchie, Anne Thackaray, 124
Roach, John P., 252, 254, 256
Robb, Charles, 174

Roberts, Helen, 69
Robins, A. H., Co., 60
Robinson, Jean, 34
Rogers, Adrian, 254
Rohrbaugh, J. B., 223
Rose, Ernestine L., 117-18, 136
Rose, Wendy, 130
Roslyn Group, 315
Rostker v. Goldberg, 165
Rothschild, E., 16
Rowe, Mary, 280
Ruether, Rosemary, 239, 240-41, 243,
     245, 247
Runcie, Robert, 253

Sagan, Mariam, 130
Saiving, Valerie, 242
Sanctified Church, The (Hurston), 246
Sandler, Bernice, 311
Sandmaier, Marion, 68
Sanger, Margaret, 126
Sappho, 133
Sarton, May, 134
Sayers, Dorothy, 126
Scaife, Richard Mellon, 304-5
Schink, Anne, 27
Schlafly, P., 4, 8, 10, 12, 14, 151, 152,
     164, 170-73, 180
Schlesinger Library (Radcliffe), 33
Scholastic Press, 28
School Book, The (Bernays), 206
School lunch programs, 99, 155
Schultz, A. P., 232
Schweiker, Richard S., 57, 65
Science, 316
Scorsese, Martin, 199
Scott, Joan W., 40
Scott, Kathryn P., 28
Sears, Roebuck and Co., 304
Sea Run (Shields), 127-28
Second Wind, 32
Section 8 housing, 99, 101
Seller, Maxine, 122
Sexton, Anne, 130
Sexual Assault Crisis Service (Hartford,
     Conn.), 274
Shakespeare and the Problem of Meaning
     (Rabkin), 134
Shakespeare's Division of Experience
     (French), 134
Shakespeare, William, 134
Shavers, Helen, 197
Shaw, Carol M., 42
Shawn, Wally, 208

Shields, Brooke, 200-201
Shields, Laurie, 181
Shields, Mary Lou, 127-28
Showalter, Elaine, 126
Siegman, Henry, 256
Signs, 130, 132, 136, 242n
Simmons, Paul D., 256-57
Simon, Neil, 199
Simons, Wood, 130
Simpson, Peggy, 2
Sirhan, J., 228
Sklar, Kathryn Kish, 246
Smith, Elizabeth Oakes, 129
Smith, William French, 169
Snider, Paul, 197
S.O.B. (Edwards), 200
Social Security and the Changing Roles
     of Men and Women (HEW), 313
Social Security benefits, 155-56,
     171-72, 313
Sojourner, 130
Sokoloff, Natalie J., 315-16
Solle, Dorothee, 237, 239, 261, 263
Southwest Institute for Research on
     Women, 33
Spencer, Scott, 200
Spielberg, Steven, 203
Spires, Elizabeth, 130
Stage, Elizabeth K., 30
Stalin, Joseph, 122
Standefer, Norman, 308
Stanley, J., 30, 316
Stanton, Elizabeth Cady, 117-18
Starr, Susan Leigh, 317
Steelworkers v. Weber, 157
Stein, Gertrude, 135
Stewart, Potter, 161
Stiehm, Judith, 39
Stimpson, Catherine, 132, 136
Stineman, Esther, 5, 117-49
Stone, Lucy, 127
Stowe, Harriet Beecher, 124, 126, 133
Stratton, Dorothy, 197-98
Stratton, Joanna, 123
Streep, Meryl, 202
Strickland, Stephanie, 130
Superman II (Lester), 194, 202-3
Surviving Sisters (Pass), 205
Swift, Carolyn Ruth, 34

TABS, 28
Tagan, Jeffrey, 277n
Technical Reports of the Commission on
     Obscenity and Pornography, 282-83

Teish, Luisah, 247
Tennis, Diane, 261, 262
Tennyson, Alfred, 128
Tennyson, Emily, 128
Terry, Ellen, 126
Tesich, Steve, 199
Thackaray, William Makepeace, 124
"Theology of Pro-Choice" (Harrison), 5
Thief (Mann), 199, 208
Third International Congress on Menopause, 69
Third Woman, The (Fisher), 106-8
Third World women, 87-116; see also individual groups
This Bridge Called My Back (Moraga et al.), 107-8, 109, 246
Thomas, Betty, 201
Thomas, David, 252
Thornton, A., 14
Title IV (Civil Rights Act), 24, 26
Title VII (Civil Rights Act), 278, 286, 311
Title IX (Educational Amendments), 2-3, 24, 25-26, 28, 31, 154, 158, 159, 171, 176, 278, 304, 310-11
Title X, 155, 178
Title XX, 31
To Change the World (Ruether), 204-41
Tolstoy, Leo, 128
Tolstoy, Sonya, 128
Tomlin, Lily, 196, 314
Tooney, Nancy, 316-17
Toward a New Psychology of Women (Miller), 222
Treatment of Men and Women Under the Social Security Program, 313

Ulanov, Ann Belford, 242

Vance, Susan Margaret, 311
Van Devanter, Lynda, 312-13
Vasa, Robert, 253
Victorian Women (Hellerstein et al.), 123
Viguerie, Richard, 8, 13
Violent Home, The (Gelles), 277
Virginia (O'Brien), 133
Vocational Education Act, 25, 27
Von Gunden, Heidi, 130-31

Wagner, Cosima, 128
Wagner, Richard, 128
Walker, L. E., 224, 225
Walker, Sarah Breedlow, 315
Wallace, Michele, 108

Wallach, Anne Tolstoi, 194-95
Wandersee, Winifred, 120
War and Peace (Tolstoy), 128
Warner, Deborah, 315
Warner, John, 164
Washington Monthly, 152
Watt, James, 154
Wealth and Poverty (Gilder), 172
Weaver, Sigourney, 200
Weinberger, C. W., 159
Weiss, Janice, 27
Weissman, Michaele, 5, 193-210
Weisstein, Naomi, 223
Weld, Tuesday, 199
Wenzel, Helene, 132
Wertheimer, Barbara, 119
Western Kentucky Coal Mining Women's Support Team, 310
Wharton, William, 206
White House Conference on Aging, 69
White, L. K., 316
Wildfire, 28
Willard, Frances, 121
Wilson, Edith Bolling Galt, 125
Wilson, Joan Hoff, 41
Wilson, Kathy, 175
Wilson, Woodrow, 125
Wisconsin Humanities Committee on Women in the Workplace, 315
Within the Whirlwind (Ginzburg), 122
Wittig, Monique, 132
Whitmire, Kathy, 175
Wider Opportunities for Women, 32
Women and American Socialism, 1870-1920 (Buhle), 121
Women and Minorities in Science and Engineering, 41
Women and Pensions, 313
Women as Interpreters of the Visual Arts (Sherman and Holcomb), 131
Women in American Theatre (Chinoy and Jenkins), 129
Women in Construction program, 310
Women, Infants, and Children's Feeding Program, 100
Women in New Worlds (Thomas and Keller), 246
Women in Science Program, 41
Women of the Church Coalition, 248
Women of the Cloth (Carroll), 253
Women of the Republic (Kerber), 120
Women's Christian Temperance Union, 121
Women's College Coalition, 36-37

Women's Division, Board of the Global Ministries of the United Methodist Church, 256
Women's Division of the Vietnam Veterans of America, 312-13
Women's Educational Equity Act, 2, 24 25, 26, 28, 31, 156
Women's Equity Action League, 310, 313
Women's History Week, 29
Women's House (St. Paul, Minn.), 276
Women's Institute for Freedom of the Press, 315
Women's Legal Defense Fund, 154
Women's Lives/Women's Work, 119
Women's Missionary Union, 254
Women's Ordination Conference, 248, 251, 252
Women's Political Times, 304
Women's Reentry Consortium, 42
Women's Re-Entry Project, 36
Women's Research and Education Institute, 177

Women's Studies, 34, 134
Women's Technical Institute, 32
Women's Work and Family Values, 1920-1940 (Wandersee), 120
Women's Work (Wallach), 194-95
Wood, Donna J., 34
Woodward, C. Vann, 125
Woolf, Virginia, 124, 133
Working on Wife Abuse, 276
Working Women (Chicago), 314
Working Women Education Fund, 32
Working Women's Institute (New York), 278, 280
Wynn Oil Co., 168

Yale French Studies, 132
Yates, Peter, 200

Zieff, Howard, 195
Zimmerman, Jan, 314